W9-BEV-587

# The Gulf War

# The Gulf War

ITS ORIGINS, HISTORY AND CONSEQUENCES

## John Bulloch and Harvey Morris

Methuen London

First published in Great Britain in 1989
by Methuen London Ltd
Michelin House, 81 Fulham Road, London SW3 6RB
Copyright © 1989 John Bulloch and Harvey Morris

Reprinted in 1991

Photoset by Rowland Phototypesetting Ltd
Bury St Edmunds, Suffolk
Printed in England by Clays Ltd, St Ives plc

A CIP catalogue record for this book
is available from the British Library

ISBN 0 413 61370 4

# Contents

# Illustrations

The photographs in this book are reproduced by kind permission of the following: Magnum Photos: 1a, 1b, 2, 3a, 3b, 7a, 7b, 10a, 10b, 12; Jill Brown: 4a; Islamic Republic News Agency: 4b, 5, 6a, 8b; Edward Fursdon: 6b; Frank Spooner Pictures: 8a, 9a, 9b; John Bulloch: 11.
The maps on pages xii and 113 were drawn by Neil Hyslop.

# Acknowledgements

Our thanks are due to many people who have helped us with this book, either with information, insights or analysis, in Tehran and Baghdad, London, Paris, Washington and New York.

We are particularly grateful to Major General Edward Fursdon for his assessment of the military strengths and weaknesses of both sides, gained from his own observation in the early months of the war; to Safa Haeri for his knowledge of Iranian politics; Adel Darwish for his equal understanding of the Arab side, as well as for his technical assistance, with Edward Poultney. Others who helped included Annika Savill, Leonard Doyle, John Roberts, Nassir Shirkhani of Reuters, Baqer Moin of the BBC Persian service and, equally important, the 'minders' of the Ministries of Information in Tehran and Baghdad, who at times frustrated us, at times terrified us, but without whose own particular dedication we would not have been able to see what we did or to meet those who could help.

All these and many others gave us valuable information, but we emphasise that the interpretation and the judgments, and above all any mistakes, are entirely our own.

Our thanks are also due to the Foreign Editor of the *Independent* for his tolerance of our devotion to extramural activities for some months, and to our colleagues who bore stoically with our obsession. Above all, we thank Jill and Sarah, who put up with our absences and our single-mindedness. To them this book is dedicated.

# Authors' note

No attempt has been made in this book to give a scholarly transliteration of Arabic or Persian names for people or places. The style adopted is the one generally used in British or French newspapers, which it is thought would be most familiar to readers of this work in the English language.

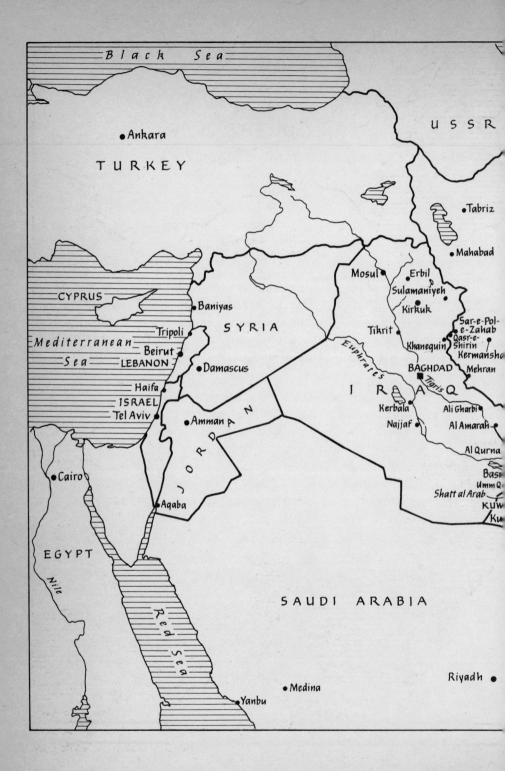

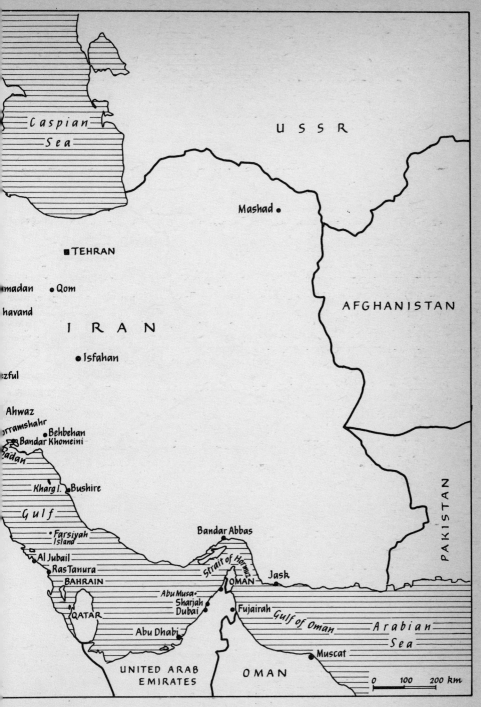

The Gulf and the Middle East

# Preface

The war in the Gulf lasted eight years, cost half a million lives, destroyed whole cities, devastated great swathes of Iran and Iraq, yet in the end settled little. Iran, for all its sudden collapse, remains an Islamic Republic. Despite his death on 3 June 1989, Ayatollah Khomeini's revolution is still being exported, with neither greater nor lesser success than in the past; more Revolutionary Guards, for example, have been dispatched to Lebanon to counter the arms being sent to that unhappy country by Iraq, that brutal state which considers itself the victor in the conflict, and now seems set to try to act the regional bully-boy. In Geneva and New York the antagonists meet, talk, disagree, meet again, while in a dozen other capitals their representatives buy more guns and rockets, shells and bombs. Oil, despite the price drop, still fuels the economies of Iran and Iraq, but the end of the fighting has failed to bring the construction bonanza that a dozen countries were hoping to exploit – anticipation of the contracts to be won when the war ended shaped the policies of many a country while the war was on.

A year after collapsing morale, lack of material and international pressure forced Ayatollah Khomeini to do what he had always sworn he would never do and bring the war to an end, how pointless it all seems. On 22 September 1980, the Iraqi army swept across the border into Iran in what was supposed to have been a blitzkrieg operation which would capture Khuzestan province with the help of its Arabic-speaking people and, by cutting off Tehran from its main refinery and port, force the mullahs to acknowledge the regional domination of Baghdad, trim their plans to export Ayatollah Khomeini's uncompromising brand of Islam, and accept the terms for peace which President Saddam Hussein would dictate, including a realignment of the border in Iraq's favour. It was not to be. By the spring of 1982 the Iraqi forces were back on their own soil, beaten by the shattered remnants of the Shah's army, by the Pasdaran, the Revolutionary Guards inspired by Khomeini, and by the children of the *basij* – the nine-, ten- and eleven-year-olds who swept the minefields with their feet or walked straight up to the Iraqi guns to fire their one shot or throw a single grenade in the sure expectation of the paradise which would follow martyrdom.

In that June of 1982 came the mistake of Khomeini's life. In Baghdad the Revolutionary Command Council, the ruling body of the Ba'ath party, met without Saddam Hussein and offered peace. Khomeini, if he had not been obsessed by hatred for the man who had been his reluctant host during his years of exile, or if he had had about him advisers powerful and brave enough to tell him the truth, could at that moment have gained peace for his people, international acceptance, the certainty that his vision of the Islamic society would be emulated in a dozen other places, and an honoured place in history, instead of the ignominy which now attends his name. This was one of the classic blunders which change the course of events for mankind. It led on to more carnage, to years of hardship for the Iranians as their leaders sought to use their numerical superiority to wear down the Iraqi defences, and to the eventual triumph which Saddam Hussein so desperately wanted as his policy of involving the superpowers eventually achieved the result he could not obtain alone.

For the war in the Gulf could not be confined to that narrow geographical region. More than half the world's oil reserves lie under the sandy deserts, the shallow seas, or the sudden unlikely cities of the Gulf littoral which the oil revenues have produced; and though America now imports only 5 per cent of its needs from the Gulf, Europe still takes 35 per cent of its consumption from the area, while Japan depends on the Gulf for 77 per cent of its supplies. Despite the desperate rush to build new pipelines, a tanker still transits the twenty-five-mile wide Strait of Hormuz between the Gulf and the Arabian Sea every two minutes. The doctrine laid down by President Jimmy Carter – that the Gulf forms part of the West's vital strategic interests, for which if necessary it would go to war – remains as true now as it was in the 1970s.

Yet when the calamity of armed conflict struck the Gulf in 1980 there was quick agreement by Washington and Moscow that they should not become involved, and for seven years America and the Soviet Union did no more than dabble, seeking rather to bolster their regional positions and to contain the war than to bring it to an end, much less to extract global advantage. The timing certainly had much to do with it. In 1980 the Soviet Union invaded Afghanistan, Solidarity was being broken in Poland, and the long ordeal of the American embassy hostages in Tehran ended only as a disillusioned electorate abandoned the President who had come to seem so ineffectual and turned to a man they believed would restore America's international reputation. Instead, President Ronald Reagan abandoned government to his often corrupt Californian cronies, and in the Irangate affair colluded, at least, with a colonel in the White House basement to sell arms to Iran in order to extract Western hostages held in Lebanon, and in order to obtain money to foment the revolution against the legitimate rulers of Nicaragua. Only when an Iraqi pilot mistook an American warship for an Iranian target did America decide to act – and then it paradoxically joined in on the side of the country which had done it the injury, using the attack on the USS *Stark* as the excuse finally to ensure the defeat of Iran.

The Soviet Union was no more positive and no more logical. Bound to Iraq by a Treaty of Friendship and Cooperation, Moscow at first held up all arms shipments to its regional client state as it tried to gain influence with the mullahs in Tehran. Desperate to ensure that the Khomeini brand of militant Islam did not spread across the border into the Soviet republics of Central Asia, where the Muslim conscripts had proved unwilling to act even against their distant cousins in Afghanistan, Moscow cynically abandoned the Tudeh party in Iran, communists loyal to the Soviet Union who were betrayed to the mullahs by the British in a last echo of the Great Game.

It was the war at sea, the tanker war, which finally drew America and the Soviet Union into the Gulf with a common aim, plus the changes in the Kremlin. The decision to pull out of Afghanistan showed that Mikhail Gorbachev was genuine in his desire to settle regional conflicts, and it also made it more important for Moscow to achieve a settlement in Iran – the military wanted no harassment, no possible side-shows, as they extricated themselves from the morass of Afghanistan. But it was the tanker war, begun by Iraq in 1984, which provided the imperative.

Iraq developed the capability for in-flight refuelling, so that its aircraft could attack ships loading at the southern end of the Gulf, at Larak and Sirri, as well as keeping up its attacks on the Kharg Island terminal and on Iranian oilfields. In response, Iran chose to sow mines in international waters, thus directly interfering with the shipment of oil from 'neutral' countries, in particular Kuwait, a state which was in fact Iraq's most loyal ally and committed supporter. Iraq's intention had always been to involve America if it could, but for all the talk of closing the Strait of Hormuz in 1984, the Americans had resisted the efforts to drag them into the conflict.

Now Kuwait succeeded where Iraq had failed. By the simple expedient of asking the Russians for help when they were turned down by the Americans, the Kuwaitis easily persuaded the Reagan administration that it had to act – the rationale in Washington was that the Soviet Union could not be permitted to move into what had always been a Western sphere of interest. So after much dithering the Americans allowed Kuwaiti tankers to be registered in the United States, and to fly the Stars and Stripes, while the Soviet Union leased three of its own ships to Kuwait. Both major powers said they would escort, guard and protect their own vessels, in effect taking sides against Iran, as that was the only country attacking neutral ships in the Gulf, its sole possible response to Iraqi attacks on its own tankers as Iraq had no vessels of its own in the Gulf.

With its friends protected, Iraq felt safe from retaliation and stepped up its attacks, causing serious difficulty to the Iranian economy, already suffering from the drop in oil prices and lower production. At the same time, Moscow and Washington began to put pressure on their client states not to supply Iran with arms, effectively cutting the flow of weapons from such places as North Korea and Israel, causing the Chinese to be less generous to Tehran, and making life even more difficult for the independent arms dealers who kept Iran supplied throughout the war. As the arms dried up, so the difficulties on the battlefield accumulated.

The Iranians were forced to abandon their human-wave tactics, which rarely gained much ground, and to try to advance by more conventional attacks. Now and again they did take some territory, but this was hard, slogging work against an Iraqi army radically improved since it was fighting to defend its own territory, protected by vast earthworks and wide man-made water obstacles, with defences in depth prepared if the front line should be overrun. The Iranians never had any hope of making the breakthrough they needed.

For much of the war, the plight of the Western hostages in Lebanon was another element affecting the conduct of the outside powers. Iran almost openly acknowledged that its men were the kidnappers, and quite cynically tried to barter the lives of the victims for arms, money or political support. Originally, the aim of the hostage-takers was to secure the release of seventeen supporters of Iran convicted and imprisoned in Kuwait for terrorist attacks there, but then, in the best-known affair of the Reagan years, Israel set up the deals which were to have provided Iran with arms, the Contras with money and the Americans with the success they sought in Beirut. Instead, it came close to bringing down the US President.

In the end, the grinding years of combat, the lack of arms and the collapse of morale forced Iran to accept the UN resolution calling for a ceasefire, a resolution accepted a year earlier by Iraq. But once the fighting stopped it was Iraq which sought to impose new conditions, a delaying tactic designed to give it time to complete one of the worst crimes of the century by a government against its own people. By concentrated use of chemical weapons the Iraqis sought to end once and for all the problem of the Kurdish dissidents in the north of their country, who for decades had been seeking autonomy. The day after the ceasefire went into effect Iraqi jets were in action strafing Kurdish villages, dropping poison gas and rocketing people trying to flee. In the end, organised Kurdish resistance was eliminated, and 100,000 refugees had been forced out of northern Iraq into Turkey and Iran. While it was all going on, the world looked carefully the other way, more concerned to do nothing to risk Iraq walking away from the Geneva ceasefire negotiations than to try to save the Kurds, a people with no voice or vote at the UN, no powerful lobbyists, no influence in the forums of the world.

The eight years of the Gulf war did have some results. It prevented what had at the beginning of the decade been seen as the main danger – that Iranian forces would sweep across the Gulf to export revolutionary Islam by the sword, much as the Arabs surged out of the Arabian peninsula 1,400 years earlier to spread the new faith. Iraq, backed by the fearful states of the lower Gulf, put an end to Khomeini's dreams of any forceful export of his ideas, and the barrenness of his vision and the consequences of his actions in Iran made it unlikely that his brand of zealotry would gain many adherents in the future. Inside Iran, the Khomeini years became even more bloodstained than the last months of the Shah's reign, with men, women and children summarily executed, torture the norm, human rights ignored. Within the Iranian government, the constant struggles for power continued as those around Khomeini sought to take over the revolution he had created. The moderates, the so-called pragmatists, were soundly defeated as extremism took over once again in the last span of the Imam's life.

In Iraq, it was a mirror image. Finally successful in the war he had deliberately begun and made entirely his own, Saddam Hussein emerged a victor – to his own people at least. There had to be some rewards for all the sacrifices, so there was some cosmetic liberalisation, quick demobilisation, an amnesty and some judicious pump-priming to get the economy moving. But at the centre of it all, Saddam Hussein remained in total control, the Ba'ath party apparatus as firmly in place as ever, Iraq still a police state, the people watched, regimented, spied upon and, if necessary, arrested, tortured or imprisoned. Still, the war was over, the country and the state intact, and the likelihood was that Iraq would play a bigger part in Arab affairs and would therefore continue to receive the backing and the practical help of the states it had saved from the dangers of Khomeinism. In Iraq, once the war was over, there was a feeling that somehow it had all been worthwhile.

One of the most dreadful facts to emerge from the eight years of war was that chemical weapons could now be used in local conflicts. Iraq first tested poison gas in real conditions in 1982, and though the fact was widely reported there was no international opposition, so that in 1984 Iraqi forces were able to move on to systematic use of chemical weapons, culminating in the massacre of the Kurds in northern Iraq in 1988. The world awoke too late to what was going on, and though efforts were made to limit possession or use of these weapons, a parallel and far more deadly trade began in organising their production and distribution. With chemical warheads being fitted to long-range missiles, the one lesson may be that the concept of local war is no longer viable.

Events since the end of the Gulf war have shown that the international community has finally realised the dangers. If this belated awakening leads to an international ban on the production as well as the use of chemical weapons, then some good will have come out of the war.

# 1

# Khomeini's
# poisoned chalice

When the end came, the old man could not bring himself to give the news in person. He was in his private mosque at his house in Jamaran performing the *asr* prayers as an announcer at the Tehran studios of the Voice of the Islamic Republic called on the Iranian nation and the Muslims of the world to stand by for an important message from Ayatollah al-Ozma Sayyed Ruhollah Mousavi Khomeini, Imam of the Ummah, the architect of Islamic Iran, the mullah who had defeated the Shah, the implacable commander who had decreed that there could be no peace until the forces of anti-Islamic Iraq were defeated. It was 2 p.m. on 20 July 1988, and though the message was a confirmation of what the world had learnt twenty-four hours earlier, it still came as a shock to the Iranian people, for without Khomeini's imprimatur, they could hardly believe the wild propaganda of foreign radio stations – that after almost eight years the war against Iraq was over. Even now, it was an announcer who was reading the text of the Imam's message, yet the words rang true, the style was his. 'Happy are those who have departed through martyrdom,' the announcer intoned. 'Happy are those who have lost their lives in this convoy of light. Unhappy am I that I still survive and have drunk the poisoned chalice. . . .'

In Baghdad there was dancing in the streets; in Tehran, a mournful resignation among a population taught to expect war until victory. And fighting did go on for weeks more, so that when the ceasefire did eventually take effect on 20 August, the two opposing armies were back to almost precisely the positions they had occupied before the 22 September 1980 invasion of Iran by Iraq. Now, eight years later, what was to have been a swift Iraqi offensive followed by a peace dictated from Baghdad could be seen as the longest conventional war of the twentieth century, a war which combined the human-wave assaults and gas attacks of the first World War with the modern horrors of long-range missile strikes on civilian targets. The precise death toll may never be established but is probably between half a million and a million.

On the Iranian side of the border entire towns were destroyed, either bulldozed into oblivion by the advancing Iraqi armies or shelled to rubble by the Iranian forces trying to liberate them, while on the Iraqi side in the final months of the war, Iraqi jets rained poison gas on their own civilians at Halabja, wiping out 5,000 Kurds in the space of a few minutes in revenge for the loss of a small town of doubtful importance. On the battlefield, the Iranians deployed poorly armed schoolchildren against tanks and artillery and the Iraqis used nerve gas for the first time in the history of warfare. In eight years, the two sides spent a total of $350 billion on a conflict which brought neither anywhere near fulfilling even its most modest war aims.

The only victory, for both Iraq and Iran, was that they avoided defeat. For the world, the tragedy was the continued strength of both brutal warring regimes. For most of the eight long years of war the opposing forces were locked in a virtual stalemate, brought about by what one Western military analyst called 'a balance of incompetence'. At one time or another, both armies were in a position to deliver the knockout blow, yet they squandered their opportunities with bad strategy and lack of preparation. The Iraqi forces which stormed across the frontier into Iran for what they believed would be a speedy victory spent the next seven and a half years on the defensive, most of that time on their own territory, while their political leaders sued for peace. Iran, which had to scrape together a makeshift defence to halt the 1980 Iraqi blitzkrieg, was carrying on an unsuccessful offensive during that time while Khomeini and the clerical leadership refused all offers of a negotiated settlement. Iran declared itself to be the victim of an 'imposed war', yet after 1982, when the invaders were thrown out and the battles moved into Iraq, the continuation of the conflict was largely self-imposed. The Iranian decision to carry the war into Iraq rather than to negotiate for peace from a position of strength proved to be the greatest single blunder of the war.

Saddam Hussein escaped the consequences of his ill-conceived adventure to contain and subdue Iran thanks to a combination of determination and ruthlessness, coupled with the indirect support of outside powers, principally the United States, which by 1987 had resolved that the Islamic Republic should not be allowed to triumph. The ceasefire, when it came, was forced on Iran when it was at its weakest, when it had lost both its capacity and its will to continue the fight – which did not prevent Saddam Hussein declaring the outcome a victory for Iraq with all the hyperbole his regime had made its own over the years. It was a war in which, in the words of the Iraqi General Command, 'the Iraqi people and their valiant armed forces resisted the force of aggression and tyranny'. The ending of the conflict was 'a great victory that has been achieved by Iraq in the name of all Arabs and in the name of humanity'.

The Iranian religious hierarchy had a much more daunting task in persuading their people that the sacrifices and sufferings of the previous eight years had not been in vain. The essence of their message was that the struggle against Iraq had consolidated the achievements of the revolution and that the decision to end the war was in order to protect those achievements. For all that, Khomeini's acceptance of the 'poisoned chalice' of peace was tantamount to an acknowledgement of defeat. 'I know that it is hard for you,' he told the Iranian people. 'But then is it not hard for your old father? I know that for you martyrdom is sweeter than honey, but then is it not the same for this servant of yours?' Those were unmistakably his own words, but when it came to justifying what had been decided the excuses of advisers took over: Iran was the victim of a plot by the enemies of Islam in which Iraq's role was merely that of a mercenary catspaw, acting on behalf of outside powers. 'Everyone knows that we did not start the war. We only defended ourselves in order to ensure the continuation of Islam in the world. It is the innocent Iranian nation that has been the target of continuous attack by the world-devourers.' For 'world-devourers' read the United States, the Soviet Union and Israel, although each one at times helped to bolster the Iranian war effort for its own geopolitical motives.

The outside powers did not start this war but they did nothing to avert it and little to end it once it had begun. Despite declarations of neutrality from the world community and occasional expressions of outraged impotence at its inability to bring the conflict to an end, a steady supply of foreign weapons reached the two belligerents throughout the war, and even when Iraq began to use chemical weapons on the battlefield, there was no more than a muted response from the rest of the world. Only on those occasions when the conflict threatened to spill over the borders of Iran and Iraq and to threaten oil supplies did the rest of the world really become concerned, though in the end it was concerted action by the outside powers which dictated the outcome.

Back in the autumn of 1980 the intensity of mistrust between the two great powers was such that neither side could afford to intervene decisively without risking the possibility of a slide towards world war. Some days before the Iraqi invasion, members of President Carter's Special Co-ordination Committee, including secretary of state Edmund Muskie, defence secretary Harold Brown and the national security adviser, Zbigniew Brzezinski, gathered in Washington to discuss intelligence reports of a build-up of Soviet troops along the Iranian frontier, possibly poised for intervention. It was less than a year since the Soviet invasion of Afghanistan which had prompted Carter to set out his new doc-trine threatening a US military response against any Soviet at-tempt to gain control of the Gulf, but in September 1980 the United States had no forces in the area to mount a conventional military response; the only possible option was nuclear. Brzezinski gives an account of the meeting in his memoirs:

> Muskie offered the judgment that Congress would not feel that a nuclear war was worth 11 per cent of our oil, and Brown rather sharply responded by asking what would happen if the Soviets invaded Iran and we did nothing. Did Muskie really believe that our losses would be only a percentage of our oil supply? Muskie retorted that the American people might even accept the loss of Europe rather than risk nuclear war. I then joined in by asking Muskie if he accepted the proposition that the loss of the Persian Gulf might lead to the loss of Europe and Muskie reluctantly agreed that that might be the case.

It was against a background of chaos in the oil markets that the Carter advisers met to discuss the challenge of a possible Soviet move into Iran and towards the Gulf, and Muskie was correct in asserting that only a small proportion of US oil consumption depended on supplies from the Gulf, but for America's allies in Western Europe and Japan, Middle East oil was of primary importance. For the world in general, the importance of Gulf oil to the global economy remains paramount and will increase in coming decades as reserves in other parts of the world run down. Middle East oil is at present calculated to represent 58 per cent of all the world's known reserves, and a quarter of those Gulf reserves lie beneath the territories of Iraq and Iran – by the next century nearly all the remaining oil in the world will be in the Gulf.

The West has already suffered two oil shocks which plunged Western economies into recession: the first in 1973 when the Organisation of Petroleum Exporting Countries (OPEC) took over price-setting from the international oil companies at a time of high demand for Middle East oil. The effects of this OPEC revolution were exacerbated by an Arab oil embargo imposed as a result of the Arab–Israeli war, so that within two years the price of a barrel of oil rose from $1.90 to $10.40. Queues at petrol stations, rationing and the US decision to reduce the speed-limit to an energy-saving 55 mph were all signs of a realisation in the West that oil supplies were not infinite and could not be taken for granted.

Ironically, it was the Shah who was one of the architects of the pricing revolution, and six years later it was his fall which occasioned the second oil shock. The disruption of Iranian production in the year leading up to the February 1979 revolution caused panic in the oil markets, although demand for oil was relatively depressed at the time. Yet despite this and the fact that Western countries had by now built up substantial strategic reserves, buyers rushed to beat the rising market; further panic set in at the time of the Iraqi invasion, with its threat of a total cut-off of Gulf supplies, so that by the autumn of 1980, the free-market price of a barrel of Gulf crude was approaching $40.

The geopolitical dilemma facing Washington in 1979 was that US inability or failure to protect the Gulf from Soviet threat would risk undermining the entire structure of the post-war Western alliance, for the underlying threat of any Soviet move into the Gulf was that the West might ultimately lose access to Saudi Arabia's oil reserves, almost twice as great as those of Iran and Iraq combined. The Americans believed the threat was real because the CIA had reported, erroneously as it turned out, that the Soviet Union would soon become a net importer of oil. In fact, the Russians wanted security and stability of supply from the Gulf in much the same way as the Americans did. Traditionally, the Soviet Union had sold its own oil and gas at favoured rates to its Eastern bloc allies, but as world prices began to rise it saw the opportunity to boost its foreign exchange earnings by selling its oil on the free market and diverting its allies towards suppliers in the Gulf.

The crisis prompted by the slide towards war in the Gulf could not have come at a worse time for the United States: its global standing was low and its relations with the Soviet Union were bad, and in the region affected Washington had lost its most powerful ally and had found no one to replace him. When the Gulf war began, fifty-two of America's diplomats had been held hostage in Iran for more than ten months after fundamentalist students seized the embassy on 4 November 1979, and President Carter's failure to extract them pointed to his almost certain defeat in the election battle with Ronald Reagan which was by now just two months away.

But the Soviet Union was also under pressure, with the process of detente with the West begun by Leonid Brezhnev in the early 1970s now on the point of collapse. The SALT I treaty which resulted from the first Strategic Arms Limitation Talks was the high point of the process, but the SALT II treaty, negotiated with the Carter administration, was doomed to founder on the rock of Congressional opposition. The Soviet desire for detente had been spurred on, in part, by the deterioration of relations between Moscow and Peking in the Maoist era, a process later exacerbated by Sino-Soviet rivalry in Indochina after the Vietnam war. Now it seemed that Washington was strengthening its ties with Peking, possibly even contemplating selling weapons to the Chinese, at a time when its relations with Moscow were drifting towards a new Cold War. The birth of the Solidarity trade union and the growth of liberalism in Poland during 1980, a process in which Moscow inevitably detected the hidden hand of Washington, was threatening Soviet dominance of the Eastern bloc. In Turkey, the Soviet Union's NATO neighbour on the southern flank, a right-wing military regime had just seized power. The American decision to lead a boycott of the 1980 Olympic Games in Moscow seemed symbolic of the new freeze between the superpowers.

Not for the first time in its history, the Soviet Union felt itself surrounded on all sides, and the theory that the opportunistic entry into Afghanistan was designed to strengthen the southern defences is as valid as Washington's worst-case scenario in which the Afghan invasion represented the first step on a Soviet march towards the warm waters of the Gulf. Moscow had its own, equally disturbing scenario: that the United States would use the excuse of the Tehran hostage crisis to mount an assault on Iran aimed at reversing the revolution and bringing Iran back even more securely into the Western camp. Alternatively, it feared that once the hostages were freed Washington might move to restore a strategic relationship with Iran, for after the Afghan invasion US officials began to hint at the possibility of future military and economic cooperation with the Iranians once the hostage crisis was resolved. A state department official was quoted in January 1980 as comparing the relationship with Iran with that between the United States and post-war Germany, and remarking: 'We ended up rearming Germany.' It was a prospect only slightly less alarming to Moscow than that of direct US intervention.

In international politics, a balance of suspicion can often serve the same purpose as a balance of trust, and in this case both Washington and Moscow understood that any attempt by either side to move into the countries of the Gulf in force would almost inevitably provoke a war between the superpowers, for neither side had a reliable surrogate in the region. Revolutionary Iran owed allegiance to no one, and US attempts to support a counter-revolutionary movement capable of unseating Khomeini had come to nothing. Iraq, so long an ally of the Soviet Union, was now marching to its own tune, so when war broke out the superpowers stood aside, and the state of relations between Moscow and Washington even made decisive action at the United Nations a virtual impossibility. Although it was clear from the spring of 1980 and certainly after August that a war was brewing between Iraq and Iran, the Security Council took no action to restrain either side. Some of the blame for this lay with Iran itself which, by its continued detention of the American hostages, had made itself a pariah state.

The Soviet Union, given the state of its relations with the United States, had opted at the start of the hostage crisis to give moral support to Iran's 'revolutionary act' (the taking of the embassy), rather than standing unequivocally by Washington on the issue of the inviolability of international law. A *Pravda* commentary published one month after the seizure of the US embassy merely noted that the action was in violation of international law, but it added that Washington was guilty of a gross violation of international norms by conducting naval manoeuvres in the

Arabian Sea. Although Moscow supported a unanimous Security
Council call for the release of the hostages, it abstained on
a further resolution threatening Iran with economic sanctions.
Britain's ambassador to the United Nations at the outbreak of
the war, Sir Anthony Parsons, has described the failure of the
permanent members of the Security Council to take swift action
when it was most needed.

> Iraq was, as I saw it, under the impression that they needed
> three or four days in which to deal Iran a knockout blow.
> Now, with that in mind, Iraq made the most strenuous efforts
> to prevent the Security Council actually from meeting at all.
> And they brought enormous pressure on the seven non-
> aligned members of the Council actually to refuse to go into
> the Chamber. And this tactic succeeded for some days. At
> that time, if Iran had not been in international disgrace
> because of the hostage holding, I simply don't believe that
> the other members of the Security Council, the permanent
> members and others, wouldn't have actually overridden this
> Iraqi pressure against a meeting.

When the Security Council eventually adopted Resolution 479
on the Gulf war in September 1980, this called only for a ceasefire
and did not call for a withdrawal of forces to the international
frontier nor condemn Iraq for its act of aggression, so that Iran
was left with the impression that the world community had abandoned it to its fate. It was something that was to colour Iranian
perceptions for the rest of the war for it sowed the seeds of the
belief that the Islamic Republic was facing the combined enmity
of the outside world. It was a belief which was enhanced by the
fact that the Security Council's collective inability at the start of
the war to rescue Iran from the consequences of Iraqi aggression
contrasted so greatly with the subsequent determination of individual states to secure their interests in the Gulf.

For most of the war, four of the five permanent members of
the Council – the United States, the Soviet Union, Britain and
France – all had warships stationed in or near the Gulf to safeguard
oil supplies and ultimately, in the case of the Americans, to bring
pressure on Iran to end the war, for this American intervention
in the Gulf, ostensibly to safeguard the security of international
shipping, was unashamedly one-sided. The White House refused

to be diverted from its chosen course even when in May 1987 an Iraqi jet mistakenly attacked the USS *Stark*, killing thirty-seven American servicemen on board. Rather, the incident was the signal for an expanded US presence which was ultimately pitted against Iran. It was a high-risk operation, which disturbed some of America's closest allies and was condemned by domestic critics, for the US presence, particularly after Kuwaiti tankers were placed under the protection of the Stars and Stripes in July 1987, actually made the Gulf less safe. It prompted the Iranians to mine international waterways and tempted the Iraqis to attack Iranian tankers in the hope of provoking Iran into entering into an unequal combat with the US fleet. Under broader rules of engagement introduced in the final year, the United States assumed the role of an undeclared belligerent in the war against Iran, while Iraq continued to carry out air strikes on Iranian shipping with impunity.

The American intervention was motivated by the desire to contain Iran at a time when it looked as if the Iranians might make a decisive breakthrough in the land war by capturing the Iraqi city of Basra. It was also prompted by the need to purge the memory of Irangate, both at home and among the United States's Arab allies. The revelation in the autumn of 1986 that Washington had secretly been supplying arms to Iran, at a time when such sales were banned, had a traumatic effect on the American public and on countries such as Saudi Arabia which had put their trust in the United States. It was an affair which threatened to destroy the Reagan presidency and undermine the US role in the Middle East, and the secret dealings revealed the views of those in the Reagan administration who saw Iran as the cornerstone of America's geopolitical strategy in the Gulf. It was a doctrine inherited from Henry Kissinger and the Nixon administration and had provided the basis of the strategic relationship between Washington and the Shah.

After the Irangate revelations, those who saw Saudi Arabia as the key US asset in the region, notably the secretary of state, George Shultz, came to the fore, and there was a sharp switch away from seeking a rapprochement with Iran towards a policy of containing it. But whatever the motivation, the results were the same: the US presence in the Gulf as an undeclared ally of Iraq was a central element of the pressure which built up on Iran to end the war. Had the Americans acted so aggressively or decisively at the beginning, they might only have succeeded in worsening the already dismal relations with Moscow and perhaps provoked a Soviet military reaction, but by the summer of 1987 Mikhail Gorbachev had taken over in the Kremlin and a new and more co-operative chapter in the superpower relationship had begun.

For the first six years of the Gulf war, both superpowers were content with the stalemate: the panic over oil supplies proved to be unfounded, for Iran's war effort depended totally on its ability to export its oil and the periodic threats of the mullahs to close the Strait of Hormuz were never more than rhetorical. The early 1980s was a period of recession in which world demand, and therefore the oil price, was generally slack; the major industrialised countries had also diversified their sources of supply after the first oil shock and were, for the time being at least, less dependent on Gulf oil. The end of the oil boom in Texas, with unaccustomed talk among the oilmen of budget-trimming and belt-tightening, symbolised the fact that the threat was now not of a sudden cut-off of Gulf supplies but rather of a flooding of the market by Iraqi and Iranian crude if the war should end suddenly.

There was therefore no economic imperative in the United States or elsewhere in the West to work for a ceasefire. There was also a feeling that while the two sides were bogged down at the battle-front they would have less opportunity to create trouble elsewhere in the region – a short-sighted view in light of the mayhem the Iranians helped to sow in Lebanon – or to pose a threat to the security of Israel. The Soviet Union gained similar satisfaction from the fact that the war kept Iran tied up on its western frontier and therefore not in a position effectively to support the Mujahedin guerrillas fighting against Soviet occupation in Afghanistan to the east. Broadly speaking, the fall of the Shah had been a geopolitical benefit to the Russians. The Soviet academic, Vladimir Shmarov, asked to sum up the Kremlin's attitude to the Iranian revolution a decade after Khomeini took power, chuckled and replied: 'We like revolutions.' Nevertheless, the Russians had no wish to see Iran's regional influence spread, so until the decision was taken to withdraw from Afghanistan, the state of general equilibrium between Iran and Iraq suited Moscow very well.

Both during and after the war, Iran's leaders made much of the supposed superpower plot against the Islamic Republic which had

led both to an imposed war and an imposed peace. Like many of
the conspiracy theories to which the revolution was so prone, this
one had an element of truth: certainly the outside world was
happy enough at the prospect of seeing the mullahs' Iran cut down
to size and only intervened to end the war once it appeared that
Iran might win. But the responsibility for the continuation of the
war for eight years lay with one man, Khomeini. His long struggle
against the Shah both in exile and at home, and his subsequent
establishment of the first modern theocracy under his own, undis-
puted rule appeared to serve as an example of the virtues of
intransigence. How could a man who had overturned 2,500 years
of monarchy compromise in the battle against someone like Saddam Hussein? After 1982, there were those in the leadership who
did argue that Iran should call a halt to the war now that it had
ousted the Iraqi invaders and regained its territory, but Khomeini
adamantly refused, insisting that the punishment of God and the
world had to be inflicted on the aggressor.

His attitude to the war and his refusal to compromise were a
natural product of a lifetime's study and teaching of Islamic
philosophy. Within the tight circle of the Shia clergy, Khomeini
had a reputation as a leading philosopher and mystic long before
his name became known to the outside world. He was a proponent
of the mystical and hermetic school of *erfan* philosophy which
teaches extreme self-discipline and single-mindedness. The
American scholar Roy Mottahedeh has written that 'teachers of
*erfan* seek to impart to their students a sense of fearlessness
toward everything external, including all the seemingly coercive
political powers of the world'. Both in the revolution and the war,
Khomeini saw his role as a warrior against Satan and the temporal
enemies of God in the form of Western imperialism and atheist
communism. While others in Tehran, including the *ulema*, came
to view the war increasingly in nationalistic terms, Khomeini saw
it as an extension of the revolution and as a defence of what he
believed was the first truly Islamic state since the time of the
Prophet. More than six months after the ceasefire, he said:

> Every day of the war we had a blessing, which we utilised in
> all aspects. We exported our revolution to the world through
> the war; we proved our oppression and the aggressor's
> tyranny through the war. It was through the war that we

unveiled the deceitful face of the world-devourers; it was through the war that we recognised our enemies and friends. It was during the war that we concluded that we must stand on our own feet. It was through the war that we broke the back of both Eastern and Western superpowers.

When it came, the impact of the revolution was not that it happened, but the form it took; for years there had been regular predictions of upheavals in Iran, of bloody revolution or of a *coup*, a popular uprising or a left-wing takeover. It was the Tudeh party and other similar far-left groups which seemed to pose the threat if there was to be violence, and the young intellectuals who saw the Shah for what he was who would provide the ideology for change. On visits to Iran in the time of the Shah, we would have clandestine meetings with such young revolutionaries, at great risk to them; often, they could not be found on subsequent trips. Not once did we visit the mosques, and when we went to Iraq we paid little attention to the activities of exiles in Kerbala or Najjaf. Like the rest of the world, we were wrong, but at that time the idea of a mullah-led upheaval was so new and strange that it did not impinge on Western consciousness. Squabbles between ayatollahs inside Iran, or between the exiled Shia leaders and those inside the country, seemed too esoteric a subject to have any practical impact. It was a mistake made not only by Western reporters, but also by the Shah, and by world leaders everywhere.

In a famously dismissive phrase when asked about the occasional bombs which went off in Tehran, symbols of the futile efforts at disruption by the tiny band of left-wing militants, the Shah spoke of those who wanted to assassinate him, and said: 'Taxi-drivers and shoeshine boys in the streets hunt them down.' That may have been so, though the Shah rarely gave anyone the opportunity to remove him – he was a physical coward, and would not venture into the streets of his own cities. One British ambassador recalled him staging a mock procession in a specially arranged set every now and then so that television cameras could film a royal progress. What neither the Shah nor anyone else realised was the potential impact of the aged exile in Najjaf, the mullah-revolutionary whose ideas of a theocratic state seemed no more than the muddled dream of a man out of touch with the world, who spent his lifetime poring over the abstruse ideas of

Islamic jurisprudence. But in his exile in Iraq Khomeini nurtured a deep hatred of the Shah and all his works, a hatred rooted in events of his youth and early years when the first stirrings of revolt were brutally crushed, and when his own attempts to defy the power of the state were brought to nothing. On top of personal animus there was a burning sense of the need for change, of the inequities of life in Iran, and of the subservient state to which the Islamic establishment had been reduced. Add to all this cunning and charisma, a natural aptitude for politics and an unshakeable belief in his own abilities, and Khomeini should have been seen as the doughty opponent he so swiftly became.

Yet right up to the end, the Shah failed to appreciate his adversary. Ill-advised by the Americans on whom he had come to depend so basically, he did not realise that bullets could not kill an idea, nor partial reforms buy off a crusade. When the end finally came early in 1979, and the Shah was forced into exile, others had the benefit of learning from his blunders, and could make their own assessments much better. Thus in the Gulf there was little hesitation: the impact of Shia fundamentalism had to be stopped. In Saudi Arabia, where the 5,000 descendants of Abdel Aziz were sustained by the wealth from the oil pumped out of the desert by the Americans, and kept the peace by allowing some of the riches to trickle down to the people, there was a swift realisation of the danger. Only some 5 per cent of the population of the Kingdom were Shia, but they were concentrated in the eastern provinces where most of the oil was found, and – quietly – it had to be admitted that they had not done quite so well as the Sunni majority. There was fertile ground here for Khomeini to export his revolution, if he carried through his promises to do so.

In Bahrain for years past the month of Muharram had produced its crises, as the 80 per cent of this small island country's population mourned the death of the third Shia Imam and on the tenth day, Ashura, marched through the streets, slashing themselves with swords and flagellating themselves with chains in a frenzy of religious devotion which all too often turned into a demonstration against Bahrain's Sunni rulers.

In Kuwait only some 30 per cent of the population were Shia, but more than half of those came from Iran and there was a huge Palestinian population there too, a variable factor in an explosive situation. The astute, rich and highly practical Kuwaiti rulers

knew very well that they would be a prime target. Nor was it only
Iran's near neighbours who felt the frisson of fear which warned
that action had to be taken to avert calamity. In Egypt, Anwar
Sadat had released members of the Muslim Brotherhood imprisoned by President Nasser, and actually encouraged the rise of
Islamic fundamentalism in the universities as a means of counter-
ing resurgent Nasserism as well as the revolutionary left. By the
time of Khomeini's triumphal return to Tehran, Sadat was trying
to put the genie back into the bottle, but his own assassination in
1981 showed how impossible that was. Even in the far-off states
of the Maghreb, in Morocco and Tunisia, Islamic fundamentalism
among both the Sunni and the tiny minority of Shia was the
growing force, far more potent than the yearning for a return of
Nasserism shown by Muammar Gaddafi in Libya, or the movement for economic reform in Algeria.

But it was in Iraq, Iran's neighbour and its constant adversary
over the centuries, that all these disparate elements had to come
together if anything were to be done. The prospect seemed
unlikely: Iraq was largely the artificial legacy of the Ottoman
Empire, a group of provinces – vilayets – united by the British
after the First World War, and containing separate ethnic and
religious groupings. In the mountainous north of the country, one
and a half million Kurds, Sunni Muslims with no affinities at all
with the ruling clique of their co-religionists from the areas of
Tikrit and Hadithah who ran the country, pursued their own
convoluted campaigns in their search for nationhood, national
identity or, at the least, the freedom to live their own lives in their
own way. Spread across the border regions of five countries –
Iraq, Syria, Iran, Turkey and the Soviet Union – the Kurds were
a constant nuisance to their host-states, yet at times an asset to
be bribed or goaded into action against a neighbour. Used by the
Shah up to 1975 when he was seeking to force Iraq to give in to
his demands (principally over the Shatt al Arab dispute), the
Kurds had been given a very limited autonomy by the Baghdad
government, but certainly could not be relied on for help in any
new cross-border adventure.

In the south of Iraq, in the region once called Mesopotamia –
the land between the two great rivers, the Tigris and Euphrates
– the country was populated by the Shia, perhaps 60 per cent of
Iraq's 14 million population, a people regarded as rather beneath

them by the Sunni rulers in Baghdad, a sub-class relegated to the less well-paid jobs, the lower grades in the armed forces, the more menial tasks. Could they be relied on to move against their fellow-Shia in Iran? Saddam Hussein, the Ba'ath party gunman and *apparatchik* who took over from the figurehead ex-General, Ahmed Hassan al-Bakr, just as Khomeini was establishing himself in Tehran, had no doubt that the attempt had to be made. If he did not move, he was certain that Shia fundamentalism would sweep across the border from Iran, gathering in the holy places of Kerbala and Najjaf with their religious establishments and thus taking over half his country and more than half his people. For Saddam Hussein, the choice was simple. If he did not act, he would not survive; either his regime would wither away, or it would be swept aside by the tide of resurgent Shia militancy.

Not only the countries of the Middle East and the Gulf region were concerned. Pakistan had a division of troops in Saudi Arabia to guard that regime against incursion from South Yemen, or against its own dissident forces, and had friendly relations with Iran. Turkey, a member of NATO, had a common border with both Iran and Iraq and was intent on maintaining existing good relations with the aim of improving its own difficult economy. Even the European countries had their interests. Britain first became involved in the early nineteenth century when it used its naval power to impose a maritime truce, and then spread its influence from sea to land. By the end of that century an imperial-minded Germany with its *drang nach osten* was seeking a toehold there, and soon the French joined in as they sought new markets.

But above all it was superpower concerns which had to be taken into account. America, with its oil interests in Saudi Arabia and other Gulf states, had quietly moved in to replace the British from 1970 onwards, and was mainly responsible for promoting the Shah as its surrogate and policeman for the region. But the Soviet Union was on Iran's northern border, and it too considered the Gulf an area of vital interest. Both countries were deeply impressed by that CIA report predicting that by early in the twenty-first century Eastern bloc oil production would have declined so much that Russia would be forced to begin importing supplies from outside its own sphere of influence, and would thus have to compete with America and other Western nations for the production of the Gulf. Later estimates, and Moscow's own assessments, ridiculed that study, but by that time the damage was done. No matter what the futurologists said, planners and politicians in both Moscow and Washington had it firmly fixed in their heads that they would sooner or later be in competition with each other in the Gulf. It mattered not that such an assessment was wrong, for once an idea is in a politician's mind it is difficult to move, and by now Russians and Americans alike were predicating their policies on a competitive, confrontational approach.

Neither Russia nor America brought much pressure to bear when Saddam Hussein sent his armies across the borders in 1980. The Russians did have a Treaty of Friendship and Cooperation with Baghdad, which meant in practice that they armed Iraq and trained its soldiers and airmen, and America was slowly beginning to mend its fences with Iraq as its influence in Iran dwindled to nothing. In a token expression of displeasure Moscow suspended arms deliveries to Iraq as long as that country's forces were inside Iranian territory, and at the same time sought to maintain links with Tehran; although it fared rather better than America, it had no spectacular successes there. In both Iran and Iraq the Russians saw their local communist parties decimated and suppressed, and did nothing about it. Ayatollah Khomeini was almost as opposed to Godless Moscow as he was to the Great Satan in Washington, and in Baghdad the Iraqi army commanders never made any effort to hide their dislike of their Russian instructors. The superpowers quickly realised that their best interests were served by leaving well alone; there was a glut of oil on the world market, so it was no bad thing if a few million barrels were taken out of production every day. Nor would it do any harm if the regional superpowers bled each other for a while; not only did Khomeini's Islamic revolution have to be contained, but Iran itself had to learn that it could not expand, no matter who was in charge.

Support for Iraq was no more altruistic, for all the talk of Arab solidarity. In the 1970s, Iraq was the trouble-maker of the area, stirring up dissidents in the lower Gulf, providing arms for rebel movements, assassinating its opponents. An Iraq obsessed with its own concerns and militarily weakened would suit the purposes of its neighbours very well – throughout the war and after its conclusion, Kuwait remained as fearful of Iraqi expansionism as it was of Iranian-inspired dissidence or straightforward invasion.

The one country which believed that its vital interests were closely affected, and which accordingly took a direct hand in the affair, was far from the battle lines. Israel saw the Gulf war as an opportunity to confound its Arab enemies and to ensure the safety of a Jewish community which it believed was at risk. At the time of the revolution in Iran, there were probably some 80,000 Jews in the country, a recognised minority along with Christians and Zoroastrians, which in general had suffered no persecution and had been able to continue its affairs undisturbed. The fervent fundamentalism of Khomeini put all that at risk: his denunciations of the Zionists and his support of the Palestinians was a deep worry to the Israelis, and the thought of the Islamic revolution spreading to Iraq was a prospect almost too awful to contemplate. But think about it they did, and the result was a clandestine support of Iran which ensured the safety of the Jewish community in the country and allowed thousands to emigrate; it also contributed substantially to Iran's successful defence of its borders, and the eventual weakening of both sides in the war.

It was the Israelis who devised and manufactured the huge, lightweight polystyrene blocks which the Iranian assault forces carried with them to build instant makeshift causeways across the shallow Iraqi water defences in front of Basra; it was Israel which kept Iranian planes flying in spite of a lack of spares; and it was Israeli instructors who taught the new young Iranian commanders how to handle troops, how to move their forces about and how to exploit the openings made by the fanatically brave young volunteers who died in their thousands in the human-wave assaults. Above all, it was the Israelis who involved the Reagan administration in the Iran–Contra affair. For all the speeches of Iranian leaders, the diatribes against Israel, the denunciations at the Friday prayers, there were never less than about a hundred Israeli advisers and technicians in Iran at any time throughout the war, living in a carefully guarded and secluded camp just north of Tehran; they remained there even after the ceasefire.

Eight years after Iraqi troops first rolled across the frontier to begin their difficult two-year occupation of some border areas, Iran finally accepted the UN ceasefire Resolution 598 which Iraq had enthusiastically endorsed a year earlier. A month later the guns fell silent, UN truce supervisors moved in, and the war was at an end – with the forces of each combatant roughly where they were back in 1980. In the world at large, and in Iran in particular,

many voices were raised. Had there been any point in it all? What
had been accomplished? In fact, the Gulf, the world and Iran and
Iraq themselves underwent profound changes in the years of desperate combat. In September 1980 the Iranian revolution was
young and the people filled with a fervour born of a new devotion
to their religion and a new belief in the wisdom and infallibility of
their leader. They were the victims, the people defending not only
their homeland but their vision of a new, just society. On the
shoulders of the young men who went off to battle with little more
than a rifle, a couple of hours' instruction and the blessing of the
Imam rested not only the future of the Islamic state but also the
new-found confidence of the down-trodden 10 per cent of the Muslim world, the Shia who had for so long been regarded as lesser
beings, the deprived of the earth, as Musa Sadr called them.

In Iraq, the attitude was very different. The conscripts who led
the first assault into Khuzestan – called Arabistan by their leaders,
who assured them of a welcome from their brothers there – did so
in a dour mood. They wanted neither death nor glory, but to return
to their homes as soon as possible. Their commanders were well-
trained professional soldiers, but they were constrained by the political officers accompanying each battalion, Ba'ath party men who
could insist on putting domestic considerations ahead of military
necessities. They were hampered too, by an instruction passed
down to them from President Saddam Hussein himself: avoid casualties. In a country of no more than 14 million people taking on an
enemy with a population then of more than 40 million, manpower
could not be squandered. In addition, the Iraqi leaders knew very
well that this was not a popular war but something they had inflicted
on their people. They were also less than sure of the loyalty of many
Iraqis, both inside and outside the armed forces, and they realised
very well that the spectacle of coffins being carried back to the towns
and villages from the front line so close to many heavily populated
areas would do nothing for morale.

This was an attitude which had other effects too: for instance, the
best troops in the Iraqi army, the Republican Guard Corps, were
not committed to the battle for years to come. Occasionally, as
in Khorramshahr, the situation became so desperate that special
Guard units had to be taken away from Baghdad and put in to try
to retrieve the situation, but in general the Republican Guard and
many other crack units were kept in their barracks close to Bagh-

dad. The reason was two-fold. Firstly, the regime had to be protected from its own people, for the Iraqi government was made up of a core of cronies of Saddam Hussein, party men who like him were Sunni Muslims in a country where the Shia formed the majority. Secondly, Baghdad itself had to be defended at all costs, and it was no more than sixty miles from Iranian forces on the border.

Perhaps one of the great Iranian mistakes of the war was to concentrate so completely on Basra, Iraq's second city and main port. The Iranians chose Basra because it was approached over a wide plain, and so was relatively easy to attack, and also because they believed that by seizing Basra and setting up an alternative government there they could bring about the collapse of the regime. Even when in later years they decided to avoid Basra, realising that it was too difficult to take, they still put in their main attacks in that southern region, attempting to by-pass the city and split the country – again, they hoped, achieving their object by rallying to their side the majority of the Shia of the southern part of Iraq.

A comparable Iraqi mistake in the first months of the war was their obsession with Abadan. The Iraqis were determined to take this huge oil refining town, the symbol of modern Iran; they thought that by seizing it they would cripple the Iranian economy and so bring the war to an end, but then it became an objective for its own sake, though it was already ruined by artillery and aerial bombardment and not worth wasting a man on. Yet for almost two years the Iraqis continued to see Abadan as the prize; they never took it, close though they got. But instead of wasting their men and firepower on this shattered oil town, they should have been driving for Dezful and Ahwaz, the provincial capital where the Iranian resistance was organised from an underground bunker at the airfield.

Even then, the whole Iraqi plan was flawed. Just as the Iranians wrongly believed that Iraq would fall to them if they could take Basra, so the Iraqis thought that Iran would give in if the province of Khuzestan was taken. But Khuzestan to the Iranians was only one small and rather difficult province out of fourteen; it was far from the capital and the major cities of the country, sheltered behind the Zagros mountain chain. Even the people of Khuzestan, for all the loyalty to the state they eventually displayed, were not of great concern to Tehran, for they were a suspect group, Arabic-speaking and alien to the Iranian élite.

# 2

# Preparations
# for war

On 8 April 1980 Iranian gendarmes patrolling near the frontier crossing at Khosravi came upon a group of middle-aged men in crumpled business suits wandering lost and bewildered in the desert scrub. None of them spoke Persian or the local Kurdish dialect. At the nearby border post, with the help of Arabic-speaking mullahs, their story slowly emerged: they were all Shia Muslims and prominent traders in the Baghdad bazaar who, by a trick of the Iraqi secret police, had been taken from their families and abandoned in the wilderness. Altogether, the Iranians rounded up some 500 men with a similar story to tell from the total of more than 16,000 Iraqis sent across the border and into involuntary exile during that one week in April, while by the time the war broke out the number expelled had swollen to 200,000. These refugees had been thrown out as part of an escalating ideological war between Iraq and Iran, a clearing of the decks before the real war which was to erupt less than six months later.

Of all the stories which the refugees brought with them of summary expulsion from their homeland, the tale of the 500 Baghdad bazaaris was the strangest. The previous day, 7 April, they had gathered at the Baghdad Chamber of Commerce after receiving individual letters from the director of the government's Commercial Affairs Department ordering them to be there at noon. 'If you fail to attend this conference, your export permit will be declared invalid and you will be deprived of your trading rights,' the letters warned. The businessmen, most of them prosperous shopkeepers and traders, put on their best suits and ties and obeyed the order to a man. At the Chamber of Commerce, they were told that buses would take them to a larger conference hall where they would be addressed by the deputy prime minister, Taha Yassin Ramadan. Some said later that they had been puzzled but not unduly concerned; they were cautious men who were used to accepting without challenge the demands of the state.

They were taken, however, not to a conference hall but to the headquarters of the secret police, where they were searched. Then, with no opportunity to tell their families of what was happening, they were bundled back on to the buses, driven ninety miles north-eastwards across the Tigris plain and abandoned in the hills of southern Kurdistan after being told by their escorts to head for the Iranian border a few miles away.

What the 500 businessmen had in common was their religion: they were all members of the Shia sect, a fact unremarkable in itself in a country where a majority of the Arab population is Shia. But the Iraqi leadership, including the President and his close family from the town of Tikrit, north of Baghdad, was predominantly Sunni, and the Iraqi leaders feared that the tide of Shia fundamentalism which, less than eighteen months before, had swept away their erstwhile enemy, the Shah, might now sweep on into Iraq and destabilise their own regime. Faced with Iranian threats to export the revolution, President Hussein decided to export potential revolutionaries.

As they shuffled aimlessly around the tented Sarabgarm refugee camp outside the Iranian border town of Sar-e-Pol-e-Zahab, it was difficult to believe that these pitiful refugees had ever presented a real threat to the Ba'athist state. But perhaps President Hussein recalled that it was the Tehran baazaris who had financed and encouraged the Khomeini revolution through their links with the Shia mosques. The refugees were a mixed bag: Kurds, ex-soldiers, tradesmen, though Iraq insisted that they were all of Iranian origin – a convenient fiction since historically the term Iranian was used in Iraq as a synonym for Shia.

In fact, nearly all of them were Iraqis. One group of Kurds had been rounded up in a Baghdad suburb, others came from just over the border. Many were ex-soldiers: a young truck-driver, Moussa Jomeh, had served three years in the Iraqi army; his friend Ahmad Hussein had served four; a third man still had two months' military service to complete when he was picked up by the secret police while on leave at his parents' home in the Iraqi border town of Khaneqin. Some of the older men produced faded

identity papers which showed that they had been born subjects of
the Ottoman Empire in the Turkish provinces of Mosul, Basra or
Baghdad before modern Iraq was even founded. It was clear that
Iraq's motive was not to rid the country of disruptive aliens but
rather to expel a potential fifth column which might side with the
enemy in the event of war; the refugees were among the first
victims of that so-far-undeclared conflict. In a tent at Sarabgarm,
a group of them sat on the ground and wept as Hojatoleslam
Seyyed Mohammad Ali Shirazi, the black-turbaned son of a
Grand Ayatollah of Mashad, told them softly in Arabic that they
would be avenged.

Tension between the two countries had been building since the
victory of the Iranian revolution in February of the previous year,
and by the spring of 1980 the ideological antagonism between the
two regimes had turned to an active campaign by each side to
destabilise the other. Iranian newspapers reported large-scale
artillery duels lasting for days at a time, though the fighting
was in fact little more than symbolic. In the week of the mass
expulsions, as Iraqi and Iranian gunners swapped artillery fire
across the border in southern Kurdistan, the official casualty list
showed that only one Iranian soldier was killed; on a single day
in the same period, ten people were killed in clashes in Beirut
between rival Lebanese supporters of Iran and Iraq.

A series of events had brought about the sudden upsurge in
tension. On 1 April a lone attacker with a grenade tried to
assassinate the Iraqi deputy prime minister, Tariq Aziz, as he
entered the Mostansirya University in Baghdad. Iran was immediately blamed for the attack, in which Aziz was slightly wounded,
though the attacker was an Iraqi student, Samir Noor-Ali, who
was killed by the security forces in the ensuing mêlée. The following day, Saddam Hussein told a meeting at the University: 'I
swear three times that the pure blood spilt here will not be
forgotten. This treacherous attack is the work of cowards who
want to avenge Qaddissiya.' The mention of Qaddissiya was an
unmistakable reference to Iran, and one that was to be used
throughout the ensuing war. Qaddissiya was the name of the
battle in 633 AD in which the advancing armies of Islam defeated
the Persian forces of Rustam, and was later used as a synonym
for the war by the Iraqi government – the official army newspaper
was even renamed *Qaddissiya*. But for all the official propaganda,

to the people of Iraq it was always 'Saddam's war'. They were clear from the beginning that it was their leader who had started it, and he would have to take any credit or blame that was due.

The same week, just after the Baghdad University attack, rumours spread to Iran from the Shia community in Iraq that an eminent pro-Khomeini Shia scholar, Mohammed Baqr al-Sadr, had disappeared, though the circumstances of his disappearance were only to emerge much later. Then, on 30 April, gunmen seized the Iranian embassy in London and took twenty-one hostages at the start of a siege which was closely connected with the events unfolding in the Gulf. The gunmen were identified as Khuzestan Arabs, Iranian citizens from the province which borders Iraq in the south-west. They were controlled, however, from Baghdad, and their mission was to publicise autonomy demands by Khuzestan Arabs and secure the release of Arab separatists held in Iranian jails. On the sixth day of the siege they killed their first hostage, press attaché Abbas Lavasani. The British authorities decided to send in the SAS, a move which saved the lives of Iranian as well as British hostages, yet the popular view in Tehran was that the embassy siege was part of a conspiracy against the Islamic Republic in which Britain was intimately involved. After all, it was reasoned, the takeover of the London mission had come only a week after America's failed attempt to rescue its own hostages from the US embassy in Tehran: such was the level of paranoia in Iran about foreign plots in the months leading up to war.

In the disorder which followed the Iranian revolution, autonomy movements had sprung up among the ethnic minorities on the fringes of the Persian heartland, leading sometimes to armed revolt among the Kurds, the Baluchis in the south-east, the Turkomans in the north, the Azerbaijanis in the north-west and Arabs in Khuzestan. What discontent existed in Khuzestan was actively encouraged by the Iraqis, who sent infiltrators across the border to sabotage pipelines and other oil installations in the province itself and further north along the border. On the Iranian side pipelines snaked along isolated border roads and could be put out of action with a grenade or a stick of dynamite. In July 1979, the month of Saddam Hussein's takeover of the presidency, the Iranians captured would-be saboteurs crossing into Khuzestan from Iraq. It was also claimed that explosives had been discovered at an Iraqi school in Khorramshahr, the main naval base in the province, and the Iranians said that the Iraqi consul in that city directly controlled the activities of the Arab Peoples' Cultural Centre, which was set up in the provincial capital of Ahwaz at the time of the revolution.

In the meantime, Baghdad actively supported the notion of autonomy for the Arabs of Khuzestan, a province which contains the bulk of Iran's oil production network and the source of most of its wealth. Iraq's clandestine Khuzestan campaign was an integral part of President Hussein's bid for regional power in the Gulf. To fill the vacuum left by the overthrow of the Shah, he sought to exploit Arab fears of revolutionary Iran in order to promote Iraq as the regional protector. The previous February he had launched a pan-Arab charter which called for all Arab states to stand together in the event of foreign aggression. President Hussein revived the demand for Iranian withdrawal from three islands in the Gulf: Great Tumb, Lesser Tumb and Abu Musa, which the Shah's forces occupied when the British withdrew from the Gulf in 1971. The islands are in the south of the waterway near the Strait of Hormuz and far from Iraqi territory, and if anyone had a claim to them it was the sheikhdoms of the United Arab Emirates on the southern shore, but by championing the cause of the three 'stolen' islands, President Hussein was staking his claim to be the natural defender of Arab interests in the region.

There was political and military provocation on both sides, and from early April, the start of the mass deportations, the number of cross-border incidents increased. That month, from a gendarmerie outpost on the Iranian side of the border near the oil town of Naft-e-Shah, Revolutionary Guards monitored a build-up of Iraqi troops and supplies across the narrow Naft river. Nearby, an armoured division from Sar-e-Pol-e-Zahab moved its M-60 tanks up to the international frontier. From 1 April until the outbreak of war, Iran listed 546 Iraqi violations of its territory in which border areas were bombed or shelled, while in the same period Iraq claimed almost 300 Iranian violations. Through speeches and broadcasts, each side appealed for the overthrow of the opposing regime.

The deportation of the 'Iranian Iraqis' was only the most visible of the preparations for war being made by the Baghdad government. From well before the time Ayatollah Khomeini returned to Tehran, President Hussein had been considering what to do in response, and he increasingly tended towards the view that military action was the best option; but he had to take into account the possibility of trouble from his own people. Discounting the Kurds of the north, who are Sunnis like the ruling élite but totally separate and distinct from them in every way, Iraq has a majority of Shia Muslims. From just south of Baghdad down to the border with Kuwait, the area is peopled almost exclusively by the Shia, followers of the same branch of Islam as that led by Khomeini in Iran. So the one restraining factor on Saddam Hussein was the danger of what this sizeable section of his own people might do, a danger made all the more real by past treatment of the Shia.

They were, in theory, as equal as any other Iraqi; but in practice it was the élite from the towns between Baghdad and the beginning of the Kurdish areas around Kirkuk which provided the leaders in every area of public life, and that included the armed forces. The Shia were the foot soldiers of the Iraqi army, the privates and corporals, while in general the Sunni provided the officer corps. Yet, surprisingly, the Baghdad government made little effort to woo this downtrodden and disadvantaged section of its own people; instead, it embarked on a policy of repression, dealing with extreme severity and brutality with the regular outbreaks of dissent which occurred. As Ayatollah Sayyed Mahdi al-Hakim noted after the execution of Mohammed Bakr al-Sadr: 'The Ba'ath history in Iraq is a history of bloodshed and killing of the *ulema* and scholars.'

Not only of *ulema* and scholars, but of any opposition or potential opposition. It can hardly be anything in the Iraqi character which so distinguishes it from other countries, yet from the time the monarchy was overthrown in 1958, successive regimes in Baghdad have used imprisonment, terrorism and assassination as methods of stifling opposition. General Abdel Karim Qassem seized power in 1958 with a violence and ruthlessness which shocked a world then unused to the excesses of violent revolution. The King and other members of the royal family were murdered, as well as such veteran and internationally known politicians as Nuri Said, and any opposition to the *coup* was dealt with swiftly and brutally. These precedents set the tone of the regime, as nationalists and communists fought for supremacy under the nominal leadership of the 'Free Officers', the ineffectual group through which Qassem tried to rule. By 1963 he was isolated, and was easily pushed aside by the nationalists and the emerging Ba'ath party, which was soon to dominate the country. For five years the various groups bickered and wrangled in obscure arguments which often spilled over into violence, before a group of Ba'athist army officers led by Ahmed Hassan al-Bakr seized power in a move which could later be seen to be the beginning of the modern history of Iraq.

For the difference from previous military regimes was that the officers led by al-Bakr realised that they had only the most rudimentary idea of how to govern – of how to run the country from day to day – and so deliberately brought in members of the civilian wing of the Ba'ath party and, notably, the man who was to prove the cuckoo in the nest, Saddam Hussein. For all his uniforms and his titles today, Saddam Hussein has never served in the Iraqi forces, never undergone military training and probably never even read a military textbook – facts which put into some perspective the regular Iraqi wartime announcements that President Hussein had taken personal control of vital battles, or was 'guiding' military staff meetings.

Saddam Hussein was an *apparatchik*, a street-gang leader and a killer: he earned his Ba'ath party revolutionary spurs at the age of twenty-three when he was one of those who waylaid Qassem's car on Rashid Street in Baghdad, stuck a pistol through the window and let off a volley of shots. It may have been a reflection of the state of over-excited panic in which the ambush was laid that Qassem escaped unhurt and it was his unfortunate chauffeur who was killed. This early episode, for which he was sentenced to death *in absentia*, perhaps set the tone for Saddam Hussein's later career – impulsive, reckless, willing to kill, but often failing in an enterprise as a result of poor planning or trying to push through some project without having worked out all the likely consequences.

Yet in the run-up to the war, what seemed to be miscalculations by Saddam Hussein had little effect. The moves against the Dawa party, the militant wing of Shia Islam, and the Islamic Liberation Movement, a loose and short-lived coalition of Iraqi opposition groups, did not lead to any general reaction by the Shia of southern Iraq, nor did the drive against the communists result in any real opposition from a group which might have been expected to be well organised and disciplined. In that case, the reason was that the Ba'ath had already established a commanding presence in all the many security organs of the state, and the communists were effectively prevented from taking action. In the case of the Shia, lack of response stemmed from the decades of preaching of secularity, the loose hold which the Shia *ulema* had on the people, and, again, the very tight security exercised by the Ba'ath party.

Yet it was a tremendous chance which the Iraqi leaders took as they set out quite deliberately to nullify or remove all potential religious opposition; the murder – or judicial killing – of the 48-year-old Ayatollah Mohammed Baqr al-Sadr in April 1980, could well have sparked mass violence, as lesser events had already caused riots in Kerbala and Najjaf, the two holy shrines of Shi'ism in Iraq. At one time there was even trouble in Baghdad itself after Sadr was removed from his home in Najjaf to stop demonstrations there, and taken to Baghdad 'for interrogation'. The people heard about it, and riots erupted in the poor Shia neighbourhood of Thawra City, a new suburb which had already been the scene of trouble because of lack of food and facilities. Yet the execution of the Ayatollah and his sister, Amina Haydar, known as Bint Huda, passed almost without incident when the government decided to act; the result was that the lack of response was taken as a message by the regime that it could get away with anything, and played its part in the continued bloodstained tale of repression of the Iraqi government.

Sadr was one of the founders of Dawa Islamiya, the Islamic Call, which was the secret, violent arm of the Shia Islam association set up by clerics in Najjaf in response to what they saw as the growing influence of 'communists and atheists' in the Qassem regime. Sadr was a leading figure in this movement, widely known for his influential books on Islamic philosophy and economy, and sharing many of the views of his senior, Khomeini, who was in Najjaf at the time Sadr was writing and preaching there, though the two had little contact. The Shia people of southern Iraq, and in particular, the *ulema* who could influence them, were the main concern of the Ba'ath party, which was seeking to build a secular state and to exert its influence over all aspects of life – political, social and religious. Thus the power and privileges of leading clergy were gradually being taken away, and the state was being put in place of the mosque, something which the Shia *ulema* could not accept, and which on more than one occasion led to bloody incidents in the holy cities.

During one Friday prayer meeting, two plain-clothes government agents were denounced, men from a special intelligence unit set up to deal with Shia dissent; the two were torn to pieces by the crowd before regular police could intervene. As a result, hundreds, perhaps thousands, of people were arrested, and many were never seen again. Yet the unrest continued, and even Saddam Hussein and the Ba'ath, never the most sensitive of interlocutors, realised that they could not simply suppress religion; so they went the other way. The Ba'ath party was always on the side of belief, Saddam Hussein now said in his speeches, but he warned that religion must not be used as a cloak for violence or dissent. Syria, the perennial enemy for reasons of geography and ideology, was being officially blamed for the violence in the holy shrines, but everyone, including the Ba'ath and the *ulema*, knew very well that this was just a convenient way to cloak the contest between the state and the mosque.

So as the conflict went on, Mohammed Baqr al-Sadr gradually emerged as the centre of opposition to the regime's attempts to secularise the country and strip the mullahs of their powers, considerable in a state where the mullah might be the only literate person in a small village. But Sadr was careful not to go too far, and the Ba'ath party seemed intent on avoiding the kind of confrontation which could lead to new bloodshed, so that for a while all was relatively well.

Then in October 1978 came the expulsion of Khomeini from Najjaf and the beginning of the process which was to result in the establishment of the Islamic Republic in Iran. It was a time of ferment in the Muslim world, particularly for the Shia; they could not stand aside and allow the Iranians to bear the brunt of the struggle alone, for in Iraq too the regime was considered un-Islamic and in direct opposition to the Shia establishment. The Dawa, which had from its inception been a secret organisation working underground, began to attack police posts and government institutions, and particularly targeted Ba'ath party offices; to the minority regime in Baghdad it seemed to be the beginning of a Shia uprising.

Fearful of making the situation worse, the Ba'ath at first reacted in a conciliatory way rather than using a big stick; Saddam Hussein, who was already beginning the cult of personality which was to become such a feature of Iraqi life in later years, was seen on televised newscasts handing out cash to the poor Shia of the south, or presenting them with television sets while mullahs could always be found to look on benevolently. At the same time, the Dawa was proscribed and its members attacked wherever they could be found – a decree was issued making it an offence punishable by death merely to belong to the movement. Sadr was interrogated, and when he refused to toe the Ba'ath line was put under house arrest in Najjaf; then in April 1980 he and his sister were executed after the attempt on the life of Tariq Aziz, though there was no suggestion of their complicity. The would-be assassin was said to be an Iranian, and that was enough to condemn those who had praised the Iranian regime.

The removal of Sadr effectively brought to an end the internal activities of Dawa for years to come, though it was to emerge in the later stages of the war as an instrument of Iranian clandestine activities. It did not, of course, put an end to the opposition in Iraq, but the loss of their leader seems to have disheartened the Shia, particularly as it came only shortly before the outbreak of the war with Iran, which like all wars everywhere served to focus the attention of the peoples of the two countries in conflict on outside affairs and away from their internal disputes. There was, too, a continuing campaign against Shia militants which also served to inculcate discipline and obedience among the party activists: according to Shia who fled Iraq at the time, at least seven Ba'ath party men were executed for refusing to obey orders to move against Shia clerical leaders, and other more senior officials were dismissed from their posts. Estimates were that in 1979 alone some 10,000 Shia militants were detained, 400 of them women; 100 were sentenced to death and thirty-six died under torture.

Once the Shia threat seemed to have been contained, at least, the Ba'ath turned its attention to its other enemies, the communists and the Kurds. The communists had originally been allies of the Ba'ath, and at various times there were communist ministers in the government, but gradually their power was whittled away, and despite the 1972 Treaty of Friendship between Iraq and the Soviet Union, the regime was moving steadily to a more central position. In a fashion which the Iraqi government made all its own, when it was decided that the final break with the communists should be made this was done in the most brutal way: twenty-one officers who had been in prison for years accused of forming communist cells among the armed forces were taken out and shot. The two communist ministers in the government at the time were not told in advance, and had to flee for their lives; hundreds of others were arrested, offices were closed and presses of party newspapers destroyed. The Iraqi communist party, which in the days of the monarchy had operated from a base in Prague, was again driven underground.

Yet even after the ruthless moves against the Shia leaders and the communists, it was clear that the rulers in Baghdad, and Saddam Hussein in particular, felt far from secure: there were constant purges in the party apparatus and in the army as Saddam Hussein, ostensibly still vice-president, sought to consolidate his hold on power. It was on the eve of the eleventh party congress in July 1979 that the struggle for control came into the open when President Hassan al Bakr appeared on television to announce his resignation, and Saddam Hussein was immediately sworn in as head of state in his place. This had long been expected, and the feeling was that Bakr, who was by this time a sick man, was only kept on as a link with the old 'Free Officers' who ousted the monarchy, and as a reassurance to the army, which might not take kindly to having an *apparatchik* as their supreme commander – Bakr had been a general. So when the change-over came, it made little impact, particularly as the few other new appointments and shifts of position seemed minor. Two weeks later, however, a very different picture emerged: Saddam Hussein announced that a plot to overthrow the government had been uncovered, masterminded by Syria. Twenty-two senior members of the Ba'ath party were arrested and immediately taken before a seven-man 'revolutionary court'. Then, when the predictable guilty verdicts were handed down, Saddam Hussein summoned other leading party members from all parts of the country. The new President and his comrades personally formed the firing squad to execute their former colleagues.

The incident was also used to bring to an end the hesitant steps towards rapprochement between Iraq and Syria which had been taken at the Baghdad summit the previous year. Though Syrian involvement in the attempted *coup* was never proved – if in fact there was a plot at all – the affair marked the definite ending of attempts at reconciliation between the two countries, each ruled by a separate wing of the Ba'ath party. The reason for this apparent miscalculation was that Saddam Hussein was then far more concerned with trying to inherit the mantle of Gamal Abdul Nasser than with worrying about Iran. It was Iraq which took the lead in condemning Egypt for its treaty with Israel, and Iraq which was bidding for the allegiance of the PLO, the 'floating vote' of the Arab world. Saddam Hussein saw himself not only as the leader of the Gulf region, but of all the Arabic–speaking people, 'from the ocean to the Gulf'. An alliance with Syria would inhibit his pan-Arab aspirations, for President Assad would never allow a rival Ba'ath party to take over. The essence of Ba'athism was pan-Arabism, so that Assad and Saddam Hussein could never co-exist. It was something that both realised, so their short-lived rapprochement was no more than a tactical manoeuvre.

Certainly it would have been useful to Iraq to have a neutral Syria on its border once the war started. Although there was never any real prospect of union between the two countries, something which was occasionally discussed, it would have been possible for Saddam Hussein to have maintained correct relations with Damascus, which would have made it more difficult for the pragmatic President Hafez Assad to side so swiftly and so practically with Iran when the war came. It was one of the questions that Saddam Hussein did not seem to consider, partly no doubt because the rivalry and mistrust of one section of the Ba-ath party for the other was so ingrained, partly because the Iraqi leader was being encouraged in his adventurism by a group of Iranian exiles. These were mainly senior, but not totally successful, military and security officers, and some tribal chiefs from border regions who saw their own freedom and authority being eroded by the Islamic revolution in Tehran. Between them, this heterogeneous group gave a great deal of bad advice: the generals swore that the Iranian army was in total disarray, and would not fight; the security men said that thousands of opponents of the Khomeini revolution would take to the streets if Iraq moved; and the tribal chiefs promised the support of their people in Khuzestan and other border regions. All the predictions were wrong, and none of the tribal chiefs was able to deliver. Just as Ayatollah Khomeini's calls to the Shia of Iraq to rally to his Islamic revolution had no effect, so too Iraqi attempts to foment trouble in Arabic-speaking areas of Iran had just as little success. On both sides wishful thinking was a substitute for intelligence or logical thought as the conflict began.

More real, and more influential, was the advice given by other Arab leaders who met Saddam Hussein. None of these men, well used to conducting their own *majlis* where what is not said is as important as what is, went so far as to advise the Iraqi leader to attack Iran. That would have been crass, and possibly dangerous if all did not go well, as the Arab politicians realised. Instead, there was much discussion of the upheaval in Iran, of the dangers of unrest in the Gulf region, of the need to ensure steady oil production and export, even of the need for common policies among the Arab states of the eastern side of the Gulf. Nothing was ever spelled out, but for Saddam Hussein the message was clear: contain the Ayatollah, prevent him from exporting his revolution, and you will have our support. Unlike the exiles from Iran, the Arabs meant what they said, and they delivered: Iraq's war effort was made possible by huge subventions from Saudi Arabia, Kuwait, Qatar and, to a lesser extent, the Emirates, while Kuwait became in effect an Iraqi port as soon as Iraq was denied access to the Shatt al Arab. Jordan opened Aqaba to the Iraqis without restriction, and organised a supply line across the desert to Baghdad for arms and ammunition produced by Egypt. It was this Arab support, more than anything else, which encouraged Saddam Hussein to embark on his adventure.

But there was another factor, too – the United States. President Jimmy Carter had set out American policy: 'Let our position be absolutely clear. Any attempt by any outside force to gain control of the Persian Gulf will be regarded as an assault on the vital interests of the United States of America.' Neither Iran nor Iraq were outside forces, so there could be no reason for American intervention, even if that were a possibility – in 1979 the Rapid Deployment Force was not a force and could certainly not be deployed rapidly. Estimates were that it would take four days to put the first American soldier into the Gulf in a crisis. That, to the Iraqis, was not the point; what was important was that the United States had laid down the Carter doctrine which, though designed for consumption by the Soviet Union, was a reassurance to Iraq. The Shah had been America's surrogate in the Gulf, taking over when Britain withdrew from the area in 1971; there was no love lost between Washington and those who had replaced Washington's protégé.

At the same time, Saddam Hussein had been distancing himself from Moscow. The Iraqi Communist Party, founded in 1934 and once the centre of opposition both to British colonial rule in Iraq and to the British-imposed monarchy, was no longer a force in the land. Always opposed by the Ba'ath, under Saddam Hussein the communists were harried, persecuted and frequently executed. Hussein, according to officials in Washington, was a man America could do business with. The Pentagon believed that his armies could defeat or at least contain Iran, and it was only the purists of the state department who noted Iraq's blood-stained history and predicted trouble.

In the north of Iraq, Saddam Hussein had moved swiftly, brutally and ruthlessly to ensure that there would be no trouble and that the Kurds would not be used by Khomeini as the Shah had used them a decade earlier, providing weapons for use against Iraq, and then withdrawing supplies as the situation demanded. More than a quarter of a million Kurds were deported, moved out of their villages along the Turkish and Iranian borders, and either concentrated in soulless new concrete garrison towns under the eyes of Iraqi troops or taken to settlements in the south of the country, down in the steamy heat around Basra, in a region and a climate quite alien to them. In some areas of the north considered vital, Iraqi settlers had moved in, and throughout the area, units of the People's Army were deployed to keep order, with a stiffening of some front-line troops based nearby to give help if needed, and to deal with any Iranian adventures in the north. Along the frontiers there were free-fire zones; no announcements were ever made about these areas – the Kurds learnt about them the hard way.

Officially, Iraq had set up an autonomous region in Kurdistan, but it was a poor sort of autonomy which deceived no one. Even the chief minister of the region was subject to the control of the Arabs from Baghdad. Once, when interviewing the minister, we were accompanied by a 'minder', a Ba'ath party official sent to ensure that journalists and writers did not learn anything the government did not want them to know. The chief minister, who spoke good English, suggested that there was no need for the party man to stay during the interview. The minder smiled thinly. And stayed.

Once the Shah had withdrawn his support for the Kurds as a result of the 1975 Algiers agreement, Mulla Mustafa Barzani, the leader of the Kurdish Democratic party, went into exile, and the Iraqis were able to set up a small Quisling group which they also called the KDP, and which supplied most of the personnel for the administration of the Autonomous Region of Kurdestan. But with Barzani's son Masoud soon raising the banner of revolt once again, it was a short-lived affair, and throughout the war the Iraqis were forced to keep large numbers of troops in the north. In general the People's Army managed to keep things quiet for most of the time, but towards the end of the war the Iraqis were in difficulties: groups of Kurds from Iran, with some trained Pasdaran, penetrated for hundreds of miles into Iraq to threaten Kirkuk itself. The practical damage they did was slight, though they made sure that any target they blew up would burn for days and thus advertise their exploit, but the psychological effect was considerable.

It was because of the danger posed by the Iraqi Kurds and by Kurds from Iran that Iraq entered into an agreement with Turkey in 1982. This officially did no more than give the Turks the right of 'hot pursuit' into Iraqi territory following any strikes by Kurds in the eastern areas of Turkey where the Kurdish Workers' party, the communist PKK, had launched a new campaign. But the secret understandings which went with the official agreement carried things a lot further: because they earned royalties from the Iraqi pipelines (doubled in capacity by the sixth year of the war) which crossed their territory to the Mediterranean, and because they wanted to ensure their supply of oil, the Turks agreed to seize and hold areas of northern Iraq if the pipelines there were threatened. And though it was not formally set out, it was accepted that in the event of an Iraqi collapse the Turks would have crossed the border to ensure that there were no hostilities close to their territory, and to see that calm prevailed. So in the early days of the war, things were relatively peaceful in the north of Iraq as the Kurds tried to recover from the brutal campaign of 'pacification' which had followed the Algiers agreement, while, on the Iranian side of the border the fighting which erupted immediately after the proclamation of the Islamic Republic was soon contained. Iran was no less anxious than Iraq to keep the Kurds quiet, and would not even consider granting them the sort of limited autonomy which Iraq had tried in case such ideas 'infected' the Baluchi, Armenian, Azerbaijani or other minority groups.

Iraq's *casus belli* was the alleged violation by the Khomeini regime of the Algiers agreement signed by the two countries five years earlier. The 1975 Treaty on State Borders and Good Neighbourly Relations was intended to put an end to a long-standing dispute over the southern frontier at the Shatt al Arab. The treaty established that the frontier at the estuary would follow the thalweg, the deep-water line of the navigable channel, so that Iranian territory now began at the centre of the estuary rather than on the eastern bank, and Iraq was denied sole control over its only outlet to the sea. Although the treaty made some minor territorial concessions to the Iraqis along the land border, Baghdad resented the fact that it had been obliged to sign under duress, for its motive in signing the Algiers agreement was to gain a commitment from the Shah that he would end his support for Barzani's rebel army. And the Shah kept his word: in one of the more cynical and brutal moves of his despotic reign, he duly cut off supplies to the Kurds from June 1975. The rebellion that Iran had fomented and supported collapsed; hundreds of Kurdish fighters, the *peshmerga*, died; and Barzani was forced into exile.

The territorial dispute over the Shatt al Arab dated far back, to before the creation of the modern Iraqi state. The Iraqi foreign minister, Saadoun Hammadi, defending his country's position before the UN Security Council one month after the outbreak of war, said: 'The problem is neither new nor simple. It goes back over 460 years of history. It is not a border problem or a minor conflict over navigational rights. It is much wider than that.'

For most of the history of the dispute, it was a struggle for territorial advantage between Persia and the Ottoman Empire. There were agreements on defining the territory of the two empires as early as 1639, but under the terms of these early accords the frontier line was left extremely vague, and it was only under British and Russian pressure and mediation that the two empires signed the Treaty of Erzerum in 1847. Under this agreement, the Ottomans accepted Persian sovereignty over the east bank of the Shatt al Arab and the right of passage for Persian vessels in the Ottoman-controlled waterway. Persia, in return, abandoned its claims to the city and province of Sulamaniyeh, now part of Iraqi Kurdistan. In a distant echo of the 1975 agreement, in which Iraq and Iran agreed to end support for cross-border subversion, in 1847 'the two Mussulman powers [undertook] to adopt and enforce the measures necessary to prevent and punish theft and brigandage on the part of the tribes and peoples settled on the frontier'.

At that time the territories on either side of the Shatt al Arab were isolated, inhabited by autonomous Arab tribes, and of little value to either power. But in 1908 oil was discovered at Masjed-e-Suleiman on the Iranian side. The port of Khorram-shahr, which the Arabs called Mohammarah, became increasingly important as a trans-shipment point for oilfield equipment and general cargo. But, because the Turks controlled the waters of the Shatt, ships bound for Persian ports were obliged to pass through Ottoman waters and pay Ottoman customs dues. A further protocol was signed in 1913, reaffirming Turkish sovereignty over the Shatt, but in the following year Persia succeeded in obtaining a verbal agreement from the Turks that the frontier at Mohammarah should be moved to the centre of the river, reflecting the new importance of the port.

From the late nineteenth century Persia and the Ottoman Empire, and later the new state of Iraq, were virtual bystanders in the development of the territories on either side of the Shatt. With the defeat of Turkey during the First World War, Britain occupied Iraq and took over navigation in the estuary through the Basra port authority. Britain also controlled the growing Iranian oil industry and the expanding refinery town of Abadan. In 1937, the thalweg principle was extended to Abadan, so that Iran now controlled the waters immediately outside its two main frontier towns, but elsewhere in the estuary ships were still obliged to fly the Iraqi flag. For three decades, it appeared as if the long-standing dispute had been settled for good, but in the mid-1960s the Shah, just then emerging as the major power in the Gulf, began to complain that, although ships using Iranian ports in the Shatt were paying most of the revenue derived from use of the waterway, Iraq was keeping all the money for itself, contrary to the 1937 border agreement. Iran claimed that the main purpose of the 1937 accord had been to facilitate the movement of British warships and that this no longer applied. In any case, said the Iranians, international river boundaries invariably followed the thalweg or median line.

On the basis of these arguments, Tehran unilaterally revoked the 1937 treaty on 19 April 1969; henceforth, Iranian vessels using the Shatt al Arab would neither fly the Iraqi flag nor pay Iraqi tolls. Baghdad responded by declaring that the Shatt was Iraqi territory but, despite threats to take action against any vessel contravening the terms of the 1937 treaty, an Iranian ship with an Iranian pilot and flying the Iranian flag sailed down the estuary without being challenged on 22 April. Others followed, and Baghdad never carried out its threats. Instead, as was to happen a decade later, several thousand undesirables said to be of Iranian origin were summarily expelled across the border. The Shah's territorial muscle-flexing over the Shatt al Arab was a prelude to his emergence as the unchallenged policeman of the Gulf when Britain withdrew from the region in 1971, for Iraq was the only other country in the area which even began to measure up to Iran in terms of population and military strength.

Another trial of strength, and another victory for Iran, came in 1971 when the Shah annexed the Tumb islands and Abu Musa. There was a two-year break in diplomatic relations with Baghdad, during which Iran steadily increased its support for Barzani's Kurds, but Iraq could do nothing in response, while the Shah succeeded in his aim of preoccupying and containing the radical and anti-Western regime which had taken power in Baghdad through his support of the Kurds.

The antipathy between the two Gulf powers was a source of concern to other members of OPEC, which was emerging as a player on the world scene following the oil price explosion of the early 1970s, so Algeria took the lead in trying to arrange a settlement, and at the OPEC conference in Algiers in March 1975 succeeded in persuading the two sides to sink their differences and reach an agreement which 'completely eliminated the conflict between the two brotherly countries'. The treaty lasted barely four years, though the interim revolutionary government which took power in Tehran in 1979 was pledged to honour international agreements reached by the old regime.

In the turmoil and euphoria of the post-revolutionary period, however, it became an article of faith to promote the export of the revolution to Iraq and elsewhere in the Muslim world. Baghdad was to argue later that by encouraging Islamic and Kurdish dissidents to overthrow the Ba'athist regime, Tehran's revolutionary leaders had effectively revoked the 1975 treaty which barred each country from promoting subversion in the other, and during April and May 1980 Iraq sought to persuade the United Nations and other international bodies that Iran had violated commitments undertaken by the Shah. Hammadi told the secretary-general of the Organisation of African Unity that 'the behaviour of the Iranian government and officials . . . prove that Iran is still pursuing the same path and the same racialist expansionist policy pursued and practised by the deposed Shah regime'. Baghdad also accused Iran of being in violation of the terms of the 1975 treaty by failing to hand over small pockets of territory along the frontier assigned to Iraq. It was ostensibly to recover this territory that the Iraqi President dispatched his forces to the border at the beginning of September.

And then on 17 September Saddam Hussein finally tore up the 1975 treaty as a prelude to the invasion, and declared the Algiers agreement null and void. 'We have taken the decision to recover all our territories by force,' he said. 'The waters of the Shatt al Arab must return to their former Iraqi and Arab rule and be placed entirely under Iraqi sovereignty.' In a theatrical touch, an order was issued that all ships plying the waterway must henceforth fly the Iraqi flag and pay dues to Baghdad. It was a rhetorical gesture: within a week the Shatt al Arab was closed by fighting and ships of many flags were stranded there for the duration of the war.

# 3

# Iraq's
# failed blitzkrieg

According to Iraq, the war began on 4 September 1980; according to Iran, 22 September was the date, as that was the day Iraqi forces began their invasion of Iranian territory. It was a well-prepared, three-pronged offensive, but Iraqis who saw the beginning of the invasion reported later that the troops showed little drive or dash as the offensive began. According to these witnesses – not totally reliable as they later left the country, but confirmed by subsequent events – the Iraqi soldiers often seemed in a sullen mood as they took up their battle positions ready for the move into Iran. Certainly there were no stirring speeches, no pep-talks from generals to enthusiastic soldiers. This was an army obeying orders, not a cheerful extension of a people's will. Oddly enough, though, at the beginning and throughout the war, the closer the troops were to the front line, the better the morale seemed; not because of any anticipation of action, but because the political commissars attached to every unit stayed carefully at rear headquarters, and were never seen at the sharp end.

These commissars, officially known as political officers, were Ba'ath party men put in place to keep an eye on the military; the lowest rank they were given was that of captain, but no matter what their rank they always had the right to attach themselves to the commanding officer and to interfere in any discussion of what they classed as political matters – treatment of prisoners or of the soldiers under command, tactical objectives, reports of actions, requests for particular supplies. The commissars made themselves extremely unpopular with the 'real' officers – an example of their insensitivity came when we were guests in a forward mess. Invited to sit with the brigadier at the 'top table', the only other place there was taken by a political captain. The regimental colonel and a number of lieutenant-colonels were ranged in order of rank at two side tables. Oddly, it was the officers who showed most dislike of the 'politicals'; the private soldiers and non-coms took little notice of them, presumably because in Iraq they were so used to the tight security system, the watchers and informers, that they would have found it odd if such men had not been present.

So it was that on 22 September Iraq launched its long-prepared and well-advertised attack with air raids on nine military bases in Iran, including Mehrabad international airport in Tehran. Two of the planes were shot down by Iranian gunners, and the Iranians also gave a swift demonstration of the naval superiority they were to hold throughout the war, sinking four of Iraq's fleet of gunboats and patrol boats. President Saddam Hussein issued a statement designed to mollify the Iranian public and drive a wedge between them and their leaders, a forlorn hope; he promised that civilian targets would be spared unless Iran chose to attack such places in Iraq, in which case there would be retaliation. He avoided declaring war, and said merely that 'the Khomeini gang' in Tehran had forced Iraq to carry out 'deterrent actions'. The response from Ayatollah Khomeini was much more direct: in his broadcast on that first day of hostilities, the Ayatollah called Saddam 'this germ of corruption', and urged Iraqis everywhere in the country to rise up against their leaders and overthrow their President as the Iranians had toppled the Shah.

The Soviet Union was given some advance warning of what was afoot. Tariq Aziz, the foreign minister, flew to Moscow on 21 September to tell the Russians that the invasion was about to be launched, and to invoke the Treaty of Friendship between them, a treaty in form alone over the past couple of years as Iraq had purged and driven underground the communist party of Iraq and tilted sharply to the West in its commercial dealings. At the same time the Russians had appeared to be taking the Iranian side in the growing dispute, but were repulsed there too, with Khomeini and his ministers making it plain that they ranked Moscow only slightly lower than Washington in the Satanic stakes.

The first Iraqi objectives were Qasr-e-Shirin in the mountains of the central sector, and Abadan, Khorramshahr and Dezful in the south. It was in these first days that the huge refinery at Abadan was set on fire and virtually destroyed by Iraqi bombing and shelling, while Iran used its air force to strike at Iraqi military targets and at the cities. Baghdad came under regular attack, and so too did the Iraqi oil refinery outside Basra, where fires raged unchecked for days. Eventually, Kuwait sent its own fire brigade up the road to help fight the fires in the first, physical demonstration of the total support it was to give Iraq over the years.

The initial Iraqi successes were minimal. Abadan and Khorramshahr were surrounded and Qasr-e-Shirin was taken, but the drive to Dezful or the Khuzestan provincial capital, Ahwaz, never even looked threatening. In the central sector the Iraqis did well with minimal effort against light defences, and succeeded within weeks in taking all the territory in dispute in the 1975 agreement, while also thickening and consolidating the defence of Baghdad against any attack from the Qasr-e-Shirin direction, feared as a possible invasion route. But nowhere did the Iraqi soldiers have their heart in it, while the Iranian defenders fought stubbornly and well. The Iraqi advance propaganda had painted a picture of a demoralised Iran, with the army in disarray and in constant competition with the Revolutionary Guards, the air force unable to fly and the navy confined to port for lack of officers, as the navy in particular had been the province of a pro-Shah officer corps and consequently heavily purged. None of those things proved true: certainly the Iranians were short of planes and pilots, but they found enough to give their men battlefield support, and to carry the war to targets deep inside Iraq. The Iranian navy quickly established its mastery of the waters of the Gulf and shelled Umm Qasr, the oil port on the Fao peninsula, in a convincing demonstration that Iraq would not be able to export any of its oil through the southern route.

Oil was the major component of the economies of both Iran and Iraq, vital to the war effort of both sides, but right from the start of the war Iran was able to prevent Iraq from using the Gulf for its oil exports, so until new pipelines could be built to pump oil to tankers in the Red Sea via the Saudi network, Iraq's export capacity was crippled and it had to rely on the good grace of Saudi Arabia and Kuwait to produce an allocation on its behalf; the two countries eventually donated all production from the neutral zone which they shared to the Iraqi war effort, while Iraq continued to pump northwards to the Mediterranean via Turkey through its one usable pipeline. The result of all this was to reduce Iraq's weight in OPEC just as Iran's influence was increasing – throughout the war the oil ministers of Iran and Iraq would meet in the same conference chamber with other members of the producers' cartel, although the convention was that they addressed each other through third parties. Early in the war, the Iranian minister, Mohammad Javad Tondgoyan, was captured by Iraqi troops near the border, so at the next OPEC meeting aides placed a cut-out of the unfortunate Tondgoyan in the seat he would have occupied. He has been in a POW camp ever since.

The oil industry and oil policy, like other aspects of Iranian affairs, had been severely disrupted by the revolution, but once the war began the Iranians displayed a remarkable realism in their attitudes within OPEC, even making common cause with the conservative Saudis when it suited them. After the revolution, Iran emerged as the arch-hawk of OPEC, demanding ever higher prices and threatening to cut off the West's oil supplies if its demands were not met. In wartime, however, it was faced with the need to obtain maximum revenue in order to finance the war effort, so Iran favoured a cartel policy of limiting production on the basis of agreed quotas in order to maintain a high price; it was the ideal policy for Iran, since its production capacity was limited by the depradations of the war and lack of maintenance, but the strategy depended on Saudi Arabia acting as a swing producer, adjusting its production upwards or downwards in order to hold the world oil price at the level decreed by OPEC as a whole. This was fine as long as demand and price remained relatively high and while the thirteen-member OPEC retained the major share of the world market, and for the first half of the war the strategy brought Iran adequate funds both to fight and to feed its people without resort to long-term credit or foreign financing, for the Iranians cheated shamelessly by offering discounts in order to squeeze as high a share of sales as possible in an increasingly glutted market.

As the Iraqi invasion began, the Iranian army and the Revolutionary Guards were in some disarray, each holding different areas, but wherever they could they stood and fought and, in the face of superior numbers, fire power and armour, stemmed the Iraqi advance. It was not what the Iraqi planners had expected, as a small change in the stream of propaganda from Baghdad Radio showed. In the first days of the war, a catchy number entitled 'Whirlwind of Victory' was constantly being played, with its verses extolling the Iraqi soldiers and speaking of 'pushing the treacherous

Persian beyond his mountains in the east'. As it rapidly became evident that the Iraqis had no hope at all of pushing the Iranians back to the mountains or anywhere else, the tune had to be quietly dropped. But it was not only in Baghdad that miscalculations had been made: around the world the estimates were that the war would be a quick affair, with negotiations forced on Iran following a swift Iraqi display of military might. Certainly some countries, notably America, must have been less than distressed at that prospect. But things did not go as the world had anticipated; the situation was transformed, and a quick reassessment had to be made.

In Moscow and in Washington, the signs that the conflict would drag on reinforced the determination of both countries to remain neutral, though at this early stage it was clear that the Russians were doing no more for Iraq than they had to under their Treaty, while inclining towards Iran, not least because it was such a firm opponent of America. In Washington the aim was much more one of 'positive neutrality', though officials could not avoid the general wish to see Iran and the Ayatollah 'punished' for the detention of the American diplomats, still locked up in the Tehran embassy. China too proclaimed its neutrality, but it was noticeable that when the Chinese agreed to make some effort to bring the war to an end, they called on Iraq alone to cease hostilities – ostensibly on the reasonable grounds that it was Iraq which had invaded Iran but, as later events showed, in fact because the Chinese favoured Tehran.

In the Gulf itself Kuwait was the only country publicly to support Baghdad, though the Iraqis claimed that King Khaled of Saudi Arabia had sent messages assuring them of the support of the Kingdom. No doubt he did, but they were not intended to be made public; Saudi diplomacy has a nineteenth-century ring about it, with the emphasis on secrecy and discretion. What is not made public does not later have to be justified – or denied. The Emirates and Qatar followed the Saudi line, with Bahrain showing greater nervousness and more support for Iraq. Bahrain has a population which is something like 80 per cent Shia, but is ruled by a Sunni minority, and it was only recently that an Iranian mullah had renewed Iran's claim to Bahrain, a claim dropped by the Shah years earlier. Though Khomeini refused to endorse the new claim, Bahrain, understandably, remained more worried than most.

At the southern end of the Gulf, Oman was the most vulnerable of the littoral states, as its tiny navy patrolled the Strait of Hormuz and its ports, airfields and cities were within a few minutes' flying time of Iranian airfields around Bandar Abbas. Oman was strictly neutral, for all its close links with Britain and developing friendship with America; Sultan Qabous remembered that it was Iranian troops which had finally turned the tide of the Dhofar insurrection at the beginning of his reign in 1971, and enabled him to take his country into the twentieth century as a united state. Gratitude, proximity and self-interest dictated Oman's attitude of even-handedness throughout the war, plus a realisation that, whatever happened, Oman would have to live with Iran in the future; the Omani foreign minister, Youssef Alawi, was to establish a warm relationship with Iranian officials which formed a valuable channel of communication as the years went on.

In the first days of the war, there was no doubt that Iraq had been well-prepared and well-organised but had made a fundamental miscalculation; to add to its troubles, the Baghdad government went in for the kind of grossly exaggerated claims which the Arab side had made during the 1967 war with Israel. In particular, the Iraqis put out false reports that Ayatollah Khomeini had died, and that the port of Khorramshahr had been taken: Ayatollah Khomeini immediately went on television, and in a speech directed to the Shia of Iraq more than his own people, called on them to stab Saddam Hussein in the back, to finish him off 'before we do'. At the same time, as international agencies were able to confirm that Khorramshahr was still in Iranian hands, the Iraqis were forced to admit that the announcement they had made of its capture had been 'premature', a true but lame explanation, as it was another month before the city finally fell.

All this heartened the Iranians, and those who had feared a swift Iraqi push which would toss aside any opposition and seize the whole of Khuzestan rallied to the national cause. The mood was beginning which allowed the Iranians to recruit huge volunteer forces, and which induced the young men to suicidal acts of bravery which courted martyrdom. And it was the defence of the towns of Khuzestan which did it, towns which the Iraqis had believed would be turned over to them by their inhabitants. Khorramshahr and later Susangerd came under terrible bombardment from Iraq, and Iraqi troops reached the outskirts of both towns, but there was never any suggestion that the people there ever did anything but help the Iranian forces. In both places the citizens asked for guns, and were given them by the military and the Revolutionary Guards. Civilians erected barricades in the streets and the men fought beside the army, while the women somehow supplied food to as many as possible without running water or electricity. Reza Mohtazemi summed it up in a rare telephone interview: Ahwaz would be the Iranian Stalingrad, he said.

In fact, it was perhaps the nearby town of Susangerd which deserved that title, for the Iraqis never did take it. A small place of no more than 20,000 inhabitants, it had no military or strategic value, but the Iraqi attack on it was launched on the eve of the first Arab summit conference to be called since the beginning of the war, and Saddam Hussein wanted a victory to announce when he got to Amman. At the same time, the Iranians had to stem the Iraqi advance if they were to hold on to the growing support they had won; the result was a horrific battle for a town of no real use to either side. It took the Iraqis a month to capture Khorramshahr, and a month to decide that they could not capture Susangerd. It was those battles in October and November of the first year of the war that created the conditions for the tide to be turned two years later, and also brought about the atmosphere in Iran which made everyone a combatant. Iraq overstated its case and defeated its objectives.

One of the surprises of the first months of the war, for Iran and Iraq as well as for the outside world, was that the predictions of mass defections by Shia soldiers from the Iraqi army and help by the 'Arabs' of Khuzestan for the invaders did not materialise. Ayatollah Khomeini certainly believed he could influence the Iraqi troops: both personally and through his lieutenants he regularly urged the Iraqi Shia to desert, and appealed to their religion. Hardly any responded, and not because the government in Baghdad had done anything to win the allegiance of a people who had always been considered the least well-off section of Iraqi society. After all, Saddam Hussein had executed their leader, and it was long before the Ba'ath government went out of its way to woo the Shia with mosques, endowments and praise. What was not realised outside Iraq was that the Shia themselves did not consider their community downtrodden or deprived; they were in the majority in the country, so their fortunes or misfortunes were the lot of everyone. The small Sunni élite from Tikrit was something quite separate, a special group to be regarded rather as the Chinese of old had considered the mandarins.

In practical terms, what mattered was the attitude of the ordinary soldier, and that was secured by the structure of the army. For in the forces merit and ability were the criteria in the junior ranks: the chief of staff at the beginning of the war was General Abdul-Jabbar al Shenshan, a Shia, a conservative, a British-trained officer who had served through all the changes of regime and had never been involved in politics. Shia officers could be found at all levels, though it was still true that able Sunnis were more likely to be noticed and given swift promotion. Yet throughout the war, about 20 per cent of the four-star generals in the Iraqi army were Shia, and during the same eight years the Shia increased their share of government posts, by the end of the war holding 45 per cent of party and militia offices.

In the 1970s there were no Shia and no Kurds on the Revolutionary Command Council, the ruling body; by 1988, there were three Shia who were active and important members, and one Kurd, who was not. The Shia have been integrated into Iraqi society, while the Kurds are still seen as a separate entity either to be subjugated or bribed into acquiescence. One of the three Shia ministers was put in charge of internal security, a key post in the Iraqi system, and the head of the Republican Guard was also a Shia. It is also noteworthy that the RCC had only one former officer, and he was there more because he was Saddam Hussein's cousin than for his military background. The lack of military men in the ruling bodies was quite deliberate: there was a careful separation between army and state, so that the army came to be seen, and to see itself, as the apolitical arm of government, an instrument to be used by the politicians in dealing with outside countries or groups, but not involved in internal matters. Equally, of course, the Sunni, Tikriti establishment took certain precautions: the 'political officers' were usually Sunni, and the security services were manned entirely by Sunnis, while Saddam Hussein's personal bodyguards were not only Sunnis from the Tikrit area, but also from his own clan of the Banaisa tribe.

The so-called 'Popular Army' was also intended in the first place as a counter-weight to the army proper, and was formed entirely from members of the Ba'ath party; 75,000-strong when the war broke out, it was commanded by Taha Yassin Ramadan, a party thug who was one of Saddam Hussein's closest henchmen. During the war the Popular Army was expanded until at its peak it reached a strength of 250,000 men, and was then given the duty of rear-area security, freeing army units for combat duties. But it was only when the tide of war had turned, when the Iraqis were behind their own borders and fighting to repel the Iranian invaders, that the loyalty and trustworthiness of the army was accepted by the ruling clique, and the systems of checks and balances among armed units was relaxed. The Republican Guard, the élite force of the Iraqi army, was not committed to battle until 1984: right up to that time the best units Iraq could muster were still kept in Baghdad in defence of the capital and the regime.

Saddam Hussein's failure to foresee the spirited resistance which Iran would put up to his lightning invasion stemmed from a combination of false assumptions and bad intelligence. The Iraqi strategy was based on the assumption that the ethnic minorities, particularly the Arabs of Khuzestan, would turn against the Tehran regime; in addition, Saddam Hussein had been told by those who encouraged him in his adventure, particularly the Shah's former generals, that the Iranian army was in a state of collapse. One more thing contributed to the Iraqi failure: according to the former Iranian president, Abolhassan Bani-Sadr, who was appointed chairman of the Supreme Defence Council soon after the Iraqi invasion, Tehran had been in possession of Saddam Hussein's war plan for almost two months. In an interview in Paris in 1988, Bani-Sadr claimed that the Iraqi plan was contained in a document purchased in August by foreign minister Sadeq Ghotbzadeh from an unnamed Latin American for the sum of $200,000. 'Everything happened as set out in this document. There had been a meeting in Paris. At this meeting were Americans, Israelis, Iranian royalists; it was there that the attack plan was prepared.' Subsequently, Iran's ambassador to Moscow, Mohammad Mokri, later jailed by Tehran as a Soviet spy, gave a similar account of the secret Paris meeting to Bani-Sadr. 'I then put it to the Soviet ambassador: "Was it you who gave us this information." He just chuckled. It was his way of confirming it.'

The contents of the Paris papers, and the suspicion that they had been deliberately leaked by Moscow in order to counter US designs in the region, squared with intelligence reports already received by Bani-Sadr of a secret meeting in Jordan earlier that Summer between the US national security adviser, Zbigniew Brzezinski and Saddam Hussein, in which the American was said to have pledged US backing for an attack on Iran. Whatever the origin of the Paris papers, they gave the Iranians a forewarning of Iraqi intentions and almost two months in which to prepare their defences. The information given to the Iranians was that the Iraqi plan was threefold: to destabilise the Iranian armed forces; to provoke civil conflict, particularly in the Iranian border provinces of Kurdistan and West Azerbaijan; to stage a blitzkrieg over a period of four to five days in order to occupy large sectors of western Iran before bringing in an exiled royalist army under the political leadership of the ousted prime minister, Shahpour Bakhtiar, who would declare a provisional government in the liberated zone.

The Iranian authorities exposed eight plots within the senior ranks of the armed forces during 1980, centring on the air force. According to Bani-Sadr:

> It wasn't feasible that these small groups should be preparing a *coup d'état*. Rather it was to destabilise the armed forces from the inside, to disorganise them, and above all to create a climate of suspicion among the mullahs, and Khomeini in particular, against the armed forces. Thus Iraq would confront a disorganised and desperate force which lacked the will to resist. That was how the first part of the plan was carried out.

Armed with the Paris documents and in the face of resistance by hardliners, Bani-Sadr managed to persuade the senior clergy to suspend the purges and executions which followed the uncovering of the military plots in order to restore the morale of the majority of troops loyal to the regime.

Part two of the Iraqi war plan, as stated by Bani-Sadr, was aimed at holding down as many Iranian troops as possible at the Kurdish front, thereby weakening the defensive line to Khuzestan. The Kurdish *peshmerga* had been in open rebellion against the central government since 1979 and the main towns of Kurdistan and West Azerbaijan regularly changed hands between Kurdish and government forces. With weapons and logistical support from the Iraqis the rebels were able to tie down a large part of the Iranian army until mid-1982. On the eve of the war the royalist army was stationed at Sulamaniyeh in Iraqi Kurdistan under the command of the royalist general, Gholam Ali Oveissi, the Shah's former military governor of Tehran. Oveissi's Iran Liberation

Front had already mounted guerrilla operations in Iranian Kurdistan during the summer and he was believed to be behind the *coup* plots in the armed forces.

> The first thing I did, when I had established the presence of these camps in Sulamaniyeh [said Bani-Sadr], was to have them bombed. This was how we dispersed the royalists. They no longer existed. Mr Bakhtiar had told Baghdad that he would be in Tehran within a few days but it never happened. This all took place in the opening days of the war.
>
> When the Iraqis attacked they thought it would all be over in a matter of days. I put it to the army: 'If Iraq attacks, how long can we hold out?' They told me four days. This wasn't a bad estimate from a military point of view. But not all calculations are military ones, there were many other things that they had not taken into consideration. I told the army: 'Do everything possible to resist for those four days, on the fifth I will hold myself responsible.' That's how we succeeded in breaking the Iraqi offensive.

After the fall of the Shah, according to Bani-Sadr, the operational capacity of the army had been allowed to fall practically to zero, that of the air force to 20 per cent and that of the navy to 10 per cent. During the first six months of his presidency, despite the purges which led to the dismissal of thousands of officers, he claimed that, unbeknown to the Iraqis, operational capacity was restored to 90 per cent of its pre-revolutionary level. President Hussein's belief in the unreliability of the Iranian armed forces was shared by hardliners in Tehran who had actively sought to undermine the role of the military. The armed forces were seen as the creatures of the Shah and therefore their loyalty was always suspect. Khomeini, however, took a more pragmatic view, resisting demands after the revolution for the army to be dismantled and replaced entirely by a popular militia. In his final weeks of exile in France, Khomeini had assured his followers that the military were not a significant threat to the revolution; either by instinct or by a subtle understanding of the sociology of the Shah's army, Khomeini understood that the loyalties of the mass of the armed forces were directed towards the nation rather than the monarch.

The modern Iranian army was the creation of Reza Pahlavi, the Shah's father; his intention was to make it the guardian of the

Pahlavi dynasty and of central power. Under Reza Shah, military governors had more authority than civilian governors and they reported directly to the monarch. The army's function was to defend the regime rather than the country. After the Second World War, however, there was a need to create a national army; Iran was now a party to international alliances, so Reza Shah's generals were pensioned off and a new generation of non-politicised career officers was recruited. The tasks of defending the state against external and internal enemies were separated, with the latter being put in the hands of the secret police, Savak. The army owed loyalty to the Shah but it had no responsibility for maintaining him in power until suddenly, in 1978, it was called upon to play a role in suppressing the revolution.

The aristocracy of generals, who owed their position to the Shah, went along with the role assigned to them. After a visit to Tehran shortly before the revolution, Senator Hubert Humphrey reported that an Iranian general had told him that, thanks to American help, the Iranian army had reached the stage where it was capable of coping with civil disturbances. That was what the generals believed, but the less privileged ranks, from colonel downwards, were open to the influences of the revolution. Only 7 per cent of the armed forces were in barracks, the remainder at home with their families; in all there were some 100,000 NCOs living in the towns and cities of Iran, in direct contact with the daily sufferings caused by the revolution. For many from religious families their first loyalty was to their ayatollah rather than to the Shah. After the revolution Khomeini removed the top echelon of the armed forces down to the rank of colonel, though in these purges no one was executed merely for having been a soldier. While other clergymen, and most of the left, pushed for the dismantling of the army, Khomeini insisted on maintaining it. He saw that it would never be an Islamic force, like the Revolutionary Guard, but its nationalist credentials were not really in question. So it was that when Iraq crossed the frontier it confronted an army that was virtually intact and dedicated to holding off the invaders.

Before the war more than half a million Arabs lived in Khuzestan, the province which the Iraqis called Arabistan. Like their near neighbours across the Shatt al Arab, they were Shia. Although the province contained the port of Khorramshahr and the refinery town of Abadan, as well as much of Iran's oil installations, the social organisation of the province was basically tribal. The population as a whole supported the Islamic revolution and had high expectations that the fall of the Shah would bring wide-ranging autonomy for the Arab minority. Immediately after the revolution, Arab representatives put forward a list of demands which included a reserved share of the province's oil revenue and recognition of Arabic as the first language in schools. When it became apparent that their demands would not quickly be met by the embryo government in Tehran, they staged mass demonstrations in the towns of Khuzestan and a minority launched guerrilla attacks on local barracks and oil installations. It was the first of a series of ethnic revolts that the new republic was to face in the first year of the revolution.

Tehran appointed the defence minister and naval commander, Admiral Ahmad Madani, to be governor-general of Khuzestan with a mandate to quell the unrest. Although he had been a career officer during the monarchy, Madani had impeccable revolutionary credentials: his father was an ayatollah, he himself was a devout Muslim and a supporter of the opposition National Front who had been jailed and dismissed from the navy by the Shah. To the Arab minority he became 'the Butcher of Khuzestan' but in the light of the subsequent injustices inflicted in the name of the Islamic Republic, it was an unfair sobriquet.

Nevertheless, Madani did use harsh methods to put down the incipient rebellion. In an interview in Paris, nine years later, he defended his record by saying that Khuzestan had been the target of a campaign not just by Iraq but also by elements of the PLO who wanted to wrest control of the province from Tehran. He said that George Habash, the leader of the Popular Front for the Liberation of Palestine, made several clandestine trips across the Iraqi border to southern Khuzestan in early 1979 to stir the Arab population into demanding autonomy. 'His message to the Arabs was to go for self-determination, to set up a republic, something like that. Maybe he hoped to find a solution for the Palestinians, to go and settle them there,' Madani said, and revealed that the PLO had opened a consulate in the provincial capital of Ahwaz in the early months of the revolution. 'Maybe that was a good solution for them. That was the beginning: first of all establishing a consulate for them, then encouraging them to come there to be settled. Maybe.' Despite Tehran's good relations with the PLO

(Yasser Arafat was the first foreign leader to travel to Iran to congratulate Khomeini on the victory of the revolution), Madani closed down the Ahwaz consulate and secured the border against infiltrators, Palestinian or otherwise.

The focus of Arab dissent in Khuzestan was the spiritual leader of the province, Sheikh Taher al-Shobeir Khaghani – 'not a bad man, but very stupid', in Madani's judgment. Khaghani not only complained about the lack of progress towards autonomy but also about the activities of the predominantly Persian revolutionary *komitehs* who policed the province. What had begun as a political dispute was threatening to turn into a racial conflict, so Madani came down hard on the Arab dissidents. At a mass demonstration in Khorramshahr in May, his troops opened fire and a number of people were killed. It was an uncomfortable reminder of the Shah's last year when the army had opened fire on the people – in future the regime would use Pasdaran and street gangs to confront their internal enemies.

The showdown between Madani and Khaghani came after Arab guerrillas threw a grenade into a crowded and predominantly Persian mosque in Khorramshahr, killing seven people, two of them Revolutionary Guards. Madani responded with a frontal assault on Khaghani's headquarters. Within twelve hours five suspects had been arrested, tried and executed for causing the mosque blast. It was the first time an Islamic revolutionary court had executed anyone for political violence committed after the revolution. 'It was said that a lot of people were killed and that we put down the rebellion very ruthlessly,' Madani said years later. 'In fact, the whole process in Khuzestan lasted a day. We lost about eight men and they lost about twelve. Altogether, in two months of dealing with the situation, forty-nine people were killed. After that there was peace.'

Madani sent Khaghani into exile in the holy city of Qom, where Khomeini had his headquarters. The Arab rebellion simmered on until the start of the war in the form of isolated guerrilla actions, but as a mass movement it had been contained. Although the central government would continue to be challenged by autonomy movements on the outer fringes of Iran, and in Kurdistan in particular, the threat in Khuzestan had been neutralised. And when Saddam Hussein's armies moved into the province in September 1980, there was no one there to greet them.

As 1980 came to an end, the battle lines were beginning to solidify. An agreement secured by Olof Palme for the release of the eighty-six foreign ships trapped in the Shatt al Arab by the fighting was ignored, the flow of oil from Iraq had decreased by more than two-thirds, Iraq's ceasefire offer made at the beginning of October had been spurned, and attention was moving away from the battle fronts to the hostages in the American embassy in Tehran as President Carter's term of office came to an end and President Reagan prepared to take over. Khorramshahr was occupied by Iraq on 10 November, and Abadan surrounded, though it was never totally occupied; the drives on Ahwaz and Dezful were halted, the battle of Susangerd was won by the Iranians, and by the end of November Iraq had reached its most forward positions on Iranian territory, facing a swiftly reinforced army which had dug in around the Iraqi objectives or withdrawn to the foothills of the Zagros mountains west of Dezful to set up a proper defensive line.

The Iraqi advance, such as it was, ran out of steam and the front stabilised. In the process, the Iranians used for the first time a weapon which was to become one of Iraq's main defences around the city of Basra when the Iranians began their advance – water. Near the village of Hamadiyeh, north-west of Ahwaz, Iraqi tanks and trucks were caught by a torrent of water when Iranian engineers opened the sluice gates on the Karkheb river to flood the plain below; the Iraqi armour and trucks became bogged down in the thick mud that was quickly created and the Iranian army was able to halt and repel the advance.

With the Iraqi army now dug in along a 170-mile line on the southern front from Dehloran down to Abadan, the political leaders in Baghdad seemed unaware of the real situation, or unwilling to acknowledge that even the limited military objectives they had set out at the beginning of the war had not been achieved. These were those contained in an old British-prepared plan of campaign which called for the occupation of all the main population centres of Khuzestan, with a break-out through the Zagros mountain passes on to the central Iranian plain in the direction of Isfahan after a major build-up. But Iraq had failed in those first objectives, not even taking the main towns of Khuzestan, and there was certainly never even any contemplation of a drive to the mountain passes.

In Baghdad, the politicians decided that the new stable front should be explained as the objective they had always wanted, not realising that the breakneck speed of the Iranian reconstitution of its armed forces meant that it was the Iraqis who were vulnerable, not the Iranian defenders. In January, the Iraqi minister of information, Latif Jassem, announced that the Iraqi army had reached the 'real' border with Iran and would not pull back even if it had to stay there for ten years, apparently a response to President Bani-Sadr's refusal of negotiations while any Iranian territory was under occupation. The reality of the rhetoric was that after its initial advance in the first two months of the war Iraq could make no gains; nor, at that time, could Iran, but it was Iran which had the advantage, for the December rains put a stop to any serious fighting for five months and gave the Iranians the valuable breathing space they needed – the opportunity to build up and reorganise their forces. Artillery exchanges went on each day, and there were regular probing attacks on both sides, though the Iranians were the more active in testing the Iraqi defences ready for a major counter-attack; the Iraqi commanders never really considered any further advance.

One consequence of the stalemate, which lasted for the whole of 1981, focused attention on a perennial question of the war: would Iraq run out of men before Iran ran out of money? Even in the quiet periods Iraq was losing between 300 and 400 men a month, a considerable total in a country of 14 million. At the same time, Iranian oil exports were at their lowest, while the country's expenditure was building up as it began its arms-purchasing campaign. President Hussein, in one of those remarkable Arabic phrases which mask reality, described the Iraqi situation in 1981 as 'a stationary offensive'. This bizarre concept was apparently designed to hide the reality from the civilians, still a worry to the Sunni/Tikriti junta which maintained its control with scant concessions to the Shia majority.

For the same reason, the restrictions imposed in Baghdad at the beginning of the war were relaxed, the black-out lifted, the airport reopened to civilian traffic, and work begun again on the building programme inspired by the agreement to hold the 1982 non-aligned summit conference in Baghdad. More foreign workers were brought in, mainly Asians, to press on with the hotels, conference centres and grandiose monuments thought necessary, as the Iraqi workers were all away at the front. Later in the war, even the humblest of these foreign workers found themselves contributing to the Iraqi war effort, whether they liked it or not. Filipino staff employed at the hotels were ordered to attend at health centres for six-monthly checks, a reasonable enough requirement. But once there, they found that they were obliged to donate blood, a ready supply for the Iraqi army medical corps hard-pressed to deal with casualties as each Iranian offensive took its toll, though not as brutal as Iran, where prisoners were 'bled' before execution.

Egyptian settlers, too, found themselves involved: brought in from the Nile delta before the war to farm the similar land in southern Iraq, they were pressed into military service, forced to enrol on the threat of having their family land confiscated. When the war came to an end, President Hosni Mubarak went along with the fiction that all the Egyptians were volunteers, but it took intense diplomacy by Turkey to secure the repatriation from Iran of those taken prisoner.

As the war which was to have been a triumphant Iraqi blitzkrieg settled into stalemate within months of the first thrusts across the border, the world too began to learn to live normally while a major conflict raged in a vital region. Bellicose early Iranian threats to halt the flow of oil from the Gulf at first contributed to panic in the oil markets, as dealers took seriously the prospect that the Strait of Hormuz might be closed. But only a few months into the war, the fears receded. The Strait was twenty-five miles wide and could not be blocked by a few scuttled ships, and surely the Iranians did not possess mines – did they? Anyway, the Iranians were even more dependent than Iraq on getting their oil out through the Gulf, so of course they would do nothing to halt free navigation there – would they? It was a hesitant accommodation with reality that the oil community reached, but it was an accommodation, and the situation had been improved by the suddenly soaring oil prices which had again contributed to a lessening in demand as economies were enforced and the world-wide drop in industrial activity began to be felt.

The flurry of diplomatic activity caused by the outbreak of war came to a halt, the special correspondents who had taken up residence in the Airport Hotel in Basra were recalled, and as 1981 went on the daily reports faded into articles about 'the forgotten war'. Israel was happy, America and Russia were warily neutral, waiting to see what developed, arms-producing nations were quietly beginning to make their sales pitch, and only in the Middle East itself did the war still command front-page headlines and the attention of the politicians. In the Gulf, the unexpressed wish of the Arab states of the western littoral that Iraq would first contain and then extinguish Ayatollah Khomeini's Islamic revolution went unfulfilled, but at least Iraq was now the focus of Iranian anger, and its military strength could prevent the Ayatollah from directing his energies to the export of his ideas. In Moscow, in Washington and in the capitals of Europe, a quiet hope emerged that two nasty regimes might exhaust each other, that it might be possible for a war to be conducted without the involvement of the superpowers. There was certainly a general humanitarian concern for what was happening, but among the policy-makers a feeling emerged that this was a war the world could live with.

The euphoria did not last long: by March 1982 the tide began to turn, and halfway through that year it was clear that Iraq was being forced on to the defensive. The twenty-one month stalemate was no more than a preparation for what was to come. In Iraq, Saddam Hussein began the consolidation of his personal authority which he was to pursue throughout the war, turning the conflict into his mission, his Qaddissiya. Iraqis accepted the war on their leader's terms: it was always called Saddam's war, an identification which the President had consciously encouraged. It was a dangerous gambit which eventually paid off – against all the odds. Perhaps Saddam Hussein saw more clearly than most that he had no choice: he had to win to survive, so he might as well risk all.

In Iran, the one undoubted leader was so much above the fray that he was hardly touched by it. The Ayatollah remained God's word on earth, the source of all laws and the arbiter of all destinies. But the mullahs who had triumphed over the Shah, over the forces of secularism and communism, had still not made their victory secure. Because the country was still divided, still in a state of chaos after the swift changes of only two years, they had an even more difficult task as they sought to ensure the continuation and success of the Islamic revolution. It was a conflict in which one side or the other had to emerge victorious, and there was no place for a man like President Bani-Sadr, who sought to span the worlds of Islam and more modern, orthodox politics, nor for those who were willing to compromise. What the world saw as a stalemate in the Gulf was a blood-stained, desperate time of struggle in Iran.

# 4

# Iran and Iraq:
# internal wars

President Abolhassan Bani-Sadr was an unlikely Bonaparte. Like the Emperor, he was small in stature but his wispy moustache and horn-rimmed glasses gave him an owlish and quizzical look which suggested more a college professor than a leader of men. Yet destiny – and Ayatollah Khomeini – had decreed that he should take the leading role in the defence of Iran against the invading Iraqis. Within a month of the outbreak of war, Khomeini appointed Bani-Sadr chairman of the Supreme Defence Council with wide-ranging powers to direct the conduct of the war and supervise foreign policy. The President rose to the challenge with vigour and little regard for his own safety: the incongruous figure of Bani-Sadr crouched in the trenches with an ill-fitting steel helmet clamped untidily on the back of his head is one of the enduring images of the first months of the war.

By the end of 1980, the military initiative had switched firmly to Iran. The Iranian armed forces, thanks in no small measure to the support of Bani-Sadr, had held together despite the pre-war purges and now had nothing to lose by biding their time for a fresh counter-attack against the Iraqi invasion force. It was on the home front that the President faced a much more serious challenge than that now posed by Saddam Hussein. It came from powerful clergymen grouped in the Islamic Republican party (IRP) and led by Ayatollah Mohammad Beheshti, the chief justice of the Supreme Court, a skilful if Machiavellian politician who was as at ease with Westerners as he was with his own countrymen and who, although he wore the black robes of a mullah, had them made up by his tailor in Europe. Within the first year of the war Beheshti was to engineer Bani-Sadr's downfall, though he had little time in which to savour his victory: within a month of the departure of Bani-Sadr into exile, Beheshti and much of the senior leadership of the I R P were wiped out in a bomb explosion which unleashed a reign of terror and counter-terror almost as bloody as the confrontation on the front line with Iraq.

A political battle for control of post-revolutionary Iran had been going on for more than a year when Iraq invaded – the image of internecine strife and internal chaos which the new regime projected was a major factor in encouraging Saddam Hussein to embark on his military adventure. The continuing power struggle was a conflict which involved liberals and leftists, nationalists and Islamic fundamentalists, those who had spent the years of opposition in exile and those who had spent them in the prisons of the Shah; it was between clergymen who sought political power for themselves and secularists who wanted the mullahs to return to their mosques. And it was largely by their skilful manipulation of the US embassy hostage crisis, in which fifty-two Americans were held for 444 days by fundamentalist pro-clergy students, that the mullahs succeeded in neutralising their liberal opponents, while by exploiting the war with Iraq, Beheshti and his allies succeeded in destroying not only Bani-Sadr but also those on the left who sought to capture the revolution for themselves.

The revolution was made by a variety of disparate forces united under the banner of Islam, although for many this was a flag of convenience which would be cast off once the Shah had been overthrown. The exiled propagandists of the revolution were predominantly Western-educated, like Bani-Sadr or the former student leader, Sadeq Ghotbzadeh. They envisaged a secular society in which Islamic values would be respected but in which the clergy would play a purely guiding role. They promoted Khomeini as a Gandhi-like figure personifying the aspirations of the Iranian people, and ignored the Imam's writings over the previous quarter of a century in which he had outlined his belief in theocratic rule. The revolutionaries were mainly left-wingers from the Fedayin movement and the People's Mujahedin, who had their own separate visions of a classless, revolutionary society. The Fedayin were secular radicals while the Mujahedin preached a synthesis of Marxism and Islam, though both believed that the internal dynamics of the revolution would sweep aside any reactionaries, whether liberal or clerical, who tried to stand in its path. All sides ignored the political knowhow and organisational abilities of the clergy and the determination of the mullahs to build up and consolidate their own power, a determination so firm that even after the war began, the mullahs appeared prepared to sacrifice the national unity created by the Iraqi invasion in order to destroy their secular opponents. Khomeini's grandson, Hossein, who for a time was one of Bani-Sadr's most fervent supporters, was later to remark of the clerical leaders of the IRP: 'I have heard them say that it is preferable to lose half of Iran than for Bani-Sadr to become the ruler.'

Bani-Sadr was elected by an overwhelming popular majority in January 1980 to become the first President of the Islamic Republic. It was never clear how much his victory owed to his own popularity and how much to the tacit endorsement of Khomeini, who seemed at the time to be keenly aware of the dangers of the clergy filling elected offices. For the time being at least Khomeini was also disposed towards checking the unrestrained growth of IRP power. Thus, he rejected the IRP's first choice for president, Jalaleddin Farsi, on the grounds that he was the son of an Afghan. Although there were eight candidates in the 25 January election, Farsi's disqualification effectively left the field to Bani-Sadr, a French-educated economist who had been part of Khomeini's close entourage during his exile in France. Khomeini may have regarded Bani-Sadr as a bridge between secularism and Islam, as Iran's first president was the son of a clergyman and was himself a devout Muslim, but he had had a secular education both in Iran and abroad. He liked to see himself as an Islamic anarchist, regarding religion as a medium of individual liberation and as a guarantor of tolerance and human rights. His main enemies were those he termed the 'fascist clerics' who sought to institutionalise the role of the clergy at the expense of other sectors of the community.

Throughout the first year of the revolution, Bani-Sadr stood outside the political fray. Mehdi Bazargan, Khomeini's choice as provisional prime minister, failed to give Bani-Sadr the cabinet post he might have hoped for, given the prominent position he had occupied in the inner circle of the Imam's secular acolytes. He was nevertheless appointed to the Revolutionary Council, a secretive body which took over the reins of government when Bazargan resigned in November 1979. And although he served briefly as foreign minister and then finance minister before his election to the presidency, he remained instinctively an outsider. As a member of the Assembly of Experts set up to draft a new Islamic constitution, he dared to speak out against the more theocratic provisions proposed by Beheshti and his followers and, after the US embassy was seized, he went against the current of popular opinion by denouncing the hostage-taking as a misguided adventure. He was, however, an economic radical and fiercely anti-American, and while he opposed the totalitarian element within both the clergy and the far left, he appeared to share their contempt for the pro-Western centrists grouped around Bazargan.

So Bani-Sadr's failure in the first year of the revolution was not in his individuality, his nonconformity, but in his lack of political understanding – and the error which was to contribute to his downfall was that he failed to establish a firm political power base. He did have his own newspaper, *Enghelab-e-Islami* (*Islamic Revolution*), through which he propagated his ideas on Islamic democracy and economic reform, but he had no political party through which to put these ideas into practice, and though he polled 75 per cent of the votes in the election, he did not have a defined constituency. He attracted the support both of the secular middle class, who saw in him a natural defence against theocratic rule, and of the Islamic proletariat, who saw him as Khomeini's spiritual son; with greater political experience he might easily have built himself the popular base he needed to maintain his power. Bani-Sadr's opponents realised this before he did, and the IRP, which for once had been out-manoeuvred, was determined to clip the new President's wings.

One of the most sinister movements spawned by the Islamic revolution was that of the *hizbollahi*, the adherents of the so-called Party of God, though there was in fact no such party. The gangs which emerged in 1979 to take the clergy's battles against their secular opponents on to the streets took their name from their war cry: '*Hezb faqt, hizbollah; rahbar yeki, Ruhollah*' – 'There is only one party, Allah's; there is only one leader, Ruhollah [Khomeini].' Their enemies nicknamed them *chomaqdar*, the clubwielders. Their organiser and mentor was Hadi Ghaffari, an IRP radical who had trained with the PLO in Lebanon, and who was to return there later in the war to act as the mentor of the Hizbollah movement in Lebanon, where it was responsible for the kidnapping of foreigners and the suicide bomb explosions which precipitated the withdrawal of US troops.

In Iran in the summer of 1979, Hizbollah's task was to intimidate and disrupt the rallies of the IRP's opponents, and a pattern of aggression and interference was soon worked out. A typical incident occurred on 13 August at the football ground of the Tehran University campus, a regular venue for political meetings. About 10,000 supporters of the centre-left, middle-class National Democratic Front had assembled to hear their leaders denounce the recent closure of opposition newspapers. Suddenly a gang of shaven-headed youths stormed through the crowd and began pelting the speakers' platform with rocks, injuring several NDF officials. Some clambered on to the platform to rip out microphone leads and tear up party leaflets. When the attack subsided and most of the crowd had fled, *hizbollahi* roamed the campus, picking on stragglers and beating them up. Then, in what became part of a cynical pattern during that summer, an arrest warrant was issued against the victim of the attack, the leader of the NDF Hedayatollah Matine-Daftari, for 'disrupting public order'.

The *hizbollahi* were a living legacy of the Shah's unrestrained modernisation programme, part of the vast lumpenproletariat from the slums of south Tehran which had been swollen by mass migration from the provinces during the boom years of the 1970s. The *hizbollahi* were illiterate, dirty and poorly dressed; some bore the scars and deformities of their dispossessed childhoods. Those of them who were prepared to speak on 13 August about their motives for attacking the rally were barely coherent, but seemed to be spurred on by a hatred of foreigners and of the rich, and by an unquestioning loyalty to Khomeini and the clergy. The militants of the IRP harnessed this aggressive energy as a potent weapon against their enemies. Later, the impoverished youth of south Tehran were to find a new outlet for their hatred in the war against Iraq in which tens of thousands of them perished in the service of Islam.

With the help of Hizbollah, the IRP succeeded in destroying the political organisations of the middle-class centre while the left looked on with rather more satisfaction than foreboding. But the left too was soon to come under attack: the clubwielders next turned their attentions to the Fedayin and the People's Mujahedin, both of which had retained the weapons captured in the revolution. A minority faction of the Marxist Fedayin went underground but the Mujahedin hung on, expressing their loyalty to Khomeini, who, in turn, continued to spurn them, dubbing them *monafeqin* (hypocrites) because they dared to promote a Marxist interpretation of Islam. The orthodox communist Tudeh party, faithful to the directives it received from Moscow, maintained a policy of supporting the regime and currying favour with the clerical party.

Throughout 1980, the IRP conducted a persistent campaign to undermine the authority of Bani-Sadr. The new President considered that the constitution gave him a powerful executive role and he interpreted his landslide victory in the election as a popular mandate for secular democratic government, but Beheshti and his fellow clerics skilfully manipulated the constitution against him. They blocked his nominees for the premiership and other cabinet posts and succeeded in forcing him to accept their own candidate, Mohammad Ali Rajai, as prime minister. The inexperienced and malleable Rajai was in practice the servant of Beheshti and with the establishment of the first Majlis after elections in the spring of 1980, it was the leader of the IRP who held most power in the land after Khomeini. It was a reflection of the situation when Bani-Sadr arrived for the inaugural session of the parliament late and alone. The electoral manoeuvrings of the IRP had ensured that a majority of the assembly were either members of, or sympathetic to, the clerical party, while Bani-Sadr's supporters had secured only a handful of seats. As the President addressed the assembly for the first time, a group of senior mullahs drifted from the chamber, either out of boredom or contempt, and settled into the armchairs of the outer gallery to sip tea and puff at their imported American cigarettes.

Not all the clergy were with the IRP. Bani-Sadr had his partisans in the mosque who shared his opposition to the excesses of the regime: the executions and arbitrary imprisonment ordered by Islamic courts, the closure of the opposition press and the intimidation practised by Ghaffari's *hizbollahi*. For a time he even enjoyed the support of close members of Khomeini's family, including the Imam's son Ahmad, and his elder brother, Ayatollah Pasandideh. But Khomeini came to accept the arguments of the leaders of the IRP that it was Bani-Sadr and not they who was responsible for the internal dissent. The diminutive President did nothing to counter their arguments: he was indeed an active polemicist against the clerical party and its attempts to monopolise power; whoever they attacked, such as the Mujahedin, he defended. In the end the IRP, more often than not, was able to remain silent and allow Bani-Sadr to dig his own grave. So it was that the outbreak of war presented Bani-Sadr with both an opportunity and a challenge. At last, he had the chance to take on the role of a truly national leader, commanding Iran's forces at the front line in defence of the national territory, and at the same time, in the armed forces, Bani-Sadr had the opportunity to build the power base against the mullahs which he had previously lacked.

The IRP was not slow to spot the dangers and they redoubled their efforts to undermine the President; so once the initial Iraqi assault was contained, Bani-Sadr came under fire for not mounting an immediate counter-offensive, and the army, despite its role in holding back the invasion force, was criticised for avoiding battle and leaving the combat to irregular volunteer militias and the Revolutionary Guard. There was an active campaign, which found an echo in the tactics of the invading Iraqis, to sow dissension between the regulars and the volunteers.

Eight years later, after the war had ended, we asked Bani-Sadr at his home in exile in Versailles whether he had not made a mistake in spending so much time with his troops at the front rather than staying in Tehran to confront the pressures that were building up against him. 'I had no alternative but to be at the front, it was my place as President. I wouldn't accept resignation. By June of 1981 Beheshti and Rafsanjani had to admit that not all the clergy united could compete with Bani-Sadr, particularly if he won the war.'

Bani-Sadr said he still believed that the war could have been ended after a few months on favourable terms for Iran.

Then Carter and I committed a capital error. On 8 October a Western European ambassador came to see me saying that Carter had sent a message stating that the United States would never accept the defeat of Iran, though that didn't mean that they would accept the victory of Iran either. It was I who passed on this message to Khomeini. That was my error. Once Khomeini was reassured that defeat was not now possible he said to himself: 'We can do what we like, why not?' Thus this reassurance changed his attitude, with grave consequences.

The President became a victim of his own success. His enemies on the left joined the clergy in attacking his alleged Bonapartist aspirations while the IRP leaders quibbled about the lack of Islamic conviction within the officer corps. The mullahs now proceeded to destroy the unity among the fighting forces which Bani-Sadr had managed to sustain in the first perilous weeks of the war. They were determined to build the Revolutionary Guard, a body of some 20,000 to 30,000 men at the start of the war, into the main fighting force at the expense of the regular army. Beheshti and the IRP made repeated attempts to have Bani-Sadr removed from the post of commander-in-chief, and any hopes the President had of building a power base within the armed forces were slowly throttled.

The first six months of 1981 saw a virtual stalemate on the front line with Iraq but a state of open warfare within Iran as the power struggle intensified. It was a period in which the middle-class secular parties and the Mujahedin and far left made their last stand against the creeping takeover of the IRP. The clerical party was by now in firm control of government, most of the media, the Islamic courts and the revolutionary *komitehs* which acted as an arbitrary and unofficial police force. Left-wing and centrist students had been ousted from the universities and the campuses closed, while *hizbollahi* roamed the cities, breaking up rallies and attacking political party headquarters with impunity.

Khomeini made repeated appeals for unity but his pronouncements invariably favoured the IRP, and though he continued to support Bani-Sadr's presidency he also took the IRP line that the President should accept the limits of his powers as defined by the constitution. So Bani-Sadr and the centre parties began to secure the backing of the powerful Tehran bazaar, whose devout but deeply conservative members were becoming increasingly concerned about the drift towards extremism. But as the opposition sought to regroup and fight back, so the repression intensified; leaders of the moderate parties railed impotently against the Stalinism of the IRP, and were answered with violence and arrest. There was evidence that the centrists and the moderate left had widespread support within the country, but they were too disorganised and intimidated to counter the power of the IRP. The Mujahedin too retained their popularity, particularly among the young, but by now had been forced into a semi-clandestine existence, ready to take up the arms which had been hidden in preparation for a possible civil war against the regime.

The leaders of the People's Mujahedin were seen by the mullahs, and indeed regarded themselves, as the main threat to the emerging clergy-dominated regime, as both sides were direct competitors in the contest for the hearts and minds of Iranian youth. A poor young man from south Tehran might as easily be recruited into the ranks of the Mujahedin as into Hadi Ghaffari's Hizbollah. The Mujahedin had served as the radical cutting edge of the revolution, they had fought against the remnants of the Shah's regime in the Battle of Tehran and had then mercilessly pursued the repression of the Shah's supporters, insisting on summary trials and executions when many mullahs were urging restraint. They backed the seizure of the US embassy in November 1979 and supported the most extreme demands of the Islamic students. They were among the first to volunteer to go to the front when the war broke out. They were part and parcel of the Islamic revolution, and indeed many who subsequently turned against them had once been among their most enthusiastic admirers. But for all their adherence to the cause of militant Islam, Khomeini still regarded the Mujahedin as hypocrites. The spring of 1981 saw almost daily clashes between the Mujahedin and Hizbollah: what had begun as a political struggle was degenerating into a small-scale civil war, with battles in the towns of the Caspian coast, traditionally a leftist stronghold, and in Tehran where armed *hizbollahi* turned out in force every time the Mujahedin tried to mount a demonstration. The toll of dead and injured mounted.

For most of Bani-Sadr's presidency he had maintained cautious and unofficial contact with the Mujahedin leader, Masoud Rajavi; the two men had profound ideological differences but both saw the benefits of an alliance of convenience against the common enemy, the IRP, so as the political crisis worsened they became more active partners; it was this relationship above everything that turned Khomeini against the President. Amid the mounting street violence, Bani-Sadr's position was becoming increasingly untenable: he was denied access to the airwaves, and demonstrations in his support were either banned or broken up. Then in May, the Majlis voted to increase the powers of the Prime Minister at the President's expense, and both Bani-Sadr and the Mujahedin began to talk in terms of active resistance to the tyranny of the clergy. By doing so, they cast themselves in the role of renegades while allowing the clerics of the IRP to pose as the guarantors of constitutional law. So, carefully following the proper procedure, in mid-June the clerical party within the Majlis moved to have Bani-Sadr dismissed on the grounds that he had called for open rebellion.

The President was invited to defend himself from the floor of the chamber but, with many of his closest supporters already in jail, he went underground before the motion for his impeachment was put to the Majlis on 21 June. The one-sided debate was held against the background of chants from the street outside of 'Death to Bani-Sadr' and among the 218 members of the assembly, only one voted against the motion, while 177 voted in favour. Within hours a warrant was issued for Bani-Sadr's arrest for provoking rebellion against the state. Among the catalogue of charges levelled against the President in his impeachment were: defiance of the Imam, factionalism, and opposing revolutionary organisations; perhaps the cruellest of all was that, as commander-in-chief, he had left Iran open to foreign aggression.

When he received news of Bani-Sadr's impeachment, Khomeini appointed a Presidential Council to replace him, made up of Prime Minister Rajai, Ayatollah Beheshti and the speaker of parliament, Hojatoleslam Ali Akbar Hashemi Rafsanjani; from now on, the mullahs were fighting the war.

The showdown with the Mujahedin had come the previous day, on 20 June. Together with their Fedayin and other leftist allies and elements of the Kurdish Democratic Party, the Mujahedin brought tens of thousands of supporters on to the streets of Tehran in a last-minute show of force on behalf of Bani-Sadr. Revolutionary Guards were immediately drafted in to break up the demonstration, and in the clashes which followed at least thirty people were killed, among them fourteen Guards. The clerical authorities struck back harshly: more than twenty people were summarily executed at Evin prison in Tehran the following day. So from 20 June the Mujahedin were in a state of war against the regime, with Bani-Sadr and the Mujahedin leader, Rajavi, smuggled out to direct the struggle from exile.

A week after Bani-Sadr's dismissal, some ninety senior officials of the IRP gathered at party headquarters in Tehran to discuss the new political situation. As they did so a powerful bomb planted in a neighbouring building exploded, killing seventy-four. Among the dead were Beheshti, four cabinet ministers and twenty-seven parliamentary deputies. The victorious IRP had been decapitated at a stroke. That 28 June attack was blamed on the Mujahedin, although the movement has never accepted or denied responsibility; an obscure monarchist group claimed to have planted the bomb, while many exiles, displaying the Iranian penchant for conspiracy theories, insisted that the attack was part of an internal power struggle within the clergy. Some of the senior leadership was spared: Rafsanjani had left the building before the explosion and other IRP leaders were absent. On 30 August, however, a second bomb claimed the lives of Mohammad Ali Rajai, who had replaced Bani-Sadr as President, and Mohammad Javad Bahonar, the new Prime Minister.

A brutal reign of terror and counter-terror had begun which was to last for two years; apart from the war, the bombings were the most serious threat which the regime had faced since the revolution. Prominent clergymen and IRP politicians became the targets of Mujahedin assassins, and Revolutionary Guards were shot dead by Mujahedin gunmen in the streets of Tehran. Yet despite the occasional direct confrontations between guerrillas and Guards and the intensive leaflet campaigns, the Mujahedin failed to provoke the popular uprising they sought, even when the regime, fearing that its lower echelons were riddled with Mujahedin sympathisers, reacted brutally. Suspects, many of them students or schoolchildren, were summarily tried and executed, some of them publicly. At times the executions averaged fifty a day, though there are conflicting claims about the total number who died on both sides in the terror.

The Iranian sociologist, Ehsan Naraghi, who was arrested three days after the bomb which killed Beheshti and spent the two years of the terror in Evin prison, has estimated that 10,000 people died, equivalent to the number of Iranians who died in the first six months of the war with Iraq. Naraghi had tenuous connections with the old regime and, as Bani-Sadr's former teacher, he had encouraged the future president to pursue his studies in France. He regarded himself as an impartial observer of the events which were unfolding, and took a clear-eyed view of his compatriots:

> After the bombing the Mujahedin were convinced that Rajavi would return, and that was why they were prepared to die. The movement thought it gained strength from the number of its martyrs; it was the policy of the Khmer Rouge. They were obsessed and fascinated by weapons, which is why they never gave them up. For them, the powerful man was the one who controlled the biggest cache of hidden weapons.

Naraghi believed that the Mujahedin policy of arbitrarily assassinating Revolutionary Guards lost them what support they might have hoped to gain for a popular rebellion, for the Guards, after all, were recruited from the ordinary people. Later, many of the Mujahedin held in Evin repented and became, according to Naraghi, more *hizbollahi* than Hizbollah. 'The Guards one could debate with, but these converts who crammed into Evin mosque and screamed support for every visiting clergyman, you couldn't reason with them. They were fanatics.'

It is clear that both Bani-Sadr and Rajavi over-estimated their popularity among the mass of the population and underestimated that of the clergy, while the President put unreasonable faith in the backing of the armed forces. As Sheikh Sadeq Khalkhali, the so-called 'hanging judge', put it: 'If Ayatollah Khomeini had not been popular, it is he who would have fled the country and not Mr Bani-Sadr.' If the clergy had succumbed to a popular uprising, then the war with Iraq might have been over much sooner, though the regime which would have succeeded Khomeini's could have been even less amenable to Western and regional interests than the one it replaced. Bani-Sadr would have been a hostage to the radical and doctrinaire policies of the Mujahedin, and domestic chaos or civil war would have invited intervention by the Soviet Union. Instead, the external threat from Iraq provided a unifying factor and a justification for the counter-terror against internal enemies, and despite the outcry in the West against Tehran's brutal disregard of human rights, Western strategists saw the value of a stable, anti-communist regime run by the mullahs but kept in check by the stalemated war with Iraq. A British-based analyst,

M. S. El Azhary, wrote in 1983 that among the reasons for the reversal of the fortunes of war in Iran's favour

> was that since the beginning of 1982 revolutionary turmoil subsided within her borders and a gradual cohesion had begun to evolve. This came as a welcome development to the United States because, with a pro-Soviet regime next door to Iran in Afghanistan, a strong anti-communist Iran was considered an important barrier to the extension of Soviet influence in the Gulf region.

In the first year or so of the war, just as at its end eight years later, the two superpowers found themselves in agreement. With its recent experience of Iran, America wanted no direct involvement in the conflict, while the Russians were content to sit back for a while to see how things went in Tehran, and to allow their difficult ally Iraq to be bloodied and made more amenable to advice from Moscow. Inside Iraq, the first years of the war were the most difficult and dangerous for Saddam Hussein as his over-optimistic forecasts of a swift campaign and a quick victory proved so wrong when the Iraqi forces were first halted and then pushed back to their own border at the end of 1982.

But even more than in Iran, the rulers in Baghdad had a huge state apparatus at their disposal to see that discontent did not spill over into action. Nor did Saddam Hussein rely on his internal intelligence forces merely to watch over the people, to detect plots and prevent *coups*; it was also used as an instrument of repression, designed to keep a restive population under control. To do so, it had not only to find dissidents and plotters, the subversives and the discontented, it also had to mete out punishment, to wreak vengeance when necessary and always to bring home to the citizens that there was a high price for any action against the regime. The result was a total police state with an elaborate system of watchers and informers in addition to the security forces; every village, every block of flats and every factory had its complement of watchers – and the watchers knew that they were being watched, but were never allowed to know the identity of those carrying out the same tasks as themselves. In the armed forces, in addition to the political commissars, soldiers of all ranks were encouraged to report 'disloyal' remarks made by colleagues, criticism of the commanders or doubts expressed about the way the war was going. Iraqis were actively discouraged from talking to foreigners, and if through some accident a person did so without any obvious motive, then a police car would be at his house next day, and there would be a long interrogation about what was said on both sides, the reason for the conversation, and so on; and everyone knew that even the most cursory brush with the police, as in such a case, meant that the individual concerned would be on a 'watch' list for evermore.

To make the system work, fear had to be instilled in the populace, and this was something that was done from the early days of the Ba'ath regime. From the time when King Feisal and his family were murdered in their palace in the original revolution of 1958, change in Iraq was always accompanied by bloodshed. But after Saddam Hussein came to power – with the initial executions in which he took a personal part – it was continuity that required violence: dissent had to be stifled, opponents dissuaded from acting, and the way to do that was to show the consequences of error.

As early as 1981, in one of the many reports on conditions in Iraq that it was to produce, Amnesty International said that for years past it had received reports of routine torture of political suspects once they were held by the security forces. Many died under torture but, rather than attempting to conceal this, the authorities returned the bodies of the victims to their families with the marks of what had been done to them plain to see. In other cases the bodies were dumped in the street outside their homes, so that not only the immediate family would be aware of what had happened, but the friends and neighbours too. If there was a dissident in one house, then the whole street was suspect.

The Revolutionary Court established in the early days of the regime dealt with crimes unknown in the West: insulting the government, selling revolutionary newspapers, inciting discontent. Those arrested were usually tortured in police stations and detention centres to make them confess, to sign statements which would then be the sole evidence against them in court; there was no appeal. Executions were commonplace: between 1978 and 1981 Amnesty had the names of 520 people executed for political offences, and there were more than 300 executions in 1982. As the war went on the totals rose as deserters joined the categories facing the death penalty; at first taken to their homes to be executed, they were later killed in such places as the increasingly notorious Abu Ghraib prison near Baghdad. According to one prisoner who survived,

> the section of Abu Ghraib reserved for those under sentence of death is a hall surrounded by rooms measuring four metres by four metres into each of which fifteen to twenty prisoners are packed. They have to use their rooms as toilets and rubbish dumps. The sun never finds its way into these rooms. A very small proportion of these prisoners are common criminals but the majority are from the military, men who have opposed the Iran–Iraq war.

Other inmates have described the department of the prison dealing with 'special sentences', a category including all opposition members, but particularly those from Dawa and the communist party. Many of these people are kept in basement dungeons, and allowed out for exercise only once a month. Again, some are there for crimes unknown outside Iraq: a sixty-year-old retired officer ordered back to the forces at the beginning of the war was sentenced to twenty years for incompetence and cowardice; a Turkish Kurd heard criticising the Ba'ath party's autonomy plans for Iraqi Kurdistan was given fifteen years.

A branch of the security service runs Abu Ghraib, not the police or regular prison service. Significantly, the executioner Abu Widad, and his assistant Sayid Medlool, both live permanently in the prison – their services are constantly needed.

The number of executions has risen since the war began because of the extra offences which carry the death penalty. In addition to the civil crimes of murder, rape, arson, armed robbery and sodomy the death penalty has been imposed for desertion, certain currency and commercial crimes, conspiracy against the state – widely interpreted – espionage, membership of Dawa, and treachery against the party by members of the Ba'ath. As in the case of Ayatollah Baqr al-Sadr, executions were used to stamp out the last vestiges of opposition from the Shia religious establishment: in 1983 there were widespread arrests of members of the family of Ayatollah Mohammed Baqr al-Hakim, the leader of the opposition in exile, SAIRI. Those picked up ranged in age from nine to seventy-six, a plain indication that this was a punitive measure, and that no real crimes were charged. Of those arrested, six were immediately executed; ten others were hanged in 1985, after having been held in prison in dreadful conditions for two years.

To ensure that the message was understood, Iraq had to publicise what had happened, so that news of the arrests and executions could reach Tehran and perhaps deter people from joining the opposition based there; this also meant that outside bodies learnt of the executions, so that when Amnesty complained to the Iraqi government there could be no denial. Instead, Iraq replied that those hanged had

> consented to arouse dissension and hateful sectarian divisions, and forming a hostile organisation known as the Iraqi Mujahedin Movement, the principal aim of which is the overthrow of the legitimate constitutional regime in Iraq. They brought in weapons and explosives from abroad and distributed them among saboteurs with the aim of causing chaos and dissension and arousing sectarian divisions. They have suspected and real links with the Iranian regime which is at war with Iraq, and this amounts to high treason against their country.

As the war went on, less and less attention was paid even to the semblance of law and judicial procedure; increasingly, summary executions were carried out by the security forces. Two groups in particular were singled out – deserters from the armed forces, and the Kurds. As the conflict turned into a war of attrition along the battle lines, more soldiers found that they could not face the relentless attacks of the Pasdaran and *basij*, Iran's teen-aged volunteers, for all their superior equipment and well-placed fortifications; but, knowing the penalty for desertion, they could not risk going back to their homes, no matter how remote. The solution, for thousands of those on the southern front, the most unremitting and dangerous of all, was to join the bands which had established themselves in the marshes of southern Iraq. There, well-armed groups lived by preying on traffic along the main roads, sallying out at night to carry out their raids, holding up lorries and taking all their contents. They exacted dues from the local people, promising in return that no government agents would get in to enforce tax payments or take the young men for military service, and they also went in for straightforward robbery. All the deserters took with them arms and ammunition when they left, so that at times the gangs operated in groups of a hundred men or more, and could not be contained by the police and other local security services. The government's solution was to make sure that there was no break-out from the marshes, but to leave them alone where they were; Iraq had enough problems without taking on armed insurgents.

The Kurds were in a different category: they could give actual help to the Iranians, they could act on behalf of Syria, and because they occupied the areas of the main oil production, and the region through which the vital pipelines to the Mediterranean passed, they could do huge damage to the economy of the country. They had to be contained, and the regime's solution was a massive programme of deportations and re-location, forcing the Kurdish villagers into settlements which could be guarded by the army, declaring a free-fire zone along the borders in which anyone found was regarded as an enemy and a target, and bringing in thousands of 'loyal' Arab Iraqis from the south.

Yet none of these measures ended the continuing Kurdish revolt, so again the regime turned to terror. When incidents occurred, there was no attempt to make arrests or go through the process of law: the practice of arbitrary execution was considered a better way of deterring others from taking similar actions. Amnesty reported that in October 1985, for instance, 300 Kurds were killed in retaliation for attacks on the Iraqi forces. In Sula-maniyeh ten young men were seized at random, lined up outside a public bath and executed in retaliation for the loss of two Iraqi airmen shot down by Kurdish insurgents that day. Next day, 20,000 Iraqi troops were sent into the city to make house-to-house searches; thirteen of the hundreds arrested were again lined up and shot, this time in a residential suburb of the city. Eight men said to be deserters or members of the *peshmerga* were buried alive in the cemetery, and when young men took to the streets to protest against the outrage, the troops fired directly into the crowds, killing more than two hundred. In Erbil, the Iraqi air force was brought in to bomb the town's old Citadel, where some of those sought by the troops had taken refuge; eighty were killed. Hundreds of others were arrested in the regular sweeps the Iraqi forces made through the Kurdish areas in the search for deserters and members of the Kurdish opposition; in many cases those picked up simply disappeared.

The situation in Iraq was summed up by a group of the moderate opposition in exile, among them Jalal Talabani, the Kurdish leader, Sadiq Alattiyah of the Liberal Democratic Party, General Hassan al Naqib and Sayyed Mohammed Baqr al Udema of the Islamic Front. In a memorandum submitted to the United Nations, they wrote:

> The dictatorship of Saddam Hussein is one of the harshest, most ruthless and most unscrupulous regimes in the world. It is a totalitarian, one-party system based on the personality cult of Saddam Hussein. This man and his family and relatives have full control of the regular army, People's Army, police and security services. All news media are under the strict control of the regime and there is no opportunity for freedom of expression. Political organisation is limited to the Ba'ath party and a number of insignificant, obsequious organisations. Trade unions do not exist. Membership of any opposition party is punishable by death. Any criticism of the President is also punishable by death. Torture is the norm. The security system is all-powerful, omnipresent, and enjoys unlimited powers.

This opposition memorandum noted that Iraq had been under martial law since the regime seized power in 1968, and that since 1976 the RCC had issued seventeen resolutions making twenty-nine political offences subject to the death penalty, some with retroactive effect. 'Persecution, torture, executions and murders are general and extend to all sections of the population.'

Proof of that statement came as early as 1980 when three leading scientists were arrested at a time when the country desperately needed their services. Amnesty reported that Dr Husain al Shahristani, a nuclear physicist at the Iraqi Nuclear Research Institute, was arrested, tortured, sentenced to death and then sent to life imprisonment in Abu Ghraib. No charges against him were ever given, but he was a member of a well-known Shia family from Kerbala, and was apparently suspected of supporting Dawa. His colleague Dr Jaafar Dhia Jaafar at the Research Institute made representations on his friend's behalf; he disappeared. Dr Hassan Muhammed Rajai, a mechanical engineer with the Iraqi National Oil Company, was another Shia from Kerbala; he was arrested and questioned about the Dawa party. He told his interrogators what he had heard, but would not reveal who had told him. For that he was sentenced to seven years in prison.

In their submission to the UN, the opposition leaders noted the 'extra-judicial' methods of the Iraq government as well as the excesses of the courts. 'Methods of the physical liquidation of opponents include poisoning, in which a thalium compound is often used, assassination, death by car accidents and disappearances.' They detailed the case of General Omar Hazaa, a supporter of the regime who lived in Tikrit, the home of the ruling clique. His offence was that he supported not Saddam Hussein, but the man the President ousted, Hassan al Bakr. Reports of the general's derisive comments about him reached Saddam Hussein. The general was arrested and died under torture; his extensive property was seized and his house bulldozed.

The lack of any real opposition once the re-structuring of the regime took place at the Ninth Party Congress in 1982 enabled the Baghdad government to breathe more easily; the Shia of the south had shown no more enthusiasm for the Iranian invaders once they crossed the border than the Arabs of Khuzestan had for the Iraqis. Apart from Dawa, which for all its repeated acts of violence was a tiny group incapable of fomenting a real rebellion, the Shia proved themselves loyal to the regime – not so much, perhaps, through any affection for Saddam Hussein, the Ba'ath party or the repressive Iraqi system, as because they liked what they saw of Iran even less.

Reports of the economic hardships in Iran, true or false, had their impact in Iraq, where the economic and social situation was quite reasonable for the mass of the people. The petrodollars were still trickling down through the structure of the state, the aid given so fully in the first years by the countries of the Arab Gulf was applied not only for the purchase of arms, but also to maintain the living conditions of the people; and from being a depressed group of near second-class citizens, the Shia suddenly found themselves in the position of being wanted and wooed.

Saddam Hussein, a natural prince in the Machiavellian sense, understood that the violence and brutality of his regime had to be matched by inducements to the people to continue their support, so the *waqf*, the religious endowments, suddenly found themselves awash with money. Najjaf, with its golden-domed mosque and the silver tomb of the Imam Ali, the most sacred place of pilgrimage for the Shia, was suddenly awarded £12 million for renovations and improvements; a similar sum was given to Kerbala, the site of the shrines of the Imams Abbas and Hussein.

The main building developments too were in the south – including the provision of entirely new settlements west of Basra, gaunt grey blocks of apartments which stood empty for many months; they were eventually filled with some of the 100,000 Kurds deported from the north as Iraq tackled its internal revolt. Even when the multi-million dollar building programme in Baghdad had finally to be abandoned, work still went on in the towns of the south, and the cancellation of the Non-Aligned Conference – Saddam Hussein was forced to admit defeat on that after a massive car-bomb exploded outside the planning ministry in Baghdad – did not end all the work in hand. Nor was there any stinting of expenditure on the social services; for all the ubiquitous secret police and the network of party cells, watchers and informers, Iraq was also a welfare state, where education was compulsory and medical care freely available to everyone.

The Shia of Iraq were as devout as their cousins in Iran, but showed that they preferred to separate religion and politics, to look to the state for the physical needs of society, and to the mosque for things spiritual. The reports from inside Iran, even when exaggerated and over-emphasised by the Iraqi media, still gave a picture of life under Ayatollah Khomeini which was less than appealing, and the nightly television pictures showed events in Iran which spoke for themselves. Life under the Ayatollah seemed precarious and difficult, while the Iraqis knew where they were: they knew that if they joined Dawa, criticised the regime too openly, or acted against the state, they would almost certainly be found out and punished.

A new hazard was added at the height of the anti-Iran propaganda campaign when it was laid down that to be of Iranian origin made an individual suspect – and the definition of Iranian used by the authorities when they wanted to get rid of anyone was wide indeed. Deportation was formally added to the penalties available to the state to maintain its authority, and in a fashion particularly Iraqi, there was even encouragement for Iraqi husbands to divorce 'Iranian' wives. Under an RCC decree any Iraqi national married to a woman of Iranian origin 'is eligible to ID4,000 if he is a member of the armed forces or ID2,500 for civilians if he divorces his wife or if she is deported'. The RCC issued another decree saying that any 'Iranian' family found to be disloyal to the Iraqi revolution would be liable to deportation even if the family held the certificate of Iraqi nationality.

Yet for all these restrictions and penalties the average Shia was untouched by the hand of the state: the ordinary people knew that in addition to the restrictions of the regime, if they went about their business, did their civic duty and steered clear of politics, they could live rather better than their fathers had done, and could see their children educated and kept in good health. For all the increasing use of posters showing Saddam Hussein at prayer, Saddam Hussein reading the Koran, or Saddam Hussein listening to the Shia clergy, it was the material benefits of the Iraqi system which kept the Shia loyal, not any sudden belief that Saddam had become a devout Muslim and a descendant of Ali, one of the wilder pieces of propaganda tried by the notoriously inept Iraqi ministry of information.

One small factor which may have contributed to Ayatollah Khomeini's lack of success in influencing the Iraqi Shia to join the revolution may also have been his own conduct while in exile in the country, which alienated the Iraqi *ulema* of Najjaf and thus inclined them against advising their followers to support the Iranian movement. Rather like the claim of Saudi Arabian rulers to have a special role as 'the keepers of the holy places of Islam' – Mecca and Medina – so the Iraqi *ulema* had a special place because it was in their country that the two holiest shrines of the Shia faith could be found, at Kerbala and Najjaf. One Shia divine went so far as to write that a pilgrimage to Najjaf was worth a thousand to Mecca. So the Iraqi *ulema* considered themselves the senior members of the Shia religious hierarchy, and were none too pleased when Khomeini arbitrarily assumed the mantle of the Imam, claiming to be the leader of all Shia everywhere, and very much accepted at his own valuation by most Shia, something which diminished the standing of the Iraqi religious leaders.

Khomeini was welcomed when he began his exile there in 1965, but was not regarded by his Iraqi peers in Najjaf as an ayatollah of pre-eminence nor one of the greatest thinkers. When he arrived in Najjaf he was regarded more as a politician than a divine by the *ulema* of Iraq, who had in the main decided that the mosque and the state should go their separate ways, and with the exception of the minority who founded Dawa, the *ulema* were content to allow the secular state to rule so long as they were allowed to maintain their religious life. Khomeini they saw as a trouble-maker, the sort of man whose activities might induce the authorities to clamp down on them as well, an ayatollah, they believed, of the second rank, a man not worthy of support or emulation. Once in Najjaf, Khomeini did nothing to win the friendship of the Iraqi *ulema*. On the contrary, he very soon set up what amounted to an opposition headquarters in the city, with messengers constantly coming and going, Iranian exiles surrounding him and agents of Savak and the Iraqi secret police always on the watch. Khomeini's arrival made life more difficult for the Iraqi Shia in Najjaf, and because of their close links with their brethren in Kerbala, there too Khomeini was unpopular. The Iraqi *ulema*, except for the tiny minority supporting Dawa, never accepted Khomeini.

Not that Khomeini had ever been a particularly charismatic figure in Iran in the earlier years. He was openly 'political', he was moody among his close associates and students, he was notoriously mean in a society which needed and expected its leaders 'to share the wealth', and his sermons were a strange mixture of mysticism, politics and orthodoxy couched in extravagant language which often sent even his most devoted supporters away puzzled to find his message. Then, after his first brushes with Savak and the Shah, Khomeini decided on the well-worn device of finding an international conspiracy on which to focus his anger, this time an unholy alliance of 'foreigners and Jews' who were seeking to bring about the destruction of Islam. This form of attack may have gained some adherents among the simpler people of Qom who heard the Ayatollah's sermons, but did nothing for Khomeini's standing in the Shia hierarchy, where his reputation was questionable among the most orthodox for his earlier practice of writing poetry, and among the liberal and modern for his fundamentalist approach and uncompromising sermons.

Khomeini took all this baggage with him when he was exiled, first to Turkey and then to Najjaf, where he set up what amounted to the headquarters of an exile movement dedicated to the overthrow of the Shah, something which suited the Iraqi government very well in the years before 1975, when the Shah was the enemy for his support of the Kurds, but which obviously could not be maintained once the Iraqis had concluded their peace agreement with the Shah: there was no way that an opponent of Khomeini's calibre and dedication could be allowed to continue his activities if the agreement between the two countries was to persist. Yet it was in the years of exile in Iraq that Khomeini brought about the revolution in Iran; if he had been allowed to remain in his own country he might well have been replaced by more moderate and more learned leaders, by men who might have been content to reform the system rather than supplant it, to allow the Shah a continuation of power so long as due regard was paid to Islam and to the rights of the poor people.

Once in exile, however, Khomeini was alone, the only one who could organise opposition, whose words did not have to be censored by himself or anyone else. No one but Khomeini would dare to call the Shah 'the Jewish agent, the snake whose head must be smashed with a stone'. No one else had unfettered access to the people of Iran, for Savak itself estimated that something like 100,000 tapes of Khomeini's speeches and sermons were distributed each year, to be played in the back rooms of mosques or in the homes of the budding revolutionaries. Privately distri-buted at first, the Khomeini tapes were later released through the reputable retail companies in Iran, with no mention of his name, but merely the designation *'sokhanrani mazhabi' – religious ser-mon* – on the cover. The faithful knew what this meant, and soon Khomeini's words were out-selling the latest albums of the most popular Persian singers.

In the early 1970s Khomeini made regular demands for a popular uprising to overthrow the Shah, but his calls were ignored, and his denunciation of such events as the extravaganza in Persepolis to celebrate the 2,500th anniversary of the monarchy in Iran had little effect. Certainly his influence was growing in Iran as the most radical of all the Shia leaders – and the publication of his book, *Islamic Government*, caused a stir among the leading *ulema* in Iran – but it was the agreement between the Shah and Saddam Hussein in 1975 which began the path to leadership of his country for Khomeini. He managed to hold on in Najjaf for another three years, but in 1977 he issued an edict 'deposing' the Shah, and the following year called for the overthrow of the faltering Iranian ruler as more riots erupted all across Iran.

At the request of the Shah, the Iraqis agreed to rid themselves of this troublesome cleric. He was ordered out, and there was a real fear in Iran that he would cross back into the country to head an armed insurrection, but Khomeini's intelligence was good – he knew that the conditions were not right at that time, and instead went into exile in France. There, in Neauphle Chateau, Khomeini was suddenly available to the media, not only to the Persian and Arabic papers and radio stations which had always been interested in him, but also to the West; and it was a Western broadcasting organisation which played a major part in his eventual return, though not by any design. At that time, the regular twice-daily broadcasts by the overseas service of the BBC in Farsi had achieved an enviable reputation for speed, accuracy and balance which was contrasted with the regular diet of propaganda which the Iranian people were fed by the organs of the state, or the equally biased information from the clandestine sources controlled by the various revolutionary factions, the Tudeh, the People's Mujahedin and other groups as well as the mullahs.

With the speed of events increasing in Iran, Khomeini and those around him were quick to see the advantages offered by the BBC and other foreign broadcasting organisations. A short statement from the Khomeini headquarters in response to an event in Iran would be heard by the faithful within hours, instead of the laborious business of making and distributing tapes which at best meant a delay of days before Khomeini's thoughts could be transmitted. The BBC in particular became a favoured medium for Khomeini, who was always ready to make a statement or give a comment or respond to something which had happened. The British Ambassador in Tehran, Sir Anthony Parsons, who like his American counterpart William Sullivan was trying to prop up the Shah, spent a great deal of time and effort in trying to persuade the BBC to stop paying such attention to Khomeini.

In the face of pressure from the ambassador, and from the Foreign Office, which finances the Overseas Service, the BBC took the most extraordinary precautions to see that the Persian language broadcasts were fair, balanced and accurate; but to their great credit they did not give in to the pressure, and the reports of Khomeini's sayings and activities were given almost as much prominence as accounts of what was going on in Iran itself.

# 5

## Exporting the
## Islamic revolution

For the ambassador, it was one of the more pleasant of the many functions he had to attend. A good dinner, as always at the Dorchester, pleasant company and an attentive audience as he made a speech dwelling on Israel's achievements and glossing over the country's difficulties. Shlomo Argov, a supporter of the Israeli Labour Alignment who, as his country's representative in London, had to explain the often tough policies of the Likud, was an able and experienced envoy, a professional who did not allow his own feelings to influence his work. He was one of the more successful of the Israeli ambassadors to London, recognised as a key post by the foreign ministry in Jerusalem.

As he put on his overcoat over his dinner jacket, Argov was relaxed and smiling, taking his leave of the other guests as his Israeli bodyguard and the policeman assigned to him by Scotland Yard hovered nearby. The three were grouped close together as they moved quickly from the entrance of the hotel to the ambassador's armoured car waiting fifteen yards away. As they did so, a lurking figure stepped forward, a single shot cracked out, and the ambassador fell. That shot, like the assassination at Sarajevo, changed the course of history, for it provided Israel with the excuse it was seeking to move into Lebanon to destroy the PLO once and for all; and it was Iraq which provided Israel with the pretext it needed.

Israeli officials immediately blamed the PLO for the attempt on Argov's life, which left him with permanent brain damage, but it was in fact one of the most extreme and bitter opponents of the PLO which had carried out the attempted assassination. Each member of the three-man squad which made the attack on the ambassador was a member of the Abu Nidal group, the most efficient and feared of all the Middle Eastern terrorist organisations, and one which had the PLO as high on its list of targets as the Israelis. In addition, the leader of the group was also an officer in the Mukhabarat, the Iraqi intelligence organisation, sent to London to activate the two sleepers who had been put in place in 1980.

One of the three operatives in the hit-squad was Marwan al-Banna, the 21-year-old nephew of Sabri al-Banna – the real name of Abu Nidal, the dissident Fatah officer who fell out with Yasser Arafat, was condemned to death *in absentia* by a court martial, and set himself up as a freelance terrorist willing to work for anyone prepared to finance operations against Israel, the official PLO, or Europeans or Americans cooperating with Israel or working for a settlement of the Middle East crisis. Abu Nidal took the view that anything except the total victory of the Palestinians was a betrayal, so he was ready to use his men to frustrate anything which looked as if it could lead to a compromise solution.

With Marwan al-Banna were Hussein Said, the actual hit-man who pulled the trigger when the attempt on Argov was made, and Nawaf Rosan, another member of the Abu Nidal group who was also an officer in Iraqi Intelligence. Unlike the other two, Rosan was not a Palestinian, but came from the East Bank of the Jordan, and had served in the Jordanian air force. He had also been to the Soviet Union on a weapons course, part of his training as an officer in the Mukhabarat. Rosan arrived in London in October 1981, almost a year after the other two, and eight months before they were to act. According to intelligence sources in London, Iraq put the team into London, and other operatives into other capitals, at the beginning of the Gulf war to be used either against the usual Israeli or Palestinian targets, the regular mission of Abu Nidal men, or against Iranians if that should be useful, or against any others chosen in Baghdad.

It was when the war began to go badly for the Iraqis that they conceived the idea of providing the incident which would enable Israel to move against the PLO in Lebanon. As usual, once the political decision was taken, instant results were expected, which was why the London hit-team was activated so quickly and with so little preparation. When police searched the room occupied by al-Banna, the armourer of the group, at the YMCA in

Wimbledon, they found two machine pistols, fragmentation grenades and ammunition, though at Said's flat in Brixton his fellow conspirators were able to remove such incriminating evidence as money, a passport and another pistol – all of which were found in a briefcase which Rosan was holding when he and al-Banna were stopped by police.

The actual assassination attempt was a professional job showing evidence of good training: Hussein Said lurked about on the pavement for a little while before Argov came out, but was not so conspicuous that any of the many people about felt it necessary to challenge him. Then, when the ambassador emerged with his two bodyguards, Said stepped forward and fired the single shot which penetrated the ambassador's brain. The Israeli bodyguard dropped down beside his charge to protect him against further attack and then to give what help he could, while Detective-Constable Colin Simpson of the Diplomatic Protection Group ran after Said, eventually firing a shot which wounded him and brought him down. At the same time, an alert employee at the nearby Hilton hotel had noted the number of a car used by al-Banna to make his getaway and to pick up Rosan. The two were stopped in Brixton after they had been to Said's flat.

The murder attempt was made late on the evening of 3 June 1982. The next day the Israeli cabinet met and ordered the bombing of targets in Lebanon; the PLO responded with a barrage of shells and rockets on Upper Galilee, the first time in ten months that they had broken the truce with Israel in any but a token way. The Israeli cabinet met again and sanctioned the invasion of Lebanon, with most of the Israeli ministers believing that the object was to advance no further than forty kilometres and so to clear southern Lebanon of Palestinian gunners capable of launching attacks on settlements inside Israel. Only Prime Minister Menachem Begin and Ariel Sharon, the minister of defence, knew at that time that the objective was to go as far as Beirut itself.

In Baghdad, the extent of the Israeli action came as a bonus. It had always been realised that Israel would invade Lebanon, but the Iraqis shared the views of many others that any new operation would be a virtual repeat of the 1978 invasion, with the Israelis seeking to surround and destroy as many Palestinians as possible in the south of the country. The drive for Beirut gave the

Iraqis a far more realistic excuse for the move they wanted to make – to bring the Gulf war to an end. On 10 June, only four days after the invasion and when the Israeli encirclement of Beirut was only just beginning, Iraq offered a unilateral ceasefire in the Gulf war and said it was ready to withdraw all its forces from Iranian soil within two weeks. The reason for the offer, the RCC in Baghdad said, lay in events in Lebanon. 'The RCC expresses its belief in the urgent necessity of directing all efforts towards confronting the ferocious Zionist aggression against the Arab world, the Palestinian people, and Lebanon.'

In Tehran, the mullahs saw the move as an attempt by Saddam Hussein to extricate himself from an increasingly difficult situation. The invasion of Lebanon, they said, was part of a plot to rescue Saddam and his 'Ba'athist-Zionist government' and to prop up his tottering dictatorship. Both the offer of a unilateral ceasefire and the withdrawal of troops were ignored.

The plan to break the PLO had been hatched by Sharon and General Rafael Eitan, the chief of staff, two men on the far right of Israeli politics who by chance found themselves in pivotal positions at the same time. Begin was the third in the triumvirate who manipulated the Israeli government and pushed through their grand design, though even Begin might not have realised just how far he was committing his forces as he endorsed the Sharon–Eitan plan. It was Begin, the best politician of the three, who chose 'Operation Peace for Galilee' as the code-name for the invasion of Lebanon, instead of the more military and uninformative 'Operation Pinetrees'. Begin's implied description of the aim of the operation was intended to still the fears of other cabinet members who might have baulked at going into Lebanon at all if they had realised that the ultimate objectives of Sharon and Eitan were not only to eradicate the PLO in the south of the country, but also to destroy its infrastructure in Beirut and replace the weak Lebanese administration with a tough government which would conclude an alliance with Israel and would bar the PLO from any activity in Lebanon. It was an ambitious, grandiose scheme, and it came within a whisker of success: just as it began with the bullet of a would-be assassin, it ended with the murder of a president.

Everything that happened resulted from the decision made in Baghdad to give Israel the excuse it wanted. It was a cynical but carefully calculated plan with clear objectives which must have seemed to the Iraqi intelligence men who dreamt it up to be easily attainable: they wanted Syria to be so involved in Lebanon that the Syrian forces could present no threat to Iraq, and they wanted the PLO cut down to size because of Yasser Arafat's early support for Ayatollah Khomeini and the continuing help which PLO men were giving to the Pasdaran. It was the sort of symmetrical operation which would be a delight to any intelligence officer – a few shots in a London street and a pressing danger to the country would be removed.

The Iraqis had a year to dream up their plot, for it was as early as the beginning of 1981 that Israeli intentions became clear. It was during the election campaign that Begin visited the northern Israeli border town of Kiryat Shmona and promised the inhabitants there that soon no more rockets would fall on their town. Israelis and Arabs alike took the Prime Minister seriously: he was not a man to speak lightly or make promises he did not intend to keep, so it was accepted on all sides that Begin intended to send the Israeli army into Lebanon to clear the PLO gunners out of the south of that country, the area from which they regularly shelled the settlements of Upper Galilee. The Palestinians themselves accepted the likelihood that they would soon be attacked, and made their plans accordingly – plans based on their experience of the earlier invasion, in 1978, when they were able to melt away as the Israeli army swept through southern Lebanon in a disorganised and ineffectual way, a hasty response to Palestinian incursions.

Within a month of Begin's re-election Kiryat Shmona again came under fire, and it seemed that the Prime Minister would have to make good on his promise. But this time the Americans intervened. Philip Habib, America's roving ambassador, a trouble-shooter whose family originated in southern Lebanon, arranged a ceasefire between the PLO and the Israelis, the first time Israel had ever dealt with what it always called a terrorist organisation. And to everyone's surprise, the ceasefire held. Arafat and his lieutenants knew very well what Sharon intended to do, and realised they were not prepared for the sort of campaign that would be launched against them. Equally, the Syrians were well aware of what was going on, and were doing all they could to restrain the Palestinian extremists over whom they had most influence. The result was absolute calm along the border at just the time the Israelis would have liked salvoes of Katyushas to give them the excuse they needed to move.

As early as December 1981 the Israeli cabinet had been given details of what was called a contingency plan to move into Lebanon as far as the Beirut–Damascus highway to link up with the Phalangist forces of Bashir Gemayel, the right-wing Christian leader whose views were very close to those of Sharon and Eitan. Israeli ministers were so alarmed at the extent of the operation envisaged that it was plain they would not countenance it, so the idea was in theory shelved. But Sharon was determined to go ahead when he could, as he made clear in meetings with Samuel Lewis, the American ambassador in Tel Aviv, and finally in Washington, where on 20 May 1982, he spelt out his plan in considerable detail to General Alexander Haig, the secretary of state, though he did not specify the extent of his territorial aims. Haig, who antagonised and puzzled Arab leaders a year earlier when he insisted to them that the Soviet Union was the main threat to the Middle East, not Israel, was sympathetic to Sharon's ideas. A dedicated anti-communist, Haig took a simplistic view of the PLO, which he saw as a monolithic structure controlled from Moscow which he would be very willing to see destroyed.

Although there is no published record of what was said at the meeting between Haig and Sharon, Israeli officials who read their ambassador's account of the conversation had no doubt that Haig had given the green light for Israel's invasion of Lebanon. Even so, there was still hesitation in Israel. The Habib-negotiated ceasefire was holding, though there was some dispute on its actual terms: the Israelis said that any terrorist action anywhere in the world by the PLO against an Israeli target would be a breach, while the Palestinians believed that the truce concerned only cross-border incidents. The Americans, directly involved for the first time through the success of the Habib mission, warned against action whenever an incident occurred, and were able to prevent the Israelis moving when an Israeli diplomat was killed in Paris in April. Instead, Israel sent its air force to bomb Palestinian refugee camps in southern Lebanon, and it was only then that the PLO responded with a few token salvoes of rockets which hit no targets, probably by design.

Then came the assassination attempt on Shlomo Argov, and

the Israeli cabinet ministers who had counselled caution in the past were now forced to sanction retaliatory action. At first, it was the air force again, sent to bomb targets in Beirut as well as in the south, something that the PLO could not allow without reacting; so the PLO gunners in the south were ordered to shell the Israeli settlements in Upper Galilee, just the sort of thing that the Israeli Prime Minister needed to make him sanction Sharon's grand design.

Thus it was that at 11 a.m. on Sunday, 6 June Israeli armour rolled north across the border in an invasion which was to cause thousands of deaths, to divide Israel, to break Syria's military power, to come close to destroying the PLO, to enable Iran to export its revolution, and to involve America militarily in the Middle East for the first time since 1958.

From the Iraqi point of view, the most important days came at the beginning of the war, when the American aircraft flown by the Israelis annihilated the Soviet planes used by the Syrian air force. The Israeli targets that day were the Sam Six missile sites close to the town of Chtaura on the main road between Beirut and Damascus, installed the previous year after the Israelis had shot down two troop-carrying helicopters in a move designed to help their Christian allies who were trying to extend their influence from Beirut to the Greek Catholic town of Zahle in the Bekaa Valley. By putting the missiles into Lebanon, with their 250-kilometre range, the Syrians were proclaiming that the country was their fiefdom, and not under Israeli control.

To the Israelis, who espoused the odd strategic notion that their own security demanded the right of unchallenged flight over Lebanon, the missiles were a defiance and a practical worry; they swore to take them out, and frequently sent radio-controlled drones over to test reactions. Foolishly, the Syrian ground defence teams could not resist opening up on these pilotless aircraft, allowing the Israelis to calibrate radio frequencies in the seconds it took a missile to strike. So on the fourth day of the Lebanon war, the Israelis carried out their promise to destroy the Syrian missiles.

The Israelis used F16s for the strike, with F15s flying top cover and a Hawkeye command and control plane directing the battle from above them all. The Syrian Mig 21s and 23s attacked as soon as the Israelis appeared, but were no match for them, and though the Sam Sixes were launched, not a single one of them hit their target. The Israelis' preliminary work in finding out radar frequencies meant that they had been able to install the appropriate electronic counter-measures, and all the missiles exploded harmlessly. On the first day of this great air battle, the Syrians lost 22 planes, and 17 of the 19 missile batteries in position were knocked out. On the second day the remaining two batteries were destroyed and another 25 Syrian planes shot down, as well as two helicopters. The Syrian air force was destroyed, which meant that for years to come the Syrian army, unable to move without air cover, could present no threat to the Iraqis or anyone else. The Iraqis were able to move badly needed combat troops away from the Syrian border to the Iranian front, and to replace them with garrison troops or units of the People's Army.

Another advantage for Iraq was that Syria, Iran's one Arab ally and the closest to it in geographical terms, could no longer send the supplies it needed; the Syrians were desperately building up their own air force for years to come, and could spare little for their ally. Even the Israeli involvement in Lebanon worked to the advantage of Iraq. At home, the Israelis were bitterly divided by events in Lebanon, where their army became bogged down just like all previous invaders who had been sucked into that quagmire. Israelis had no stomach for further adventures, and would not have taken kindly to any open alignment with Iran, although the planners were clear that they had to do what they could to ensure the continuation of a war which was bleeding two of their potential enemies to death. The result was that Israeli aid to Iran had to be given covertly, resulting in the whole Iran–Contra scam which did so much to damage the Reagan administration.

The Israeli invasion of Lebanon, with its savage siege of Beirut, ruthless air strikes against civilian areas and shelling of towns and villages, finally came to an end on 21 August when men of the Second Foreign Parachute Regiment of the French Foreign Legion landed at Beirut port to take over from the Palestine Liberation Army men who had been stationed there. They formed the advance guard of the Multi-National Force which was to be composed of American, Italian and British troops as well as the French.

Many in America opposed the dispatch of the Marines to Beirut, and there was a national sigh of relief when after ten days – instead of the thirty days originally planned – the Marines sailed away again after supervising the evacuation of the Palestinians, a large banner on the last boat carrying the proud slogan: 'Mission Accomplished'. The next few horrific days proved how idle that boast was. The newly elected President of Lebanon, Bashir Gemayel, was killed by a carefully rigged, remote-controlled bomb as he addressed a party meeting – a dissident member of his own Phalangist party detonated the device, but Syrian hands arranged it all. The immediate result was that Israeli troops moved into West Beirut in direct contravention of the agreement made when the PLO pulled out, and by Thursday 16 September, Israel was in control of the whole of West Beirut. On that day the first units of Elie Hobeika's special force of Christian Phalangist fighters moved into the Palestine refugee camps of Sabra and Chatila to massacre the families of the fighters who had been forced out, families whose safety Philip Habib had guaranteed to Yasser Arafat. With less fanfare and more determination, the Americans returned to Beirut.

Also moving into Beirut now, but with no publicity at all, were some of the Iranians who had arrived in Lebanon during the war. Dispatched by Ayatollah Khomeini to help the Palestinians, the 500 picked Revolutionary Guards established their headquarters at Zabdani in Syria, and from there moved into Baalbek in Lebanon. At first, according to local people, they spent more time praying than doing anything else, but gradually, as time went on, they turned Baalbek into a facsimile of a modern Iranian town, run by *komitehs*, policed by black-bearded Revolutionary Guards, and inspired and guided by the mullahs. It was a strange fate for a town which boasted the beautiful Roman Temple of Bacchus, and which had once been the site of so many performances by some of the world's great artistes. Now, it was the selection centre and training ground for Iran's surrogates in Lebanon, men who were to export the Islamic revolution for the first time, and to humble the Great Satan just as their colleagues in Tehran had rooted out the Nest of Spies – the US embassy.

At the start of the Lebanese civil war in 1975, the Shia were the largest but also the most downtrodden community in that factionalised country, though they had made some progress towards achieving a more effective political role under their spiritual leader, Imam Musa Sadr, a charismatic mullah born in the

Iranian holy city of Qom in 1928. His ancestors, like those of many of the Shia clergymen of modern Iraq and Iran, fled Lebanon during the Sunni Ottoman repression of the eighteenth century. Because of these intimate religious and family links, the Lebanese Shia often regarded Iran rather than the Lebanese state as their natural protector. Mousa Sadr was among a number of Shia clergy dispatched to Africa and the Middle East by the religious hierarchy in the late 1950s and 1960s – ironically, with the blessing of the Shah – to counter the ideological rise of 'atheistic' Nasserism which was spreading through the region from Egypt. Mousa Sadr encountered a deeply conservative Shia clergy and an impoverished Shia population which was subject to the will of the more powerful Sunni establishment.

By the mid-1970s he had helped to revitalise the community and persuaded parliament to establish the Higher Shia Council, of which he was elected President in 1969, and under his auspices the Amal militia, which was to become the armed wing of the Shia community, was secretly founded. Mousa Sadr, a former pupil of Khomeini to whom he was related by marriage, was the archetype of the clergyman–politician at a time when Khomeini was virtually unknown outside Iran: he arranged for funds from Iran to be channelled to Lebanon to finance schools, hospitals and community centres in Shia areas. Despite the links which then existed between the Shia clergy and the Shah, Mousa Sadr expressed his opposition to the Iranian monarch and indeed smoothed the way for anti-Shah groups to train in Lebanon at the camps of Yasser Arafat's Fatah group.

Among those in Lebanon in the early 1970s were Mustafa Chamran, a future Iranian defence minister killed early in the Gulf war, Jalaleddin Farsi, who was to try unsuccessfully to stand for president against Bani-Sadr, and Hojatoleslam Mohammad Montazeri, the son of Ayatollah Montazeri, later to be named Khomeini's successor; Hojatoleslam Montazeri, who was to die in the 1981 bombing of the Islamic Republican Party headquarters in Tehran, was an eccentric pan-Islamic internationalist who refused to acknowledge frontiers between Muslim states. These and other Iranian militants served their revolutionary apprenticeship in Lebanon, though intimate links existed between the Lebanese Shia and the Iranian opposition long before the Islamic revolution, and were developed further once Khomeini came to power.

Mousa Sadr went missing on a visit to Libya in 1978 and, although it has never been proved, is assumed to have been murdered on the orders of his erstwhile supporter, Colonel Muammar Gaddafi. His disappearance left a vacuum in the Shia hierarchy which allowed the post-revolutionary Iranian leadership to take an increasingly direct role in the affairs of Lebanon in the 1980s. During the Israeli invasion, for instance, more Revolutionary Guards were sent from Iran to fight alongside the Palestinian and Lebanese forces, and though the Amal men also fought, that organisation was now a movement under the secular leadership of the militia commander, Nabih Berri, who was rightly seen by the Shia fundamentalists as loyal to the concept of the Lebanese state rather than to any idea of establishing an Islamic republic on Lebanese territory.

The resulting friction between the secularists and the Iranian-backed fundamentalists led to the emergence of Hizbollah, the Party of God, which shared its name with the unstructured organisation of street-fighters who had opposed the leftists and liberals in the streets of Tehran in 1980–1. The *hizbollahi* were the infantry of Iran's second front: financed and controlled by the Iranian embassy, they sponsored and carried out the kidnappings of Westerners and terrorist attacks on Western targets. Their aim was to take over the state and to spread the Islamic revolution beyond the frontiers of Iran, but America, it seemed, was in their way, and would have to be dealt with first.

To everyone else, the Americans in Beirut seemed to be men without a mission. Their role was merely to be there, now and then exchanging fire with the Amal guerrillas whose territory swept close up to the airport headquarters of the Marines, or to get into arguments with the Israelis who held the area to the south. A year later, the Americans were still there, the men who came in as protectors and guarantors now the besieged, surrounded by hostile forces as the country they were supposed to be helping crumbled around them. A bemused American public learnt that a small hill resort town called Souk al Gharb had suddenly become the front line of freedom, a bastion whose fall would bring down the Western world.

Syria had decided to act, to show that it was Damascus, not Washington, which could dictate the course of events in Lebanon – Greater Syria, as it saw it. Above all, Syria had to prevent the conclusion of the new peace accord which America was seeking to arrange, a second Camp David, a peace treaty which would give Israel huge power in Lebanon and unfettered control over the south of that country, an area the Syrian leader considered to be vital to Syria's interests. Assad set himself the task of forcing Lebanon to abrogate the agreement with Israel signed at Khalde on 17 May 1983, and if possible to bring down the government of President Amin Gemayel.

The 17 May accord accepted by Lebanon was the result of tremendous pressure from America, but one consequence of the negotiations between Lebanon and Israel gave Assad the opportunity he wanted: the Israelis pulled out of the Chouf, the mountainous region inhabited by the Druse which had been colonised by the Phalangists during the Israeli occupation. With Syrian backing, the Druse swiftly expelled the Christian inter-lopers, then arranged a pact with Amal, Nabih Berri's Shia guer-rillas who controlled the southern suburbs of Beirut next to the American military positions. With other Amal groups and some *hizbollahi* active in the south of the country, and the Syrians holding the northern and eastern sections, the Lebanese govern-ment was left with very little – except American support.

It was to prop up that tottering regime that the American fleet off Beirut eventually fired its salvoes at the Druse positions in the mountains, American helicopter gunships flew missions in support of the Lebanese army trying to prevent the Druse and their allies totally encircling Beirut and moving into Yarze and Baabda, the army headquarters and presidential palace, and American gunners at the airport gave their artillery support. So it was that Souk al Gharb suddenly became so important; Colonel Fintel, the American military adviser who was in fact running the Lebanese army's defence of the place, went a lot further than the Pentagon, the White House or Congress might have liked and would have committed US troops if he had had his way. In the end he and the men of General Michel Aoun's First Brigade managed to hold up the attackers, but they could not defend the Americans as well.

In April 1983 a suicide bomber rammed his vehicle into the American embassy on the sea front in Beirut. Among the sixty-three killed were the CIA station chief and his deputy, and the Agency's chief Middle East analyst, Robert Ames, who was on a visit to discuss the rising danger posed by Islamic fundamentalism. Ames was a regular adviser to George Shultz, the secretary of state, and his loss may well have contributed to the eventual American decision to pull out, and to the administration's shaky handling of the region for years to come.

Then in October 1983 another car-bomber struck at the ill-defended American Marine headquarters at the airport; 241 men were killed. On the same day a second bomber hit the French contingent of the Multi-National Force, killing fifty-six soldiers. Investigations into the explosion turned up Syrian and Palestinian connections, but the guiding hand behind this worst-ever terrorist attack against an American target was Iran and its Hizbollah allies. According to some reports the Revolutionary Guards minister, Mohsen Rafiqdoost, gave the order for the operation and Ali Akbar Mohtashemi, at that time the Iranian ambassador to Damascus, provided the funds. For those who organised the bombing, the MNF barracks were legitimate military targets. For them, the suicide bombers had died in action against Iran's greatest enemy, the United States, and against France, a key provider of arms to Iraq. By their presence in Lebanon, these two outside powers were seen as engaged in halting the spread of the Islamic revolution.

It was a shattering blow for the Americans, to see so many of their élite force wiped out by a lone fanatic, though the domestic impact of the Lebanese disaster on the Reagan administration was nullified two days later by the news that US troops had invaded the tiny Marxist-run island of Grenada in the Caribbean. In Lebanon itself, a mounting toll of American and other Western casualties and the realisation that nothing was being achieved contributed to the pressure on governments to take their troops out of Beirut, and early in 1984 the withdrawal of the MNF began.

The Americans left on 1 April, and in a day of rich symbolism conducted a classic fighting retreat – with no one to fight against. The Marines gradually contracted their perimeter from the airport to their supply beach, pulling out company by company until only one unit was left, watched by dozens of journalists and hundreds of local children, with bearded Amal militiamen cruising up and down in jeeps as they waited for the last American to go. As that man, a captain, stepped on to the amphibious vehicle taking him and his men out to the mother ship, he shook hands briefly with the Amal commander whose men ran up the green flag of Islam in place of the Stars and Stripes before the Americans were a dozen yards off-shore.

It was the handshake of the victor and the vanquished, but the real winner was in Damascus. With ruthlessness, cunning and lack of scruple, it was President Assad who had engineered the downfall of the Americans. Within weeks President Gemayel was in the Syrian capital to acknowledge the error of his ways to Assad, his effective overlord, and to promise that the hated accord with Israel would not be ratified.

The American withdrawal from Lebanon seemed to the planners in Washington to be something like straightening the line in a military sense. America was committed to Israel, and so had a firm base and what it saw as a dependable ally in the eastern Mediterranean, but equally America had a conflict on its hands in the Gulf, where Saudi Arabia was an ally, though one much less committed and much less able than Israel, but where Iran was still a dedicated enemy. Now, the tidy men in Washington believed, they were shot of a messy situation in Lebanon, which could be left to its own devices, ignored while America dealt with its real problems elsewhere. But the Pasdaran who had moved into Baalbek had done their work well: the men who drove the bomb-laden cars into the targets in Beirut had been chosen by Iranian mullahs preaching in the mosques of the Bekaa and trained by Revolutionary Guards.

Soon, the Israelis in the south of Lebanon were to feel the effects of the new fanaticism inculcated by the Iranian missionaries: young girls riding donkeys towards Israeli checkpoints could prove as dangerous as any car-bomber. But the Americans were not to be spared either. In December 1983 bombings spread to Kuwait, the Gulf state which had in effect become the main port for Iraq, and one of President Saddam Hussein's most dedicated supporters. The French and American embassies were attacked, and the Emir narrowly missed assassination when a car-bomber attempted to crash into his motorcade. After hundreds of suspects were rounded up – all Shia – seventeen were eventually convicted of responsibility for the attacks, and were found to be members of Dawa. Two of them belonged to a Lebanese family prominent in the growing Iranian-backed Hizbollah movement, and the leader of one of these families, Imad Mughniyeh, was at the time the chief bodyguard of Sheikh Mohammed Hussein Fadlallah, a man often described as the spiritual guide of Hizbollah in Lebanon but, in true Shia style, actually its leader and chief organiser. Fadlallah had been an associate of Khomeini in Najjaf, where he studied before moving to Lebanon, and shared the Ayatollah's views. Hizbollah in Lebanon, under Sheikh Fadlallah, became an extension of the Iranian regime. And on 16 March 1984, Hizbollah began its campaign of kidnappings.

As he left his Beirut apartment to drive the short distance to the American embassy, William Buckley, the new CIA station chief, was quickly bundled into a car and driven away. He was the first of many captives who were to play such a part in relations between the West and Iran, and to come close to bringing down the American administration, but Buckley was also the one whose kidnapping had most effect in Washington. His captors, with good information from locally employed people working in the embassy, knew who Buckley was and the job he did, and exploited that knowledge in the most savage way. The Americans were soon given a video tape of Buckley under 'interrogation' – being tortured while answering questions being put by a man off-screen. The tape was widely shown at the Langley headquarters of the CIA and, not surprisingly, had a huge effect there. The Agency was ready to take any chances to get Buckley out, or to wreak vengeance for the way he had been treated.

Despite the rivalry between the National Security Council and the Agency, some thoughts of events in Beirut must have been in the minds of the CIA men who set up national security adviser Robert McFarlane's bizarre trip to Tehran to set up the Iran–Contra arms deal, and of McFarlane himself as he sought to outwit the mullahs. In itself, the Irangate affair was proof enough that both sides acknowledged the degree of Iranian involvement, though at that time the Americans did not realise that operations in Lebanon were the responsibility of specific radicals in the Iranian regime, particularly Mohtashemi; Rafiqdoost, the Revolutionary Guards minister; Hadi Ghaffari, the founder of the Iranian Hizbollah; and Hossein Sheikholeslamzadeh, the deputy foreign minister who had once guarded the gates of the occupied US embassy in Tehran. But Lebanon was an enterprise which had the support of the higher leadership, including Rafsanjani and Ayatollah Montazeri, who sponsored the Office for the Export of the Islamic Revolution.

In the West, the strange Iran–Contra affair attracted most attention for the light it shone on the workings of the American administration, where a lieutenant-colonel in the White House basement could make and carry through a policy of his own involving several agencies of the government. Certainly Colonel Oliver North was the organiser of the affair, but it was Israel which first floated the idea of exchanging arms for hostages, and North and his friends – and there were many – who added the extra dimension of channelling off the money so generated to the Nicaraguan Contras.

Yet the most remarkable aspect was the insight given for the first time into the workings of the Iranian government, for it was Hashemi Rafsanjani who brought the affair into the open. He did so not because he wanted to, but because his hand was forced by the militant opposition of those who believed that Rafsanjani and his faction were 'corrupting' the revolution, cheapening and debasing the pure Islamic spirit which they saw as its driving force. The journalistic scoop which broke the Iran–Contra affair has now passed into legend, with the Beirut weekly *Al Shiraa* generally being given credit for first publication – a bizarre story which would never have been believed if it had not quickly been confirmed by Rafsanjani. The editor of *Al Shiraa* claimed in an interview that he was tipped off by an Iranian friend with whom he had studied, but later information makes it likely that this was a *post-facto* explanation of what had happened, as a mention of the McFarlane mission to Tehran was given in a small Hizbollah magazine circulated in Baalbek, the east Lebanon stronghold of pro-Iranian elements, a week before *Al Shiraa* published.

Equally, the Syrians, who controlled that area, claimed that it was they who first gave the news, for their own purposes. In his biography of Assad, Patrick Seale says that a Syrian intelligence officer in Tehran, Iyad al Mahmud, learnt of the McFarlane trip to Tehran, and sent full details to Damascus. Then Mahmud was kidnapped by the group led by Mehdi Hashemi, a protégé of Montazeri with close links with Hizbollah in Lebanon. This only coincidentally touched on the arms-for-hostages deal, and was a ham-fisted effort to stop Syria moving against Hizbollah in Lebanon. Syria protested, and Mahmud was quickly released, but Assad thought he saw an opportunity to gain kudos with America, a nation he was seeking to ingratiate himself with at that time. Assad asked the Iranians to let him have one of the American hostages in Lebanon, so that he could claim the credit for obtaining a release. Instead, the Iranians chose to set free David Jacobsen, and handed him directly to the Americans in Beirut without any Syrian intervention. In pique at what had happened, and to get even both with the Iranians and to embarrass America – still vocal in its criticism of Syria's human rights record – Assad, Seale says, leaked the story to the Beirut paper.

According to our researches, the *Al Shiraa* story was a piece of straightforward journalistic enterprise, picking up an unnoticed item from the Baalbek sheet, and that in turn was published on the instructions of Mehdi Hashemi to embarrass Hashemi Rafsanjani. Rafsanjani had emerged as the most pragmatic of the Iranian leaders, a man willing to cooperate with the West if that seemed in the interests of his country, a man not bound by the dogma of a particular doctrine, and for all his undoubted commitment to the Islamic revolution and to the Ayatollah, no hide-bound Muslim looking to the Koran to settle twentieth-century problems.

Rafsanjani had another driving force besides his determination to see his country survive: as a hojatoleslam, 'a Vicar of God', he could not immediately aspire to the highest rank in the land or succeed Ayatollah Khomeini, nor even be one of a Board of Guardians or other form of regency which might follow the Ayatollah's total rule. So Rafsanjani saw himself as the king-maker, the practical twentieth-century man who would make and break others, see that his policies were the ones adopted, his solutions the ones chosen. In 1985 he had not achieved that position, though every politician in Iran knew of his driving ambition and recognised him as the man who had to be beaten if policies he opposed were to be pushed through. So Rafsanjani was taking a great risk when he agreed to deal with the Israelis and the Americans in setting up the exchange of hostages for arms: not only was he admitting that he had actual control over those who held the hostages, he was also laying himself open to obloquy at home if it all emerged. Others saw that, and tried to exploit the situation. During McFarlane's stay in Tehran, Mehdi Hashemi organised a violent demonstration near the hotel in which the Americans were incarcerated during their trip, undoubtedly given the go-ahead by Montazeri, then in near-open revolt against the authoritarian pronouncements of Khomeini.

With all the emphasis of the Irangate affair on the consequences in Washington, few analysts looked in any depth at the picture in Tehran. When they did, a paradox emerged. What became apparent was that the affair had brought into the open for the first time the evidence of the bitter power struggle which was beginning to emerge, not only over the succession to Khomeini, but also over the direction in which the revolution should go – continued fundamental devotion to Islam and efforts to export the Khomeini brand of Islamic rule, or a gradual shift towards a more pragmatic approach, perhaps a watering-down of the more extreme aspects of the revolution to return Iran to the mainstream of world affairs, with links with the West while retaining its non-aligned role.

At the same time, it became clear that the Americans were not talking to just one faction of the Iranian government, as they so steadily claimed; when it came to acquiring much-needed arms for the battle with Iraq, the Iranians at all levels of the government were united. While holding that what they were doing was designed to bolster moderate elements in Tehran, the Americans were in fact dealing with an administration working together; it was only afterwards that Rafsanjani exploited what had happened to protect and enhance his own position. Once ensconced in his suite at the top of the Hilton in the northern suburbs of Tehran – by this time renamed the Esteghlal, or Independence Hotel – Robert McFarlane found himself facing a series of messengers from the Iranian government, not the leaders of a particular faction he had expected to be meeting.

It was made clear quite early on that there was no question of Rafsanjani showing up to talk directly to the Americans, who did not seem aware that one of their main interlocutors, Hadi Najafabbadi, was actually an associate of the Prime Minister, Mir Hossein Mousavi, although he was regarded by the Americans as a Rafsanjani man. Nor did the American party appear to understand the significance of the demonstration outside the hotel organised by Mehdi Hashemi. It was a small crowd which Hashemi had managed to gather together, and in the quiet area around the hotel there were no local people to swell its ranks, but in Tehran at that time the fact that the demonstration took place showed that there had been a serious leak of what was going on, that there was deep opposition to any dealing with the Americans, and that important figures were prepared to make their opposition known – only the certainty of powerful support would persuade anyone to take to the streets. As it was, the incident was quickly contained by the hundreds of security men who had been drafted in to seal off the hotel, and although a number of people saw what had happened, none seemed to realise the significance of it.

What emerged from all the endless investigations and recriminations in Washington once it all came out was that the two sides had fundamentally different ideas. The Americans, for all their talk of opening up channels of communication with moderate elements in Iran, were seeking freedom for their hostages in Lebanon; the Iranian negotiators believed that they were buying arms, arranging delivery times and methods, and ensuring a steady supply of sophisticated weaponry in the future. To complicate matters, the meeting was arranged in the middle of Ramadan, and the Americans, with their Israeli companion Amiram Nir, were also constrained by the need to leave their forward base in Israel before the sabbath, and to return on a working day. During the negotiations, it also became clear that Manuchir Ghorbanifar, the Iranian-born intermediary, had given the Iranians one set of promises as an agenda, and the Americans another – he stood to make a lot of money if the deal went through. Perhaps the final difficulty was as important as all the others. George Cave, the Farsi-speaking former CIA man on the American team, noted that one of the Iranians had breath that could curl rhino hide.

Once the story broke in *Al Shiraa*, Rafsanjani moved swiftly to capitalise on the affair. There was no doubt that he was the central figure, but inside the Iranian government it was also clear that both the Prime Minister, Mousavi, and the President, Ali Khamenei, had known of deals being done with Israel – indeed, Khomeini himself had approved the purchase of arms from Israel – and had also known of Rafsanjani's efforts to get the Americans to supply weapons directly to Iran. Given the rivalry between the three – with Rafsanjani representing the 'pragmatists' (those prepared to mould the revolution to accommodate policy, rather than the other way about), Mousavi, the leader of the leftist grouping within the government, and Khamenei, the least bright of the three and wedded to the purest principles of Islam – Rafsanjani had to seize the high ground by claiming credit for what might have been.

His method was to portray the Americans as the ones knocking on the door – he made great play of the minor elements, of the cake sent as a present from Reagan. It was such apparently incredible details which gave it all such verisimilitude. Eventually it was to emerge that Rafsanjani's account erred on the side of moderation – not only did the Americans take a cake to Tehran, they arranged for this very special chocolate cake to be provided by a kosher bakery in Tel Aviv. It was eaten without apparent ill-effect by the devout Shia guards around the American plane at Mehrabad airport. A few months later, we attended the news conference at which Rafsanjani produced the Bible also sent as a gift by President Reagan, with its inscription to Ayatollah Khomeini taken from one of St Paul's epistles: 'In thee shall all nations be justified.'

Both at that remarkable press conference, and in private meetings, Rafsanjani came as close as he could to acknowledging his control over those who had taken the hostages in Lebanon, and virtually set out the terms for the release of the prisoners: America would have to deliver the arms already bought and paid for by Iran in the time of the Shah, and in the case of France, repayment of a large outstanding loan due to Tehran. A year later France complied with that requirement, and the last French hostages were subsequently released in May 1988.

# 6

## Khorramshahr:
## the City of Blood

By the end of the first month of fighting in the autumn of 1980, Iraqi forces had succeeded in occupying some 7,000 square miles of Iranian territory. It was too little, too late. For the rest of the war, Iraq never managed to improve on its early gains and within two years the bulk of the invasion force had been pushed back and the war taken into Iraqi territory. Saddam Hussein's war plan had established a ten-to-fourteen day timetable for the capture of the main cities of Khuzestan: Khorramshahr, Ahwaz, Dezful, Masjed-e-Suleiman and the refinery town of Abadan, while in the north, a third of Iran's Kurdish provinces were targeted by the invasion force.

The first impetus of the Iraqi invasion foundered on the rock of Khorramshahr, which fell only after twenty-four days of bitter house-to-house fighting. Thereafter, until its recapture in the Iranian spring offensive of 1982, it was known in Iran as Khunin-shahr – the City of Blood. For more than three weeks, a force of only 3,000 Iranian troops and Revolutionary Guards in the port city held out against a vastly superior attacking force. By the time the Iraqis broke into Khorramshahr, 2,000 of their troops had been killed and 6,000 wounded. Neighbouring Abadan, situated on an island formed by the Bahmanshir river and the Shatt al Arab, held out thanks to a much more powerful defence force which managed to keep open a single supply road. By holding Abadan, the Iranian forces stayed within artillery range of the Shatt al Arab and ensured that the waterway remained closed for the duration of the war.

Deeper inside Iran, at Ahwaz and Dezful, the Iraqis made repeated probing attacks accompanied by blanket shelling, but despite occasional claims from Baghdad that one or other had been captured, the cities never fell. The Arab population of Khuzestan, far from welcoming the invaders, either joined the defenders or moved eastwards to join the growing army of refugees. President Hussein had overestimated the disintegration of the Iranian armed forces and underestimated the level of patriotic fervour with which the Iranians would respond to external attack. Khomeini had successfully resisted left-wing demands for the dissolution of the conventional army and the process of restoring military pride through allegiance to the new Islamic Republic was already under way by the time war broke out. The war also obliged the Iranians to impose higher standards of training and discipline on the enthusiastic but anarchic groups who made up the irregular guerrilla forces of the emerging Revolutionary Guard Corps.

A certain antipathy was to remain between the regular army and the Corps, not least because part of the task of the latter was to act as an internal security force to prevent future plots within the military. But whatever ill-feeling persisted never resulted in a terminal split between the two wings of the Iranian fighting forces, despite the best efforts of the Iraqi propaganda machine. In some engagements, the Iraqis used loud-hailers to appeal to Iranian troops to lay down their arms because Iraq's fight, they claimed, was only with the Revolutionary Guards. But such tactics did not succeed in shaking the morale of the regular forces. Until the ousting in 1981 of President Bani-Sadr, who saw the conventional armed forces as a potential power base, there was constant bickering within the Supreme Defence Council between partisans of the army and the Guard Corps. After his departure and the direct takeover of the war effort by the clergy and its representatives, there were increased efforts, never totally successful, to integrate the fighting forces and to Islamicise the army. Mullahs were appointed to army units to instil Islamic values into the officer corps and even to improve their knowledge of Arabic, the language of the enemy but also the language of the Koran.

Once the early Iraqi onslaught had been halted, the conflict settled into a relatively low-key war of attrition, an ostensibly encouraging development for the international peace missions which were already shuttling between capitals to promote an early end to the war. At this stage, both sides might have achieved an honourable settlement of the differences which had brought them into conflict and the war might have been over within a year. President Hussein had failed to achieve his maximalist designs: Khomeini was still in power and the Tehran regime looked, if anything, stronger than when the war had begun. In Baghdad, peace at a price was beginning to look more desirable than the doubtful benefits that might accrue from a long and unpredictable war. There was less urgency for the Iranians to end the war, but they too might have retreated with honour from the battlefield and settled for Iraqi withdrawal and a return to the pre-war *status quo*.

Now, however, it was Khomeini's turn to maximise his war aims: what had begun as an 'imposed war' which Iran had fought in self-defence now became a *jihad* against heretics and outside powers who had sought to thwart the reconstruction on earth of the pure Islamic state. Nothing less than the overthrow of Saddam Hussein would satisfy Khomeini, and this in itself would be only the first step on the road to the 'liberation' of Jerusalem. These expectations were coupled, as ever, with a down-to-earth and pragmatic view of political realities, for the war provided a degree of national unity which had been lacking in the immediate post-revolutionary period. What is more, it had instilled a sense of purpose into the army and was allowing for the rapid build-up of an alternative force, the Revolutionary Guard Corps, which was totally loyal to the clerical regime. The need to confront the enemy allowed the clergy to monopolise power and impose controls which might have been resisted in peacetime. Once the immediate Iraqi threat had been contained, the war became a means of consolidating and extending the Islamic revolution and of establishing the succession in the event of Khomeini's death.

The Iraqi troops who manned the front line along the 720-mile border were obliged to fight a stolidly conventional campaign on foreign soil against tenacious and highly unconventional defenders. Although the Iraqi invasion had been planned as a blitzkrieg, the lumbering advance of the invaders reflected the textbook strategy of their Soviet instructors and suppliers. When the initial assaults became bogged down, the Iraqi army dug in with its tanks and fought an essentially defensive war, allowing the more numerous and mobile Iranians to go on to the offensive. These Iranian counter-offensives were marked by a gifted but often foolhardy amateurism: tens of thousands of men would be

assigned to attack seemingly impregnable targets, would capture
them against all the odds and would then be forced to retreat
because no follow-up strategy had been prepared. As often as
not, this was the result of Revolutionary Guard commanders and
clergymen–commissars overruling the more conventionally-
minded Iranian officer corps. The Iraqis, schooled to believe that
the enemy would follow the textbook conventions of warfare,
were repeatedly taken by surprise, for the Iranians regularly chose
to mount major offensives at night and often in bad weather when
the enemy was off its guard.

The pattern of Iranian counter-offensives to recover captured
territory began in earnest in September 1981, and the next two
years were to witness some of the most bloody fighting of the
conflict, characterised by massive human-wave attacks and appalling casualties on both sides as Iran sought to oust the invader.
Although Iran now had the initiative on the battlefield, it was
severely hampered by the lack of spare parts, particularly for its
air force. The Iranian air force had performed well at the start of
the war, raiding targets as far away as Baghdad, but a lack of
spares caused by the international embargoes against Tehran
reduced its capacity to supply even the most elementary air cover
to the advancing Iranian ground forces. By now Iran was operating
with a three-pronged fighting force made up of the regular armed
forces, the Revolutionary Guard Corps and the *basij* mobilisation
brigade made up of enthusiastic but usually inexperienced volunteers who had responded to Khomeini's call, first issued before
the outbreak of war, for a 20-million-strong army to defend the
revolution. They were often teenagers or old men who would
serve either at the front line or in rearguard duties for tours of
three months, if they should survive that long. The volunteers were
invariably poor; mosques and factories acted as their recruiting
centres. Groups of boys would often join up together, opting for
the camaraderie of the front line in preference to the grinding
poverty of the Tehran slums. They became the cannon-fodder of
the Iranian counter-attack.

War-time Iran was a strange mixture, and its heart was to be
found at the University grounds each Friday. Always in Iran, in
town or village, there was the Shia martyrdom complex – the
death-wish – demonstrated most graphically by 'the fountain of
blood' in the martyrs's cemetery in Tehran, and by the children

not yet in their teens who paraded in uniforms with headbands proclaiming their devotion to Khomeini and their readiness for death. But there was also the normality, the sense of everyday life going on, of people largely untouched by the revolution, paying lip-service to it if necessary, but in general getting on with their own affairs and doing their best not to attract the notice of anyone in authority. The bazaaris, the merchants who did so much to put Khomeini in power, were left very much to themselves, and went on trying to earn money as best they could throughout the war. Very successful most of them were; in Tehran and in most other major cities everything was always available – consumer goods, luxury goods even, for those who could pay, and the essentials of life too for those with less money but enough to avoid the queues and quotas. The rationing system was fair, and fairly administered, and nowhere in the country did anyone go short; but for the poorest people the business of living became a burden as the years went on and the queues got no shorter, the rations no bigger.

The vibrant heart of the revolution all over Iran could be felt in those Friday prayer meetings, in the mosques of villages and the huge open-air gatherings in the big cities. The mullahs had made the revolution, and now they had to preserve it, to expand it and export it if possible, at least to maintain the devotion and fervour of the people. It was a remarkable performance each week, carefully orchestrated from Tehran. The Association of Friday Prayer Leaders was a powerful political instrument, set up and organised by the central government. Each week the theme of the addresses to be given in mosques throughout the country was laid down, while in Tehran, at the University, the scene of so many now-legendary exploits during the struggle to oust the Shah, one of the leaders gave the address. Before that, in Tehran and everywhere else, lesser figures worked the crowd up into an occasional frenzy, or prepared them for what was to come in much the same way that a warm-up man prepares the audience for the big-name performer in the West.

There were chants of familiar slogans, lines from the Koran which the crowd completed, ritual questions and answers and then the rhythmic, frightening chest-beating audible far away as the hundreds of thousands, sometimes millions, beat their left chest with their right hand while chanting the slogans dedicating themselves to the revolution, to Khomeini, to death. The mullahs were in the front row, very publicly above such performances, merely going through the gestures; hard-eyed Revolutionary Guards stood facing the crowds, ready for any trouble; the small boys in their cut-down uniforms were there; the Iraqi prisoners of war said to have recanted and joined the revolution; the wounded on crutches or in wheel-chairs. But it was the crowds of hundreds of thousands of men – the women always carefully segregated – the simple people of the countryside or the manual workers in the towns, who gave the Friday prayer meetings their special flavour. These were the committed, who had no doubts.

This was the raw material of a society being changed and moulded, something the leaders realised very well. Always the Friday prayer leader in the usual black robes of the mullah stood on the dais with his hands resting on a rifle just visible to the crowd, the symbol of Islam militant, the revolution on the march. Khamenei was an elegant speaker, and Ardebili could get a crowd going better than most, but the favourite was always Rafsanjani with his quiet delivery, down-to-earth use of language and his ability to play on the crowd's emotions. He would sense when attention was flagging and drop into his talk, apparently casually, a phrase which had come to be associated with him, something to which the crowd knew the answer and could have a break from concentration as they chanted the slogans or roared out the responses. It was a brilliant performance, week after week.

In the towns all round the country, the situation was repeated, and television carried live the scene from Tehran. In the villages, the mullahs may have performed with less panache, but their message was just as compelling, for in many of the smaller places the only people able to read and write with ease might be the mullah and the schoolmaster, and they were the ones to translate the messages from Tehran into practical terms for the villagers. In Shi'ism, the mosque had always been more than a mere place of worship; it was the centre of life, the place for social contact, for the politics inseparable from the religion, for argument and explanation. It was in the mosques that Khomeini's message had been heard, as his speeches were played in the back rooms on cassette recorders, and it was in the mosques that the battles with the Shah's men had been planned and directed; the *komitehs* had their headquarters there, so that now the mullahs had the ear of the people as never before. For most of the eight years of the war the mullahs were the highly effective recruiting sergeants of the regime, the translators of the directives from Tehran, the revolutionary guides who shaped the generation which grew up knowing nothing of the Shah and his times, but everything of the Imam, Khomeini, and the war.

Much has been made of the martyrdom complex associated with the Iranian revolution and the Gulf war, and attempts have been made to identify a peculiarly Shia and oriental element in the apparent willingness of tens of thousands of young Iranians to accept almost certain death at the battlefront. This, however, is to simplify the motivations that lie behind the decision to fight in any war. In the cause of nationalism, the peoples of Europe in 1914–18 fought a war even more bloody and suicidal than that which was fought in the Gulf in the name of Islam, and yet the First World War is scarcely cited as proof of an innately fanatical streak in the Western character. Yet the mullahs did use Shia doctrine and myth in order to sustain enthusiasm for the war and to enhance the people's hatred of Saddam Hussein. The various Shia sects represent perhaps 10 per cent of Muslims in the world, the overwhelming majority of whom are orthodox Sunnis. Only in Iran is Shi'ism the dominant religion – it has in fact been the state religion since its introduction by the Safavid dynasty in the sixteenth century. Shi'ism, therefore, along with the Persian language, is a national characteristic which distinguishes Iran from its neighbours.

The Shia, or partisans of Ali, were on the losing side of a war of succession which divided the Muslim world after the death of the Prophet Mohammed. The dominant Sunni branch of Islam holds that religious sovereignty was passed to elected caliphs while the Shia contend that the rightful leaders of Islam are the descendants of Ali, the Prophet's cousin and son-in-law, whose rights they believe were usurped by the caliphs. Ali was succeeded by eleven Imams, all of whom died violent deaths, while the twelfth, an infant, is believed to be in supernatural hiding – occultation – and will return to establish justice on earth. Khomeini, in common with other Grand Ayatollahs and a host of lesser clergy besides, wears a black turban to denote his line of descent from the Prophet's family.

There are those who saw his determination to pursue the war and carry it into and even beyond Iraq as proof of his grand design to re-establish the Muslim caliphate throughout the Middle East, this time under the leadership of the descendants of Ali. Whether this was his ultimate dream or whether his war aims were more conservative, the idea of resurgent Persian Shi'ism righting ancient wrongs was a powerful weapon of internal propaganda, for the struggle against the Iraqis found a reflection in Shia traditions and myths. In popular lore, Saddam Hussein became Saddam Yazid to identify him with the Caliph Yazid who slaughtered the Shia leader Hossein at the battle of Kerbala in the year 680 AD. Each year, in the month of Muharram, devout Shia act out the martyrdom of Hossein and slash themselves as an act of penance for not having stood by him in his hour of need. The annual self-mutilation is a recognition of the sufferings of the Shia and their exploitation at the hands of more powerful groups, but after the Islamic revolution the myth was subtly reinterpreted: henceforward, the Shia would be at the forefront of a worldwide army of the dispossessed. In a symbolic glorification of the over-throw of the Shah, one year after the revolution, a Tehran radio commentary proclaimed: 'Imam Hossein was not killed again, but he defeated Yazid in Iran last year. Imam Hossein, who is now leading a battle against a greater Yazid, will also triumph, God willing. The revolutionary Imam Hussein in Iran, who is fighting imperialism, is not alone now.'

In an effort to show that Khomeini, and not he, was the enemy of God, President Hussein adopted his own symbolic role as Sardar Qaddissiya, the commander of Qaddissiya, the battle at which a small Arab army defeated the imperial forces of Zoro-astrian Persia and obliged it to embrace Islam. He cast himself as the defender of Arab values against an age-old Persian enemy and, in Iraqi propaganda the Iranians became 'pagan Zoroastrians' and 'Persian racists'. The war revived historical antipathies which had little to do with Islam or with the territorial dispute which had provided the motive for the conflict.

The Shah and his father, Reza Khan, had sought to construct their modern nation state on the bones of an ancient pre-Islamic empire which had once stretched from Egypt to India. Their new national myth had strong racial overtones: Persia became Iran, the land of the Aryans, and the Shah took the title Aryamehr, the light of the Aryans. Within the training schools of the Imperial Army there was a concerted effort to Persianise the language and to rid it of Arabic and Turkish borrowings, rather as the Nazis purged German of English and French words. The implication of this imperialist mythology was that the Iranian nation was a superior entity among backward neighbours and the natural master of the region.

The Islamic revolution eradicated this élitist self-image. The mullahs, in their black turbans, glorified their Arab antecedents and Arabic became the second language in schools. The Islamic Republic declared itself at the forefront of an international liberation movement of Muslims and until President Ali Khamenei made a revealing speech in the final year of the war, there was no mention of the glories of Iran's imperial past. For Iraq and its Arab allies, however, there appeared to be little to choose between the domineering Shah and the expansionist Khomeini – the Shah in a turban, in Saddam Hussein's phrase. In their propaganda, the Iranians promised to 'liberate' the holy cities of Najjaf and Kerbala, and to march on Baghdad.

Although Saddam Hussein attempted to give the war a pan-Arab dimension and to cast himself as the leader of the struggle of the Arab people against an ancient Persian foe, Iraq's war aims were essentially those of a modern nation state: to seek regional domination by attacking an ostensibly weaker neighbour and later, when that project failed, to defend its frontiers against invasion. The motives of the Iranians were more complex. Khomeini and the radical mullahs, like the early Bolsheviks in Russia, feared that their revolution would not survive if it were confined to one country; reactionary forces would surely conspire to overthrow the new order. This was the impetus behind the early attempts to export the Islamic revolution and to regard it as a pan-Islamic rather than a purely Iranian phenomenon. Although the reverberations of the revolution were felt most strongly among the Shia populations of the Arab Gulf and Lebanon, Khomeini made no distinction between Shia and Sunni when calling on the Islamic peoples to rise up against their oppressors.

When Iraq invaded, however, Iran found itself fighting a strictly national war against a neighbouring state, and apart from its strategic alliances with Syria and, at times, Libya, Iran did not receive direct backing from any other Islamic state. It also rapidly became apparent that there would be no general uprising by Iran's Shia co-religionists in Iraq and that in this war, like in almost every other in the twentieth century, nationalism rather than inter-nationalism was to be the key factor motivating both sides. Although Iranian propaganda portrayed the Islamic Republic as a victim of imperialist aggression and the war as a struggle between Islam and heresy, the reality was that, as the conflict dragged on, the two sides found themselves slogging it out in a classical modern struggle for regional dominance.

In the face of this reality the myths were sustained, particularly on the Iranian side: the *basij* volunteers would kiss the Koran before marching to the front, vowing to capture Kerbala and to avenge Imam Hossein. On the sleeves of the Revolutionary Guards were stitched keyholes, and they carried keys which would allow them to pass into paradise when they died in the service of Islam. As in other wars, these symbols reflected a mixture of fervour and bravado, rather like the death's head emblems of other armies. For the most part, the Iranian soldiers performed like any others. When told to attack, they attacked; when told to retreat, they retreated; and, as with the Iraqis, they fought best when they were fighting on their own national soil. The expla-nation for the great human-wave offensives which drove the Iraqis back is not only in the desire of ordinary volunteers to be martyrs to Islam but also in the fact that the Iranians were forced to employ their greatest, perhaps their only military advantage: manpower.

The successful Iranian counter-offensive began in earnest soon after Khomeini assumed the role of commander-in-chief after the ousting of Bani-Sadr. In September 1981 a combined force of regular troops and Revolutionary Guards succeeded in lifting the siege of Abadan in a twelve-hour battle against the well-entrenched Iraqi forces. Two thousand prisoners were taken with their equipment intact and the invaders had to withdraw across the Karun river. The acknowledgement that they had been forced to retreat was a significant setback for the Iraqis and an equally significant victory for the new Iranian strategy of planning and operational coordination between the regular army and the Revo-lutionary Guard. At Abadan, the army provided 30 per cent of the fighting force and the Guard Corps 70 per cent, and the Revolutionary Guard role was even greater in later offensives as the Corps developed into a more sophisticated military force and its ranks were augmented by *basij* volunteers.

Two months after Abadan, in the second major Iranian offensive, this time north-west of Ahwaz, 80 per cent of the attack force of up to 100,000 men were either Guards or *basij* who had received intensive training from the Guard Corps. In a series of coordinated offensives, the Iranians steadily recovered hundreds of square miles of territory captured at the start of the war, growing increasingly confident of their ability to mount and sustain large-scale operations. The vast armies which the Iranians assembled were almost impossible to disguise – the CIA, for instance, invariably gave its allies intelligence on impending Iranian offensives derived from satellite photographs of troop concentrations, while Tehran itself made little secret of its intention to mount new offensives, often timing them to coincide with major anniversaries of the Islamic Republican calendar, as if to unsettle the enemy in advance.

The tactic sometimes appeared to have an effect. In September 1982, to mark the third anniversary of the revolution, Iran declared a 'war week' in apparent preparation for a new offensive. The Revolutionary Guard commander, Mohsen Rezai, announced that he was confident that Iranian forces would soon capture Kerbala, and the Prime Minister, Mir Hossein Mousavi, pledged that an imminent Iranian victory would decide the fate of the region. The Iraqis were convinced that they faced a massive new attack; the president of Iraq's National Assembly, Naim Haddad, said Baghdad believed that the Iranians were poised to strike deep into Iraqi territory, and Saddam Hussein's government redoubled its international efforts to achieve backing for a cease-fire.

When it came, the much-heralded offensive turned out to be a relatively minor affair, but the Iraqis were understandably nervous. They had been on the run since late March, when Iran had launched perhaps its most effective offensive against the invaders, ousting the Iraqis from territory west of Shush and Dezful. In the al-Fatholmobin or Inevitable Victory offensive, the Iranians attacked during a sandstorm and took the Iraqi troops completely by surprise to the extent that the Iraqi defence effectively collapsed, with casualties on the Iranian side relatively low, both among the 120,000-strong forward line of troops, Guards and *basij* and among a 30,000-strong rag-tag army of refugees and local townspeople – including women, and led by mullah-commissars – which provided the rear-guard and helped to speed up the Iranian advance. More than 15,000 Iraqi troops and more than 300 tanks and armoured vehicles were captured and 1,500 square miles of territory recovered in the three-phase offensive which lasted from 22–29 March. It was, to that date, Iraq's most ignominious defeat of the war.

But worse was to come. The following month, the Iranians launched the Beit al Moqaddas, or Jerusalem, offensive, which was to deprive the Iraqis of their single greatest prize, the port of Khorramshahr. The Iraqis had had twenty months in which to transform the gutted ruins of Khorramshahr into a seemingly impregnable fortress. The port was linked to the well-fortified road and rail junction of Hamid to the north and protected by Jofeir, from which the Iraqis had built a network of new roads linking occupied areas. Khorramshahr represented both a strategic and a symbolic target for the Iranians, but also one which it seemed almost impossible for them to recapture. Yet in a twenty-five-day campaign, they split the Iraqi army and captured its main bases between the Karun river and the international border.

On day one of the offensive, 30 April 1982, a combined force crossed the Karun river and advanced towards the Ahwaz–Khorramshahr highway west of the Karun. The road had been mined on either side and was protected by fifteen-foot earth embankments. After almost two days of fighting the Iranians succeeded in cutting the 60,000 force of Iraqi defenders in two, half in the north on the Hamid–Jofeir axis and the remainder in the south towards the port itself. Hamid fell on 6 May and Jofeir was abandoned. The Iraqis mounted a series of counter-attacks and halted the advance at Shalamcheh, but this failed to blunt the offensive. On the morning of 22 May the Iranians captured the paved road built by the Iraqis along the Shatt al Arab, cutting off 19,000 troops in Khorramshahr from the rest of the Iraqi forces. Two days later, the demoralised Iraqi forces laid down their arms and walked to the Iranian lines to surrender. Ecstatic Revolutionary Guards and *basij* volunteers, chanting '*Allah-o-akbar*', entered to reclaim the City of Blood.

More than 3,000 square miles of territory were recovered in the

The furthest extent of the Iraqi advance into Iran

Beit al Moqaddas offensive, and apart from a few remaining pockets, the invaders had been virtually ousted from Iranian soil. From now on, it would be Iraq's turn to defend its land. In June, President Hussein announced his unilateral decision to withdraw the remaining Iraqi forces to the international frontier, but Khomeini instantly retorted that Iran did not consider the war over. He was still demanding the punishment of the 'aggressor', in effect the overthrow of Saddam Hussein, perhaps encouraged by reports that Arab leaders were secretly discussing how the Iraqi President might be replaced in order to placate Iran. Iranian officials said the war would continue until payment of reparations, which by now they calculated as running between $50bn and $150bn. Iran also demanded the establishment of an international commission to assign responsibility for the war.

On 26 October, Saddam Hussein announced that he now accepted the frontier line as defined by the 1975 Algiers agreement, the document he had torn up on the eve of the outbreak of war just two years before. The prevalent view in the West and among the conservative Arab states in the Gulf which had backed Iraq was that the Iranians had effectively won the war but that a negotiated settlement was as far off as ever. Having successfully repelled the invaders, the Iranians might now have chosen to sue for peace from a position of strength. But, given Khomeini's characteristic intransigence and the natural tendency of victorious forces to wish to press their advantage, the Iranians took the fateful decision to continue the war.

The internal situation remained fluid. The Tehran regime was still engaged in a war of terror and counter-terror against the People's Mujahedin and in the spring, at the time of the Khorramshahr offensive, yet another plot against Khomeini was discovered, this time involving the former foreign minister, Sadeq Ghotbzadeh, and the conservative Azerbaijani clergyman, Grand Ayatollah Kazem Shariatmadari. The bungled *coup* attempt, which Iran blamed on the CIA, involved only a handful of military officers but it was an indication that the consolidation of the revolution and the eradication of the mullahs' enemies was not complete. The war still served its domestic purpose, and the prospect of continued conflict gave a fresh impetus to the various peace efforts that had been under way from the start.

The initiative which was deemed to have the best chance of success was that of Algeria, a country respected by all sides in the Middle East because of its liberation war against the French. Algeria had played a central role in the settlement of the hostage crisis between Iran and the United States, resolved the previous year. On 3 May, however, at the height of the Khorramshahr campaign, a plane carrying the Algerian foreign minister, Mohamed Benyahiya, was shot down just inside the Iranian border as it headed for Tehran. Iran blamed the Iraqis; Baghdad denied the charge. Whether the incident was accidental or a deliberate assassination by one or other side, the peace initiative died with Benyahiya.

Four years later, another peace-maker was to die even more dramatically and just as mysteriously. The Swedish Prime Minister, Olof Palme, decided to go with his wife to a cinema in the centre of Stockholm, giving his detective the evening off. Two hours later, as the couple left after the show and were walking home, a gunman shot the Prime Minister dead in a killing which caused turmoil in the Swedish government, the police force and the security service, and appeared to have close links with the Gulf war. At first a group of Kurds emerged as the main suspects in the case, and Iran was believed to be behind the killing, for the motive was thought to lie in the efforts Palme had made to bring the war to an end.

The Swedish Prime Minister, then out of office, had been appointed as the special UN representative in November 1980 after the failure of the initial efforts by the Security Council to obtain a ceasefire in the Gulf – feeble efforts which Iran was to use years later as its own justification for refusing new mediation attempts. All that the Security Council did at first was to issue a formal request to the parties to stop fighting and withdraw to the international border, making no distinction between Iraq, whose troops were advancing into Iranian territory, and Iran, which was desperately trying to organise its own defence. Even this weak Resolution 479 calling for a ceasefire took days to hammer out, and Iran over the years pointed to this delay and to the wording of the resolution as an indication of the one-sidedness of the international body, where, it claimed, there was an in-built prejudice against Tehran. There was also, it seemed, more concern at the international effects of the war than real desire to bring it to a speedy end: the first priority of the Secretary-General, Dr Kurt Waldheim, was to try to extricate the ships trapped in the Shatt al Arab, not to find ways of halting the Iraqi invasion. Even this attempt failed when Iraq refused to allow the ships to be moved under the UN flag, claiming that recognising such a flag in the waterway would undermine its own claim to sovereignty over the Shatt al Arab.

Between June 1981 and March 1982 Palme paid a number of visits to Tehran and Baghdad, meeting the leaders on both sides as well as many lesser figures; it was from some of these, it was thought, that he learnt facts which were to lead to his death. The murder of the Prime Minister threw the Swedish police and intelligence agencies into disarray, leading to resignations, accusations of incompetence and political uproar. The favoured explanation at the end of it all was that he had been told of arms deals involving the Swedish Bofors company, and of Iran's plans to finance weapons purchases through illegal drug exports. Right up to the time a known criminal was arrested at the end of 1988 and identified as the killer by Mrs Palme – an accusation he strenuously denied – all the Swedish investigators, official and unofficial, believed that the Palme assassination was the work of members of the PKK, the violent and extreme Kurdish Workers' Party which since 1984 has been carrying on a terrorist war against Turkey in the eastern provinces of that country from its bases in Iran and Syria.

The PKK would have been willing to carry out a contract killing on behalf of Iran anywhere in the world in order to ingratiate themselves with the authorities in Tehran and ensure their own freedom of movement in that country, but they had a particular dislike of Olof Palme and his Social Democratic government in Sweden which had barred the PKK leader, Abdullah Ocalan, from entering the country, where he wanted to establish a base among the many Kurdish refugees who were resident there; and the police chief, Hans Holmer, was particularly tough on Kurdish activities. Swedish police said later that they had a list of ten Kurds living in Sweden who were kept under constant surveillance as they were thought to be high security risks, though it later emerged that these individuals were all linked to feuds between various Kurdish factions, and were not regarded as threatening the Swedish state.

Very soon after the murder police leaked the fact that Kurds were high on their list of suspects, yet it was twenty-four hours before a café called Kurdiska Bokkafeet was visited by the police. That café was known to be the unofficial headquarters of the

PKK in Stockholm, it was only a few minutes away from the place at which Palme was killed, and the man who shot the Prime Minister ran off in that direction, according to eye-witnesses. Again, dozens of Kurds were rounded up for questioning. Hans Holmer and a friend of Palme's who conducted his own private investigation, Ebbe Carlsson, both said they knew how the murder had been carried out, and claimed that ten men had been involved, all with walkie-talkies, monitoring the Prime Minister's movements and directing the assassin when to strike. To complicate matters further, two officers of SAPO, the Sakerhetspolisen or Swedish Secret Police, Valter Kego and Jan-Henrik Barrling, said they knew of a meeting in Damascus at which the Palme assassination had been arranged. The two claimed that representatives of Iran, Syria and the PKK were at the meeting in August 1985, and that British Intelligence and the American CIA were told what went on there by a Turk who was involved, Mehmet Ali Iula. The Swedes went so far as to send a senior representative to London to get the British version of this story, but he totally failed to make contact with any officials.

In the end, the Palme murder was attributed to an unbalanced Swede with a grudge against the Prime Minister, yet doubts remain. Both the circumstantial evidence, the testimony of witnesses, and the leaks from the intelligence services of Sweden, Turkey, America and Britain all point to the fact that this was a political killing, that the Kurds were involved, and that they were working at the behest of Iran. The Kurdish motive is plain: they wanted to ensure the gratitude of Iran, and probably to get the support of that country for an eventual Kurdish state which would take in some Iranian territory as well as most of the south-eastern provinces of Turkey. What remains unclear is the Iranian motive. In war-time, it is normal for governments to make promises in order to win support against their enemies (witness the British treatment of the Arabs in the 1914–18 war), but Iran could derive no profit and might be embarrassed if it was found to be supporting the PKK, which was fighting Turkey, not Iraq.

Olof Palme's attempts to mediate in the Gulf war ended in death and drama, while most other efforts dribbled away into the sand. The Islamic Conference Organisation, the Non-Aligned Movement, the Arab League, Algeria, Turkey, the PLO, President Castro of Cuba, Syria and Kuwait all at various times tried to bring the war to an end, but none achieved the slightest success. The trouble was, of course, that the two sides had totally different aims and quite separate perceptions at different times of the war. Iraq was always the most ready to observe a ceasefire, initially because it was winning, then because it was losing, while Iran took a much more steady course. After the first few days of the war Iraq proclaimed itself ready for peace on the basis of the situation on the ground, and announced a unilateral ceasefire; but it was quite obviously something the Iranians could not accept, for by that time the Iraqis had captured the territory they claimed along the border, and had also crossed the Shatt to establish themselves on the west bank, improving even on the pre-Algiers situation. Any ceasefire then would have put the Iraqis in a very powerful position in any negotiations, controlling all the areas they wanted and in total command of the waterway; no Iranian government could accept such a situation.

Once the tables were turned, the Iraqis were even more eager for a settlement, this time on the basis of the frontiers as demarcated in the Algiers agreement. They realised that there was a real danger at that time that the Iranians would make the threatened breakthrough and either take Basra or split the country, something which would have brought an end to Ba'ath rule in Baghdad. Only at the very end, when America had virtually entered the battle on Iraq's side, did Saddam Hussein revert to his pre-war intransigence. Once Iran announced its acceptance of Resolution 598 in the remarkable volte-face by Khomeini, Iraq, which had accepted that resolution a year earlier, began hedging it around with all sorts of conditions, trying to re-write parts of it and altering the order in which things were to take place. Meanwhile the world failed to take any action to stop the massacre of the Kurds for fear of driving Iraq away from the negotiating table altogether.

Earlier attempts at mediation foundered either because of the special interests of those trying to mediate or, more usually, because the United States and the Soviet Union did not line up behind the efforts to bring the conflict to an end. America suffered for years from the effects of the Tehran hostage crisis and the public perception of the brutal Iranian regime propagated at that time, while Reagan during his first term was still in his 'evil empire' era in his attitude to Moscow, determined not to pull back anywhere in the world in case the Soviets moved in. Others in the administration took the same view for better reasons, holding that the danger was not the Russians but the Iranians themselves, and seeing the export of the Islamic revolution to the Arab states of the Gulf as the real concern for the West.

The Soviet Union was much more concerned than it ever admitted about the effect Ayatollah Khomeini's takeover in Tehran was having on its own Muslim groups, which will make up the majority in the Soviet Union by the end of this century. Equally, Moscow had to maintain its links with Iraq, to honour its treaty, if it were not to lose credibility with Iraq's backers, the more conservative Arab countries with which Moscow wanted to improve its relations. Again, Moscow had constantly to think of the effect of what it was doing on Syria, its one active and reliable client state in the Middle East, for although Syria was becoming more economically dependent, President Assad had in the past shown himself to be a leader who would not hesitate to act against his own short-term, narrow interests in the hope of long-term gain.

The Islamic Conference Organisation, dominated by Saudi Arabia, made more efforts than most to find a solution, but had no success. This disparate group was linked only by the fact that the majority of people in its member countries were Muslims, but this was less of a unifying factor than might have been supposed. Countries as diverse as Pakistan and Bangladesh, Senegal and Guinea shared little except religion, and had difficulty in finding a common approach, so that they were never taken particularly seriously by the Iranians. Equally, the Arab League could make no headway, not least because Libya and Syria were there to see that it did not take a totally one-sided view, while all the other Arab countries firmly supported Iraq.

The one group which tried harder than most to find a settlement was the PLO. Yasser Arafat was one of the first to visit Tehran after the triumph of the revolution, and he was assiduous in the Arab League, in the Islamic Conference Organisation, the Non-Aligned Movement and on his own in trying to bring the war to an end. The reason was plain: the war in the Gulf was diverting Arab attention and Arab effort from the root conflict of the area, the continuing crisis between Israel and the Palestinians. Without Arab backing, and in particular Arab money and Arab arms, the PLO could hardly maintain itself even as a propaganda machine, so Arafat had to try to end the 'diversion', and once again to put the Palestinian issue back in the forefront of Arab affairs. In November 1987, just a month before the *intifada* (uprising) broke out, Arafat was at the nadir of his career as he sat in a hotel room in Amman, ignored by his fellow leaders at the Arab summit conference called to consider the Gulf war. It was the only time that the question of Palestine or Israel had not been at the top of a summit agenda since the first meeting of Arab heads of state was held in 1964. Not only did the Gulf war marginalise the Palestine issue, it also actually threatened the Palestinians of Lebanon, who were caught in the ideological – and actual – cross-fire between the Syrians and the Iranians there, and brought them new danger when at the end of the war Saddam Hussein sought to take revenge on the Syrians at one remove by arming and encouraging the Phalangists.

Another half-hearted mediator was Turgut Ozal of Turkey, who went to Baghdad and Tehran at the beginning of 1988, carefully waiting until the first signs had appeared that the super-powers were at last united in wanting an end to the war, and that Iran was at least preparing to consider peace. As leader of the one country bordering both Iran and Iraq, Ozal had had to tread a most careful path from 1980 onwards, and succeeded remarkably well in doing so. Although his relations with Iraq were rather closer than with Iran, he still managed to have correct relations with Tehran, and to derive considerable profit for his country from the transit trade which increased so dramatically as the passage through the Gulf became more dangerous.

Turkish policy towards both Iraq and Iran was conditioned by its own fear of its Kurdish minority, a group of six or seven million not even acknowledged as a separate ethnic group until Ozal himself broke the ban on talking about them towards the end of 1988. Because of the special Turkish position, the Arab League had asked Turkey to intervene as early as 1982, but, quickly realising that there was no hope of any success then, the Turks extricated themselves, got on with trade, and left it until almost the end of the war before appearing on the scene again – no mean feat. Even the formal agreement between Ankara and Baghdad to allow the Turks the right to pursue Kurdish rebels into Iraqi territory, with the secret provisions of the agreement providing for Turkish protection of the oil pipeline from Kirkuk to the Mediterranean in certain circumstances, failed to upset the Iranians. Iran had to keep open the supply route through Turkey, and because of that, Turkey was able to do much as it liked. Turkey even went so far in the early days of the war as to allow the CIA and MIT, the Turkish military intelligence organisation, to set up the nucleus of a monarchist 'liberation army' in eastern Turkey.

All the international peace efforts proved ineffective because there was no will towards peace in the two countries at the same time. Right up to 1988 Iraq was ready for negotiations so long as Iran did not insist on all the conditions it had earlier made, particularly the demand that Saddam Hussein should be removed and the system of government changed in Baghdad. That was something that no head of state and no government could accept, so that Iraq had no choice but to go on fighting while proclaiming its willingness to talk peace. Iran believed that it could win and there were those in the government who adhered to the old Islamic belief that converts could be gained by the sword; they still believed they could export their revolution to Iraq, and that the Shia there would eventually come under theocratic rule.

Once inside Iraqi territory, the Iranians soon came to realise that the Shia of southern Iraq were not about to overthrow the Iraqi government and join the Ayatollah. The so-called 'war of the cities', beginning with random shelling of Basra by the Iranians, plainly indicated Iran's acceptance that it was now involved in a conventional nationalist war. Iraq responded with regular air raids on Tehran, which were answered by Iranian missiles on Baghdad. Iraq was certainly making no effort to hit economic targets in the attacks it carried out at this time. We watched Iraqi planes fly over power stations and factories to drop their bombs on residential areas, a plain effort to damage the morale of the civilians – and a successful one, too. Night after night thousands of Iranians left their homes in Tehran to take refuge in the hills above the city, disrupting the working day at both ends.

In Baghdad, military attachés at a number of embassies plotted the position of the various hits, and became convinced that the Iranians were trying to hit Saddam Hussein's palace. The President believed it too, and took to sleeping in various 'safe houses' in the suburbs, though in fact the fall of the missiles seemed to be quite random within a very large circle. After three months of increasingly bitter confrontation, it was Iraq which blinked. In June 1985 Iraq called an end to the war of the cities, though it continued to attack economic targets, and Iran still shelled Basra at times.

Iraq launched a new and more bitter duel at the beginning of 1987 once it had acquired missiles capable of reaching Tehran. The missile strikes caused huge panic among the city's ten million inhabitants and a nightly exodus. The Iraqis appeared to think that they could bomb Iran to the conference table, and in February of 1987 put that to the test by offering a two-week halt in the attacks during which Iran could start to talk peace on the basis of Saddam Hussein's 'five principles'. These were: an immediate ceasefire, troop withdrawals to recognised international borders, a full prisoner-of-war exchange, signing of a peace treaty, and a pledge of non-interference in each other's affairs. Eighteen months later, suddenly feeling strong, Iraq was to spend months arguing about conditions less exact than those. Iran agreed to go along with the pause in the bombing, but took no notice of the Iraqi offer of peace. It was all propaganda to cover up Iraqi failures to break the Iranian spirit, and was forced on Baghdad by the success of the Iranian 'Kerbala' offensive against Basra, said Rafsanjani. In fact, the Iraqi bombing did a great deal of damage to Iranian morale, and the Kerbala offensive was getting nowhere at very high cost, while Iraq was desperately looking for a way out of the war to avoid the much-feared Iranian break-through. Iranian officials themselves estimated that the Iraqi attacks killed 3,000 civilians in two months, and wounded 9,000 others.

The other thing which had a significant effect on Iranian morale was the use by Iraq of poison gas; it was an efficient weapon when used against large masses of men in confined spaces, such as the Majnoon marshes, but its effect was much more widespread than its actual area of use. Iran had to spend large amounts of money in buying masks and other protective gear, but the major result of the use of gas was on the attitude of the young men of the country. News of the gas attacks, carried to every town and village by survivors, played a significant part in slowing the flow of volunteers to the *basij*, so that by 1987 Iran was in no position to try once again the human-wave tactics which had succeeded very well in the early years.

# 7

# America:
# the Great Satan

The strident shout of '*Marg bar Amrika*' – 'Death to America' – echoes through the Iranian revolution and the Gulf war. The *basij* volunteers who went to almost certain death in the great human-wave attacks were sacrificing themselves in a holy war against all the enemies of Islam, not just the Iraqis but also the Zionists, the atheist communists and above all 'the world devourer', the 'Great Satan' – the United States. After the fall of the Shah in 1979, the relationship which had held the two countries together over a quarter of a century gave way to an un-paralleled antipathy and hatred which would affect American perceptions of the war. In the end, it was the United States which would do more than any other power to dictate the out-come of the conflict and to halt the tide of a revolution which had inflicted upon it so many humiliations. It was America which pushed Resolution 598 through the UN Security Council; it was America, not Iraq, which confronted the Iranian navy in the Gulf; and it was America, having failed to find support for a one-sided arms embargo against Tehran, which put in train an unofficial but highly successful operation to starve Iran of weapons.

Yet even after the humiliations of the hostage crisis and the Iranian-inspired US retreat from Lebanon, there was an ambiva-lence in American attitudes towards Tehran. Iran remained, after all, the great strategic prize that it had been in the Shah's time. The mullahs, for all their medievalist obscurantism, were dedicated anti-communists; hence one of the reasons for Irangate and the bungled efforts to find potential interlocutors in the Islamic regime. Irangate had to be the last humiliation. From then on,

American policy towards the war was dictated by one simple aim: Iran would not be allowed to win.

The slogans of 'Death to America' and 'Death to the Shah' were almost synonymous to the millions who poured on to the streets of Tehran and other Iranian cities in 1978 in the revolution which was to end 2,500 years of monarchy. Mohammad Reza Pahlavi was, for the demonstrators, the American Shah, a foreign puppet dancing on the strings of the CIA to a tune composed in Washington. The Americans, like the Greeks, the Mongols, the Russians and the British before them, had sought to enslave the Persians, but this time Islam would defeat the foreign devils. Such was the propaganda inspired by the mosque and endorsed, partly from conviction and partly from political expediency, by both Westernised moderates and left-wing radicals who sought political power under the banner of Islam. In reality, it was the mullahs themselves who would use anti-Americanism as a potent weapon to destroy their rivals and monopolise the revolution. In a country where disasters are always blamed, and often rightly, on the machinations of foreign powers, anti-Americanism became the central article of faith.

The close involvement of the United States in the affairs of Iran began, benignly enough, at the end of 1943 when President Franklin D. Roosevelt travelled to Tehran for the wartime summit with Churchill and Stalin. Although their discussions focused on the planned invasion of Europe and the shape of the post-war settlement, Roosevelt also won a commitment that Iran's independence would be respected once the war was over. The Soviet Union and Britain had deposed the pro-German Shah, Reza Pahlavi, two years earlier and placed his son Mohammad Reza on the Peacock Throne. The country had been invaded and divided into British and Soviet occupied zones, so at the Tehran conference Roosevelt secured a timetable for the early departure of all the occupying forces once the war was won, for this was a period when the United States, loyal to its Wilsonian and anti-imperialist traditions, presented itself as the guardian of the emergent nations against a re-establishment of the old pre-war hegemonies.

It was only later, in Iran and elsewhere, that a growing fear of the spread of communism led the United States to take on the mantle of the old imperialism and to see behind every nationalist movement the hidden hand of Moscow. In the closing years of the war, however, the United States had no desire to establish its own hegemony over Iran but rather sought, through aid and encouragement, to safeguard the future independence and territorial integrity of the post-war Iranian state. The effort was not entirely altruistic, for the Americans already had important oil interests in the Gulf which they were eager to protect. And in Iran, at least, the fear of Soviet intentions appeared to have been justified at an early stage. Going back on its earlier commitment, when the end of the war came, the Soviet Union tried to perpetuate an occupation which is still remembered with bitterness by older Iranians for its tyranny, impoverishment and repression.

The Soviet Union delayed its departure and set up puppet regimes in the provinces of Azerbaijan and Kurdistan, either as a prelude to annexation or as a means of winning oil concessions from the Tehran government. In what was one of the most serious crises of the post-war period, the United States stood firm against Moscow, using the machinery of the newly created United Nations, and forced a Soviet climbdown. Assured of US backing, the young Shah sent his army into Azerbaijan and deposed the pro-Moscow government. In their first contact with Iran, the Americans had played the unsolicited role of saviour. This Iranian crisis of 1946 was one of the opening campaigns of the Cold War, the first time that the new post-war powers, the United States and the Soviet Union, had collided outside the European theatre. It heralded the start of forty years of superpower rivalry in the Middle East which only began to dissipate at the height of the Gulf war with the advent of the Gorbachev era.

In 1946, one of the main priorities of the US strategists was to plan for an expected oil drought and to find new sources from which to supplement traditional domestic and Caribbean supplies. This led the Americans to seek a stronger role in the economic and political destinies of Middle Eastern states, including Iran. Towards the end of 1953, Vice-President Richard Nixon, then an enthusiastic and active cold warrior, paid an official visit to Tehran at the end of a cataclysmic year for Iran in which the Shah had almost lost his throne and in which the popular perception of the United States had changed from one of disinterested benefactor to that of alien manipulator.

The crisis began in 1951 when the Iranian parliament under the leadership of Mohammad Mossadeq nationalised the holdings of the British-owned Anglo-Iranian Oil Company (AIOC), the forerunner of BP, which had controlled all the country's oil resources since 1909. Britain responded by imposing an international boycott of Iranian oil, claiming that it was, in effect, stolen property. In the tide of popular support for Mossadeq which followed the nationalisation, the Shah was obliged to appoint him Prime Minister, but Mossadeq's demands for increased governmental powers put him on a collision course with the Shah, who dismissed him only to be forced, under popular pressure, to reinstate him.

America's attitude to the crisis was ambivalent. On the one hand, it was ideologically opposed to the concept of nationalisation; on the other, it did not see its role as that of propping up Britain's waning imperial power. The deciding factor was the threat of communist subversion, as the pro-Moscow Tudeh party was supporting Mossadeq against the monarchy and there was the ever-present threat of Soviet intervention under the terms of the 1921 Soviet-Iranian treaty. The death of Stalin in March 1953 appeared to provide a limited window of opportunity for action, so in collusion with the British intelligence service, the CIA mounted a counter-*coup*, codenamed Operation Ajax, which ousted Mossadeq and restored the Shah to his full powers, although he and his family were briefly obliged to seek exile in Rome. There followed a period of repression in which those loyal to the nationalist cause, including Mossadeq himself, were hunted down and imprisoned while those who cooperated in the counter-*coup* were rewarded with high office at court and in government – and the gang leader who had brought pro-Shah mobs on to the streets was given a gymnasium much patronised by the élite. By the time of Nixon's visit to Tehran, the United States had become, in the minds of the millions of supporters of the nationalist cause, the protector of the Shah and the enemy of the people. It was America's first step on the road to becoming the Great Satan.

Nixon and the Shah shared the same view of Iran's role as a regional bastion against communism, and both saw the opportunities for a close strategic alliance. In addition, the 1953 visit established a personal tie which led to the special strategic relationship which blossomed almost twenty years later during Nixon's own presidency. Until then, successive presidents from Eisenhower onwards had much more modest expectations of Iran. Under the terms of a 1959 bilateral security agreement, the United States became a major arms supplier but always held back from giving the Shah as much as he demanded in terms of weapons and military technology. During John Kennedy's presidency, in particular, the policy was to encourage the Shah to develop the country's political institutions and infrastructure rather than its military might. This the Shah tried to do, and the decade which followed his proclamation of the White Revolution in January 1963 saw a gigantic surge in the Shah's influence and international prestige.

In that period, oil revenue grew tenfold to reach $5 billion a year and the new-found wealth fuelled an explosion of construction and modernisation. A revolt by the clergy, led by Ayatollah Khomeini, was foiled in 1963 and Iran's enemies, both internal and external, were held at bay, so that by the time of President Nixon's visit to Tehran in May 1972, after his triumphal summits in Peking and Moscow, the Shah was at the height of his power. The previous year he had staged an opulent pageant at the ruins of Persepolis to mark 2,500 years of the Persian monarchy, an ostentatious display of wealth and power designed to show the rest of the world that Iran had arrived as a major player on the world scene. The early 1970s was a time when Iran was spoken of as a future world power which would rank alongside China and Japan by the end of the century. It was a powerful illusion.

When President Nixon and his national security adviser Henry Kissinger arrived in Tehran in 1972, their purpose was to seal a new and more intimate relationship with the pre-eminent power in the Middle East. Hardly anyone took any notice when twenty-one small bombs exploded in different parts of Tehran on the morning of Nixon's arrival, including one at a tomb he was to visit an hour later. The White House spokesman dismissed the incidents as local protests of no significance. 'We are assured this is of no importance and those behind these small demonstrations do not amount to anything,' he said airily. That evening Kissinger and the Prime Minister, Abbas Hoveida, were the guests of honour at a lavish banquet, served to guests reclining on cushions on the floor; Kissinger was much taken with a talented and beautiful belly-dancer who chose him as her personal audience. When the

Americans left next day, it was that image of opulence and security which they seemed to take back with them to Washington, not the warnings given by the explosions.

The relationship established between Tehran and America carried the seeds of the Shah's downfall just seven years later, swept away on a tide of anti-Americanism. Under the terms of the new relationship, the Shah was given *carte blanche* to purchase the most sophisticated US weaponry outside the nuclear sector, and in return he was to act as the custodian of the Gulf on behalf of the West, a role he quickly and enthusiastically adopted. Britain's withdrawal from east of Suez in 1971 had made it imperative to ensure the defence of the Gulf, so Nixon's motive was to control an area of vital American interest through a surrogate, rather than through the direct presence of US forces – the United States was still entangled in the Vietnam war and needed no new foreign commitments.

The US doctrine of the time is summed up in a confidential briefing paper, contained in the thousands of documents uncovered by the Islamic students who seized the US embassy in 1979. The document said that 'flanked as it is by the volatile Arab–Israeli conflict to the west and the continuing animosity between Pakistan and India on the sub-continent to the east, Iran stands as an island of stability and progress in a part of the world where these conditions are in short supply'. Perhaps even more tellingly, it noted that 'balance of payments has been a chronic problem for the US economy. In addition to the sale of military equipment, Iran is a thriving market for US capital and commercial goods. At present, over 200 US companies have resident offices in Tehran.' It was a period which saw a substantial increase in the numbers of American and civilian technicians in Iran – by 1978, there were 58,000 Americans living there.

Yet the bolstered relationship was not so much between two countries as between the White House and the Peacock Throne. The US Defence Department was told to accede to all the Shah's requests for weaponry, whatever its own views about the ability of the Iranian armed forces to absorb the vast purchases of arms. US sales alone in the five years after the Nixon visit reached $10 billion dollars as American and other arms producers flocked to join the gravy train; it was an era of extravagance and corruption in which the West showed its worst face to a nation increasingly disenchanted at the failure of modernisation and expansion to fulfil its rising expectations.

The perceived benefits of the strategic relationship with the Shah, coupled with the enormous profits to be made by America's military-industrial complex eclipsed the doubts of those in the administration who believed that the pace of progress in Iran was too rapid for such a fundamentally unsophisticated and traditionalist country. But even the doubters did not predict the cataclysm which was to strike in 1978 and sweep away the special relationship for ever. America became so entirely dependent on the Shah to protect its interests in the Gulf that its leaders were blinded to the realities of what was happening inside the country. Added to wishful thinking, this could produce bizarre results. At a state dinner in Tehran on New Year's Eve 1977, little more than a year before the Shah was to depart his country for ever, President Carter still felt able to describe Iran as 'an island of stability in a turbulent corner of the world' – to the relief of the Shah, who had had reason to fear the advent of the Carter presidency.

The Democratic challenger was elected in 1976 on a foreign policy platform linking America's relations with developing countries to their adherence to human rights, yet the special relationship between Tehran and Washington survived into the Carter presidency, for the Shah pre-empted possible pressure from the new US administration by introducing a series of institutional reforms and ordering an end to torture in Iranian jails. Although the changes were more to do with image than substance, they appeared to persuade Carter that the Shah was moving in the right direction towards a more open society. The Shah's instincts, however, remained absolutist, and he was unwilling to abandon any of his supreme power to the unpredictable mercies of a democratic system. Although he sought to bring new faces into parliament and government he did it through the medium of a single party, the Rastakhiz (National Resurgence), founded in 1975 and to which all loyal Iranians were urged to belong.

So, ignoring the muted rumblings of internal dissent, the American administration continued to regard the Shah as a bulwark of US strategy in the Middle East. Carter's secretary of state, Cyrus Vance, assured the Iranian monarch on a visit to Tehran in May 1977 that the administration would honour US commitments on arms supplies and was, in fact, ready to initiate new contracts. To the revolutionaries who were to take power in February 1979, Carter came to be seen not, as he was elsewhere, as a champion of human rights, but rather as a partner in the repression exercised by the Shah – according to Khomeini, Carter was 'the vilest man on earth'. This Iranian view of Carter's role helps to explain the virulence with which he personally was attacked during the hostage crisis of 1979–81, a crisis which dominated the latter half of his presidency and wrecked his chances of a second term.

In the beginning, however, the Shah's opponents had allowed themselves to believe that Carter's election represented a setback to the strategic alliance between the White House and the Peacock Throne. They were encouraged by the scenes outside the White House in November 1977, during a state visit by the Iranian monarch, when police were forced to use tear gas to break up clashes between rival groups of Iranian students. That the Americans should allow the Shah's opponents to humiliate him so publicly in the very seat of US power was taken as a clear sign that Carter intended to humble the Shah. This belief that the Shah might no longer be able to count on the total and unquestioning support of the Americans encouraged some of the opposition, particularly those in the secular centre, to seek contacts with Washington through the US embassy, something which was later to cost them dearly when the clerical leadership and its radical supporters exposed these contacts in order to destroy their secular opponents.

As domestic opposition to the Shah grew during 1978, the United States was hopelessly ill-prepared to assess the threat to its ally's throne. Its intelligence operation in Iran was geared to looking north to the Soviet Union; internal dissent was a matter for the Shah with which he was considered well able to cope, and spying on such a trusted ally was seen as bad form, so US interest in domestic affairs was limited to monitoring the machinations within the Shah's entourage in government and at court. For this reason, the signals of turmoil and unrest went virtually unheeded in Washington, and indeed in other Western capitals which had an interest in the survival of the Shah. In late 1978, when the Shah finally embarked on positive measures to liberalise his regime by releasing political prisoners and dismissing corrupt officials, it was already too late to stem the tide of revolution.

Gary Sick, President Carter's adviser on Iranian affairs during the revolution and the hostage crisis, noted that in late 1978, among the lists of problem areas monitored by various government agencies, 'the question of "domestic instability" in Iran was assigned a priority of three on a scale of six on one such list and, on another, a priority of three on a descending scale of one to three'. When the reality finally dawned that the Shah's days were numbered, Washington had to scramble to find a new strategy and, in the process, succeeded in increasing the mistrust of American motives which already existed on both sides of the Iranian political divide.

Nothing illustrated more clearly the panic and confusion within the Carter administration than the ill-fated Huyser mission to Tehran in the first days of 1979. General Robert 'Dutch' Huyser, a Second World War conscript who rose to be a four-star general and deputy commander of US forces in Europe, had made numerous visits to Iran in the years immediately before the revolution on missions involving the Iranian military programme. In April 1978 he was in Tehran helping the Shah to reorganise his armed forces structure and to introduce a new command and control system which the Shah insisted must be proof against *coups*. In the dying days of the Pahlavi dynasty, therefore, Huyser probably knew as much as anyone in the United States about the Iranian armed forces and about the military consequences if the Shah should be toppled.

At the same time that the general was reorganising the command of the Imperial Army – November 1978 – the truth of the situation was finally dawning on some US officials, as witnessed by the title of an analysis prepared by the American ambassador in Tehran, William Sullivan: 'Thinking the Unthinkable'. For the first time, a senior diplomat appeared to be encouraging the administration to accept the possibility that the Shah could not survive and that the best course open to the United States might be to salvage what it could from the crisis by maintaining the cohesion of the Iranian armed forces and encouraging moderate elements within the opposition. But while Sullivan's report outlined a number of scenarios, it failed to reach any firm conclusions. In any case, the White House and the State Department could not countenance such a fundamental policy change: if the impression was given that the United States was ready to abandon the Shah, then it would undermine confidence among America's other allies in the Middle East and elsewhere. Sullivan, however, was by this time convinced that the Shah's departure was inevitable and that the best course open to Washington was to initiate a dialogue with Khomeini in Paris at the same time as supervising a purge of senior figures in the military command, and their replacement by officers more acceptable to the revolutionaries. The ambassador, who had been no more far-sighted than other Western diplomats in predicting the demise of the Iranian monarchy, was now proposing that the United States should effectively join the revolution.

While largely at his own initiative, Sullivan was making plans to send the military top brass into exile, Huyser, unaware of the rift between the ambassador and the administration, was dispatched on his secret mission to Tehran to try to hold the Iranian armed forces together and to support the formation of a government headed by Shahpour Bakhtiar. The purpose was to prevent Iran from falling into the hands of an anti-Western regime even if the Shah himself should fall, but Huyser's mission was doomed from the outset. During his one-month trip, which saw the departure of the Shah and the return of Khomeini, Huyser never once met Bakhtiar, largely because amid the violence and turmoil of the revolution, he was a marked man. Wearing a bullet-proof vest, he moved around Tehran in an unmarked car, while at anti-Shah demonstrations the crowds chanted 'Death to Huyser'. The General believed that the Iranian military, with or without Bakhtiar, was the key to salvaging the situation for the United States, though he has since complained that the American administration lacked the political will to support the military option. 'I believe that my trust and faith in the upper strata of our government was a real weakness on my part,' he wrote in his memoirs. 'My naivety in assuming that if I carried out the tasks assigned to me with the Iranian military, then the political wing of our government would march smartly along in lock-step, was a gross mistake.'

The final triumph of the revolution came on 11 February in the battle of Tehran, when the Imperial Iranian army collapsed in the face of strike squads of street fighters and deserters. The senior officer corps, trained in America and in American ways during the quarter century of the US–Iranian alliance, were gunned

down in the streets or hauled into custody to face trial and
execution. Back in the United States, Huyser's unrealistic political
masters asked him if he was prepared even at this late stage to
return to Tehran and mount a military *coup*. He told them
he would need unlimited funds, the support of ten to twelve
handpicked US generals and 10,000 American troops and, most
important of all, undivided national support. There was a long
pause before Huyser added that he did not believe the administration was ready to contemplate that kind of action nor that the
American people would support it. As a strategic asset on the
global chessboard, Iran had been lost.

Yet the future shape of the country was still in doubt, the
struggle for control was only beginning, and the outcome was
once again to include the involvement of America. When Iraq's
armies drove into Iran on 22 September 1980, the fact that the
fifty-two American hostages in Tehran had been in captivity for
324 days played its part in shaping America's response. The
seizure of the embassy by Islamic students fanatically loyal to
Khomeini, and America's failure firstly to grasp the implications
of the crisis and secondly to extricate its citizens from their plight
was a new humiliation for the Carter administration. On the day
of the embassy takeover, it was already being said that this
was the second revolution, for the students were acting as the
storm-troopers of a mullahs' *putsch* which, under the banner of
anti-Americanism, was eventually to sweep away the last remnants
of the moderate centre which had supported Khomeini.

In the week before the embassy takeover, powerful clergymen
grouped in the newly formed Islamic Republican Party received
word that the moderates were planning a direct appeal to
Khomeini to end the chaos and dissent which had marked the
first months of the revolution; they wanted him to abandon the
divisive debate on a new Islamic constitution and to restore
the liberal constitution of 1906. This would have guaranteed the
emergence of a secular government, with the mullahs consigned
to a spiritual and supervisory role. Mehdi Bazargan, Khomeini's
provisional Prime Minister, who had acknowledged his inability
to control the revolutionary tide by declaring that Iran was 'like
a town with a hundred sheriffs', reluctantly agreed to back the
appeal. Within a few days, however, Bazargan was out of the
country attending the anniversary celebrations of Algerian

independence. There, together with his foreign minister, Ibrahim Yazdi, he met Zbigniew Brzezinski, Carter's hawkish national security adviser. While the American used the occasion to stress the common strategic interests which the two countries still shared, the Iranians took the opportunity to voice their opposition to the recent decision to allow the Shah to enter the United States. Brzezinski saw in Bazargan and his foreign minister the type of rational men through whom Washington might hope to establish a working relationship with revolutionary Iran.

It was a fatal error which the United States was to commit repeatedly in the coming months and years, as Washington failed to realise that the least endorsement or kind word from America could represent a political kiss of death for any potential Iranian interlocutor. When news of the Algiers meeting reached Tehran, it brought Bazargan one step nearer his political downfall, and for him the embassy takeover was the last straw. Within hours of the compound being stormed on the morning of 4 November 1979, the students received the backing of Bazargan's greatest rival and Iran's most powerful clergyman after Khomeini, Ayatollah Mohammad Beheshti, who gave his endorsement from the chair of the Assembly of Experts. The following day, as the hunched and diminutive figure of Bazargan paced the prime minister's office in downtown Tehran, a foreign visitor was asked by an aide: 'What is going on at the American embassy? No one keeps us informed.' A day later the demoralised Bazargan resigned, and America's main hope for a new relationship with Iran disappeared with him.

Before the revolution, the US compound in Tehran, a drab assortment of low-rise modern buildings occupying an entire block on the northern fringe of the city centre, was the focus of US diplomatic activity in the region. After the fall of the Shah, diplomatic relations were maintained but the embassy staff was drastically reduced following the temporary seizure of the compound by left-wing radicals in the first month of the revolution. Throughout the summer, however, the embassy staff was gradually built back up to about seventy, including diplomats, support personnel and marine guards. Despite the constant threat of another takeover, little was done either to destroy or to ship out the reams of confidential and secret files dating back to the 1960s stored in the embassy archives. They proved a rich haul for the students who seized the compound in November, providing them with ample evidence of what they saw as the active collusion of moderate Iranians with the Great Satan. Many of the files were captured intact, while others were painstakingly put together from the piles of shredded papers which the embassy staff had managed to destroy in their final moments of freedom.

By 1988 publication of the captured documents in book form had reached volume sixty-four, but they did not merely provide employment for the Revolutionary Guards and entertainment for those who read them; some resulted in the summary executions for which the regime soon became notorious. The students found, for instance, records of payments made by the embassy to Simon Farzami, a gentle Swiss-educated lawyer who ran a small business translating new laws and decrees from Persian into English and French for the benefit of businessmen and embassies. The Americans were among his subscribers, and the records they kept of the fees paid to him were enough to ensure the execution of this former editor of the *Journal de Teheran*.

The occupied embassy soon became the physical symbol of the anti-Americanism of the revolution. In the first months, crowds would gather daily to scream invective against the US administration, often for the benefit of the US television cameramen who maintained a twenty-four-hour vigil at the embassy gates. Parents would bring their children up from the poor suburbs of south Tehran and buy them hot beetroot from the roadside stalls and crude cardboard cutouts of the hated Carter wrapped in the American flag. The guardian of the gate was invariably a giant Cerberus of a man with a large gap between his front teeth: Hossein Sheikholeslamzadeh was later to become a deputy foreign minister, with special responsibility for liaising with the anti-American Hizbollah faction in Lebanon. Ali Reza Moayeri, another leader of the students, was to become a wartime deputy premier, while Hojatoleslam Mousavi Khoiniha, the spiritual mentor of the students, was later to be appointed prosecutor-general by Khomeini.

The scenes in Tehran were reflected in the United States, where anti-Khomeini demonstrations, born of humiliation and frustration, occasionally led to violence. Innocent Iranians, or people taken to be Iranian, were picked on and beaten up, and street traders did lively business with T-shirts proclaiming: 'Khomeini is a perfect Shiite'. *Time* magazine chose the Iranian leader as its 1979 man of the year and printed a cover portrait which showed him as evil and fanatical, a perception which was to remain in the American consciousness for years to come. Carter's failure to get the hostages home was a central factor in his loss of the 1980 election, as Ronald Reagan's promise to restore American pride struck a powerful chord with a people who had seen their flag burnt and trampled in the dirt in Tehran. It therefore came as all the more of a shock to discover, in the autumn of 1986, that the Reagan administration had been dealing secretly with Iran in an attempt to free American hostages held by Iran's Hizbollah allies in Lebanon.

The US policy towards post-revolutionary Iran from the fall of the Shah to the end of the Gulf war went through four phases. Faced with the collapse of its staunchest and most powerful ally in the regime, Washington was obliged to try to seek an accommodation with his successors; hence the approaches to Bazargan and Yazdi and the decision to maintain a sizeable embassy in place, for the Carter administration feared that a hostile attitude towards the new regime would play into the hands of pro-Soviet leftists and invite the prospect of Soviet intervention in Iranian affairs. This policy foundered on the rocks of the US embassy takeover and the hostage crisis. Relations were broken and Washington was placed against its will in a situation of conflict with the increasingly radical regime in Tehran. Each night on its television screens, the American public was exposed to the humiliating scenes from Tehran, a situation which led to a ground-swell of public opinion in support of direct military action against Khomeini's regime. The administration was fully aware, however, that an attack on Iran or an attempt to occupy Iranian territory would almost certainly provoke Soviet retaliation and might even spark a war between the superpowers.

This second phase spanned the start of the war with Iraq, which Iran always maintained was imposed on it as a function of US imperialist designs in the Gulf. Then, when it became apparent, during Reagan's presidency, that Iran was in the ascendancy and that the war had actually strengthened the clerical leadership, Washington once again sought an accommodation with Iran. The Irangate scandal, although it was dismissed as a bungled and illicit attempt to gain short-term political advantage by securing the freedom of the hostages in Lebanon, nevertheless reflected the longer-term strategic necessity of establishing links with such an important regional power. The initiative foundered, however, and the Reagan administration was forced to fall back on a policy of hostility aimed at containing the Khomeini regime, if necessary by actively supporting Iraq's war effort, in order to ensure that the Iranians did not emerge triumphant.

There were those in Iran, such as Hojatoleslam Rafsanjani, who accepted the long-term necessity of a renewal of ties with the West, but the overriding attitude in Iran throughout the revolution and the war was one of deep suspicion of American motives: Iranians became convinced that Washington was set on returning a pro-American regime to power.

In April 1980, the month which saw an acceleration in the build-up of tension with Iraq, the United States mounted its abortive mission to rescue the hostages in Tehran, which Iranians saw as proof that America was out to destroy the revolution. The question remains, years later: was the rescue attempt merely aimed at freeing the hostages or was it to have been used as cover for a *coup* by US sympathisers within the armed forces, as was perceived by elements of the Iranian leadership? Such a possibility was raised in the early days of the hostage crisis, and Brzezinski records in his memoirs: 'I recommended a number of steps designed to enhance our security presence in the region and to place greater pressure on Iran, including the possibility of assisting efforts to unseat Khomeini.'

These policy options were being discussed against the background of the Soviet invasion of Afghanistan, which had shocked the United States into the realisation that, in the turmoil and instability fostered by the Iranian revolution and the embassy hostage crisis, the Soviet Union might seize the opportunity to extend its sphere of influence to the waters of the Gulf and threaten the West's oil lifeline. In his State of the Union address on 23 January, one month after Soviet troops entered Afghanistan, the President enunciated what became known as the Carter doctrine: 'Let our position be absolutely clear. Any attempt by any outside force to gain control of the Persian Gulf will be regarded as an assault on the vital interests of the United States of America and such an assault will be repelled by any means necessary, including military force.'

The Carter doctrine represented both a direct warning to

Moscow in the wake of Afghanistan and a commitment to the conservative Arab states of the Gulf, and indeed to America's oil-consuming European allies, that it was taking responsibility for protecting Western interests in the Gulf in the absence of the Shah. The implications, should the United States ever feel obliged to put the terms of the Carter doctrine into effect, would be alarming, for it carried with it the possibility of a superpower conflict in the Gulf, and the most likely battlefield would be Iran. But as long as Khomeini remained in power, Iran was hostile territory where the United States had no means of determining events. Even if the Soviet Union could be warned off from any military adventure, there was no guarantee that Iran would not drift into the Soviet sphere.

A rescue mission was one of a variety of military options placed before Carter from the moment the embassy hostages were taken on 4 November 1979. Hawks in the Pentagon favoured more direct punitive action such as a naval blockade or the bombing of Iranian oil facilities, but because of concern about Soviet intervention, which might now come from Afghanistan as well as from the north, and the possible threat to the West's own oil supplies, such options were rejected. By the spring of 1980 Carter was nevertheless determined to take some positive action to break the stalemate on the hostages, for apart from the humanitarian concerns, there was a political need to score a victory before the November presidential election. So, at a meeting of the National Security Council at Camp David on 11 April, the decision was taken to go ahead with the rescue plan.

On the morning of 25 April, an Iranian journalist, alerted by a report from Washington that a military mission to rescue the American hostages had been aborted in the Dasht-e-Kavir desert, telephoned the armed forces high command. It was a Friday, the Muslim holiday, and only a junior officer was on hand to take the call. The duty officer was taken aback. What attack? Nothing had happened; this was more American propaganda, the journalist was told, and it was several hours before the Iranian military started to backpedal. A group of bus passengers who had been held by the US Marines in the desert were found, and gave first-hand reports of what had happened. By now the armed forces were claiming that the air force had seen off attacking US planes and that 'Allah's radar' had foiled an American attack.

**1a** and **1b**
Images of Saddam Hussein:
soldier and statesman.

**2** Ayatollah Khomeini after the triumph of the revolution, March 1979.

**3a** The Shah at a military parade in the final months of his reign.

**3b** Bani-Sadr during his successful campaign for election as Iran's first president.

**4a** An Iraqi look-out monitors enemy positions
in the plain below Qasr-e-Shirin.
**4b** An Iranian machine-gunner in action on the central front.

**5** Relatives of the Iranian war dead
gather at Behesht Zahra cemetery near Tehran.

**6a** Pack animals were used by Iranian troops
to carry weapons to remote areas of the Kurdistan front.

**6b** Iraqi troops in their defensive positions near Majnoon.

**7a** Iranian troops celebrate their capture of Fao, February 1986.

**7b** Iraqi prisoners-of-war hang an effigy
of Saddam Hussein
bearing the emblems of the three 'Satans':
the USA, the USSR and Israel.

**8a** USS *Stark:* Iraq's apparently accidental attack on the American frigate
helped to bring the United States into the war.

**8b** Iran's Nasra oil platform after an attack by the American navy
in the final months of the war.

**9a** More than 400 people died in clashes between Iranian pilgrims and Saudi security forces during the 1987 *haj* at Mecca.

**9b** The funeral procession in Tehran for the victims of the Iran Airbus, shot down by the USS *Vincennes*, July 1988.

**10a** President Ali Khamenei, a conservative nationalist
who helped to restore the prestige of the army.

**10b** The leaders of the Islamic Republic *l. to r.*: President Khamenei;
Ayatollah Khomeini's elder brother, Ayatollah Pasandideh; Khomeini's son, Ahmad;
Hojatoleslam Rafsanjani; Ayatollah Mousavi Ardebili, the Chief Justice.
The senior non-cleric in the regime is Prime Minister Mir Hossein Mousavi (*second from r.*).

11 A portrait of Ayatollah Montazeri, defaced by the bullets
of Iraqi troops who recaptured Fao in April 1988.

12 Rafsanjani, the parliamentary speaker, who convinced Khomeini
that the war must end, pictured here shortly after
the Ayatollah's death on 3 June 1989.

It was clear from the contradictory statements that US helicopters and C-130 transport planes had crossed half Iran without their presence being detected. The CIA, with its intimate knowledge of Iran's air defences before the revolution, plotted a course that would avoid radar detection, though President Bani-Sadr claimed that the Americans had acted with the assistance of agents within the air force. Certainly the CIA had agents on the ground: they provided intelligence information about the occupied embassy and obtained vehicles for use in the rescue operation. In the event the mission was aborted because of helicopter failure, and then in the scramble to evacuate from the Desert One landing site an RH-53D helicopter collided with a C-130 transport and eight members of the American commando force were killed.

As news of what had happened came into Tehran from Washington the Iranian air force commander, General Bahman Amir-Baqeri, ordered the site to be bombed, an order immediately countermanded by the government. Amir-Baqeri was dismissed and later arrested on suspicion that he had acted to try to conceal valuable intelligence information abandoned by the Americans at Desert One. Khomeini sent the revolutionary court judge, Sheikh Sadeq Khalkhali, to investigate and to retrieve the bodies, and with his characteristic predilection for the dramatic, Iran's 'hanging judge' dispatched the incinerated remains of the dead Americans to the courtyard of the occupied US embassy, where he personally unpacked them from their plastic wrappings in an attempt to prove that there were nine dead rather than eight. Film of this event was considered potentially so inflammatory and offensive to American public opinion that the US television networks voluntarily kept it off American television screens.

Nevertheless, Khalkhali's actions reinforced the American perception of revolutionary Iran as a savage and fanatical place; his obsession with the corpses also obscured the far more intriguing material which he had salvaged at Desert One, for the US task force had left without destroying its operational plans. Although there was nothing to implicate any member of the Iranian armed forces, items were found which implied a more extensive operation than a mere rescue mission. There were aerial photographs of potential targets which appeared to be unconnected with the immediate operation, including Khomeini's house north of

Tehran. There were also adhesive aircraft decals in the colours of the Iranian air force and wads of dollar bills.

Despite its failure, the mission created a mood of insecurity and tension in Tehran, which was heightened four days later when a group of F-4 fighters swooped low across the capital late at night. Tehranis thought that a *coup* had begun, or else that the Americans were attacking. In fact, the Iranian air force, which had failed so miserably to detect the US intruders, were in pursuit of an unidentified aircraft said to have been spotted on its radar screens.

The rescue mission, whatever its ultimate purpose, gave rise to *coup* fever in Iran, coinciding with growing concern about the possibility of war with Iraq. Bani-Sadr claimed that he had information from undisclosed sources in the United States that Washington planned a further military incursion, and US Marines did undergo training for a second rescue mission which never took place. The Iranian President said that, as part of its 'plots', the United States was sending weapons to Kurdistan, where *peshmerga* guerrillas were battling against government forces for control of the provincial capital of Sanandaj. There were almost daily claims of incursions by US aircraft, foreigners were detained on suspicion and in the eastern province of Khorasan, thirty alleged American agents were arrested in the vicinity of Desert One. Others were said to have been infiltrated into the mountains of western Iran, where they were preparing a campaign of sabotage and guerrilla war.

The Crusaders of the Islamic Revolution, a militant faction of the Islamic Republican Party, alerted Iranians to the threat of a US-inspired *coup* which would be carried out in Khomeini's name: 'If the Imam is not reachable, we must obey only those forces that are genuinely in the Imam's line,' it directed. Intentionally or not, Washington's failed mission had succeeded in creating an atmosphere of fear and suspicion, not least against the armed forces, as Iran drifted inexorably towards total war. The left-wing Fedayin movement and the People's Mujahedin used the situation to promote the concept of a popular army to replace the professional armed forces, as they joined the chorus warning of *coups*. Plots were indeed uncovered. In July two former generals and some 300 alleged co-conspirators were rounded up after the discovery of operation 'Red Alert', a *coup* plan aimed at seizing strategic points in Tehran, bombing Khomeini's home, detaining the revolutionary leadership and restoring to power Shahpour Bakhtiar, whose supporters operated from Iraq with the support of the authorities there. The key conspirators were executed.

In the year leading up to the outbreak of war, the US perception of its role in the region changed radically. Until the fall of the Shah, the security of the Gulf had been considered a secondary concern compared with that of Western Europe and the Far East, for with the Shah in power, the Gulf was effectively sealed off from Soviet influence. The Shah's Iran, Turkey and Pakistan provided a pro-Western *cordon sanitaire* between the Soviet Union and the warm waters of the Gulf, with Afghanistan as a neutral buffer. But in the changed strategic situation after the fall of the Shah and the Soviet invasion of Afghanistan, the United States did not have the military means available to halt a Soviet advance to the Gulf, short of nuclear war. So a reappraisal of the US military position in the region to counter the Soviet threat began immediately after the Iranian revolution, a time when there was also concern at a possible invasion of North Yemen by the Moscow-backed Marxist government of South Yemen.

A US aircraft carrier was dispatched to the Arabian Sea, supplies were airlifted to North Yemen and two AWACS reconnaissance planes were sent to Saudi Arabia, while in Washington planning began on the formation of a US Rapid Deployment Force to respond swiftly to crises in the region; but this was carried out against the background of the realisation that, in the final analysis, the United States did not have the ability to defend the Gulf by conventional means. During 1980, the United States was granted base facilities at Masirah Island, off the Arabian Sea coast of Oman, with support bases at Berbera, Mombasa and Ras Banias in Egypt. The shift in US strategy towards a more combative approach to Soviet interference in the Third World was a symptom of the deteriorating relationship with Moscow; added to the growth of Soviet military power in general, Washington was now faced with the erosion of Western power in the Gulf.

The prospect of US troops becoming embroiled in foreign wars was nevertheless disturbing to post-Vietnam America, and the Carter doctrine was not enthusiastically received. Those who took a more isolationist approach argued that the United States depended to an almost insignificant degree on oil supplies from the Gulf, ignoring the fact that some of its closest allies, in Western Europe and Japan, were almost totally dependent on Gulf oil. The motive of the Carter administration in displaying its readiness to defend Gulf oil supplies was, in large part, to ensure that those allies did not become dependent on vital supplies from a region which had fallen into the Soviet sphere of influence. The American academic Robert W. Tucker reflected on the dilemma facing the incoming Reagan administration in the early months of the war: 'It is the Gulf that forms the indispensable key to the defence of the American global position, just as it forms the indispensable key without which the Soviet Union cannot seriously aspire to global predominance.'

Towards the end of August 1980, Washington began receiving intelligence reports that the Soviet Union was moving troops up to the border with Iran in preparation for a possible intervention, while at the same time Saudi Arabia was expressing concern that the increasingly violent border skirmishes between Iraqi and Iranian forces posed a threat to the Saudi oilfields. Carter's crisis-management Special Co-ordination Committee met on 5 September to determine the US response. Brzezinski argued in favour of a tough warning to Moscow of US military retaliation should Soviet troops enter Iran, but Carter's new secretary of state, Edmund Muskie, cautioned that the crisis could lead to an outright war with the Soviet Union. He doubted that Congress would risk nuclear war to protect 11 per cent of US oil supplies, so the following day Carter went no further than approving a stiff note to the Kremlin. By the time the war began in earnest on 22 September, both superpowers had stepped back from the brink.

Part of the US dilemma in the Gulf was that the United States was committed to the territorial integrity of a state, Iran, whose rulers were implacably hostile to it. Washington wished to protect other states in the region from Iranian expansionism as well as protecting Iran from that of the Soviet Union, so that coupled with a natural and publicly supported wish to do down the Khomeini regime was a more pragmatic need to see the survival of a stable, independent and anti-communist Iran. The central importance of Iran in America's geopolitical strategy, until the advent of the Gorbachev era forced a reappraisal, was outlined by Henry Kissinger in 1982:

The focus of Iranian pressure at this moment is Iraq. There are few governments in the world less deserving of our support and less capable of using it. Had Iraq won the war, the fear in the Gulf and the threat to our interest would be scarcely less than it is today. Still, given the importance of a balance of power in the area, it is in our interests to promote a ceasefire in that conflict; though not at a cost that will preclude an eventual rapprochement with Iran either if a more moderate regime replaces Khomeini's or if the present rulers wake up to the geopolitical reality that the historic threat to Iran's independence has always come from the country with which it shares a border of 1,500 miles: the Soviet Union. A rapprochement with Iran, of course, must await at a minimum Iran's abandonment of hegemonic aspirations in the Gulf.

Iran, in other words, should be befriended if possible but must, above all, be contained.

# 8

# The turn
# of the tide

The defeats of spring 1982 left the Iraqis floundering. For all the brave words of their leaders, the Iraqi people realised very well what had happened, knew that they had suffered a serious defeat, and feared for the future. The June 'voluntary withdrawal' fooled no one. We were in Baghdad at the time of the announcement, made in the course of a long and rambling speech by Saddam Hussein, who on this occasion showed none of his usual flair and assurance. Sitting with a group of journalists, civil servants and professional men to watch the television relay, it was clear that Iraqis had become adept at interpreting their President's pro-nouncements. And at a time when the *mukhabarat*, the internal security service, was omnipresent and hyper-active, the magnitude of the occasion made the audience careless of their reactions – indeed, a uniformed senior police officer who happened to have come into the building just before the broadcast began and stayed to watch was as outspoken as anyone. 'This is a real defeat,' he said. 'We are being pushed out,' said another. 'We are in real danger now,' said a third.

Yet for all the outspoken comments, words which no one would have dared to utter in other circumstances, the interesting thing was the immediate assumption that this meant trouble for everyone, not that it was a defeat for the army. After two years of uncertainties – both among the people and the leadership – Iranian successes seemed to achieve immediately what the Iraqi government had failed to do: to unite the people. With their backs to the wall, as they saw it, fighting to defend their own territory and to prevent an invasion by the Iranians, the people of Iraq were transformed. Not only did the army fight with greater tenacity, there was also an immediate drop in the volume of dissent on the home front; the activities of Dawa continued – always blamed on Syria – but even the small opposition to the war which had manifested itself disappeared. From the time the Iraqi army withdrew to its own borders (a few small enclaves of Iranian territory were still held, but in the main it was a withdrawal to the international frontier) the Iraqi people were more united than ever before in their brief national history, which can be dated from 1946.

For Saddam Hussein and the inner group of Iraqi politicians who were running the country it was a fraught period. For two years they had been boasting of the lesson they would teach 'the Persians', as they always called the Iranians in an attempt to capitalise on old enmities and underline the racial divide along the border. Now all their speeches could be thrown back at them, all their threats to topple Ayatollah Khomeini's government shown to be hollow. Suddenly, it was Iraq which was on the defensive, so that the whole tenor and style of the leaders' speeches and pronouncements had to be changed. For Saddam Hussein in particular, this was the most difficult moment of the war. His deliberate domestic strategy of identifying himself with the state and with the war had gained a momentum which could not be reversed. The ordinary people called it 'Saddam's war', not 'the new Qaddissiya', as the President would have liked, and though they noted with private, inward amusement the vast effort made to show Saddam as the embodiment of the Iraqi people, they understood very well the implicit message of the propaganda: that Saddam Hussein was their ruler, not the RCC or the National Assembly or the ministers or even the party, but Saddam himself. It was this which made things so dangerous for the President, for just as he had built up his personal position to benefit from what he thought would be the fruits of the conflict with Iran, so now he had to deal with the problems of defeat.

It was during the 1981 period of stalemate that Saddam Hussein had sought to widen the base of his rule by holding elections for a National Assembly, the first elections in Iraq since the overthrow of the monarchy in 1958, a move designed largely to give the Shia a forum in which they could legitimately express minority views, even a measure of dissent. The 250-member Assembly was never designed to wield any legislative power, but merely to have 'an advisory function'. In fact, no one ever took any notice at all of what the Assembly said or did – which in any case was not much; those elected realised early on what was expected of them, and took care not to overstep the narrow bounds which had been set. The object, people quickly realised, was to give the Shia a place in which they could express some views and even exercise a little pressure; that was all.

At the same time, Saddam Hussein began his personal campaign to identify himself with the state and the people. He was Iraq, he was saying to the outside world, to justify his dictatorial powers and autocratic style of rule. He was the nation state, he was saying to the Iraqis, the father-figure, the compatriot, the elder brother but, above all, the embodiment of Iraq-ism – an idea which had to be built up in an artificially created country, and a country made up of such diverse ethnic groups: the Kurds of the north with their separatist tendencies, the Sunnis of the mid-region with their traditionally privileged and special position, and the Shia of the southern half of Iraq, the majority, who were still in the main the farmers and manual workers. So gradually the country became swamped with images of Saddam Hussein: Saddam wearing the turban of the Kurds, the *keffiyeh* of the southern Arabs, the uniform of the Field-Marshal he made himself, the business suit of the international statesman he aspired to become. On every hoarding, in every town and village, the jowly face of Saddam smiled or scowled – and was even seen in one pose kissing a small child. It was all quite deliberate, it was effective, but it was also dangerous: this cult of personality meant that the leader could be identified as scapegoat as well as benefactor, the leader to disaster as well as to victory.

So it was in 1982. Everyone realised that the 'voluntary withdrawal', as Saddam Hussein called it, was a real defeat, and no amount of rhetoric from the leaders could alter that perception. The trick, Saddam Hussein decided, would be to let others pull the chestnuts out of the fire, so the unprecedented step was taken of holding a joint meeting of the RCC, the national and regional commands of the Ba'ath party and the Military Command Council without the participation of the President – who was and remained the chairman of the RCC. At the end of this meeting on 10 June an offer of a ceasefire was made to Iran. The statement, issued in the name of the RCC, said that Iraq was willing to withdraw its troops within two weeks from all territory still held. It also offered to abide by decisions of the Islamic Conference Organisation on matters in dispute if the two sides could not reach agreement. The Iraqis used the excuse of the Israeli invasion of Lebanon to justify what in effect was a plea to the Iranians for peace: all Islamic forces should unite to face the Zionist aggression, the statement said rather weakly.

If the leaders in Tehran had accepted, they might have gained at the conference table what over the next six years they failed to achieve at a huge cost in men and material; but true to the bitterness and intransigence shown by both sides, Ayatollah Khomeini rejected the ceasefire offer, and the Iranian troops fought on. Iran would remain at war until all its demands were met, the Ayatollah said – and one of those demands was the removal of Saddam Hussein, the one condition which the Iraqi President could never accept. Yet there were those in the Iraqi regime who could consider such a step, notably the minister of health, Riyadh Ibrahim Hussein. During a cabinet meeting, Saddam Hussein said he had heard that some ministers felt he should step down so that negotiations could go on – did anyone agree with that? Yes, said the minister of health, he thought it might be a good tactic for Saddam Hussein to step down, temporarily of course, so that talks could begin; then when a satisfactory agreement was reached, the President could resume his proper position. How many agreed with that idea, Saddam Hussein asked? No hands were raised; the minister of health was alone. He was executed that day for high treason.

In Tehran, the sudden spate of victories caused just as many misconceptions as the Iraqi successes had in Baghdad in the first weeks of the war. Then the Iraqi leaders really believed that the painful advance of their forces those comparatively few miles into Khuzestan would so shake the Islamic government that it would be forced to sue for peace, not realising that from Tehran's point of view only a few hundred square miles of a distant and unimportant province were concerned. Now the Iranians made the same mistake: they thought that the Iraqis would collapse because their troops had been thrown out of the Iranian towns they had occupied and forced back to their own side of the border. Certainly the situation was worse for the Iraqis than it had been for the Iranians in 1980, for Iraq's second city, the port of Basra, was now within Iranian artillery range and was on the direct line of advance if the Iranians tried to move into Iraq.

It was a worrying time for the leaders in Baghdad, but apart from the few who thought the time had come for a negotiated peace, there was no great pressure on them to deal with the mullahs. This was mainly because the army command had anticipated what had happened: during the whole two years that the Iraqi troops were in Iran, the Iraqi army engineers were the hardest worked units of the armed forces, constructing a series of vast and complicated defences not in Iran, to hold the line reached, but along the border between the two countries, and in support lines behind the frontier in Iraq. Huge areas of land were prepared for flooding, roads were built, artillery towers and gun emplacements constructed, and all along the southern front a series of earthworks bulldozed into place. So when the withdrawal took place, though it was often forced and hurried, it was to a line of prepared positions which the Iranians spent the next unsuccessful six years in trying to overcome.

In Tehran, none of this seemed to have been known. Instead, in mirror image of what had happened in Baghdad two years before, the Iranians were discussing their terms for ending the war, and talking of their victory. They even consulted with the Syrians about the shape of the government they proposed to install in Baghdad, and chose a dissident Iraqi army officer, General Hassan al-Naqib, as the Quisling they would use if the Iraqi army rose against Saddam Hussein. And if, as the Iranian leaders believed, the experience of Iran were repeated and the Shia masses of the south revolted against the Ba'ath party, then they had ready the man they really wanted to put in charge in Baghdad, Abdel Bakr al-Hakim, son of the murdered Iraqi ayatollah and a man who would faithfully transform secular Iraq into an extension of Ayatollah Khomeini's Islamic empire.

It was not to be. The Iraqi forces pulled back to their prepared positions, and with their tanks hull down behind the prepared earth barriers and the artillery lined up behind, the frontier became as formidable a series of defences as anything devised since the set-piece battles of the First World War. And very like the First World War it seemed to be, the winter landscape of southern Iraq recalling the pictures of the Somme in 1916: long lines of laden men moved in single file up to the front, the non-coms shouting at them to hurry past gaps in the ramparts where Iranian snipers 1,000 yards away might pick them off. Mud everywhere, clinging soft mud that worked its way into the operating rooms in the forward casualty posts and field hospitals, mud that got into the mess tins and made all food taste the gritty same. Where the groves of date palms had broken up the landscape there were now only the blackened stumps and burned trunks of the trees, the tops blown off by shell fire and cut down by heavy machine gun bursts. Where the mud ended the water began, great man-made lakes where the Iraqi engineers flooded the low-lying land to form vast barriers to troops or tanks, only a few feet deep to make it difficult for assault boats to be used, a tremendous feat of engineering skill and sheer back-breaking labour as the pioneer battalions built the raised roads which allowed troops and vehicles to move about. There was constant danger, as the Iranians quickly found the co-ordinates and dropped shells and mortar bombs on to the bottle-necks where traffic was held up, the narrow bridges over streams, the crossroads where the new tracks converged. In the summer, when the land baked hard and sand replaced the mud, there was yet greater risk as every moving vehicle carried its tell-tale plume of dust, an invitation to every bored gunner on the other side to try his luck.

Within weeks of forcing the Iraqis out of their land, the Iranians launched their own attack, buoyed up by their victories and inspired by the rhetoric of Khomeini. The *basij*, some as young as twelve, charged joyfully to martyrdom, red bands around their heads proclaiming their allegiance to the Ayatollah, a piece of white cloth pinned somewhere to their uniforms as the symbol of a shroud, each one carrying his death with him and, later in the war, a special key too, issued personally by Khomeini, the symbol of their sure entrance into paradise. In the Koran, those who fall in battle are assured of special treatment; what no one now mentioned was that paradise is guaranteed for those who fall in spreading Islam, battling against the infidel – nothing is said about fighting other Muslims, about Shia fighting Shia. For on both sides now the Shia made up the overwhelming majority of those fighting on the ground; all the Iranians were Shia, and on the Iraqi side something like 90 per cent of front line infantry companies were Shia. The Sunnis were the senior officers, the air force and navy men and, above all, the security men and Republican Guards, the élite units still kept safely in Baghdad to protect the regime, not to be committed until more years of desperate warfare had convinced Saddam Hussein of the loyalty and dependability of his Shia subjects.

It was these Iraqi Shia who now had to withstand the onslaught of the *basij*, the children who marched to death with one clip for the rifles that were sometimes almost as big as they were, or with a grenade in one hand and a couple more on their belt. One unusual and haggard Iraqi captain told us the effect it had on him and his men:

> They come on in their hundreds, often walking straight across the mine-fields, triggering them with their feet as they are supposed to do. They chant 'Allahu Akhbar' and they keep coming, and we keep shouting, sweeping our 50 mills [.50 millimetre machine guns] around like sickles. My men are eighteen, nineteen, just a few years older than these kids. I've seen them crying, and at times the officers have had to kick them back to their guns. Once we had Iranian kids on bikes cycling towards us, and my men all started laughing, and then these kids started lobbing their hand grenades and we stopped laughing and started firing.

The three-pronged drive on Basra just a month after Iraq's withdrawal was the pattern for dozens of others that were to follow: the Iranians gained ground – in this instance about four miles – but were eventually stopped, and lost large numbers of men. Once behind their fortifications the Iraqis showed a new spirit, fighting with skill and determination as they defended their homeland rather than having to hold some nebulous, unnatural line inside Iran. It was a sign of the time that the Iraqi success in halting the Iranian onslaught was treated as a great victory in Iraq, with rallies and celebrations – carefully orchestrated – in Baghdad and in towns and villages throughout the country. For after the ceasefire offer made by the party and the military in the absence of Saddam Hussein, the President had to re-establish his authority and build a new myth of what had happened and was happening. Thus, speeches of the leaders now concentrated on portraying Iran as the aggressor in 1980, claiming that the war broke out at the beginning of September that year, and that the Iraqi move into Iranian territory was defensive, designed to pre-empt a major Iranian strike, and to defend Basra and the other Iraqi border cities by fighting inside Iran.

These assertions had little to do with the facts, and were certainly not accepted by the intelligentsia, but served to provide some kind of a rationale which would do for the mass of the people and for the army. Those who could work such things out – and they were many, for all their silence – noted that Iraq's war aims seemed to have been dramatically reduced, and that all the leaders wanted now was a return to the situation before 1980, with no mention of taking over Khuzestan, realigning the border along the Shatt al Arab, or toppling the Iranian government. But as the Iranian thrusts were repulsed, even those things began to be talked about again, as the Baghdad government gradually regained its nerve. Now the thesis was advanced that merely by staying in place and holding firm, and in the process inflicting heavy casualties on the enemy, Iraq could wear down Iranian resolve and force the mullahs to the negotiating table. In 1982 it seemed far-fetched, though in 1988 it succeeded. But it succeeded then with the help of a more potent force than Iraq's static defences: attacks on Iran's economy.

It was in August 1982 that Iraq signalled what its real strategy was to be when it announced an 'exclusion zone' in the north of the Gulf, and for the first time attacked the Iranian oil terminal at Kharg Island. The Iraqi announcement at this time was hasty and ill-considered, a response to the Iranian victories rather than a serious effort to weaken the Iranian economy. Iraq did not then have mastery of the skies, nor the aircraft capable of inflicting real damage on Iran. At the beginning of the war the Iraqi air force was dispersed to Jordan, to be held in reserve until 1983, when the leaders felt it safe to commit it to battle; in 1982 the Iraqi air force was certainly neither capable nor willing to enforce the announced exclusion zone, and the Iraqi navy, such as it was, remained bottled up in port as it was throughout the war.

Officially, the reason for the announcement of the new zone was to protect innocent ships from being hit – a Greek tanker, the *Litsion Bride* was sunk, and the South Korean cargo ship *Sambow Banner* badly damaged by rocket and artillery fire from Iraqi sources. But without the means to enforce its orders, the Iraqis in the most desperate months of the war believed that by turning their attention to the international waters of the Gulf they could widen the conflict and bring in the Western powers, something that was to be a constant strategic aim of the Baghdad government until Kuwait succeeded where it had failed. Equally, there was in Iraq now a sense that something, anything, had to be done to show that the country was still capable of fighting. In April, Syria had closed down the pipeline from the Kirkuk oilfields to the Mediterranean, assured of its own oil supplies and credit from Iran. Iraq felt that it had to react in kind, and so announced that it was targeting Iran's economic infrastructure, an offensive which was not to become serious for another two years.

In August 1982 Iraqi planes three times raided Kharg Island but, despite the claims of heavy damage inflicted, appeared to have had little effect on the sixteen loading quays there. The Iranians had installed formidable anti-aircraft defences around the terminal, forcing the Iraqi pilots to go in high and make their attacking runs without much preliminary reconnaissance. Although little damage was done to Kharg, the Iraqi campaign did frighten the shippers, with insurance rates soaring and crews chary of making the run to Kharg; in the first month of the new Iraqi campaign, Iranian oil exports fell from 1.8 million b/d (barrels per day) during July to 700,000 b/d during the second half of August. With the world oil glut beginning, Iraq calculated that action against Kharg or against tankers bound to Iran would halt that country's exports, and thus make it impossible for it to prosecute the war by destroying its economic capabilities and cutting its revenues.

Iran countered this effectively by a massive discount on the world price, at times as high as $3 a barrel, so that the Iraqi threats were soon seen to be hollow as Kharg continued to operate and owners had no difficulty in finding ships to send there. Then, as so often, Iran did the wrong thing. Officials in Tehran started taking the matter as seriously as the Iraqis did, and threatening retaliation: if Iranian ships and ships bound to Iran could not use the Gulf, or if Iran could not export its oil, then nor would anyone else, they said. With the Iranian navy in control of the Strait of Hormuz, the narrow waterway through which 10 million barrels of oil passed each day for the Western world, outside powers took the statements from Tehran more literally than they had taken the Iraqi threats. The war was back on the front pages and on the minds of Western statesmen.

In Washington, the Americans began talking about the principle of freedom of navigation and said that they were considering holding manoeuvres in the Gulf – with Oman – as a sign that they would not stand idly by if any attempt were made to close the Strait. In London, contingency plans were drawn up to run escorted convoys through the Gulf, but were not to be put into effect for another five years. Just as the world had learned to live with the war on the land, so very quickly it also learned to live with the war at sea. Crews of merchant ships began earning two and three times their normal pay for the time they spent in the Gulf, Iranian discounts on the oil it sold made lifting it worth while, and at the same time Iran began chartering its own tankers in preparation for moving its main terminals to the southern end of the waterway. The flurry caused by Iraq's premature announcement of its exclusion zone around Kharg Island quickly faded as it was realised that Iraq did not have the means to enforce it, or to deliver the kind of blow which would knock Kharg out. The hastily-made plans for convoys and manoeuvres were quietly put back on the shelf.

In Baghdad, Saddam Hussein had to re-establish his authority after effectively allowing the RCC and the military to take over for a week or two – as the ceasefire offer was made and Saddam Hussein remained invisible. Now, the dictator had to re-exert control, and he did it by his usual mixture of terror and political machinations. First, a wide-ranging purge of the party and the senior command of the army was initiated: the doubters who had been the most active and the most vocal in arguing for the ceasefire with Iran were the first to go, then those who at some stage had expressed doubts about the conduct of the war. Senior officers who had complained of the lack of air cover for their troops, or the shortage of weapons, were dismissed, and throughout the country the local Ba'ath organisation was overhauled, streamlined and purged of those who might cause trouble.

The President was able to get away with it at a time of defeat for his armies and personal loss of stature because of the intricately interwoven nature of his administration: those closest to him at the top of the structure were not only the party activists who had grown up with him in the service of the Ba'ath, they were also usually from his own clan, or at least from the provincial town of Tikrit which provided the core leadership of party and state. Saddam Hussein relied on ties of blood and of shared experience, but just as potent a binding force was the knowledge shared by those closest to him that if the leader fell, then so too did they. The years of oil wealth meant that mere membership of the party was rewarding, and to be an official or a politician carried real benefits and privileges. But just as Saddam Hussein had insisted when he took over

that his colleagues should join him in forming an execution squad –
and letting that fact be publicly known – so always he ensured that
people realised there was a collective responsibility for the way the
country was run, that all party members shared in the decision-
making process, and had a hand in the executions carried out, the
purges, tortures and disappearances.

It was a difficult trick for Saddam to pull off, for he had to
spread the fear of retribution among his comrades if he should
fall, yet to appear to the mass of the people to be the supreme
commander, the one fount of patronage as well as the father-figure
who would punish as well as reward. Before 1982, and the changes
he initiated, Saddam Hussein had not quite got it right – he was
not seen by the people as he wanted to be seen – but with his
reforms at a time of defeat he refined his system and style of
government and concentrated absolute control in his own hands
while allowing the appearance and trappings of power to those
around him. It was not something thought out, but the instinctive
actions of the natural politician Saddam Hussein had always been.
And as those closest to the leader saw the success of his methods,
they adopted the same tactics, so that there were ever-widening
circles dependent on the continuation of the established order,
men who would fall just as fast and as far as the leader if the man
at the top were removed.

Having successfully completed his purge, which included the
execution of a few generals said to have failed in their duties –
men considered powerful and dangerous enough to present a
threat – Saddam Hussein set about overhauling the party structure
to ensure even closer control. He called a special meeting of the
Regional Command of the party, that is, the national or Iraqi
section as opposed to the pan-Arab. At this Ninth Party Congress
Saddam Hussein was confirmed in his absolute control of the
machinery of government, and given the vote of confidence he
sought to continue his autocratic ways. The opposition had been
weeded out, and any who still had doubts quickly realised they
had better keep quiet and go along with the majority, the wary
but committed party men who had decided that loyalty to Saddam
Hussein gave the better prospect of success, rather than any
adventures with other personalities or other methods. After two
years in which the Shia had put nationalism first, and neither the
dissidents of Dawa, nor the communists or the Kurds had been

able to have any effect on the regime, only a *coup* mounted from within the heart of the party, or a widespread plot within the army, could have toppled Saddam Hussein.

Occasionally, such things were tried, and were quickly detected by the efficient, loyal and ever-watchful security apparatus. The following year Saddam Hussein's own half-brother Barzan Tikriti was involved in such an attempt, quickly suppressed, but in 1982 Saddam Hussein was in absolute control, using defeat to consolidate his hold on the party and the country, and playing on the nationalistic feelings of the people to mobilise them behind him for the defence of the state – which increasingly meant Saddam himself. One of his most important innovations was to slim the RCC down from fifteen to nine members, and to appoint six special 'advisers to the President' with the rank of minister, in effect signalling that all decisions would in future come from the Presidential Palace and that the party and the government were no more than instruments of the Presidency.

The final report of the Ninth Congress spelt it out in detail: 'Saddam Hussein is the symbol of freedom, independence, pride, integrity and hope for a better future for Iraq and the Arab nation.' From the Ninth Congress onwards the cult of the leader was given full rein. Not only did his picture appear everywhere – even the English-language newspaper in Baghdad read only by expatriates was ordered always to have a photograph of the President on the front page above the fold – but his words were also to be heard every day. If the great man was not speaking at that particular time, then old speeches were played over by Baghdad Radio; and every night on television there he was again, if not in the portly flesh, then in recordings of past appearances.

There was, too, a quite deliberate break with the earlier days of the state and the revolution. A new suburb of Baghdad built in the 1960s under the Qassem regime, and named Madinat al-Thawra – Revolution Township – was renamed Madinat Saddam. There was also now an open acceptance of the draconian punishments which had always been available and always used. Public decrees were issued imposing the death penalty for desertion from the army, defined as absence from a unit without leave for more than five days; this sanction was enforced with a particularly sadistic twist in certain cases where it was felt that an example was needed. The deserter was taken to his home village or suburb to be shot – and then his relatives were charged eleven Iraqi dinars for the cost of the ammunition used. But preserving the carrot-and-stick approach, the father who rewards as well as punishes, the families of those who fell in battle were well compensated. Officers' relatives were given cars and houses, and the dependants of private soldiers were allocated plots of land or cash sums. It was a system which worked well for a few years, until the casualties became too great for it to be continued, though even then families of the fallen were given priority for housing allocations; but while it lasted, it spread the wealth downwards through the poor Shia community in particular, and so helped the regime consolidate its hold.

The Iraqi pull-back from Iranian territory – the army's 're-deployment to the rear', in Saddam Hussein's marvellous phrase in the 4,000-word speech in which he announced what was happening – also had the effect of mobilising regional support for the regime. Arab leaders knew very well the extent of the setback, but far from shaking their support for President Hussein, it made them all the more eager to assure him of their continued help. King Hussein of Jordan immediately flew to Baghdad to show the Iraqis that the Kingdom remained their ally, and Prince Sultan, the Saudi Arabian defence minister, arrived with promises of more help. The rulers of the lower Gulf states, and particularly Kuwait, realised very well that they were in worse danger than ever with the Iranian forces on the Iraqi border. They knew, too, that Iraq was their only shield, though even then there were those in Kuwait who made little secret of their ambivalent attitude towards the Baghdad regime, and would have been happy to have found some alternative protector.

King Hussein had nailed his colours to the mast as soon as the war started, not only for the economic benefits to his country which its position brought, but also to consolidate his own position, to confirm his 'Arabism' after the difficult decade of the 1970s which had seen his battles with the Palestinians and his falling out with Syria, and to secure the backing of a powerful ally in case President Hafez Assad should again decide to intervene in Jordan. The King had even dispatched troops to Iraq with some fanfare, the so-called Yarmouk Brigade, but they were never in combat, merely supplementing the Iraqi training courses. The only 'foreign' Arabs who fought with the Iraqis were the Egyptians, both the thousands of Egyptian settlers forced into the Iraqi army and a considerable number of 'volunteers' from the Egyptian army seconded to Iraq.

Behind their own lines now, the Iraqis had little need of foreign manpower. Well dug in, their supply lines shortened, with plentiful stocks as the Russians quietly began a massive programme of resupply now that the Iraqis were out of Iranian territory, the Iraqi army was in a better position than ever before. The forward defences constructed by their engineers were constantly reinforced, with two other major defensive lines built in case there should be a need to fall back. Flying from Baghdad to Basra was like flying over a sand-table at a staff college: on the desert below could be seen the gun parks and the bunkers, the 'scrapes' bulldozed out to protect vehicles, the raised dykes topped with tarmac roads as the Iraqis prepared new areas to flood if there should be an Iranian breakthrough, the anti-aircraft guns around the towns, the missile sites out in the desert. On the eastern side of the Shatt opposite Basra, vast areas had already been inundated to form some of the biggest tank barriers ever made, while out in the desert where the shimmering heat haze of the summer played tricks with shapes and made it seem as if huge ships were approaching, the Iraqis formed their secondary defensive lines out of interlocking circular positions, laagers of earth with tanks and artillery inside, the field of fire of each one meshing with its neighbour.

Basra itself became one vast army camp, a military base as well as the country's second city, a place where life went on amid military occupation. As the fighting gradually drew nearer to Basra, many of the richer people decamped to Baghdad and their houses were taken over by the army; yet the size of the population remained the same, as thousands of Egyptians were drafted in to repair the hundreds of canals which criss-cross the town and which were regularly damaged by shell fire. Despite it all, the Iraqis demonstrated their faith that they could hold Basra by building a new hotel in the town, complete with swimming pool, a vast concourse for receptions, and cocktail bars manned by Filipino waiters. It was eventually so badly damaged that it had to be closed down, but for some years it was a symbol of confidence, just as the building programme in Baghdad was designed to reassure people at home and abroad that life was going on.

For a time, Baghdad was like a building site, and the people

joked that there were more cranes than palm trees as Saddam
Hussein ordered hotels and monuments in preparation for the
Non-Aligned Summit Conference he was so eager to host, a
meeting at which he hoped to take over the mantle of Nasser in
the Arab world, or Tito in the Non-Aligned Movement – and at
which, he secretly hoped too, his fellow rulers might come up
with a formula which would enable him to bring the whole costly
affair to an end, a compromise which the weight of Third World
opinion, including Muslim states, might force on the intransigent
old ruler in Tehran. It was not to be. With Iran warning the
statesmen of the Third World not to go to Baghdad, and clearly
having the means to make life uncomfortable if they did go there,
the conference was transferred to Delhi, and Saddam Hussein's
pleasure domes stayed empty.

Iran's 'Ramadan' offensive in July 1982, launched just after the
Iraqis had pulled out of all Iranian territory, was aimed at Basra.
It was halted with a huge toll of lives on both sides, but it was to
set the pattern for years to come: the Iranian strategy was to
invest the town and destroy its garrison or force it to surrender,
or to by-pass it and drive on to the west, effectively cutting Iraq
in two. The Iranian theory was that by seizing a sizeable slice of
territory in southern Iraq, the Shia heartland, it would be possible
to announce a provisional government to which the opponents of
Saddam Hussein could rally. At the same time, by cutting the
main route up from Kuwait, Iraq would be denied the large
amounts of material that came in through that port – Kuwait had
early on become an alternative to Basra, no matter how much the
Kuwaitis denied it. So as different attacks were launched in
different sectors, each one gaining a little ground and nibbling
away at the Iraqi border areas, the main Iranian strategy remained
constant: Basra was the first prize, the goal for which great
sacrifices would be made.

Around the world strategists shared the Iranian assessment, so
the more successes the Iranians achieved, the more the outside
powers were inclined to help Iraq. In the Western capitals certainly, and even in some quarters in the East, a consensus was
gradually emerging that Iran could not be allowed to win, and
that ultimately the Iranians would have to be prevented from
achieving any breakthrough. So it was that the Americans began
passing on to Iraq the intelligence they gained from their satellite

pictures, warning of Iranian troop concentrations or unexpected movements, and the Russians were soon back in their old role as Iraq's main suppliers, providing all the arms needed as the Gulf states made sure that Iraq was able to pay for its purchases, no matter what the state of the oil market.

At the beginning of the war, the oil producers of the lower Gulf were flush with money and Iraq itself was exporting all it could produce, then something like 3.7 million b/d to provide revenues of $25 billion. The development programme begun in Iraq in 1974 was stepped up at the beginning of the war, rather than being cut or modified. For internal and external reasons, Saddam Hussein had to try to pull off the trick of providing both guns and butter – in the early days of the war one of the many propaganda cartoons put out by the Ministry of Information showed two Iraqis in front of a portrait of the President. One says to the other: 'They say he's got hold of Aladdin's lamp. How else can he manage the war and all the building that's going on?' For a couple of years Saddam Hussein did manage it by using the Iraqi financial reserves, and through the aid given by Saudi Arabia and the other Gulf countries, which amounted to about $20 billion in the first three years of the war, by which time Iraq's oil exports had fallen to less than 1 million b/d. Unsure of the loyalty of the Shia, Saddam Hussein's concern in the early years was to keep his people happy, something he also tried to do by supporting the families of casualties; but he also wanted to win friends in the Non-Aligned Movement, so he sought influence there by awarding lucrative contracts to some of the developing countries, Yugoslavia in particular, a move also designed to enhance his prestige in the Arab world by portraying himself as a leader who could successfully manage the economy and the war. Preparations for the Non-Aligned Conference, the hotels, roads, conference halls and all the rest, took a huge slice of the available resources and turned Iraq into one of the most lucrative markets in the world where contractors were queuing up for the available jobs. An indication of the size of the market was that in the peak year, 1982, Iraq became the second most important British customer in the Middle East after Saudi Arabia.

Not for the first time, it was Syria which pricked the bubble, in this instance by the simple expedient of closing the Iraqi oil pipeline to the Mediterranean in 1982. With the southern outlets all blocked, Iraq was forced to rely on the one pipeline north through Turkey which had a capacity of only 500,000 b/d. In 1983 revenues from oil were down to about $7 billion, with the export of dates, Iraq's other main product, bringing in about another $80 million. The building boom collapsed, with severe losses for many contractors which forced their own governments to bail them out; but Iraq itself seemed untouched, largely because Saudi Arabia maintained its subsidy of about $1 billion a month, Saudi Arabia and Kuwait together donated the income derived from oil exported from the Neutral Zone to the war effort, and all three countries quietly, quickly and very efficiently began constructing an alternative network to Iraq's northern oil exporting lines. Pipelines were built to enable Iraqi oil to be fed into the Saudi system for export from Yanbu on the Red Sea, and the capacity of the Turkish line was increased to 1.5 million b/d in 1986, with a third line in prospect. By the time the war ended Iraqi exports were back to where they were in volume terms in 1980, though like all oil-exporting countries, Iraqi revenues were well down because of the collapse of the oil price.

During these same years OPEC saw its overall share of the world market shrink as consumers who had suffered two oil shocks diversified their sources of supply. This trend, coupled with a general decline of prices caused by the glut, panicked OPEC into going into battle for a larger share of the market. At the same time, Saudi Arabia, which had seen its production forced down during 1985 from a 4 million b/d target to little more than 2 million, abandoned its role as swing producer, so that oil flooded on to the world market to provoke a price collapse, with OPEC crude plummeting from $28 a barrel in November 1985 to $9 the following year. At the end of 1986 OPEC managed to halt the slide by reintroducing a tight production quota system, but was only able to institute a price of $18, a third less than pre-crash levels, and even then the deal was only possible because Iran was forced by other OPEC members to agree to Iraq remaining outside the compulsory quota system. The net result was economic belt-tightening in all the oil-producing states, but the consequences were particularly hard on Iran, which was already producing at the peak of its capacity and would now have to fight the war with strictly limited funds.

# 9

# Reluctant allies:
# the threat to
# the Arab Gulf

The ceremony which heralded the eventual defeat of Iran took place not in the Gulf, but out on the oily waters of the Arabian Sea, twenty miles off the port of Khor Fakhan. There, on Tuesday, 21 July 1987, a few Americans, Kuwaitis, Filipinos and other assorted seamen watched as the Stars and Stripes were hoisted aboard the tankers *al-Rekkah* and *Gas-al-Minagish*, which immediately became the *Bridgeton* and the *Gas Prince* respectively. This was the turning point which signalled that Iran would not be allowed to win, that America and the Soviet Union had decided to act together, and that the seven-year-old policy of avoiding involvement in the Gulf was finally being abandoned. The build-up to this low-key moment of decision had been a slow one, with America and Kuwait, the Soviet Union and the United Nations all engaged in a stately minuet of intentions as each party made sure the other knew what was happening, and was prepared to go along with it, to give support, or at least not to throw a spanner in the works.

From 1984 on, when Iraq began attacking Iranian tankers, the aim of the Baghdad government was to internationalise the conflict, to draw in America if possible, but certainly the Arab states of the Gulf, which were already supporting Iraq without being formally on its side. Iraq had no active navy, and so had somehow to arrange that others should do its work for it, restraining the Iranian navy and ensuring that shipping bound to or from the ports of Iraq's friends was able to pass in safety. By 1987 Iran had a more complicated role to play: above all, it wanted to export its oil through the Gulf, the only route it could command, but it also wanted to stop Arab ports, in Kuwait in particular but also in Saudi Arabia, from being used to supply Iraq. Equally, Iran did not want the great powers in the Gulf; Iran and Iraq were the regional powers, almost in balance, the one with naval supremacy and the other now with mastery of the air. The introduction of an outside force would be bound to tip that balance decisively one way or another.

From the beginning, both Iran and Iraq had ambivalent relations with the Gulf states, while the countries of the Arab littoral twisted and turned as they sought to accommodate both the regional superpowers. Geography played a large part in shaping the responses of the Arab countries – close proximity to the combatants made Kuwait more fearful than others of the consequences – but population make-up was just as important. In addition to being next door to Iraq and Iran, Kuwait had a 30 per cent Shia population, with the native-born forming only 40 per cent of the total, and a long-established group of residents of Iranian origin plus the powerful presence of some 250,000 Palestinians, a community which had close links with the PLO and access, it was assumed, to the extremist groups within that organisation.

Kuwait took the view that if Iran won, it was next on the list, a prize which Iran would take by open aggression if need be, or by internal subversion if that proved easier. Kuwait had no doubts where its immediate interests lay – in halting the spread of the Islamic revolution, cutting Khomeini down to size, and doing all it could to help the return of a more 'moderate' government in Tehran. Kuwait had to give wholehearted practical support to Iraq. Yet the decision to support Iraq was a fraught one, taken reluctantly and with full knowledge of the possible consequences – the Kuwaitis have always been acknowledged as the most accomplished politicians of the area. Kuwait's interest in stopping Iran was a short-term goal dictated by the imperative of national survival; the problem was that stopping Iran meant helping Iraq, seen by Kuwaitis as a threatening and intransigent neighbour potentially quite as dangerous as the mullahs in Tehran. So Kuwait's long-term objective was to protect itself against both the regional powers, and to do that it had to involve a third party.

Saudi Arabia was a possibility, but was only slightly less concerned than Kuwait about the consequences of a victory by Iran and, for all the build-up of its armed forces, never became a credible defender of the Gulf or even of itself. Only some 5 per cent of Saudi Arabians are Shia, concentrated mainly along the country's eastern seaboard and among the tribes of the central area, but they had an effect on the thinking of the Saudi government out of proportion to their numbers, particularly after the seizure of the Great Mosque at Mecca by a self-proclaimed – Sunni – Mahdi in 1979. At the same time, there was unrest among the Shia of the Eastern Province, and incitement from Iran to dissidents within the Kingdom to revolt. Throughout the years of the Gulf war, Ayatollah Khomeini and the leaders of the Islamic revolution cast the Saudis as the villains of the region, hypocrites who were not the true protectors of the holy places of Islam that they claimed to be. The Ayatollah referred to the Saudis dismissively as 'Wahhabis', as if that were an insult, and called their leaders 'palace dwellers', a more accurate and telling epithet.

The virulent Iranian campaign, which at its peak seemed to be making the overthrow of the Saudi regime a war aim on a par with the defeat of Iraq, did have an effect in the Kingdom, but not the one the Iranians wanted: instead of becoming more conciliatory, the Saudis became tougher, more self-confident and less prone always to seek compromise. One result of the Iranian strictures was to make Saudi leaders more concerned to give the appearance of devotion to Islam, so that King Fahd, for instance, decreed that he should no longer be referred to as 'King' but as 'Keeper of the Two Holy Places', a reference to Mecca and Medina – a title, incidentally, which was later amended to 'Servant of the Two Holy Places' to avoid all suggestion of proprietorship. The Saudis were quite consciously aligning themselves with the overwhelming majority of the Islamic world, where the Shia form only 10 per cent of the total, and with the Arab countries, where the Shia are in an even smaller minority. By their actions and attitudes, the Saudis were saying that it was the Persians who were the odd men out, the minority at war with the mainstream of Islam, the foreigners trying to invade and subvert the Arab nation.

The Kingdom was even firmer in its support of Iraq than Kuwait, not least because it was insulted from immediate contact with the combatants by its small neighbour, and by the vast distances between the rulers in Riyadh and the war on its frontier. It was also less fearful of the consequences of an Iraqi victory, confident that it could deal with any post-war adventurism from Baghdad with greater ease than it could contain the incitements to subversion which came from Tehran. The Kingdom did take practical steps as well as emphasising its devotion to Islam: it sought the most modern equipment for its armed forces from whatever source was best able to supply it. Thus traditional dependence on America was broken when Saudi Arabia ordered Tornado aircraft from Britain, with all the back-up equipment needed.

One reason for turning to Britain was annoyance at the actions of the American Congress in banning or holding up certain arms sales because, it was claimed, they might be used against Israel, not Iran. Later, there was a deliberate policy of diversification, of changing from the United States to other suppliers for practical reasons, and to demonstrate that the Kingdom was not a client state of America. There was both annoyance and unease in Washington when it was discovered that the Saudis had, in 1988, secretly bought surface-to-surface missiles from the Chinese, a move made as a result of the concern caused in the Kingdom at the use by both Iran and Iraq of rockets against each other's cities. The Saudis felt they had to have their own deterrent capability after seeing the devastation caused to their two neighbours.

The result of the Saudi arms build-up should have been to make the Kingdom a third force in the Gulf, a counterweight to either Iran or Iraq, and this was certainly one intention when Saudi Arabia took the lead in establishing the Gulf Co-operation Council, the six-country alliance which was the first reaction of the lower Gulf states to the outbreak of fighting in the north. But the primary function of the GCC was to have been to deal with internal troubles, to prevent known agitators travelling freely, to pool intelligence, and to deal with dissidence in any of the member countries. As the GCC evolved and the differences which had separated its members at the beginning were gradually ironed out, a defensive pact was agreed, with an attack on any state being construed as an aggression against them all. A regional 'Rapid Deployment Force' was established, but it was always recognised that the GCC countries would never be able on their own to contain or deter an attack by one of the regional superpowers – Iran, Iraq or even Israel, which at times made menacing comments about the bases being set up in the northern part of Saudi Arabia.

The great hindrance to the Gulf states, and the reason that Saudi Arabia itself could not become a military power to match Iran or Iraq, was the lack of manpower. The population of Saudi Arabia was no more than 11 million, and though service in the armed forces was considered by the Bedouin to be a respectable occupation, the demand for Saudi nationals in all the professions meant that the army was not given high priority by the brightest and best. In an attempt to overcome this, the Kingdom made a deal with Pakistan, which at one time had an infantry division stationed near the Yemen border, as well as supplying technical officers to the Saudi army. But once the war began, the Pakistanis could envisage a situation in which they might be called upon to repel Iranian invaders, and as they found themselves pursuing the same policies as Iran in their response to the Soviet occupation of Afghanistan, that was something they could not risk. The Pakistanis pulled out, and negotiations to replace them with Egyptians came to nothing.

As the Iranians surveyed the Gulf from north to south, so their resentment and animosity towards the Arab states diminished from Kuwait down to Oman. Kuwait was considered by the Iranians as a full partner with Iraq in the war, the country whose ports had been opened to Iraqi arms and whose territory was regularly over-flown by the Iraqi air force as its planes attacked targets in the Gulf. Saudi Arabia was an enemy, but not quite in the same league as Kuwait, while Qatar and the United Arab Emirates were considered merely misguided, small countries led astray by their powerful neighbour. Dubai, with its traditional links with Iran, was a valuable entrepôt, and the dhow trade from the Dubai creek to Iran flourished throughout the war, sometimes legally, sometimes in smuggled goods as the Iranians tried to prevent the import of items considered either blasphemous – videos, music tapes – or unnecessary luxuries which the hard-pressed economy could not afford.

Oman, right at the south of the Gulf, had the best relations of all with Iran, though its small navy shared with the Iranians control of the Strait of Hormuz, while Bahrain, for all Iran's past claims to the territory, was regarded more with sorrow than anything else. The Iranian attitude was that the good Shia, 80 per cent of the population, were suppressed by the Sunni ruling group, who were in turn under the domination of Saudi Arabia, particularly from 1984 onwards, after the causeway linking the two countries was completed. The Bahrainis took a different view. The detection and suppression of an attempted *coup* in the island – directed and supplied by Iran – at the end of 1981 was an early success by the GCC, and from then on Iranian attempts to subvert the Shia population of Bahrain never had any effect. The ruler, Sheikh Isa bin Khalifa, remained personally popular and accessible to his people despite some poor government appointments, and as the war failed to have much impact the Bahrainis became more self-confident, allowing the American navy to use the facilities at the Jufair shore base abandoned by the British, and regularly giving port facilities to the ships of the Western flotillas which eventually moved into the Gulf.

The situation in Bahrain was a lesson for the Iranians. With 80 per cent of the island Shia, a large expatriate community, reasonable prosperity and, as it appeared from Tehran, close police control of the people, the Iranians saw Bahrain as a natural place for the Islamic revolution to spread, so in the early days militant mullahs were sent to Bahrain, often secretly or in the guise of businessmen, and contacts were made between them and the tiny number of activists contacted through the mosques. No success was achieved. In every case, their emissaries were soon picked up and deported, with no fuss. Even more tellingly, these Iranian envoys failed to strike a spark among the Bahrainis: they were listened to with respect for what they were, but there was no welcome for their message. For all the occasional unrest of the past, the Bahrainis were now reasonably prosperous and reasonably content, and in no mood for desperate adventures.

Bahrain remained quiet and increasingly Western-oriented as the war went on, with its confidence strengthened by its physical link with Saudi Arabia along the causeway first mooted by King Saud in 1950, initiated by King Feisal in 1965, and completed by King Fahd in 1982, for the system of bridges and embankments was more than a quick and easy way to travel from the islands of Bahrain to the mainland. It was also a symbol of Saudi Arabia's decision to exert itself as a power in the Gulf, and it set the boundary between the Arabic west and the Persian east down the middle-line of the waterway, not as before on the Saudi shore. If trouble came to Bahrain, Tehran was implicitly warned, it would be Saudi tanks and troop-carriers using the causeway instead of vegetable lorries and tourists.

In the first years of the war, once the tide of battle had turned and the Iraqis had been expelled from Iranian territory, the Gulf states were treated with something like contempt by the politicians in Tehran. They made no effort to win them over, nor did they bother to disguise the Iranian influence behind various acts of terrorism which occurred, particularly in Kuwait, the state they had elevated to a position of co-belligerent with Iraq. In 1983 a series of bomb attacks in Kuwait City shook the Emirate more than any event of the past. The French and American embassies, the airport and a power station were the targets, with five people killed and more than sixty injured. The Kuwaiti police had no doubt who was responsible: hundreds of Shia were rounded up, and eventually seventeen of them were tried and convicted after admitting that they were members of Dawa.

At the same time, hundreds, perhaps thousands, of others were quietly deported to Iran at the beginning of a campaign which was to be pursued for years, and which divided the Kuwaitis into second- and first-class citizens more effectively than the legislation allowing only the native-born to vote. For the Kuwait authorities now openly identified the Shia population of the state as a fifth column, allies of Iran waiting for the right moment to strike, to extend the Islamic revolution to the Emirate by subversion from within as well as pressure from outside. In many cases that was true, but by their actions the Kuwait government drove many loyal Shia into the embrace of fundamentalism. Certainly many Kuwaiti Shia supported Khomeini and would have welcomed an Iranian victory; it was never difficult to find members of all classes who would say in private that they were biding their time in the hope of the victory of Islam, but it was equally possible to find Kuwaiti Shia who were totally loyal to the state and the Emir and viewed with considerable distaste the regime in Iran.

By the policy of deportation of suspects, of moving Shia from sensitive posts to less prestigious ones, and above all by making it plain that the whole Shia community was suspect, the Kuwaitis alienated a large proportion of their own population, and made it all the easier for the Iranian extremists to recruit their agents in the Emirate. Yet it was a dilemma which the Kuwaitis could not resolve, a situation made much worse by the car-bomb attempt on the Emir's life in 1985, or the sabotage attempts at oil instal-lations which followed.

Nor were the Kuwaitis helped by the Iraqis. Saddam Hussein spoke as early as 1981 of 'leasing' Bubiyan Island, something the Iranians warned would be regarded as a hostile act. When a few years later Kuwait announced that this island at the mouth of the

Shatt had been 'militarised' and barred to visitors, Iranian protests were ritual only, as the Iranians realised as well as anyone else that the Kuwaiti move was a signal to Iraq not to interfere rather than a real defence against Iranian invasion. For Kuwait was in many ways like Lebanon, relying on its weakness for its defence, knowing that it did not have the means to protect itself and so relying on others to come to its aid if necessary. Like Lebanon, too, the deep divisions between the various communities carried the threat of civil strife, though the Kuwaitis were politically more mature than the Lebanese, and looked constantly for ways to prevent tension and avoid any show-down. Cushioned by vast wealth – Kuwait has one of the highest *per capita* incomes on earth – the Kuwait authorities were remarkably successful in maintaining the *status quo*, but at the cost of alienating the Shia population in a way which will take generations to overcome.

The Kuwaitis were always clear that they had made the right decision in backing Iraq in 1980, accepting that Iran was the immediate threat, but they were equally clear from the start that eventually they would have to have some means of curbing Iraq if that country should turn out to be the victor. The Kuwaitis, active in the GCC, hoped that that organisation might do collectively what its individual members could not, but quickly became disillusioned with the defence potential of the alliance, and began to look elsewhere. Kuwait had always had diplomatic relations with the Soviet Union and China as well as America, and so naturally began thinking of how to get one or other involved; but in the early years of the war this seemed impossible. Both Russia and the United States had proclaimed their neutrality – it was not until 1982 that America showed the first signs of an eventual tilt to Baghdad by allowing the Iraqi government credits to purchase American goods, and only in 1984 did the Americans re-establish diplomatic relations.

The euphoria of those first Iraqi successes quickly wore off in Kuwait and was replaced by growing concern as the war turned against Iraq and gradually, mile by bloody mile, the Iranians carried the conflict ever closer to the border. After driving out the Iraqi invaders in the spring of 1982, Iran had only limited successes the following year, concentrated mainly in the north and central areas, with one major gain when it captured Haj Omran, once the stronghold of Mulla Mustafa Barzani in his fight for independence from Iraq, now an Iraqi army base from which

Kurdish guerrillas fighting for the Baghdad government were armed and directed. But it was in the south that Iran consistently made its main effort, throwing tens of thousands of *basij* and Pasdaran into the battles there, with the army often kept in reserve to exploit any openings gained by the human-wave tactics of the irregulars. Satellite pictures showed that at times the Iranians had as many as 150,000 men opposite Basra, always the first prize in the struggle for control of southern Iraq. Against all the military rules they were able to keep the volunteer battalions encamped close to the frontier while launching probing attacks, swiftly changing the apparent direction of their main offensives, and generally keeping the Iraqis off balance.

But just as the Iranians were building up their forces, improving their techniques and insisting on better liaison between the army, the Pasdaran and the *basij*, so the Iraqis were constantly improving their defences, flooding new areas, reinforcing their front lines and constructing rear-support facilities and fall-back positions. With Soviet arms again available almost on demand, there was no shortage of artillery or armour, and at the same time the Iraqis were gaining the upper hand in the air, as the Iranians ran short of spares for their American planes.

After their failure to achieve the swift victory expected, the Iraqis had, as we have seen, to face an economic problem they had not anticipated: unable to export their oil through the Gulf as they had in the past, they were left with only the one small-capacity pipeline to Turkey, and even that was threatened by the battles with the Kurds in the north. There were sufficient reserves, but as it became clear that the war might grind endlessly on, new measures had to be taken, and an early decision was made to double the capacity of the pipeline to the Mediterranean and to link into the Saudi network in the south. There was a comparable problem in Iran, and one of the odder aspects of the economies in both Iran and Iraq was the contrasting methods each government used to raise extra cash. In Tehran, the mullahs announced that the Crown Jewels would be sold, the fabulous treasure amassed by Iranian rulers over the centuries, including the Peacock Throne and hundreds of exotic pieces of jewellery which used to be one of the tourist attractions of the Iranian capital. In fact, nothing appears to have been done, largely because right up to the end Iran was solvent; one of the strengths of the Iranian clandestine arms-buying missions was that payment was always offered in cash, and was made promptly and fully. Even at the end of the war, Iran's credit remained good, and suggestions of selling national treasure was no more than internal propaganda to demonstrate the seriousness of the situation.

In Baghdad, the difficulty was real, with the crunch coming in 1983 when Iraqi oil exports were at their lowest – oil pumped was at a third of the pre-war level, and at the same time falling prices were bringing on the recession in the Gulf, so that Iraq's backers were more reluctant than in the past to send the large donations needed. One Iraqi response, just as in Tehran, for psychological as well as practical reasons, was to call on the people of the country to donate their personal jewellery and savings to the nation, 'to allow women or elderly people to take part in the battle for the homeland, each according to his or her ability', according to the official announcement. Taha Yassin Ramadan put it more distinctly: 'This is more a referendum in favour of the party,' he said, as women queued to hand over gold necklaces. 'It is more a referendum in favour of the revolution and the leadership of President Saddam Hussein than a source of revenue or currency cover.' Yet the response was immense, and even as we watched peasant farmers donating their life savings or elegant Baghdad ladies carrying their Moroccan leather jewel cases into the collecting centres, it was impossible to tell how much was being done out of patriotism and how much because non-compliance would bring retribution, or at least discrimination from the party.

The finance minister, Thamir Razzouki, seemed as surprised as outsiders at the amount collected: 'The response has been so great that the gold amassed will be an extra reserve to strengthen the Iraqi currency,' he said. Night after night on Iraqi television pictures were shown of the donations coming in: smart businessmen writing cheques, the ladies with their jewellery, and farmers arriving with bundles of crumpled notes – one was so impressed with the President that after handing over his money he went back and said he was giving his Mercedes as well. In theory, all the money and valuables handed over were merely on loan for the duration of the war, and would be handed back or credits given when the war ended. Nothing has yet been heard of any move in that direction.

Iraqi success in halting the Iranian advance, the continued backing of the Gulf states, the news of the situation in Iran and the demonstrations of 'steadfastness' on the home front all contributed to a slow but steady improvement in Iraqi morale after the disasters of 1982, and increased confidence from commanders aware that the penalties for failure might be much worse than mere loss of command. Now a new breed of Iraqi general began to appear, militarily competent, often flamboyant like General Maher Abdul al Rashid of the Seventh Corps, or not afraid to indulge a taste for luxury, like General Balah al Durri of the Third Corps. The generals were still firmly subject to political control – with few exceptions, generals were changed round about every eighteen months – and army officers never made it to the top of the party, even after they had retired; but the commanders were able to insist that they were running the war, not the politicians. Saddam Hussein now rarely spent long at meetings of the Supreme Defence Council, and though he often visited the front it was plain that his trips were to raise morale among the troops, and the fiction of Saddam Hussein personally directing successful operations was quietly dropped.

While Iraq tried to sort out its internal problems, Iran stepped up its effort on land, the one area in which it had a clear superiority through its pool of manpower, several times that available to Iraq. For more than a year the Iranian leaders had been pursuing a policy of attrition, hoping to wear Iraq down by repeated small-scale attacks, proclaiming that the aim was the destruction of the Iraqi war machine, while in fact retaining the main objective of getting rid of the government in Baghdad. Now in February and March 1984, the Iranians decided to make a major effort, and after diversions on the northern front, launched two offensives on the vital southern sector in quick succession, Val Fajr VI and Khaibar. The human-wave tactics and the unorthodox switches of emphasis enabled the Iranians to get through the Iraqi defences, but the reserve lines proved their worth, halting the Iranian push and enabling the Iraqis to launch counter-attacks which forced the Iranians back in all but one sector, the Majnoon marshes.

It was in the battle for the marshes that Iraq first used gas on a large scale, after its small field test on the southern front two years earlier, but in some ways it was counter-productive. Certainly the first widespread use came as a surprise to the Iranians, and caused heavy casualties, yet the conditions were not right; some blew back on the Iraqi troops, and Iran was able to hold on to its gains in the marshes. It was also able to learn from what had happened. A year later when Iraq again used gas, the Iranians were prepared: all the front-line troops were equipped with good West German respirators and with personal phials of Atropin, the drug used to counter nerve gases. The Iranian commanders learnt fast, and the Iranian arms buyers always managed to find what was needed.

As the Iranian attacks, so costly to both sides, foundered on the seemingly impregnable Iraqi defences, the Iraqi leaders were gradually persuaded that their army would stand firm, and that they need not fear an Iranian breakthrough. But that was not enough: still beleaguered, still fighting a war which was decimating the population and preventing all development, somehow the Iraqi leadership had to find a way of bringing it to an end. No offers of an accommodation came from Tehran. Ayatollah Khomeini injected the personal venom he felt for Saddam Hussein into his pronouncements, and made plain his determination to see the fall of 'the Iraqi dictator' and the dismantling of the Ba'ath structure before he would agree to any compromise. Something extra was needed, and with their new confidence that the army could withstand the Iranian attacks, even with the huge toll of human life on both sides, the Iraqis began to move the focus from land to sea.

So in March, with the Iranians halted for the time being, the Iraqis made a new bid to internationalise the war, serving formal notice that they intended to attack the Kharg Island terminal and the ships serving Iran. The tanker war was launched, and in the first months some seventy ships were hit. Iran was bound to react but, given Iraqi air superiority and the absence of any Iraqi ships in the Gulf, could only retaliate against the 'neutral' targets of Iraq's allies, the Gulf states whose oil also went out by sea. The initial Iranian calculation was that Kuwait and Saudi Arabia, Iraq's two main financial backers as well as the countries through which supplies reached Baghdad, would put pressure on Iraq to stop attacking Iranian tankers once their own trade was affected; but Saudi Arabia was enjoying one of its closest relationships with America, and that country was just beginning to show signs of moving away from neutrality to support of Iraq.

Instead of reining in Baghdad, on 4 June 1984, Saudi Arabian fighters shot down an Iranian F4 attempting to attack a target in Saudi territorial waters, an unprecedented show of daring by the ever-cautious Saudis, while Washington acknowledged that this small but significant air battle had been directed from one of the Saudi AWACS planes manned by American personnel. Instead of bluster and threats, Tehran responded with moderation; it protested to Riyadh, of course, but the protest was well within international norms, and there was a notable lack of the usual bombast. Iran was beginning to feel isolated, and instead of issuing threats in the hope of preventing the Gulf states from siding with Iraq, it began to take a much more gentle approach with the aim of maintaining, at least, the official neutrality which the Arab states of the Gulf had so far practised.

With the Iranian thrust blocked, Basra for the first time was exposed to shelling by the Iranians, something they had avoided in the past. Basra was not only the second city of Iraq, it was the biggest Shia centre in the country, and the Iranians avoided attacking it as long as they felt there was still a chance of the Iraqi Shia heeding Ayatolla Khomeini's calls to them to revolt against Baghdad. Now it was plain even to the Iranians that any hopes of an internal uprising in Iraq had to be abandoned. The result was the beginning of the regular bombardment of the city, a steady pounding which never brought its life to a stop, but which did in the end reduce much of it to rubble.

Iraq's first threats to attack Kharg Island and Iran's economic infrastructure were almost as hollow as its declaration of the exclusion zone in the north of the Gulf. Iraqi planes did make a few raids, but the Iranian defences were good, little damage was done and the Iranians were always able to make quick repairs. The Iraqis needed planes from which more powerful missiles could be launched, so in 1983 they concluded an odd deal with France to lease five Super Etendard planes – the French said they needed the planes back as they were no longer being produced, though what would have happened if they had all been shot down was not clear. By October 1983 the Iraqi pilots, trained by the French airmen who delivered the planes, began the new offensive against Iranian terminals and tankers, though it was not until the middle of 1985 that the Iraqi air force felt strong enough to launch a real assault against the Iranian facilities, with a concentrated series of raids against Kharg Island in September that year. With the Super Etendard planes and with Exocet missiles, also supplied by France in 1983, as well as the less effective Soviet-supplied air to surface weapons, Iraq was able to inflict serious demage on

Iran's oil-loading capacity, and to hit its tankers almost at will. Aware of what was brewing, the Iranians had threatened to 'close the Strait to all shipping' if their merchant fleet was attacked, but it soon became clear that this was something beyond their capacity.

Instead, Iran responded to the massive Iraqi attacks of August 1985 by exercising its right to stop and search vessels suspected of carrying arms to Iraq, a policy it had announced in July but only put into force now that it was under pressure. It was a practice to which it was entitled under international law, but it was clear that the application was now intended to make life more difficult for ships using the Gulf, a policy of harassment to back up its by now regular retaliatory strikes against ships sailing to Kuwait or occasionally to Saudi Arabia. Iran invoked accepted international law to stop, search, and sometimes impound ships passing through the Strait of Hormuz. It was a risky policy which was bound to bring it into conflict with outside powers, and could give excuses to some to intervene if they wanted to do so.

As early as 1980 Britain had formed a naval squadron for the Gulf – the oddly-named Armilla Patrol, incidentally, was so-called merely because that was the next name available in the book of code-words – while America had had a small presence since British withdrawal from the area in 1971. France now had a couple of ships there, and the small Omani navy – usually with British commanders – regularly patrolled the Strait. To stop and search ships which might be carrying war material to an enemy was legally permitted, but clearly could be used to cause trouble, to score points or to try to deter some shippers or ship-masters from trading in the region. In the event, like so many other things which looked dangerous, Iranian actions provoked few confrontations.

Constantly under pressure on land, Iraq realised that its one hope of forcing Iran to the negotiating table lay in the Gulf, and so maintained the pressure. By the beginning of 1988 Iraq had launched attacks against 189 tankers, with 164 of the targets being damaged, while Iran had answered with 171 strikes which hit 127 ships. All this had an effect. Insurance rates rose, and such costs as crew wages rose with them, while at a time of oil glut and worldwide lack of demand even the massive Iranian discounts did not make it easy to sell on the world market – other countries too were discounting to maintain their revenues. So to make things a little easier for shippers, Iran set up a new oil terminal at Sirri in 1986, chartering some of the world's biggest ships to act as floating storage tanks there, while also chartering its own fleet of tankers to run the shuttle from Kharg Island down to the new loading point.

Even that was not safe. On 12 August 1986, Iraqi planes bombed three of the Iranian tankers at Sirri, having refuelled in mid-air, according to the Iraqi announcement. There was some scepticism in Iran, and charges that the Iraqis had been given facilities in Saudi Arabia. At times that was true, but it was also true that the Iraqis had converted a couple of their Antonov transports to have a refuelling capability. As a result of this August attack, Iran moved its terminal to Larak Island so that ships would be under the protection of the anti-aircraft batteries around Bandar Abbas.

The new Iraqi policy did have an effect, for all the lack of determination which seemed to characterise it in the early days, at least, when attacks were not followed up, Iran was regularly given time to repair damage, what seemed to be sustained campaigns of air attack were unaccountably broken off, and pilots did not press home their attacking runs. There were reasons for all this. Iraq wanted to preserve its air force, it had no surplus of pilots, but above all it feared Iranian retaliation if it went beyond a certain point. Perhaps most important of all, Iraq was kept in check by its Gulf allies: Kuwait, Saudi Arabia and the Emirates in particular feared that if Iraq went too far, Iran would answer not with attacks against tankers, but by destroying their production capacity. Kuwait knew that it was always vulnerable to missile attacks. The Saudis feared that Iran might do among the Shia of the Eastern Province what it had shown it could do in Kuwait, and arrange for installations to be sabotaged. The Emirates felt most vulnerable of all with so much of their production coming from off-shore platforms, totally at the mercy of the Iranian navy.

So the Iraqi campaign was kept at what was felt to be an 'acceptable' level, damaging but not deadly – enough, Iraq hoped, to bring Iran to the negotiating table but not so damaging that it would push it over into all-out war. And at times it seemed to be working. In the first month of relatively sustained Iraqi attacks on Kharg Island, Iranian exports fell from 1.5 million b/d to only 1 million. Coming on top of the 10 per cent revenue drop caused earlier by the need to discount so heavily, this was a bad blow to the Iranian economy, and thus to its ability to wage war, for all the constant pressure it was maintaining on land.

From 1984 Iran and Iraq pursued 'the tanker war' with varying degrees of ferocity. Finally realising that it had control of the skies, Iraq committed its air force much more than in the past, developing the ability to carry out long-range raids against the new Iranian oil installations at the southern end of the Gulf – the 1983 arrival of the French Super Etendards gave the Iraqis the capacity to use the Exocet missiles they had already bought, then from 1984 on regular deliveries of Mirage F1s with in-flight refuelling capability enabled them to threaten the whole Gulf.

The only response Iran could make was to strike 'neutral' ships, particularly those sailing to or from Kuwait, by now placed only slightly lower than Iraq in the Iranian scale of demonology. Iran also threatened to close the Strait of Hormuz, without ever actually attempting to do so – something which in any case would have been difficult given the wide channels and the difficulties of mining in deep waters. This appeared to be part of Iran's effort to put pressure on the Arab Gulf countries to force Iraq to stop its attacks in case their own exports were interrupted. The Iranian navy had always been active in the southern Gulf, stopping and searching ships, but in 1986 pressure was increased when a missile was fired into the crew quarters of the Panamanian tanker *Five Brooks*. This was the first Iranian response to Iraq's long-distance raids on the Iranian storage facilities at Sirri and Larak which began on 12 August 1986.

Kuwait remained the main culprit as far as Iran was concerned, and tankers bound for Kuwait suffered most. It was at this point that Kuwait began the quiet negotiations which were to shift the balance of power in the Gulf when it approached the United States to ask for protection for its twenty-two-strong tanker fleet. The way to assure this, the Kuwaitis suggested, would be for all its ships to be put under the American flag, obliging the US navy to afford them protection. The Iranians made major pushes in the land war in 1986 and 1987, and scored some of their biggest victories opposite Basra in their Kerbala series of operations, getting closer and closer to Basra and taking Fao to bring them within striking distance of Kuwait.

America was slow to take up the Kuwaiti suggestion of re-flagging, and it appeared that the American ambassador in Kuwait had been told to stall. There were all kinds of legal difficulties, he pointed out: the Stars and Stripes could only be

flown on ships with American masters, and that would mean
formal registration in America with all the examinations and
stipulations demanded by the regulating authority, the Coast-
guard. The Kuwaitis smiled politely, said little, and began talking
to the Russians, who had always had diplomatic relations with
Kuwait, the only Gulf state until 1987 to allow them an embassy.
The Russians saw the possibilities more quickly than the Americans, and immediately offered to charter three of their own
tankers, with Russian crews, to the Kuwaitis – those ships would
of course enjoy the protection of the Soviet navy, the ambassador
said.

The Kuwaitis did not go out of their way to let the Americans
know this, relying instead on the US embassy's very good information network in the Emirate. Very soon, the Americans got
the message, but still there was opposition from Congress and
from some sections of the American public concerned at getting
involved once again in a far-off war in which American interests
were difficult to identify. The Kuwaitis quietly stepped up the
pressure to test the new-found resolve, after the attack on the
*Stark*, of the Reagan administration to become directly involved.
Sheikh Ali Khalifa, the quietly spoken oil minister, became more
accessible to the press than ever before: 'It is a purely American
business,' he said. 'It is up to the Congress to determine what is
in the best interests of the United States. . . . But if the Congress
decides the re-flagging should not go ahead, then we will have to
request other countries to help us protect our shipping. We would
be satisfied to get them re-flagged by the Soviet Union. . . .'
Sheikh Ali knew very well the pressure he was so discreetly
applying in Washington. The affair was given more urgency by
the discovery of mines in Kuwaiti waters. Both Iran and Iraq had
laid minefields in areas of the northern Gulf early in the war, and
some of these had often broken loose in storms and drifted south
into international waterways, but in a few weeks during May and
June four ships hit mines off Kuwait in what was seen as the first
indication that Iran was actually planning to try to block channels
used solely by 'neutral' shipping.

In Washington, the debate went on, and it was perhaps a symbol
of the uncertainty of those in charge that the plan was to re-flag
just half the Kuwaiti tanker fleet, though why eleven ships should
be less of a challenge than twenty-two was not explained. Gradu-

ally, too, the real motive emerged. For all the talk of maintaining the freedom of international navigation, administration spokesmen now talked openly of the need to prevent the Russians from taking over the Gulf. If America refused the Kuwaiti request, it would be a golden opportunity which the Soviet Union would immediately seize, the argument went, and there was much play on the increasing Soviet presence in the area, the diplomatic relations established with Oman and the Emirates, the Russian trade missions; even the *Tass* correspondents were seen as symbols of the evil empire. The Reagan of 1987 seemed to be adopting the language of the Nixon of the 1970s. It was a justification for what was being done; a change in American policy was being engineered, and there had to be a rationalisation.

President Carter had already laid down the fundamental American line in the area in his 1980 declaration aimed at the Soviet Union, but now there was a dawning realisation in Washington that the Soviet Union, too, had legitimate interests in the Middle East, even that it was to Moscow's advantage to have peace in the region. But because America was tilting, Russia had once again to be portrayed as a bear on the prowl, a predator waiting to slip into America's place if an opportunity were offered. It was nonsense, but it was the sort of nonsense which impresses congressmen, and the administration had to get backing for its decision to support Iraq, something which had been resisted over the years. In 1984 Richard Murphy, the Assistant Secretary of State, had testified to Congress that the administration believed a victory by either side in the Gulf war to be 'neither militarily feasible nor strategically desirable'. Gradually, this basic concept was moved on so that the American aim became to prevent Iran winning, an idea which carried with it the justification for more help for Iraq. Nothing could be allowed to stand in the way. It was in 1984, for instance, at a time when international concern was being expressed at Iraqi use of chemical weapons, that Washington and Baghdad renewed the diplomatic relations which had been cut in 1967. A decision had been taken.

Yet if Iran had to be stopped from winning, a way had also to be found to bring the conflict to an end, and for that the United Nations was used. As early as September 1980 the Security Council had passed the first resolution calling for an end to hostilities, and this Resolution 479 was followed over the years by Resolutions

514, 522, 540 and 552, all expressing pious hopes but little more. They addressed neither the Iranian demand that the aggressor should be identified, nor did they condemn the use of gas. In 1985 Perez de Cuellar became more directly involved, and that led to Resolution 582 in 1986, which did deplore the initial attack as well as calling for a ceasefire. And then at last, on 20 July 1987 came the Security Council resolution which was to be the final instrument enabling the conflict to be brought to an end – 598.

And in a very British way, it all began with a tea party. The British ambassador to the United Nations, Sir John Thompson, invited the representatives of the other permanent members of the Security Council – the United States, the Soviet Union, China and France – to join him for afternoon tea in his apartment overlooking the East river. Vernon Walters was there for America, the former general and secret agent who was always his country's top trouble-shooter, with the long-serving representatives of the other permanent members of the Security Council. And over the tea-cups, they worked out a strategy. In the debates they would all pay lip-service to the American idea of imposing an embargo on Iran if that country did not accept the peace call, though it was understood between them that in fact neither the Soviet Union nor the Chinese could go along with such a move. But the psychological effect of the threat, they believed, would achieve what they wanted: Iran would be forced to negotiate.

It did not work out quite like that, for there was no bargaining, but rather an Iranian collapse a year hence; yet it was the pressure quietly applied by these five professional diplomats which led to the Iranian collapse, for in the margins of their talks about the UN resolution, there were also quiet words about the need to prevent any more arms reaching the combatants. It had to be put in this way, but everyone knew that it was only Iran which was intended.

High above the East river, overlooking the UN building, the five men sipped their tea, nibbled at the delicate sandwiches handed around by the Filipino waiters, and quietly sealed Iran's fate. It was at this sophisticated and genteel tea party that the decision was finally taken that Iran could not be allowed to win the war.

# 10

# Secret
# arms deals

One of the early policy decisions of the military wing of the Ba'ath when they took over was to give Iraq a nuclear capability: it was, of course, to be peaceful, for research purposes only . . . Yet when Saddam Hussein was first put in charge of negotiations to obtain a reactor from France, the suspicion was that the Iraqis were considering nuclear weapons. They did sign the Nuclear Non-Proliferation Treaty, something which Israel steadfastly refused to do, but by 1975 when the first agreement was reached with France, suspicion began to harden into certainty as it was noted that France was to supply not only two reactors, but also 84 kilograms of highly enriched, weapons-grade uranium. From the moment news of the Iraqi–French deal leaked, Israel at least never had any doubt that Iraq intended to produce its own nuclear bombs. That conclusion was quickly passed on to the Shah, and in Iran, too, work was stepped up on the nuclear facility being built by the Germans at Bushehr.

The first steps had been taken towards the spread of nuclear arms in the Middle East – for it was a near-open secret that Israel possessed the weapons. And Israel intended to maintain its monopoly of the unique weapon it regarded as the ultimate deterrent; thus it was that the clandestine war began to try to stop Iraq going ahead with the project. At first, Israel seemed at a loss, and the only overt reaction was to publicise what was happening, seeking international pressure to halt the Iraqi nuclear programme. But Iraq always maintained that the programme was a peaceful one, that there was no cause for alarm, and that the work being done was open to inspection. That was eventually done: Iraq allowed inspectors from the International Atomic Energy

Authority access to the site of its Nuclear Research Institute, and those neutral inspectors consistently reported that they found no evidence of any misuse of materials provided. The Israelis – who would not even allow Norway to visit their Dimona plant, though it was a condition of Norway's supply of heavy water to them that they should be allowed to do so – replied that at the last minute Iraq would tear up its treaty, refuse to allow inspection and quickly begin producing bombs. Certainly the scale of the Iraqi work was enough to raise fears, particularly when in 1978 the Baghdad government concluded a deal with Italy for a radio-chemistry laboratory capable of extracting plutonium and other fission products from the used fuel, while also providing purified enriched uranium for re-use, both products used to manufacture weapons. At the same time, the reactors ordered from France had been manufactured and were awaiting delivery.

In April 1979 Israel decided that international pressure was not going to work, and it would have to take direct action: a commando squad of Israeli special agents was sent to Toulon to sabotage the reactors waiting there for shipment. They were only partially successful – the bombs they planted exploded and caused damage, but not enough to prevent the reactors from being shipped, merely to delay delivery. Next came the murder of the Egyptian head of the Iraqi nuclear research programme, Professor Yaha el Meshad, battered to death in room 1074 at the Meridien Hotel in Paris where he was negotiating Iraqi participation in Eurodif, the consortium set up to manufacture enriched uranium. Professor Meshad spent his last night with a French call-girl; she was run down and killed in the Boulevard St Germain the following week. In Rome, bombs went off in the offices of the company which had contracted to sell Iraq the hot-cell radio chemistry laboratory, while back in Paris another bomb blew out the shop front of a bookseller named Graf – also the name of the chief French scientist in charge of the team helping Iraq set up its nuclear facility on the banks of the Tigris fifteen miles from Baghdad. Some twenty others Grafs in the Paris telephone book received death threats over the next weeks.

News of the deal between France and Iraq caused a storm when all its ramifications became known – such as a clause in the agreement that neither side would speak publicly of the contract for twenty-five years, or that no Frenchmen of Jewish extraction were to be allowed to work on it. But for France the deal was worth more than £700 million in 1975; that was not something to be lightly discarded. President Giscard d'Estaing protested that he had not been told what was going on, the French Assembly noted that it had been kept in ignorance as there was no need for funds to be voted, and very soon the affair was forgotten. Except by Israel – and soon after the Gulf war broke out it made what appeared to be its first attempt to end the Iraqi nuclear capacity once and for all.

Two Phantoms with Iranian markings penetrated the Iraqi air defences by flying at minimum height, under the radar screen, to bomb the Osirak reactor – so named by the French, though the Iraqis called it Tammuz, after the ancient river god. On this occasion, the god of the Tigris protected the plant; the bombs did little damage and merely alerted the Iraqis to the need for additional defences around this important site. That may have been the intention: there were seventy French technicians still working at the site out of the 400 originally employed when this first raid was launched on 30 September 1980. Immediately afterwards the French pulled out most of them, and also moved their staff from living quarters close to the plant to accommodation in Baghdad. By this early and apparently abortive raid the attackers made sure that when the real strike went in, there would be few foreigners involved, thus minimising the risk of worsening relations with European countries, France in particular. The French and the Iraqis were given ten months to improve the defences, but seemed only to have taken particular precautions over the small amount of fissionable material then on site, about two kilos.

The real strike came on 7 June 1981, when fifteen Israeli planes were used, and this time made no mistake. Their bombs hit the target and, according to the video pictures taken by the attack group, destroyed the main part of the plant, the reactor itself and various other buildings. Fissionable material was not damaged in the raid, as it was stored in a deep underground canal some way away, in the subterranean link between the main reactor and the second, smaller installation. The Israeli story was that their planes had flown from Israel over Jordan, Saudi Arabia and Iraq without once being detected by hostile radar, and were refuelled in flight, a claim which even sympathetic American experts described as 'frankly incredible'. In fact, there can be little doubt that the raid was mounted from Iranian territory, perhaps the second reimbursement for Israeli supplies and help – the first was the trial raid by 'Iranian' planes against Osirak, that reconnaissance and warning by Israeli pilots on 30 September which paved the way for the real attack in 1981.

From the beginning, the anti-Israeli rhetoric of the mullahs was not matched by their practice. Iran had been armed by America, and so had to search the world for American spares for its planes, guns, tanks and armoured vehicles. Israel was both the nearest supplier, and the most willing: the 80,000 Jews in Iran gave the mullahs a hold over Israel that they were quite ready to exploit, while Israeli eagerness to see the Gulf war continue – to see two of their main potential enemies bleed each other to death – meant that Israel was a willing supplier.

In the event, the 1981 raid on the Osirak reactor taught Israel a number of lessons which were to shape its future conduct, and which in turn affected the course of the Gulf war, though the evidence is that the attack set back the Iraqi nuclear programme, but did not knock it out for good. A year later when we visited the plant everything seemed to be going ahead normally, the difference being that we had to make this deduction from the traffic going in and out and the number of people at work: nothing could be seen from ground level as a huge earth rampart about a hundred feet high had been bulldozed into position all round Osirak – a defensive wall so wide and thick that a road was built on top of it on which to site anti-aircraft guns. This vast earthwork was designed to prevent the penetration of bombs, which when dropped from today's high-speed planes, strike their targets at an extreme angle. One indication of its success may be that – so far – the Israelis have not attempted to repeat their 1981 exploit, although reports of the Atomic Energy Authority make it clear that damage has been repaired and work continues.

The main lesson for Israel was that where it mattered – in America – it could get away with anything. Immediately after the raid there was a worldwide outcry at the Israeli action, an apparently unprovoked attack on a facility which Iraq said was for peaceful purposes, a claim supported by France and by the international watchdogs. A major public concern was that Israel should apparently have been ready to carry through an attack

which could have released a radioactive cloud in a densely populated area of the countryside, and close to the capital with its
population at that time of 3.5 million inhabitants. In America,
Israel's main backer, as in Europe and the rest of the world, the
initial reaction to the strike was shock and horror that such risks
could have been run, that Israel was willing to go so far on such
thin evidence – much of the carefully leaked information from
Israel about Iraqi intentions was later found to be untrue. Yet in
two days, thanks largely to the work of the American–Israeli
Public Affairs Committee in Washington, the opinions of those
in the United States who mattered – the senators and representatives, the newspapermen and broadcasters – had been changed
completely. From condemnation and outrage the speeches and
editorials now turned to admiration and praise: the world, the
Americans concluded, was a safer place since the Israelis had
made it impossible for Iraq to produce an atomic bomb. What
was little noted was a quiet announcement in Riyadh six months
later: Saudi Arabia had agreed to pay for the rebuilding of the
reactor, a decision taken by King Khaled personally, according
to Saudi officials. France had been informed. In Paris, President
François Mitterrand had succeeded President Giscard d'Estaing,
and the new head of state was thought to have Israeli sympathies.
Perhaps things would not be quite so easy for the Iraqis after all?
But President Mitterrand, like many others in France, had been
outraged by Israeli allegations that France had conspired with
Iraq to build a secret, bomb-producing installation under the
main, visible reactor, and he also had as lively a sense of where
France's advantage lay as did his predecessor. Iraq was not only
a main oil supplier, it was also a huge arms buyer: both self-interest
and sentiment made it certain that France would agree to rebuild
the nuclear plant.

But in the years to come, it was not nuclear power but conventional arms which provided France with such a lucrative trade.
Between 1980 and 1986, for instance, France delivered more than
eighty Mirage aircraft to Baghdad, as well as millions of dollars'
worth of other equipment. France also pioneered such new ways
of supplying weapons as the lease of the Super Etendard planes,
an arrangement which allowed Baghdad to spread the war to all
parts of the Gulf and which had a direct bearing on the course of
events – the attacks on neutral shipping by Iran in retaliation for

the Iraqi strikes on Iranian tankers, for example, and thus the decision by Kuwait to re-flag its fleet, and the eventual involvement of America.

Throughout the war the Soviet Union remained Iraq's main supplier, as it had always been – the Treaty of Friendship and Cooperation signed by Moscow and Baghdad in 1972 was a formalisation of the special relationship between the two countries which had existed from the time of the overthrow of the monarchy, and survived the rift between the Ba'ath and the communist party of Iraq, with all the bloodshed that entailed. But estimates were that about a quarter of all arms imports to Iraq were from France, with a heavy emphasis on the most advanced and sophisticated weapons systems. The Soviet Union and other Eastern bloc countries provided about 35 per cent, with the remainder coming from a variety of sources – including China, which became a major supplier to Iran as well. Egypt, which throughout the decade was building up its own arms industry, provided such everyday items as ammunition, grenades etc.

By the time Iran accepted Resolution 598, Iraq was thought to have imported $10 billion-worth of arms from the Soviet Union, more than $5 billion from France, and another $5 billion from various sources. Another $5 billion probably went on ancillary equipment such as computer software and non-military supplies for the armed forces. For several years Iraq was spending 50 per cent of its budget on arms imports, and was able to do so even when oil exports were severely disrupted in the first years of the war by its inability to export through the Gulf, as Saudi Arabia, Kuwait and to a lesser extent Qatar and the Emirates gave financial support. Even that did not have to last long, as there was an early realisation in Baghdad of the need to find new routes to get the oil out. The development of new pipelines and the decision by Saudi Arabia and Kuwait to assign to Iraq oil produced from the Neutral Zone meant that Iraq was able to maintain its arms-purchasing programme even when the oil price slumped so badly.

In the first years of the war, the situation in his own country was as worrying to Saddam Hussein as the reverses he soon began to suffer on the battlefield. Uncertain of the continuing loyalty of the Shia who made up the bulk of the armed forces, the government could not afford to introduce an all-out war economy, to call on the people to put up with austerity so that nothing should be denied the army. There were some shortages, of course, but they were caused by inefficient or disrupted distribution systems, not by lack of imports – merchants had to compete for transport from Jordan with the army, which always had priority. In those days in Baghdad there were queues outside many shops, but the housewives standing in line were cheerful about it all; they knew that they would get what they needed, and a system of rationing fairly applied meant that even the poorest did not go short. The soldiers on leave and the men at home also found the things they wanted – Iraqis, unlike many Arabs, are drinkers, and in the summer in particular like to sit beside the Tigris with bottles of beer. Their national poet, Abu Nuwas, is celebrated in a garden beside the Tigris by a statue showing him with a drinking cup in his hand – so throughout the war the authorities made sure that when the soldiers on leave called for bottles of Farida, there was never any shortage.

Only for a period of about eighteen months at the beginning of the war did Iraq have the sort of trouble in getting arms supplies which affected Iran for the whole eight years of the conflict. In those early days the Soviet Union demonstrated its displeasure by holding up all shipments, refusing requests for spares, and putting pressure on its allies not to supply either. At the same time, the Iraqi oil exports were at their lowest, with the new pipelines not yet built and the routes through the Gulf closed; it was a time of huge difficulty for the Iraqis, who were rescued mainly by the efforts of Egypt and Jordan.

Egypt dramatically increased its flow of arms and spares, taking items out of its own reserve stocks and even cannibalising some of its equipment to find desperately needed spares. Jordan helped by seconding senior technical officers from the Jordanian army to Iraq; once there, many of them abandoned the army – by agreement with their own government and Iraq – and set themselves up as the kind of middlemen needed in the arms business, men who knew from experience where to find the weapons needed, who to approach and how to arrange deals. Some of these former Jordanian officers became very rich in the process, but their gains were not begrudged by the Iraqis, who realised to the full how badly they needed help in the vital first eighteen months of the war. It was then too that the Arab Gulf states proved their worth, freely subsidising Iraqi purchases and starting the regular payments to Iraq which allowed it to continue for so long its guns-and-butter policy, to keep its own people happy while pursuing the war.

After its initial difficulties, Iraq rarely had trouble. The Soviet Union did use its dominant position at times to apply pressure, but never again cut off the flow of arms. On occasion, the Russians even used their special position to reassure Iraq. When a Soviet trade delegation went to Tehran in 1987 to the dismay of the Iraqis, the Russians chose the day their representatives crossed the border into Iran to deliver a particular consignment of arms to Baghdad ahead of schedule.

It was Iran which had to search the world for arms supplies, to devise ingenious schemes to locate and pay for desperately needed spare parts, and to set up a whole network of clandestine buyers to keep its forces equipped – in 1986 and the beginning of 1987 Iran was finding 70 per cent of its needs on the black or grey markets, and only in the last phase of the war did China and South Korea step up shipments significantly. Nor could Iran devote the same proportion of its GNP to arms as Iraq was able to do. Its larger population and the disorganisation resulting from the revolution meant that it never managed to devote more than 25 per cent of its GNP to the war, compared to Iraq's 50 per cent.

Iran's strength, and its problem, was the huge spending spree indulged in by the Shah before 1978. Determined throughout the 1970s to make himself the policeman of the Gulf and to carve out a special relationship with the United States, the Shah insisted on buying far more than his country could absorb. The result was that there were large stockpiles of all sorts of items when the Shah went and the mullahs took over, but few who knew how to handle them, and total dependence on American spares. In the early days, the Iranian army and air force was purged and purged again – at one time air force pilots were even taken out of prison to fly the planes – so that even the whereabouts of some items were lost. Then, when things did settle down, came the problems of finding and paying for the items wanted; because almost everything had to be bought on the black market Iran had to pay over the odds, was often cheated and never got full value for money. American experts estimated that Iran had to pay $3 for a dollar's worth of goods.

The Iranians did remarkably well in finding arms, but they were also cheated time after time. Once, F5 spares were found to be cases of dog food tins; on another occasion, Iran bought back through middlemen US-made M48 tanks originally captured from its own forces by the Iraqis. Again, Iran was involved for three years in a complicated deal through which Israel and America were to get captured Iraqi T72 tanks in exchange for an officially sanctioned private sale of F4 planes, M48 tanks and attack helicopters. No tanks were delivered to America and Israel and none of the supplies due from them ever materialised. Iranians involved still do not know if the whole affair was a private scam or an elaborate affair run by one of the intelligence agencies. On another occasion Iran was caught in a $2 billion sting by the US customs which netted dozens of Iranian middlemen – apparently an American ploy to emphasise the Iranian need for arms and to show that only America could produce, a preparation for Robert McFarlane's Iran–Contra deal.

In the wake of the Tehran embassy siege, America organised the embargo on arms sales to Iran, and launched Operation Staunch to enforce it. Despite the well-publicised breaches, and the whole Iran–Contra affair, the embargo was reasonably effective, forcing Iran always to devote great energy and large sums of money to its search for arms. Of course, there was a good deal of cynicism about too. The Stockholm International Peace Research Institute regularly noted about fifty countries which sold arms to both sides in the Gulf war: these included China and most East and West European countries, including Britain, France, Germany, Austria and Spain, America (in the Iran–Contra deal), North Korea, Pakistan, South Africa and Sweden itself. The only countries dealing exclusively with Iraq were its close allies Egypt, Kuwait and Jordan, while states which dealt only with Iran included neighbouring Turkey, Israel, a Japan constantly worried about its investments, Libya and Syria (its two Arab allies), and Portugal and South Korea.

Britain, with its holier-than-thou attitude, presented a particularly extreme example of the cynicism with which the Europeans operated. The official British policy was that it obeyed the embargo on arms to Iran, and sold only non-lethal weapons to Iraq. Yet until 1987 Iran maintained the Iranian Air Force Logistics Office in the National Iranian Oil Company office in Westminster, staffed by Iranian military officers and officials of the various purchasing ministries, and linked to similar satellite Iranian offices all over the world. Britain agreed to direct sales of replacement parts for the Chieftains which were the main Iranian battle tank. The spares were shipped from London in crates marked simply 'vehicle parts', and were later justified by officials in London as being 'unconnected with the lethal systems of the tanks'. To match the Iranian arms-buying office in London, Britain kept its own military sales office in Tehran throughout the war, an office originally set up when the Chieftain deal was done with the Shah, but certainly used by the Iranians to find replacement parts and spares when they wanted them. British spokesmen claimed that the sales office was not concerned with supplies any more. 'Their work is taken up in chasing debts incurred before the Islamic revolution,' they said. But it was International Military Services Ltd., the arms-selling branch of the Ministry of Defence, which maintained the office in Tehran throughout the eight years of war, and military officers who staffed it.

Significantly, perhaps, there was never any mention of this strange office at the British embassy, no acknowledgement of the existence of this odd debt-collecting agency; equally, those who staffed the office never needed the services of the embassy. As most useful guests, the officers of this unique British mission suffered none of the difficulties experienced by British diplomats. But in the end, no one in the British government was able to produce a balance sheet of how much it had cost to maintain the office, and the amount of those old debts collected. Albion at its transparent worst. To underline the hypocrisy of it all, the British company Plessey was also allowed to sell a £100-million radar-defence system to Iran on the grounds that it would be deployed not along the Iraqi front, but on the Soviet and Turkish borders.

Portugal and Spain were the main sources of Western-manufactured ammunition and small arms for Iran, with most being sent by sea from such Portuguese ports as Setubal. But it was Israel which was the most interesting supplier for the militantly anti-Zionist Islamic Republic, sending shipments either directly or via third parties. As early as 1981 Israel delivered a consignment of aircraft tyres directly from Tel Aviv to Tehran, but after that shipments were usually routed either through such European airports as Frankfurt, Vienna, or military airfields in Portugal, or indirectly from China, which by the end of the war was Iran's main supplier.

In 1983, a year in which the International Institute for Strategic Studies in London managed to collate statistics, Israel sold more than $100 million worth of arms to Iran. So great was the volume of trade between Israel and Iran that a special Israeli arms-sales office was set up in Cyprus to deal with the Iranian middlemen who carried out the actual purchases – because there were restrictions on the movement of Iranian nationals Iran called in Iranians who had emigrated to other countries but remained loyal to Tehran. A number of Americans of Iranian origin were pressed into service, and regularly dealt with the Israelis through the Cyprus office. The best known intermediary of all, Adnan Kashoggi, the Saudi Arabian, did not even bother to dissemble so far as to go to Cyprus – when necessary, he flew to Tel Aviv and met face to face with the Israelis.

Kashoggi, with David Kimche, the former Mossad man in East Africa who had become director of the Israeli foreign ministry, was responsible for the initial stages of the Iran–Contra deal. In an account of the role played by Kashoggi made available to us, the Saudi Arabian dealer said that it was in June 1985 that he sent a memorandum to Robert McFarlane dealing with the whole Middle East situation. Copies were also sent to King Fahd, King Hussein, President Mubarak of Egypt, the Israeli Prime Minister (then Shimon Peres), and Saddam Hussein – perhaps a rather strange assortment of recipients, but an indication of the way Kashoggi and the few like him work, and of his standing, for all those on his list read and took note of his ideas. According to Kashoggi, the thoughts he set out had as their starting point the security of his own country, Saudi Arabia, and dealt with the whole geopolitical region, with the problem of Iranian–American relations merely a small segment. He wrote later:

> Understandably, however, each recipient took an inordinate interest in those parts of direct concern to his particular country. In particular, it suggested to McFarlane a framework within which he might solve a problem of pressing domestic concern, the freeing of the hostages held by groups in Lebanon known to be under the influence of Ayatollah Khomeini's Iran. The Israeli reaction to my letter was similarly

understandable. The Israelis with whom I discussed it saw in it opportunities lying entirely outside of my general intent. First, my remarks on Iran suggested to them a rationale with which to justify the shipment of arms to Iran they were already making. Second, they saw that if the Americans were to accept the plan they could turn their on-going secret arms deals with Iran into a means of helping the US government to solve one of its greatest geopolitical problems. Third, they had yet another means to prolong the stalemate in the Iran–Iraq war. Fourth, they would have a major customer for the items being manufactured by their burgeoning arms industry, now amounting to over a third of Israel's exports.

Kashoggi's plan, refined, he says, by his friend Manuchir Ghorbanifar, was to bring moderate Iranians together with the Americans to try to work out a *modus vivendi* which would provide for a new relationship after the death of Ayatollah Khomeini and the transition to the post-Imam Iran. Ghorbanifar, acknowledged even by his American friends to be one of the trickiest pieces of work to come out of the Middle East in a long time, said that he wanted representatives of America and Iran to agree on a course of action which would boost Iranian leaders who would be amenable to such an agreement at 'the expense of the fanatics bent on Iran's present course towards chaos'. In the process, both Ghorbanifar and Kashoggi would, of course, make considerable profits.

The Iran–Contra deal went its way, and had little effect on the battlefield – in eight years of war, 1,000 TOW missiles are less than a footnote. What was important for the Iranians was the daily supply, the provision of spare parts to keep the whole war machine going, the ability to find the best equipment possible. In the opinion of international arms dealers with whom we have discussed the situation, it was not ultimately Iraq's numerical superiority in weapons which gave them the edge, but the quality of the weapons systems they had. Iran constantly had to make do with second best, or sometimes with equipment which no army in the world would wish to have foisted on it. Certainly that was true in the early days, when teams of mullahs with little experience were dispatched all over the world to buy anything they could find. The Iranian army then was highly suspect to the new regime, and technical officers were only included in buying missions most reluctantly, their advice treated with suspicion, and at times disregarded.

Another difficulty for Iran was that those few countries willing to deal with it directly could not provide the quality of goods wanted; thus the Iranians bought a consignment of Jeeps from India which were defective. From China in the early days they made a huge purchase of tracked armoured personnel carriers, which proved useless. They bought Sam 5 missiles from North Korea on which the guidance systems did not work. All those ready to deal directly were not in a position to supply the quality of hardware the Iranians needed, and unlike the Iraqis, the Iranians did not have 'respectable' friends to act for them. Jordan, Egypt or any of the Gulf states could and did make purchases on behalf of the Iraqis in the first two years of the war, but Iran had only Syria and Libya to front for it, and those two countries were as suspect and subject to as many constraints as Iran itself.

So Iran was driven to the private dealers, the middlemen who claimed to be able to deliver. But what Iran needed could not be supplied by individuals; Iran needed tanks, planes, ships, billion-dollar deals outside the scope of even the biggest of the private dealers. So great was the demand that at times even Israel, which became one of its main suppliers, could not deliver. The Israelis were always willing to offer, but took so many orders that they found their own inventories were exhausted; they promised more than they could deliver. So Iran was driven further and further afield, constantly trying to reach deals with governments, and because it could deal only with certain types of government, always having to put up with inferior equipment.

Iran dealt with Brazil, and with Argentina, which provided jet trainers, but their main suppliers remained the North Koreans and the Chinese, two countries driven more by their need for foreign exchange than by ideological considerations. In 1986 Chinese government officials contacted some sixty arms dealers around the world and issued them with official documents showing them to be sales agents of the People's Republic authorised to deal in military equipment. After their early unfortunate experiences, the Iranian army was unwilling to deal with China, but was over-ruled. Rafsanjani, the Imam's representative on the Supreme War Council, argued strongly that everything possible should be done to further the country's links with China, not only to ensure regular arms supplies, but also to have a powerful political ally wary of both the Soviet Union and the United States. But because of their circumstances, the Iranians were basically willing to deal with anyone who could, or said they could, provide the goods. Thus, many of those who had worked for the Shah were re-activated, international arms dealers who had made their fortunes at the Shah's expense were now given the opportunity to make new fortunes from the Shah's Islamic successors. Albert Hakim, for example, acted both for the Shah and for the mullahs.

Most Iranian arms purchases were made in the name of the Prime Minister's office, with army officers brought in to check that the goods on offer were actually available and of the type specified, and money deposited in a Swiss bank for release when delivery was taken. Some very large purchases were also made in the name of the Islamic Economic Organisation, a shadowy outfit which in addition to buying arms set aside a proportion of the value of each deal done to helping Islamic organisations in other Middle East countries – organisations dedicated to spreading the Khomeini brand of Islam, and doing so by all means possible.

One of the oddities of the war was the way in which the Soviet Union tried so hard to keep its lines open to both sides, at times risking its links with Iraq, its long-standing client. The Russians, for instance, took the dangerous step of making some direct shipments to Iran, shipments which were easily detected by the Americans, who promptly passed the information on to the Iraqis in the hope of further detaching Saddam Hussein from Moscow. Iran had 203mm, 155mm and 130mm cannon, with the smaller calibre forming the backbone of the artillery, vital in battlefield support of infantry. At one stage in 1987 the Iranian stocks ran dangerously low, and the Russians stepped in to supply them directly, promising a second delivery of 100,000 as well. It was the non-delivery of the second consignment which played a significant part in forcing the Iranians to accept Resolution 598 when they found more avenues for buying closed to them in 1988. In earlier years the Soviet Union also supplied items to Iran via Yugoslavia, and Czechoslovakia and Bulgaria sold directly to Iran.

While Iran was scouring the international arms markets for its supplies – mainly from its procurement office in London – Iraq had to make only one major clandestine purchase. This was to set up its poison-gas manufacturing plant. At the same time that he negotiated Iraq's entry into the nuclear field, Saddam Hussein was also put in charge of a second secret project to give the country the capacity to produce gas, but no real effort was made to do so until the war began. Then, with no idea how to set about it, the Iraqis at first tried to buy 'off the peg' factories, plants ostensibly to produce pesticide which could easily be converted to produce gas – in effect, the processes of making pesticide have only to be taken one step further to obtain gas. The trouble was that the size of the plant needed was a giveaway to anyone in the business, and the need to buy protective clothing also made it clear what the Iraqis were doing.

One of the first companies to be contacted was in Rochester, NY, but officials quietly passed the word to the state department, and the American government made sure that no sale was made. Similarly, when a British company was approached, the Foreign Office was consulted and, again, strong 'advice' was given that the sale should not go through. In the end, the Iraqis got what they wanted bit by bit. As a first step, chemists, chemical engineers, and nuclear scientists of Arab origin were approached and offered remarkably attractive terms to work in Iraq – usually at double the salaries they were earning in the West, with the promise of free housing, cars and so on. Many accepted the offers made. The Ba'ath party, after all, stood for pan-Arabism and Iraq, in theory, could be a home for any Arab. So many were tempted to work in Baghdad, and by the time some of them realised what they were doing it was too late to back out. The result was that equipment bought mainly in Italy and West Germany, with the vital components sent by air from Austria, was assembled in Iraq and produced at least three different kinds of gas. By the end of the war Iraq had three plants producing chemical warfare products, one near Baghdad, one at Samarra and one in the Syrian desert at Rutbah, dangerously near the Jordanian–Syrian borders and thus vulnerable to Israeli attack, but close to the sources of raw materials used.

By the end of the war Iran had more than a million men under arms, with the 300,000 Revolutionary Guards almost matching in numbers the total in the army, and deploying equipment just as sophisticated – and not only on land. It was Revolutionary Guards who manned the small motor boats bought from Sweden which caused such havoc in the Gulf: these 13-metre Boghammar fast patrol boats were fitted with posts for a heavy machine gun, and were usually manned by two or three Pasdaran who also used RPGs against their targets – neutral tankers attacked in retaliation for Iraqi strikes on ships on the Iranian oil shuttle. Some of the boats were based at Abu Musa, one of the disputed islands in the Gulf, but most came out of Farsiyah in the central Gulf on their swift forays. More formally, Iran also used helicopters in the Gulf to put boarding parties on vessels suspected of carrying arms for Iraq, and at times took ships into port to be searched, though arms for Iraq were in fact never found, nor did the Iranians expect to find any; this was entirely psychological warfare. In the last months of the war, after America had moved into the Gulf in strength, the Iranian navy was more active than ever before, the regular navy as well as the Pasdaran, and officers of the Western ships who came in contact with the Iranians were full of praise for the professionalism, daring and courtesy of the Iranian navy men; the Pasdaran, not surprisingly, did not stop to chat to others in the Gulf.

One of the oddities of the war was the effect of purchases by Iran and Iraq on the international arms market. Singapore, for instance, became on paper a major centre, apparently at one time importing almost 20 per cent of total Swedish production in the year. Cyprus was another country which on paper became a major arms importer, but the biggest effect of all was in Iran itself. At the beginning of the war it had no more than a couple of small factories producing small arms and ammunition, but by 1988 it had at least a dozen large factories and thousands of small workshops producing specialised items. It was able to make at least 60 per cent of all the ammunition it used, including RPGs and mortar bombs, and developed its radio industry to provide almost all the communications equipment needed. By the end of the war it was also nearing success in producing its own missiles, but these never went into production. At the same time, Iraq had been able to modify its SCUD B missiles by reducing the warhead and fitting additional boosters so that it was able to strafe Tehran itself during the final stage of the 'war of the cities'.

Still with far more men than Iraq, by the end of the war Iran was woefully deficient in equipment. Starting the war with more than 400 combat aircraft, it had no more than 50 operational by

1988; similarly, out of 500 combat helicopters in 1980, only a couple of dozen remained serviceable eight years later. While Iran had less than 1,000 main battle tanks in 1988, barely half its 1980 inventory, Iraq had doubled the number available to nearly 5,000. Again, the Iraqi air force had far more combat aircraft and helicopters in 1988 than it had at the beginning of the war, while the Iranians were desperately searching for new aircraft as late as 1987. In December of that year Iranian middlemen located sixteen American-built F5s owned by Chile which they believed could be bought. The Chileans confirmed this, and a price of $170 million was agreed, but then Chilean air force officers pointed out that under the original terms of sale from the US to Chile, Washington had to be informed of any proposal to pass the planes on to a third country. More intermediaries were brought in, and eventually offered to obtain the release of four of the American hostages in Beirut in addition to paying the full price to Chile if America would approve the sale. After the Iran–Contra scandal, secretary of state George Shultz did not hesitate: he ordered an emphatic 'No', and the new national security adviser, Colin Powell, said that no response at all should be made to the approaches.

All in all, the fact that Iran was able to carry on a major war for eight years showed how shallow were the international efforts to ban arms sales so long as the two superpowers were not in agreement. Private arms dealers willing to sell could always be found, but in general they did not have the heavy equipment needed, nor the quantities. Only governments could supply all Iran's needs, and as long as a mentor government, the Soviet Union in this case, gave the go-ahead, then states could be found who would provide what was needed. In the early days, when it was subject to an embargo, Iraq too showed how easy it was to get around any ban, in this case turning to Western governments, notably France, which had the green light from Washington. Only when American and Russian interests converged did the ban on arms sales to Iran become effective. When that happened, the conflict came to an end, a fact which may in the future provide the main lesson of the war.

# 11

# The Soviet Union:
# the other Satan

The Soviet Union played a double game for most of the Gulf war, arming its ally, Iraq, while trying to court the fiercely anti-American mullahs in Iran. As well as through its formal links with Tehran, the Russians hoped to keep abreast of what was happening in the clerical regime through the communist Tudeh party which, on Moscow's orders, followed a slavishly pro-Khomeini policy to the point of supporting the suppression of other secular and left-wing groups. This the clergy exploited in the battle against their other leftist opponents. The secretary-general of the Tudeh party, Nureddin Kianuri, who took over leadership of the party in 1978, was the grandson of a prominent mullah, and so closely did he cleave to the Imam's line that he earned himself the nickname Ayatollah Kianuri.

Two years into the war Britain, Russia's historical rival for influence in central Asia and the Gulf, saw a chance to undermine its old foe. In June 1982 a diplomat at the Soviet embassy in Tehran, Vladimir Kuzichkin, defected to the British. During the final months before his defection he had already been passing secrets to his British controller, and later in Britain, at his de-briefing, he revealed details of the Soviet espionage network in Iran, both inside and outside the Tudeh party, and also identified the diplomats at the embassy who ran the spy ring. The British saw a rare opportunity to set back the Soviet espionage operation in Iran, so a meeting was arranged on neutral territory in the Middle East at which the British handed over to the Iranians a list of some thirty people, both Soviet and Iranian, involved in the network. The British action was a straightforward exercise in East–West realpolitik: the Iranians were asked nothing in return and there was no change in the relations between the two countries.

It is unlikely that the thirty or so names handed to the Iranians represented the entire list which Kuzichkin had provided, but it gave Tehran enough information with which to act against Tudeh and the Russians. So on 6 February 1983, eighty senior members of the party were rounded up, including the secretary-general, Kianuri. Two and a half months later, on 30 April, he was taken before the television cameras to confess that he and some of his colleagues had spied for the Soviet Union. The following week, Tudeh was dissolved and the government announced the expulsion of eighteen Soviet diplomats on the grounds of espionage and interference in Iran's internal affairs. Then in swift hearings, 101 leading members of Tudeh cells in the military were put on trial; of these eighty-seven were jailed and ten were executed.

Moscow tried unsuccessfully to intervene on behalf of Tudeh, dispatching the head of the foreign ministry's Middle East section, Vasily Safronchuk, to Tehran in April 1983. But the repression continued. In all, 8,000 people were said to have been detained in the anti-Tudeh crackdown; there were mob lynchings of Tudeh suspects and the homes of Tudeh members were set on fire, but the suppression of the communist apparatus did not lead to a breakdown of relations with the Soviet Union. Moscow had grown accustomed to seeing sister parties repressed in the volatile states of the Middle East; in Iraq, for instance, there had been public hangings of communist party members for organising within the military. Both Moscow and Tehran seemed prepared to keep relations on as normal a basis as possible.

Moscow's attempts to remain on good terms with both sides was an almost impossible balancing act. Iraq had been, to a greater or lesser degree, an asset to the Soviet Union ever since the overthrow of the pro-Western monarchy in 1958. The twenty-year Friendship and Cooperation Treaty signed with Baghdad in 1972 was one of the cornerstones of Soviet policy in the Middle East, for at the time of the signing the Iraqi regime was one of the most radical and anti-Western in the region, rejecting all moves towards a negotiated settlement of the Arab–Israeli conflict. After 1975, however, and the signing of the Algiers agreement with the Shah, there were indications that the Iraqis wanted to mend their fences with the West and to become more genuinely non-aligned. This process was hastened by the war, which obliged Baghdad to seek support from whatever quarter it could, and particularly from the pro-Western regimes of the Arab Gulf. The Soviet Union, as Baghdad's chief arms supplier, was aware of Saddam Hussein's war plans and may have sought to dissuade him from launching the invasion.

The Kremlin's ideologues had difficulty in coping with the phenomenon of the Iranian revolution. In geopolitical terms the change of regime in Tehran represented a benefit for the Soviet Union. The pro-Western Shah was toppled and replaced by vehemently anti-Western forces, but the theocracy which was set up under Khomeini was also deeply inimical to communism. The regime's commitment to exporting the revolution represented a potential threat to the stability of the predominantly Muslim southern republics of the Soviet Union, and Khomeini's support for the Mujahedin went actively against Soviet interests in Afghanistan. On balance, however, the Kremlin was disposed to regard the regime in Tehran in a positive light. Trade and industrial deals were signed with the new Islamic Republic and, although Khomeini railed against atheistic communism and eventually ordered the suppression of the Tudeh party, the Soviet Union never suffered the aggression which was directed against its rival superpower. When fundamentalist students occupied the US embassy in Tehran in November 1979, extra guards were posted around the Soviet compound so that it should not suffer the same fate, and when Afghan refugees threatened to storm the building after the Soviet invasion of their country, they were dispersed by Revolutionary Guards.

There was nevertheless an underlying antipathy between Iran and the Soviet Union which had both ideological and historical roots. On the ideological front, Khomeini's creed was: 'Neither East nor West'. He regarded both superpowers with equal contempt and, if anything, saw the Russians, who suppressed Muslims both inside and outside their borders, as a worse option than the capitalist Americans. But for historical reasons, Iran could not afford to be too openly antagonistic; the previous 250 years had taught the Iranians to beware of the giant to the north.

In the eighteenth and nineteenth centuries the decaying Persian Empire was the target of Russian expansionism in central Asia. After the Great Northern War in which Russia defeated Sweden and gained access to the West through the Baltic Sea, Peter the Great turned his attentions in 1722 to the Persian territories of the southern Caucasus, an imperialist enterprise which reflected Russia's rivalry with both the Persian and the Ottoman empires. Peter the Great was frequently quoted, almost three centuries later, by those who sought to argue that the Soviet Union still held on to the dream of breaking through to the warm waters of the Gulf. Robert Huyser, the US general dispatched to Tehran to try to prop up the Shah's regime, records how the Shah once told him that a long-term Russian plan to gain control of Iran, and through it, the world's economy, dated back to the reign of Peter the Great, who said in 1725: 'Whoever controls the area between Constantinople and India will rule the world. The doctrine should be to excite continual wars in Turkey and Persia, and then penetrate as far as the Persian Gulf.'

After the Soviet invasion of Afghanistan and the outbreak of hostilities in the Gulf, it became an axiom among many Western commentators that Peter the Great's doctrine remained the guiding principle of Soviet policy in the region. During the period of the Russo-Persian wars it was only the determination of Britain to protect the passage to India that prevented the fulfilment of Peter the Great's dream. As it was, Persia found itself squeezed between two imperial powers, with Russia pushing from the north and Britain interfering ever more persistently in Iranian affairs in an attempt to hold the Czar at bay.

In the late nineteenth century the Russians turned their attentions to the tribes and *khanates* beyond the Caspian Sea in territories which had been protectorates of the Persian Empire and which were eventually to become the Muslim southern republics of the Soviet Union.

When Khomeini was born in 1902, Persia could barely aspire to being described as an independent state. Because of the balance of power between Russia and Britain, it had never been taken over by either empire; but in all other respects it was a virtual colony, divided into unofficial spheres of influence, though the Shah and his government were effectively tools of the British. Already in the 1890s, the Shia clergy had led a successful revolt against Nassreddin Shah's granting of a tobacco monopoly to a British subject. During the latter half of the nineteenth century, British influence at the Qajar court was so extensive that Baron

Julius de Reuter, the founder of the international news agency which bears his name, won a concession which gave him a majority share of customs receipts and the right to build roads and railways, to run banking and the telegraph system and to exploit minerals and forests. Even in Britain there was opposition to the extent of the concession, which effectively gave Reuter control of the Persian economy, and the deal had to be curtailed. The controversy nevertheless succeeded in provoking resentment against the outside powers.

Russia was scarcely less influential at this time. After a visit to Russia, Nassreddin Shah formed a Cossack Brigade under Russian officers which acted as an imperial guard, and which, until 1920, was always commanded by a Russian – Reza Khan, the founder of the short-lived Pahlavi dynasty, was to come to power as a colonel in the Cossacks. In 1906, the Cossack Brigade was used to put down a demonstration of theology students campaigning against foreign domination and in favour of constitutional change. For three weeks, some 16,000 mullahs and bazaaris took advantage of the right of sanctuary within the walls of the British legation until the Shah was obliged to grant a constitution and create a Majlis. Britain gained much credit among the Persians at the expense of the Russians but the granting of sanctuary may have helped to create the myth, still widespread in the 1980s, that the mullahs were the agents of the British. Both powers were nevertheless concerned by the spread of constitutionalism in Persia as well as by Germany's attempt to extend its influence there. As a result, they drew up the secret Anglo-Russian agreement of 1907 which formally divided the country into spheres of influence. Russia would hold sway in the northern half of the country, including the capital Tehran, while Britain's sphere was in the south-eastern corner from the Gulf coast to the Indian and Afghan borders. The remainder of the country was a neutral zone in which both powers would have the right to seek economic concessions. Russia acknowledged Britain's influence in Afghanistan and agreed that it would remain outside the Russian sphere.

The new Shah, Mohammad Ali, tried to suppress the constitutional movement with the help of his Russian allies but only succeeded in provoking a civil war. On his behalf the Cossacks shelled the Majlis building and, when the constitutional leaders sought refuge in the British legation, surrounded the building and threatened to shell it as well. The constitutionalist forces nevertheless succeeded in taking Tehran in 1909 and forced the Shah to abdicate, though their victory was short-lived. Two years later, incensed at the Tehran government's attempts to introduce taxation into its zone, Russian forces entered northern Persia and began a march on Tehran to force the cancellation of the order. William Shuster, the American adviser who suggested the attempt at taxation, later wrote in his memoirs that British and Russian imperialism were crushing the life out of Persia.

At the outbreak of the First World War, all pretence that Persia enjoyed independence from the outside powers was abandoned, and Persia's declaration of neutrality in the European war was ignored. Revolutionary Russia was in turmoil and Britain now ran the Cossack Brigade, and by 1918 the country had been completely occupied by British troops. There were moves to make Persia a British protectorate, part of a vast post-war Asian empire which would stretch from Palestine to India, and in 1919 a secret Anglo-Persian agreement, signed by a group of the Shah's ministers, virtually handed the country over to the British. But Britain had underestimated the strength of nationalist feeling and also the opposition which it was to encounter from its wartime allies, so plans to put the agreement to the Majlis for ratification had to be abandoned.

Part of Britain's purpose in wanting to extend its control over Persia was to contain the spread of the Bolshevik revolution. In 1920, British and Indian troops were deployed in northern Persia after Bolshevik forces landed on the Caspian coast; since the collapse of the Anglo-Persian accord the intention had been to withdraw British forces from the country. Doubting the continued loyalty of the Russian officers in the Cossack Brigade and unwilling to leave Persia to its fate, the British commander, Major-General Sir Edmund Ironside, who had commanded allied forces fighting the Bolsheviks in northern Russia, found a strongman in the person of Reza Khan. Ironside dismissed the Russian officers and put the future Shah in charge of the country's only effective fighting force; in February 1921, Reza Khan marched with his troops to Tehran to seek control of the whole country. The Qajar monarchy lingered on for another four years, but in 1925 Ahmad Shah was deposed, and the following year Reza Khan crowned himself Reza Shah Pahlavi, Shahanshah of Persia.

For a brief period the era of Russian and British interference in Persia appeared to be over, for Reza Khan was widely viewed as a nationalist in the mould of Turkey's Kemal Ataturk. Jawaharlal Nehru, the future prime minister of India, wrote in 1933: 'Persia has changed greatly during the last few years, and Reza Khan is bent on many reforms so that the country might be modernised. . . . The people of Persia are, of course, Muslims – Shia Muslims – but in so far as their country is concerned, nationalism is a more powerful force.' Nehru hit upon the religion-versus-nationalism dichotomy which was to influence events in Iran in the latter half of the century. To many of the clergy of Khomeini's generation, Reza Khan was an imperialist creation who had come to power in a Russian officer's uniform with the connivance of the British. The mullahs never forgave his manipulation and suppression of religion, and shortly after the Iranian revolution, one of Reza Khan's former officers, General Atapour, then in his nineties, was dispatched to Evin prison on the grounds that more than sixty years earlier he had forcibly cut off the beard of a mullah.

The first quarter of the twentieth century was a period which helped to form the world view of Khomeini and his generation of clerics. They grew up in a country which was subjected to the whims of outside powers and in which the borders imposed by the Europeans were, to them, largely an irrelevance. Their Shia horizons were defined by the holy cities of Najjaf and Kerbala in the west, at that time slumbering under the decaying tutelage of the Ottoman Empire, and, in the east, by Qom and Mashad, nominally in the control of the Persian Shah. The Shia of Mesopotamia did not gain their political independence with the collapse of the Ottoman Empire after the First World War but instead became subjects of a Sunni king from the Hejaz, Emir Faisal, within the British protectorate of Iraq.

The Bolshevik revolution and the coming to power of Reza Khan did not end the era of Russian involvement in Iran, as Persia was renamed by the new Shah, although the rulers in Moscow swiftly announced their renunciation of all Czarist treaties involving their southern neighbour. They opposed the provisions of the Anglo-Persian agreement of 1919 and proceeded to draft their own treaty of friendship which was signed in 1921 and is still technically valid. The treaty gave Soviet Russia the right to

intervene militarily in Iran if that country were to be used by
hostile third parties, including a foreign power, as a base for
operations against the Russian Federation. Russia would only
intervene if Iran were itself unable to contain the threat and it
pledged to withdraw its troops as soon as the threat was removed.
The treaty was drafted at a time when the young Bolshevik regime
was still struggling for its survival against foreign intervention and
fending off the attacks of White Russian forces. It was only in
the spring of 1920 that the Red Army succeeded in ousting
counter-revolutionary forces from the Caucasus. In 1927 a treaty
of guarantee and neutrality was signed which further pledged that
each side would refrain from attacking the other and would remain
neutral in the event of aggression by a third party.

The Soviet-Iranian treaties were, from the Soviet point of view,
essentially defensive; they helped to guarantee the frontiers of
the Soviet Union at a time when it was under threat from outside
powers. Later, during the Second World War, they were cited in
justification of direct intervention by Moscow, at that time an ally
of the Western powers. The Soviet Union was considered by the
West to be an expansionist power, and it was for this reason that
the West attempted to establish a *cordon sanitaire* along the Soviet
Union's southern frontier in the form of the Baghdad Pact which
grouped together Britain and its regional allies, Turkey, Iraq,
Iran and Pakistan. Moscow countered this threat by supporting
anti-Western forces, firstly Colonel Nasser in Egypt and then the
anti-monarchists in Baghdad. Until the advent of the Gorbachev
era, the Western analysis was still the Peter the Great thesis that
the Soviet Union intended to extend its influence in the Middle
East in order to move southwards towards the warm waters of the
Gulf. To counter the Russian design, Shah Mohammad Pahlavi's
Iran was fortified by the United States as a bulwark against the
Soviet Union. The Kremlin saw the geopolitical situation quite
differently. For Moscow, the pro-Western states on its southern
border, grouped in the Central Treaty Organisation, CENTO,
the successor to the Baghdad Pact, formed a hostile alliance
directed by the West against the Soviet Union.

These contrasting superpower perceptions were to persist
throughout the post-war period and right into the mid-1980s when,
at last, both Moscow and Washington came to recognise that they
had a mutual interest in defusing tension in the Third World and

in containing such potentially uncontrollable forces as Islamic fundamentalism.

Once he had consolidated his rule, Reza Shah tried to repeal the interventionist provisions of the Soviet-Iranian treaties, which were seen as perpetuating Russian influence in Iran's affairs. But the treaties could only be nullified with the agreement of both parliaments, and so they remained in force – though in 1979, the day after the US embassy storming, the Bazargan government announced that it was abrogating the 1921 treaty; the Kremlin took no notice. In August 1941, Iran was once again occupied by Russian and British troops, this time in order to establish an allied supply line to the Soviet Union. Reza Shah, who was regarded as pro-German, was forced to abdicate and was succeeded by his son, Mohammad Reza, who inherited an occupied country and a throne which he did not control.

Stalin's attempt to maintain Soviet control of northern Iran after the end of the war by keeping his troops in Azerbaijan and Kurdistan was a factor which hastened the advent of the Cold War by convincing the Western allies of the Soviet dictator's expansionist intentions. The Autonomous Republic of Azerbaijan and the Kurdish People's Republic declared in December 1945 were Soviet puppet regimes, and the United States and Britain made it clear to Moscow that they were prepared to use force to dislodge Soviet troops from both areas. It was at the height of the Iran crisis, the first serious international confrontation after the end of the war, that Churchill made his celebrated 'Iron Curtain' speech at Fulton, Missouri.

The firm Western response in 1946 brought about the withdrawal of Soviet forces and ensured that Iran remained in the Western camp, and the Kremlin was obliged to accept that it had been effectively shut out of the Middle East. The Soviet Union was powerless to intervene in 1953 when the United States and Britain conspired to overthrow the nationalist government of Mossadeq and could only look on with alarm as the two Western powers proceeded to draw up collective security alliances with the countries along the Soviet Union's southern frontier. It protested against these developments all the same, claiming in 1955 that the formation of such alliances and the establishment of foreign bases in the countries of the Middle East were a direct threat to Soviet security.

The Western strategy, however, began to come apart in the late 1950s with the growth of pan-Arabism, the rise of Nasser and, in 1958, the anti-monarchist *coup* in Iraq by General Qassem, which led to that country withdrawing from the Baghdad pact. The Iraqi crisis prompted the United States to send troops to Lebanon to prop up the pro-Western government there, while Moscow responded to Western moves by staging military exercises along the Iranian and Turkish borders. After 1958, the volatile situation in the Arab countries made it increasingly important for the United States to build up the Shah as the main anti-Soviet bastion in the region, but, conscious of the historical relationship with his northern neighbour, the Shah still took care to maintain good relations with the Soviet Union and visited Moscow in 1956. In 1959, however, despite veiled Soviet threats of intervention, he concluded a defence agreement with the United States in response to the events in neighbouring Iraq.

Throughout the 1960s, the Soviet Union adopted a twin-track policy towards the Middle East. While lending its support to radical regimes and movements in th Arab world, it sought to build ties of neutrality and cooperation with the pro-Western countries on its southern border, specifically Iran. The Shah again visited Moscow in 1965 and signed a $290m credit agreement; subsequently, the two countries signed a five-year trade agreement and arranged for the sale of Iranian natural gas to the Soviet Union. The Shah, for his part, agreed not to allow his territory to be used as a base for American missiles, but this did not prevent him from allowing the United States to use Iran for US espionage against the Soviet Union through the installation of the sophisticated Ibex electronic listening post. Despite his growing self-confidence, the Shah kept Iran firmly in the Western camp and saw his role as one of holding off any Soviet attempt to strike southwards to the Gulf for as long as it took for help to arrive from the West.

The Russians were no more successful than the United States and the Western allies in predicting the Iranian revolution. Moscow saw the positive benefits of the departure of the pro-American Shah but hedged its bets throughout 1978 and refrained from trying to undermine him as long as it appeared possible that he might hold on to power. Washington feared that the Soviet Union might try to exploit events in Iran to its own advantage, while the Kremlin was afraid that the United States might respond to the revolutionary turmoil by intervening militarily. Leonid Brezhnev warned the United States on 18 November 1978: 'It must be made clear that any interference, let alone military intervention in the affairs of Iran – a state which has a common frontier with the Soviet Union – would be regarded by the USSR as a matter affecting its security interests.'

Despite divisions within the US administration on how to respond to Moscow, it was decided that Carter should send a tough reply to Brezhnev in which he reaffirmed support for the Shah and stressed the US commitment to the independence and integrity of Iran. He told Brezhnev that incorrect allegations about Washington's intentions to intervene should not be used as a basis for Soviet interference. This level of mistrust persisted after the revolution and was exacerbated by the US embassy hostage crisis at the end of 1979. Carter was constrained from taking military action against the Islamic Republic for fear of a response by Moscow, and yet, when he took the lesser option of mounting a rescue mission the following April, the Soviet Union interpreted the move as a prelude to further US intervention. When the Shah's regime did collapse, Moscow moved quickly to recognise the new revolutionary government in Tehran. Despite the ideological differences between the two countries, Moscow could claim that, through Brezhnev's stand in 1978, the Soviet Union had acted as a guarantor of Iran's independence at a crucial moment of the revolution.

One major factor disturbing Soviet-Iranian relations was Afghanistan. The Tehran regime was committed to the victory of the Mujahedin forces there and provided support to Shia groups in the resistance; and it gave sanctuary to up to two million Afghan refugees, some of whom fought at the Gulf war fronts. Throughout the Gulf war, news of the fighting in Afghanistan would often take precedence over news from the Iraqi front in the broadcasts of Tehran radio. The Iranian position on Afghanistan at least reflected a degree of ideological consistency. Moscow, on the other hand, having paid lip-service to the progressive nature of the Islamic revolution, was now involved in suppressing just such a revolution in the country next door. The United States, by the same token, regarded Islamic fundamentalism in Iran as a force to be feared and yet described fundamentalists in Afghanistan as freedom-fighters. As with its relations with Russia, Iran's position on Afghanistan was influenced by both ideological and historical factors, for Afghanistan had been both a part of the Persian Empire and its rival for supremacy in central Asia and the sub-continent.

In particular, the western city of Herat was claimed by the Persians until the late nineteenth century as rightfully part of their territory – in 1838 Persian forces laid siege to Herat and withdrew only when the British occupied Kharg Island in the Gulf and threatened to invade the mainland. In 1856, they took the city again and this time Britain declared war on Persia, capturing Kharg and Bushire and marching inland. Naval forces sailed up the Shatt al Arab and stormed Mohammarah, later Khorramshahr. Persia was forced to withdraw from Herat and to abandon its claims to Afghanistan.

The country which the Soviet Union invaded in December 1979 was therefore one with which Iran had the most intimate historical and cultural connections; the second most important language of the country is Dari, a dialect of Persian, and Persian is spoken by the Shia minority of the central highlands. It was inevitable that Iran would oppose the invasion and indeed do what it could to help those trying to oust Soviet troops. Tehran infiltrated Revolutionary Guards into the Shia areas and began supplying the rebel groups. The first stirrings of the rebellion against Marxist rule in Afghanistan coincided with the final months of the Iranian revolution; portraits of Khomeini began appearing all over the Shia areas of Afghanistan. Among the clerical leadership in these regions were mullahs who had been educated in both Iran and Iraq and therefore had close connections with those ruling in Tehran. Soviet troops moved into Afghanistan less than a year after the fall of the Shah and just nine months before the outbreak of war in the Gulf. Moscow took advantage of the fact that the US position in the region had been weakened by the Islamic revolution and the subsequent Tehran embassy hostage crisis. When the last Soviet troops withdrew in February 1989, the war in the Gulf had been over less than six months. It may be that the breakdown of superpower relations after the Soviet invasion contributed to the failure of the international community, and the United States and the Soviet Union in particular, to take any pre-emptive action in the first half of 1980 to stave off the likelihood of war breaking out between Iran and Iraq. Certainly, concerted action aimed at ending the war came about only when Moscow had already signalled its desire to disentangle itself from Afghanistan.

The Soviet decision to invade Afghanistan reflected in part Moscow's concern about the growth of Islamic fundamentalism in central Asia, a trend which was confirmed by the triumph of the Iranian revolution. The southern regions of the Russian Empire conquered by the Czars were now home to more than thirty million Muslims of Persian or Turkish origin who still had more in common with their neighbours in Iran and Afghanistan than with their fellow citizens in Russia or the Ukraine. The Bolshevik leadership had been engaged until 1928 in a military campaign to subdue Muslim separatists in the Caucasus and central Asia and there were further risings as late as 1941, after which Stalin purged even the pro-regime leaders of the Muslim republics. Under Brezhnev there were efforts to modernise the backward Asian republics and to allow a measure of Islamic cultural expression among populations which had never been satisfactorily converted to the doctrines of Marxism–Leninism. After the Iranian revolution, however, Brezhnev's liberal policies towards the Muslim republics was dropped in favour of a revival of anti-religious campaigns. There were grounds for Moscow's fears that the events in Iran would spill over into Afghanistan and the southern Soviet Union. Fundamentalist movements, inspired by the example of Khomeini, had begun to appear in the Caucasian and central Asian republics and were attracting more adherents than the communist party. This process appeared to accelerate after the invasion of Afghanistan and the Soviet Union's failure to eradicate the Mujahedin rebels. The Gulf war indirectly served the Soviet Union's purposes by keeping Iran as much as possible out of the Afghan equation. Much as the Islamic Republic might have wished to involve itself more deeply in Afghanistan, it was constrained by its more pressing conflict with the Iraqis and there was no way in which the leadership, despite their constant expressions of support for the Mujahedin, could afford to risk a war on two fronts.

For the most part, practical Iranian assistance to the rebel cause was confined to the Shia minority in Afghanistan, which was less involved in the direct confrontation with the Soviet invasion force

than were the larger Sunni-led groups. In addition, this aid was
kept strictly under the control of Revolutionary Guards infiltrated
into Afghanistan. Officially, the borders between Iran and
Afghanistan were closed, although there was a relatively free
movement of people, and the Iranian authorities kept a tight rein
on the smuggling of arms to the rebels. This relatively low-key
Iranian policy was designed to prevent any unnecessary friction
with the Soviet Union on the Afghan border and to avoid giving
Moscow any excuse to retaliate against Iranian interference in
Afghanistan by increasing its support for Iraq. On the other
hand, Iranian support to the Mujahedin increased somewhat once
Moscow resumed its supply of weapons to Iraq in July 1982.
A commentary published in the Tehran newspaper *Kayhan* in
December 1988 reflected on the relationship between the war in
the Gulf and events in Afghanistan:

> The eight-year war with Iraq meant that Afghanistan was not
> the prime concern of the country's foreign policy, yet during
> these eight years Iran never cut short its fidelity and support
> for the Mujahedin. Many political analysts believe that if Iran
> had shown a degree of flexibility in the Afghan issue the
> developments in the war with Iraq would have taken a differ-
> ent form.
>   During the last years of the war, the West's support for
> Iraq had become obvious and at the same time Iran's relations
> with Moscow were becoming warmer. But at the same time
> Soviet military help for Iraq continued. The reason for this,
> as mentioned time and again by Kremlin leaders, was because
> of Iran's insistence on a Soviet withdrawal from Afghanistan
> and the establishment of a regime in Kabul that would be
> freely elected by the people. . . . The war with Iraq was
> preventing Iran from carrying on its necessary role in Afghan
> developments. This was because Iran did not want to increase
> its activity and cause more sensitivity among the Soviets,
> thereby causing more danger in the process of the war, of
> which the Soviets were capable.

The Iranians may have overestimated the apparent warming in
relations with Moscow in the latter years of the war, though it is
true that by 1987, with the obvious failure of its intervention in
Afghanistan, Moscow was eager to ensure a smooth disengage-

ment. In order to cover its withdrawal Moscow needed the maximum of goodwill from Iran and could not afford to see an increase in Iranian assistance to the Mujahedin or an upsurge in Islamic propaganda directed against its own southern republics, for the invasion had failed not only militarily but also politically. It damaged relations with other Muslim states and, far from discouraging the revival of Islam within the Soviet Union, only served to enhance it. In the new mood of *glasnost* Soviet officials began to confess privately that Afghanistan had been a mistake.

It was against the background of Moscow's preparations for withdrawal from Afghanistan that the Soviet deputy foreign minister, Yuli Vorontsov, who was to be appointed ambassador to Kabul in the autumn of 1988, began his intensive diplomatic activity in the Gulf. For a time it appeared that Moscow was shifting its diplomatic weight behind Iran, but ultimately this proved to be an illusion. The Kremlin's tactic during 1987 was to play both sides in order to facilitate an ending of the war. The Soviet Union had given a commitment to Saddam Hussein that it would not allow Iraq to be defeated and the best that Iran could realistically hope for was that Moscow would stave off the imposition of a one-sided arms embargo and perhaps represent Tehran's viewpoint within the Security Council. But at the same time Moscow was prepared to capitalise on Iran's desire to publicise an apparent rapprochement, so there was talk of Rafsanjani visiting Moscow, and a series of bilateral deals were signed which appeared to indicate a radical shift towards the Soviet Union, though on closer inspection many of the projects were seen to be extremely tentative.

One of the protocols signed by Vorontsov was an agreement to import 700,000 b/d of Iranian crude via an existing gas pipeline to the Soviet border, a deal implying a major economic shift towards the Soviet Union, making Iran less dependent on the Gulf waterway but more closely tied to Moscow; but in fact the project was impractical, at least in the short-term, as the pipeline could not easily be adapted. There was also a more realistic agreement to build a new pipeline and two dams on the Araxes river and to undertake joint oil exploration in the Caspian Sea – but that was carefully left as no more than an intention for the future, with no dates set for commencement. It was all an attempt to put pressure on the Americans, so the Iranian propaganda machine went to work letting everyone know what had been done, and spreading the rumour of a secret friendship and cooperation treaty between the Soviet Union and Iran, and of Soviet commitments to sell warplanes, missiles and other weapons to Tehran. Neither side denied the rumours and the Soviet spokesman, Gennady Gerasimov, said carefully that 'both sides have expressed interest in expanding cooperation and mutual friendship'.

Tehran hoped to frighten the United States into thinking twice about a military escalation in the Gulf in Iraq's favour by implying that such a move was likely either to push it into the Soviet orbit or to provoke Soviet military action to defend Iran. But the Americans knew Moscow had no intention of becoming involved in a conflict with them over the Gulf, but now wanted to see the war ended as quickly as possible in order to avert an even greater expansion of US power in the region. The Iranian leaders had chosen the wrong time to play their Soviet card. Although Moscow and Washington remained suspicious of each other's intentions in the Gulf, a broad consensus was emerging on the need to end the war, exemplified in the unanimous support for Resolution 598. So as pressure built up from the US navy in the Gulf, it was quite apparent that the Soviet Union had no plans to come to the aid of Iran. Indeed, behind the scenes, in the last six months of the war, Moscow put into effect an unofficial ban throughout the Eastern bloc aimed at starving Iran of arms.

Within two weeks of the adoption by the Security Council of Resolution 598, Vorontsov travelled to Baghdad and then to Tehran to explain the Kremlin's position on the international efforts to end the war. Vorontsov's shuttle mission, which lasted until the war was over, was to put pressure on Iran on two fronts, Afghanistan and the Gulf. He arrived on one of his regular visits to Tehran in July 1988 just as Iran finally announced its acceptance of 598; he offered the Iranians a straight deal linking a reduction of weapons supplies to Iraq with Iranian cooperation in implementing the Afghan peace accord which had been signed in Geneva three months earlier. The Kremlin seemed, however, to have miscalculated the mood in Tehran. Rafsanjani rejected the deal and in doing so castigated Moscow for having stood by while Iran was invaded, and for having armed the aggressor. The Russians, he said, were now proposing to reduce these arms supplies in return for Tehran's acceptance of the Kabul regime.

'They are directly telling us: "Afghanistan for Iraq." However, we will not step down from our principles.' In publicly rebuffing the Soviet overture, he was showing that the doctrine of 'neither East nor West' remained in force, despite earlier indications of a shift towards Moscow. The regime would point to its lack of dependence on either superpower as one of the 'victories' of the Gulf war.

As with so much else in the Soviet Union since the accession of Mikhail Gorbachev two years before, foreign policy had undergone a fundamental reappraisal directed towards a scaling down of tension with the West and the advent of a new era of detente. The old cold warrior, Andrei Gromyko, was kicked upstairs to the presidency to be replaced by a new foreign minister, Eduard Shevardnadze, the very image of *glasnost* and reasonableness. Soviet support for the Western-sponsored UN resolution was unprecedented and reflected the realities of the emerging new relationship between the superpowers. The Kremlin remained perturbed by the level of the US naval build-up in the Gulf and baulked at imposing a one-sided arms embargo against Iran, but these reservations did not undermine the fact that both Moscow and Washington were now agreed that a continuation of the Gulf war, far from serving the interests of either superpower, was a positive hindrance to world peace.

In the summer of 1987, Gorbachev's main foreign policy objectives were to secure a medium-range nuclear missile treaty at the Washington summit with President Reagan in December that year, and to extract the Soviet Union from its military entanglement in Afghanistan, so cooperation with the United States on ending the Gulf war served his purposes on both counts: it would remove an area of potential superpower friction and would also demonstrate Moscow's new flexibility in confronting problems of mutual concern. When Gorbachev took over, he inherited the foreign policy of the Brezhnev era in which the belief was that the United States wanted to see a perpetuation of a regional war on the Soviet Union's southern border. This perception had undergone a sea change by the summer of 1987. Shortly after the Security Council's unanimous adoption of Resolution 598, a Soviet commentator acknowledged that 'the United States has no stake in the continuation of the Iran–Iraq war'.

# 12

# The struggle for
# power in Tehran

The Iranian Majlis has been compared to the British Parliament and the Israeli Knesset for the acerbity of its debates and the occasional pungency of its wit. When Speaker Rafsanjani rose one day to demand that every able-bodied young man should immediately volunteer for the front, an irate deputy shouted from the back of the assembly: 'What's your son doing in Switzerland, then?'

What had been, under the Shah, a rubber-stamp assembly became a forum for often divisive debate among radicals and conservatives, pragmatists and zealots about the future of the revolution. Despite the repression which accompanied the counter-terror and the restrictions imposed in the course of the war, there still existed within the narrow clergy-dominated political circle an element of democracy and freedom of speech, though the war had given an opportunity to the Islamic leadership to pick off its internal enemies one by one: firstly Bani-Sadr, then the People's Mujahedin and later the Tudeh party. But as the conflict entered its eighth year, and the prospect of victory looked increasingly remote, the deep divisions within the regime itself appeared to worsen. The war was a unifying factor as long as a military outcome seemed possible, and the existence of an outside enemy was regularly cited by Khomeini as a reason to put aside factional arguments, but by 1987 the war had become yet another factor fuelling the inter-clergy division. Within the senior leadership there were those, including Rafsanjani, who were beginning to recognise the inevitability of a negotiated settlement, although such an outcome seemed impossible while Khomeini was still alive. To argue too forcibly for peace, as Rafsanjani was at one point reminded during a stormy meeting with hardline radical students, was to challenge the Imam.

General elections to the third post-revolution Majlis were due in the spring of 1988. The first two parliaments had been marked by a constant battle between a government committed to greater state control and social reform and a deeply conservative Council of Guardians, the constitutional watchdog committee whose task it was to reject legislation which did not conform to the tenets of Islam. The traditionalist mullahs on the Council took a broad view of their duties and regularly used their veto powers to hold up land reform, labour legislation and nationalisation – on the grounds that legitimately held private property is inviolable in Islam. The activities of the Guardians, who had many partisans within the Majlis, frustrated not only the radical advocates of outright state control, such as the dour Prime Minister, Mir Hossein Mousavi, but also the modernising pragmatists, such as Rafsanjani, whose job it was to ensure the smooth passage of government legislation.

So in June 1987 Rafsanjani appealed to Khomeini to intervene to stop the Guardians and their conservative allies playing a spoiling role in the functions of government. The subsequent events of the summer – the US intervention in the Gulf and the deaths of Iranian pilgrims at Mecca – served to radicalise political opinion and to bring hardliners such as Hojatoleslam Mohtashemi to the fore. The mood in the country and within the mass of the clergy pointed to a radical victory in the forthcoming elections. In October there was an attempt by some conservatives to have the elections postponed on the grounds that in the current crisis in the war they threatened to exacerbate factional divisions and undermine national unity, but this ploy did not work; even President Khamenei, who was identified with the conservative wing, argued that the elections should go ahead. Ayatollah Khomeini also intervened with a series of decrees which favoured the government over the Guardians: he unblocked a contentious Labour Law by approving the government's right to impose statutory guarantees for workers in private employment and he confirmed the legitimacy of state control of underground minerals. These otherwise unremarkable edicts were a clear signal to the conservatives that they would no longer be allowed to obstruct the work of government.

Khomeini also rejected the view of the Guardians that the powers vested in the government were already too great and posed a threat to Islam. President Khamenei attempted to fight a rearguard action on behalf of the conservatives but was forced to recant when Khomeini issued a further directive which authorised the government to disregard minor rulings of Islam if these were shown to run counter to the national interests. He also set up a new Assembly of Discernment to arbitrate in disputes between parliament and the Guardians.

Khomeini's edicts failed, however, to end the factional differences, so that at one of the most crucial junctures of the war the clerical leadership was engaged in a complex politico-theological dispute and facing the most divisive elections since the revolution. If it had been a simple radical–conservative split, then Khomeini's intervention might have ended it. But there were no homogeneous groupings; the divisions tended to be on individual issues rather than along rigid factional lines, and in the jockeying for power there were shifting alliances which appeared to defy political logic. Among the proponents of greater state control were those, such as Mohtashemi, the interior minister, who took an extreme line on foreign policy and a continuation of the war, and others, such as Rafsanjani, who believed in an eventual rapprochement with the West and a negotiated settlement with Iraq. Among the conservative mullahs were zealots who sought stricter adherence to Islamic morality in broadcasting and total observance by women of the rules of Islamic dress, while others argued for greater personal freedoms.

In essence, the multi-factional conflict represented the beginning of a war of succession for control of the revolution after Khomeini's death, a struggle in which personal antagonisms were often more important than political differences. There were those who inclined towards a one-party, centralised state of Stalinist rigidity and others, notably Rafsanjani – and perhaps even Khomeini, who was otherwise above the factional fray – who recognised a degree of plurality within a single Islamic cause. Beyond the strictly political dispute there existed a more philosophical division between two competing ideologies of the revolution. The first represented a pragmatic recognition of Iran's position as a nation state, subject to the influences of the outside world; the second visualised a return to a utopian Islamic society, on the lines believed to have existed at the time of the Prophet, and which would either act as a catalyst for the resurgence of Islam or else would stand alone against the world.

The elections to the Majlis in the spring of 1988 forced the internal divisions in the regime out into the open for the first time, and although other factors were to combine to force Iran finally to accept a ceasefire, the power struggle played its part in persuading Khomeini that the revolution was as much at risk from within as from outside forces. In March there was a split in the previously monolithic Tehran Militant Clergy Association which had been founded at Khomeini's behest during his exile in Iraq – many of the senior clergymen who took positions of power after the revolution, including Rafsanjani and Khamenei, had been founding members. The Association represented all shades of opinion among the mullahs who supported the revolution, but during the course of the war it had come increasingly under the sway of its traditionalist conservative wing.

With the elections approaching, the radical-progressive faction of the Association announced that it was breaking away to form a rival group called the Tehran Militant Clerics, with the aim of presenting younger and more radical non-clergy candidates from the worker and student movements at the forthcoming poll. The movement had the tacit backing of Khomeini and the active support of his son, Ahmad, and its leadership included several members of Khomeini's private office and a number of the most hardline ministers. A leading radical, Hojatoleslam Mehdi Karrubi, who was in charge of the Iranian contingent at the Mecca pilgrimage, was appointed secretary-general.

The emergence of the Tehran Militant Clerics was a factor in ensuring electoral victory for the radicals, but the elections themselves were a disaster, marked by disputes over ballot-rigging and a running squabble between Mohtashemi's interior ministry and the Council of Guardians over who was responsible for supervising electoral law; for many war-weary Iranians, here was further proof that the concept of Islamic democracy was a charade. Political tensions which surrounded the elections were exacerbated by the activities of Hojatoleslam Mohtashemi, a middle-ranking cleric who espoused extreme political ideas and who saw in the elections an opportunity to further his own position.

The interior minister was later blamed by his rivals for having promoted dissent at a time when it was vital for Iran to concentrate on critical policy decisions regarding the future of the war. Mohtashemi had been ambassador in Damascus until 1985, an important wartime post in view of Syria's support for Iran, and was also closely involved in the activities of the pro-Iranian Hizbollah movement in Lebanon; his critics accused him of viewing the Iranian situation in Lebanese terms as one of outright conflict between irreconcilable factions. A Tehran deputy, Mohammad Reza Bahonar, said of him:

> Mr Mohtashemi has gained his experience from the internal strife in Lebanon and in his own mind he has divided the entire country's officials into two groups: those who oppose and those who favour the regime. He has made himself the measuring stick for this definition and equates those who oppose or favour the regime with those who oppose or favour him.

In the eight months leading up to the elections, Mohtashemi placed his own people in important provincial governorships and district administrations, provoking conflicts with generally more traditionalist local clerical leaders. Bahonar and others accused Mohtashemi of making such an issue of the elections that the campaign overshadowed the war effort, and after the elections the conflict erupted into clashes between rival clergymen in a number of towns, including the holy city of Qom. Denouncing the interior minister in the Majlis after the war had ended, Bahonar said: 'The fact that we must have clean elections was so much stressed, it seemed that before Mr Mohtashemi became minister there had been no clean elections held in Iran. Perhaps the sum total of this issue was that there was the least number of people present on the sensitive front lines of the war during election time.'

The bitterly disputed elections resulted in a virtual landslide for the radicals and brought more than 140 new members into the Majlis, mainly young candidates who had come up through the revolutionary institutions, such as the Revolutionary Guard Corps. This was a mixed blessing for those like Rafsanjani, who tended towards radicalism on economic issues but pragmatism when it came to foreign policy and the war. The elections had routed the more obstructive conservatives but, at the same time, the results threatened to enhance the standing of the clique around Mohtashemi and Prime Minister Mousavi, who were opposed both to better relations with the West and to a negotiated settlement with Iraq. It became more important than ever for Rafsanjani and his fellow foreign policy moderates to pursue a diplomatic settlement before the pro-war factions had a chance to consolidate their power.

Ali Akbar Hashemi Rafsanjani was one of a handful of Iranian politicians whom the bewildered United States identified from afar as a 'moderate'. As with Bazargan and Bani-Sadr before him, Rafsanjani was seen as a man with whom Washington hoped it could do business, but this analysis was only partly right. Rafsanjani was certainly a pragmatist who understood the international pressures weighing on wartime Iran, and he had been prepared to risk the wrath of the radicals by authorising the Irangate dealings in order to gain much needed weapons, but the truth was that there were no longer any moderates in the Western sense in the Tehran regime. Rafsanjani's career was a rebuke to those who were later to claim that the 1979 revolution had been belatedly hijacked by the clergy. Long before the revolution, Rafsanjani had a reputation as one of the most uncompromising supporters of Khomeini, and like many of Iran's post-revolutionary leaders he had studied under the Imam; but unlike most of them, he had refused to collaborate in the slightest degree with the Shah's regime. He was jailed for operating a revolutionary cell in the 1960s with fellow clerics and when he was subsequently forced into military service, almost as a punishment for his revolutionary activities, he took to proselytising his fellow conscripts and had to be dispatched back to Qom. For almost twenty years he struggled unquestioningly in the Khomeini cause and made close contacts with all the competing factions who were to make up the revolutionary forces, as well as raising money for the Islamic cause through the trading connections of his relatively prosperous family.

By 1987, at the age of fifty-three, Rafsanjani had become the most powerful figure in Iran after Khomeini. Politically and intellectually he far outstripped most of his fellow clerics, including Ayatollah Hossein Ali Montazeri, Khomeini's designated successor, though as a hojatoleslam Rafsanjani was relatively junior in the religious hierarchy. But in the manner of the Grand

Ayatollahs, he was capable of attracting a personal following, and among the increasingly cynical population many still retained confidence in the abilities of Brother Hashemi or, as he was less affectionately known, Akbar Shah.

Rafsanjani's position derived from his own undoubted political talents but also from his close relationship with Khomeini, shown when the Ayatollah protected him over the Irangate affair when he became the target of both the radicals and the conservatives. Rafsanjani was accused by his critics of wanting to be all things to all men, and his speeches certainly gave that impression. From the podium of the Tehran University prayer ground he would preach Friday sermons denouncing imperialism and demanding social justice and a redistribution of wealth – but he would always assure the businessmen of the bazaar that he shared their belief in the sanctity of private property. This ambiguous populism was not unusual in Iran, and was very much a reflection of Khomeini's own political style. Although the Ayatollah had little interest in economic affairs, once remarking that the revolution was not made in order to lower the price of watermelons, in other areas of national concern he invariably sought to reconcile all the competing viewpoints and rarely came down too vigorously on one side or the other.

Rafsanjani was among the first to recognise the political realities facing Iran in the summer of 1987 after the adoption by the Security Council of Resolution 598. He and other pragmatists realised that the violently rejectionist rhetoric of some Iranian leaders was harming the country's true foreign policy interests. Tehran had consistently dismissed the right of the UN and outside powers to intervene in the affairs of the Gulf, but now at last the outside world was making concerted efforts to end the war in a manner which could harm the long-term interests of Iran. Although Iran neither accepted nor rejected Resolution 598, the leadership gave a freer hand to the moderate elements within the foreign ministry to pursue diplomatic alternatives.

The purpose of Iranian foreign policy had, until now, been to sever what were described as 'dependent links' with the industrialised powers, the United States in particular, and to foster closer relations with the Third World. Since the revolution, the conduct of Iranian diplomacy had always been far more conventional than the extremist rhetoric of the ayatollahs had implied. Although Iran was responsible for supporting terrorism in Lebanon and some of the Gulf states and even, on occasions, in Western Europe, diplomatic relations between Iranian embassies and host countries were on the whole correct. By the summer of 1987, however, the pragmatists realised that Iran had no real friends in the United Nations to protect its interests. After the revolution Tehran had always tried to keep a line open to the European Community, firstly through Britain, then France and then West Germany, but events in Lebanon, above all the taking of hostages, by pro-Iranian groups, served to isolate Iran from Western Europe. Lebanon, the one country where Iran had enjoyed some success in exporting the revolution, was becoming a diplomatic millstone around the regime's neck.

Since the revolution Iran had concentrated on cultivating its relationships with the Third World and as a result gained consider-able international goodwill from countries with which it had not historically had close ties. Among the permanent members of the Security Council, however, where the power lay, it had no real friends. The relationship with the Soviet Union was problematic, and though China, which was supplying Silkworm missiles and low-level military technology, was willing to oppose a one-sided arms embargo, it was not a central player in the Gulf, while the United States, France and Britain appeared, despite their protestations of neutrality, to be actively hostile to the Tehran regime. Although the best efforts of Tehran's diplomats were now directed at improving Iran's international image, it was still regarded in the West as a sponsor of terrorism through its support of bombings, hijackings and hostage-taking, and the Western perception of Iran fostered by the US embassy hostage crisis still persisted. This state of affairs was exacerbated by the continued incarceration of the American, French and British hostages in Lebanon.

The idea of trying to re-establish ties with the Western powers was anathema to the foreign policy radicals, who believed that the pragmatists were betraying the ideals of the revolution by bargaining with its enemies. They favoured a foreign policy in which Iran's only really close ties would be with the so-called progressive Muslim countries, notably Syria and Libya, Algeria and South Yemen. According to this radical doctrine, Iran would continue to undermine the conservative Arab regimes of the Gulf rather than seek their friendship; relations with Western Europe and 'dependent' regimes such as Turkey and Pakistan would be kept to an absolute minimum.

The kidnapping of Western hostages in Lebanon began before the departure of the multinational peace force in 1983, but the process accelerated after the takeover of west Beirut by the Shia fundamentalists and their allies. The kidnappers operated behind a variety of names, including that of Islamic Jihad. Some pressed for the release of Shia prisoners held in Israel, Kuwait or Europe; others demanded changes in Western policy towards the Gulf war. Those involved were a loose alliance of individuals and groups linked by their common antipathy towards the West, though there were also opportunistic street gangs which would target any foreigner in west Beirut and then sell their captive to the highest bidder. The agents of Libya, Syria and radical Palestinian organisations were occasionally involved with specific operations but the overall and most powerful sponsor of the kidnappers was Iran, working through its embassy in Beirut, through Revolutionary Guards stationed in the Bekaa valley and through Hizbollah, the Lebanese offshoot of the Party of God.

In the worst period of the kidnapping scourge, from early 1985 to early 1987, more than twenty foreigners, of whom the largest number were Americans and French, went missing in Lebanon. Some abductions were claimed by groups whose names implied a Libyan or Palestinian connection, while others were claimed directly by Islamic Jihad; in some cases, such as that of the Anglican Church envoy, Terry Waite, no claim of responsibility was ever received. Some captives, such as the West Germans Alfred Schmidt and Rudolph Cordes, were abducted by the relatives of pro-Iranian Shia militants held in jails abroad. Although hostage-taking, like hijacking, was condemned by the hierarchy in Tehran, it was an open secret that Iran was deeply involved in supporting the activities of its Shia surrogates in Beirut and was therefore the key to securing the release of the kidnapped Westerners – the Irangate affair was proof enough that both sides acknowledged the degree of Iranian involvement.

It was Iran's growing need for sophisticated weapons, and later for diplomatic support in the West, which encouraged the pragmatists in Tehran to try to use the hostages as bargaining chips. After the Irangate dealings with Washington were aborted, efforts were concentrated on renewing ties with Western Europe, and France was an obvious target, since the French were eager, for domestic political reasons, to secure the release of their hostages in Lebanon and Iran wanted to see a reduction in French military support for Iraq. Iran also sought the repayment of outstanding debts by the French and a curb on the activities of Paris-based Iranian opposition groups, notably the People's Mujahedin. At its creation, the Islamic Republic had been relatively well-disposed towards France because the French had never played a colonialist role in Iran and had given asylum to Khomeini in 1978 until his return to Iran. During the war, however, France's policy of selling arms to Iraq led to a serious deterioration in relations and in Lebanon, ten Frenchmen were hostages of pro-Iranian and other extremist groups by early 1986. In the spring of that year, Prime Minister Jacques Chirac announced that France sought to improve its relations with Iran, and in June the government 'showed its goodwill' by expelling the Mujahedin leadership to Iraq. Within two weeks two French hostages, Philippe Rochot and Georges Hansen, were freed by their kidnappers, the Revolutionary Justice Organisation.

In September 1986 Tehran put a set of conditions to the French, including a demand for a more neutral policy on the Gulf war, on the tacit understanding that this would lead to the release of the remaining French hostages in Beirut. In the same month, the French government prevailed upon Saddam Hussein to pardon two opposition Iraqis whose expulsion from Paris to Baghdad the previous March had been condemned by Islamic Jihad. Within three months of the return of the two Iraqis to France, three more French hostages were released in recognition of what the Revolutionary Justice Organisation described as 'the evolution of French policy in the Middle East'. By contrast, the following March the same group threatened to execute one of its remaining hostages in revenge for what it regarded as a pro-Iraqi tilt by President Mitterrand. The link between the hostage-takers, whatever they cared to call themselves, Iran and French attitudes on the Gulf war was crystal clear.

In response to public demands for greater action to secure the release of the remaining hostages, Chirac set up a team under the direction of the interior minister, Charles Pasqua, which was to deal secretly both with Iran and the kidnappers. Pasqua created a network of middlemen in France, the Middle East and Africa to make the necessary contacts on France's behalf and to establish the terms of a deal. It was a complex and laborious process. At one point, in order to establish their credentials with the kidnappers, the negotiators had to summon up a French warship and have it sail along the Lebanese coast at a pre-arranged time. One of the last French hostages to be freed, the journalist Jean-Paul Kauffmann, said after his release in May 1988 that he had been aware of a growing direct involvement by the Iranians in the final year of his captivity. He described how a group of men came to interrogate him and his fellow French hostages on 10 April 1987; none of the visitors understood Arabic and they insisted on putting their questions in English. It was clear to Kauffmann that the newcomers were Iranians.

Although the Chirac government was prepared to strike a deal, it was only ready to go so far in satisfying the demands of the kidnappers and their Iranian mentors, particularly after a series of terrorist bombings in Paris in September 1986 which left eleven people dead. A six-month investigation uncovered a pro-Iranian network suspected of operating on the orders of Tehran, a discovery which played into the hands of the hawks in the Chirac government, notably Pasqua, who believed that the best way to deal with Iran was with toughness. Then in the summer of 1987 an Iranian embassy interpreter, Vahid Gordji, was ordered to appear before an investigating magistrate to answer questions about the bombing campaign the previous autumn. Gordji claimed diplomatic immunity and sought refuge in his embassy, when to the horror of the professional diplomats at the Quai d'Orsay, Pasqua ordered armed police to besiege the building. In retaliation, the Iranians put the French embassy in Tehran under siege, and on 17 July Paris broke diplomatic relations. Two weeks later the government dispatched the aircraft carrier *Clemenceau* and its support ships to join the Western naval build-up in the Gulf.

It is likely that Pasqua deliberately provoked the Gordji crisis in order to force a break in diplomatic relations. It came at a time when Iran was already faced with the American naval build-up and needed international support more than ever before, so the last thing Tehran wanted in the summer of 1987 was for France to turn its back on the developing rapprochement and to side actively with the Americans.

Four months later, two more Frenchmen were freed, and then when the last three hostages were released in May 1988, it was the restoration of diplomatic relations between the two countries which formed a central part of the deal. The day after the last three came out, Chirac announced that ties would be renewed; but although the Iranians also secured agreement to the repayment of the remainder of a $1 billion loan made by the Shah to the French Eurodif nuclear programme and the resumption of French oil purchases, suspended during the break in relations, the dealings with the French were only partially successful. They did not lead to a significant shift in France's policy towards the Gulf war, nor to a withdrawal of French naval forces from the area. France kept to its promise of restoring diplomatic relations but by that time the war was virtually over. During the last stages one of the French negotiators, a Lebanese-born physician, Dr Raza Raad, was summoned to the telephone in Beirut. It was Rafsanjani in Tehran. Iran had no further objections, he told Raad, to the release of the last three hostages.

At almost the same time that France broke diplomatic relations with Iran, two further events occurred which were to contribute to Iran's international isolation. In the summer of 1987, one of the few British diplomats posted at the British interests section of the Swedish embassy, Edward Chaplin, was briefly detained and beaten up by Revolutionary Guards. Iran maintained that the incident was a response to the unlawful detention of an Iranian member of its consulate in Manchester, who, it was alleged, had been unlawfully detained on shoplifting charges and beaten up by British police. Whatever the motive, Chaplin was withdrawn and for the first time since the revolution Britain's limited diplomatic presence in Tehran came to an end. As a permanent member of the UN Security Council, like France, Britain was a central player in the diplomatic manoeuvrings to end the war and party to the Western naval presence in the Gulf, but just when the pragmatists in Tehran needed goodwill at the UN, the link with Britain was all but severed.

Although Britain resisted any temptation to bargain with Iran for the freedom of its hostages in Lebanon, Rafsanjani nevertheless sponsored an indirect approach to London in early 1988, indicating a desire for improved relations. The British, who were eager to re-establish a relationship in view of the economic and strategic importance of Iran, but were nevertheless wary of Iranian intentions, responded cautiously. Again, as in the case of France, it was not until the very end of the war that the tentative contacts persuaded the British government of the desirability of sending its diplomats back to Tehran.

Shortly after the Chaplin affair, a much more serious event occurred which widened the existing rift between Iran and its southern Gulf neighbours and fed the by now paranoid belief of the Iranian leadership that Iran was the target of an international conspiracy. On 31 July, at the height of the pilgrimage to Mecca, there were clashes in the streets of the holy city between Iranian pilgrims and Saudi security forces which left more than 400 people dead, though what Iran was to describe as 'a massacre of innocents' had its background in events at the previous Haj which had been kept secret for a year. According to an Iranian account, some weeks after the 1986 McFarlane–North mission to Tehran which the radical Mehdi Hashemi had attempted to disrupt, Hashemi and his associates devised a plot to assassinate senior figures in the regime and at the same time wreck any further attempts at rapprochement with the outside world. If the plot had succeeded, it might well have brought other states into the war.

The plan, again according to the Iranian version, was to smuggle high explosives into Saudi Arabia in order to carry out bombing attacks against Iranian religious, government and military officials at Mecca during the pilgrimage. The bombings would then be blamed on the Saudis. The explosives were concealed in the luggage of unsuspecting Iranian pilgrims travelling to Saudi Arabia on a charter flight from Isfahan, but the Saudi authorities discovered them during a search of the pilgrims' bags carried out, according to Iranian sources, because Tehran had tipped the Saudis off to the possibility of a terrorist plot by a radical faction. The Saudis, apparently satisfied that the plot did not have the sanction of the Tehran leadership, did not publicly announce their find. Riyadh kept the secret of the explosives find for over a year, only to reveal it on television within a few hours of the bloody events of 31 July 1987. Mehdi Hashemi had by then been arrested and was put on trial for a series of crimes stemming from the Mecca plot and his role in exposing Irangate. He was charged, among other things, with attempting to disrupt Iranian foreign policy, and his fate became a test of strength between rival factions. As head of the Office for the Export of the Revolution, he had a powerful mentor in Ayatollah Montazeri, although it seems unlikely that Khomeini's successor was fully aware of his protégé's activities.

The Office was nevertheless closed down and Hashemi was sentenced to death, but it was not until September 1987 that Rafsanjani won Khomeini's authorisation to carry out the sentence. Hashemi became the first clerical member of the regime to be executed since the revolution. His arrest helped to restore Rafsanjani's authority after the setbacks caused by the Irangate revelations, and for a time the Speaker had a freer hand to pursue the pragmatic foreign policy line. By the summer of 1987, however, Iran's position was seriously weakened. Apart from the diplomatic setbacks, it had failed to make a decisive breakthrough in the land war and money was beginning to run short, and now its enemies appeared to be ganging up against it. The United States was visibly tilting towards Iraq and planning to enter the Gulf in strength, ostensibly to safeguard freedom of navigation but in practice to close the net on Iran. The UN Security Council unanimously passed what Tehran saw as a one-sided ceasefire resolution – 598 – and was contemplating an arms embargo against Iran. Khomeini reacted to the crisis characteristically by going on the offensive: in a speech to Iranian pilgrims on the eve of the Haj, he called on them to 'smash the teeth of the Americans in their mouth'.

Each year at Mecca since Khomeini's return to power, the Iranian contingent used the Haj as an occasion to propagate the political ideas of the revolution. Demonstrations by Iranian pilgrims often led to friction with the Saudi authorities, who insisted that the pilgrimage must remain a purely religious event, though in Khomeini's philosophy there was no distinction between politics and religion and he considered the Haj the right and proper occasion for proselytising the Muslim masses. In July 1987 the Saudi authorities were more than ever on their guard against trouble from the Iranians, not only because of the uncovering of the bombing plot the previous year, but also because of the rising tension in the Gulf with the build-up of the US fleet.

Among the two million Muslims attending the Haj, the 155,000 Iranians were the largest single contingent, and despite their reservations, the Saudis granted permission for the Iranians to stage what was effectively a political rally, the theme of which was a denunciation of the United States, the Soviet Union and Israel. The distance of the march, about one mile, and the duration, from 4.30 to 6.30 on the afternoon of 31 July, was agreed in negotiations between the Saudi Haj ministry and Karrubi, the leader of the Iranian pilgrims and Khomeini's representative. The Iranians rejected, however, a last-minute Saudi restriction on the size of the demonstration and a ban on the participation of non-Iranians, so that leaders of Lebanese Hizbollah and a number of Afghan Mujahedin representatives also took part alongside members of the Revolutionary Guard Corps. Women and war victims in wheelchairs were at the head of the demonstration, and bore the brunt of the violence when the march degenerated into running battles between Iranians and Saudi security forces which left 402 people dead, 275 of them Iranians.

Many victims were crushed to death as they fled in panic from the tear gas of the Saudi riot police. Independent witnesses have described hearing shots fired and some of the Iranian dead bore bullet wounds, although the Saudis denied that police fired into the crowds. How the violence started is also still a matter of dispute: the Saudis appear to have been guilty at least of an excess of zeal in containing the crowd and in responding to provocation from the demonstrators. The Iranians were certainly in a fervent mood which was stirred up by cheer-leaders who announced triumphantly at the height of the demonstration that a US helicopter had been shot down in the Gulf, but non-Iranian witnesses have described the march as a peaceful one until it reached the vicinity of the multi-storey car park of the Mecca city hall. It was from this building, the Iranians allege, that the crowd were pelted with rocks and other missiles and that this unprovoked attack led to the panic and rioting which followed.

The Iranians claimed, without presenting any direct proof, that the trouble was initiated by Iraqi and Jordanian agents who had been infiltrated into Mecca at the instigation of the Americans and with the connivance of the Saudi authorities. It was a version which was readily accepted back in Iran and fed the popular view that the violence was a deliberate attack on Iranians by Iraq and its allies. The demonstration had been against America and 'American Islam', therefore America and its reactionary Arab allies, according to the Iranian logic, must have been responsible for the attack. The incident had a profound effect in Iran and was seen as part of an international plot, already apparent from the presence of US forces in the Gulf, to attack the revolution. The pragmatists in Tehran vied with the radicals in the virulence of their denunciations of the treacherous Saudis and their allies. The Kuwaiti embassy building was stormed by *hizbollahi* and a 'Day of Hatred against America' was declared, while Rafsanjani threatened that Iran would avenge its dead by 'uprooting Saudi rulers from the region'. 'To take revenge for the sacred blood,' he said, 'is to free the holy shrines from the mischievous and wicked Wahhabis.' Mohtashemi, the interior minister, railed against 'the pioneers of paganism and apostasy, that is the United States, the Soviet Union and Israel'.

The incident at Mecca brought to the surface the latent religious and ethnic prejudice between Shia Iran and its Sunni Arab neighbours which Khomeini's universalist Islamic message had attempted to gloss over. The conflict between Iranian Shi'ism and Wahhabism, the puritanical doctrine of the ruling al Saud, was particularly deep: the Shia, with their saints and their holy tombs, were to the Wahhabis little better than idol-worshippers. The House of Saud had tried to stamp out Shi'ism in the peninsula in the nineteenth century and its forces had sacked the holy city of Kerbala in 1801, slaughtering 5,000 of its Shia inhabitants and destroying the shrines.

The Mecca riots represented one of the psychological turning points of the last year of the war in that Iranians could feel the international pressure building up against them. Although the events of the Haj provoked a temporary revival of revolutionary fervour, they also brought about a break in the already tense relations with Saudi Arabia and Kuwait.

The internal debate between foreign policy radicals and pragmatists which formed, in part, the background to the 1988 elections was less about means than about tactics. Hijackings and kidnappings had at one time or another been at least tacitly condoned by even the most senior members of the regime as an expression of revolutionary justice. But the pragmatists, with their eyes firmly set on a favourable diplomatic settlement of the war, were now more concerned about Iran's international image. Indirect contact had even been maintained with the United States, despite the trauma of Irangate, through Geneva, Algiers and Beirut. All this was anathema to the radicals, who saw no benefit in attempting to woo the traditional enemies of the revolution; they believed in the uncompromising export of the revolution and continued support for revolutionary action, particularly among the Shia of Lebanon. And just three days before the election a Kuwaiti 747 was hijacked to the Iranian city of Mashad and an uncharacteristically ruffled Rafsanjani, without referring to his internal rivals, described the hijacking as a plot against Iran.

A team of highly professional gunmen seized Kuwait Airways flight 422 and its ninety-six passengers and fifteen crew over the Arabian Sea during a flight from Bangkok to Kuwait on 5 April and ordered the Iraqi pilot to fly to Mashad. The hijackers were assumed to be Lebanese Shia on the grounds that they repeated the standing demand of the Islamic Jihad kidnappers for the release of the seventeen Shia militants, the members of Dawa, held in Kuwaiti jails for the series of bomb attacks in 1983. The deputy prime minister, Ali Reza Moayeri, a former US embassy student militant turned moderate, was dispatched to Mashad to negotiate and was apparently responsible for securing the release of most of the non-Kuwaitis on board, including twenty-two Britons. What later emerged, however, during the plane's two-week odyssey from Mashad to Larnaca and finally to Algiers, was that extra weapons and possibly men had been taken aboard at Mashad. The choice of Mashad, a religious centre in the far north-east and deep inside Iran, raised immediate suspicions that the gunmen had collaborators on the ground there. Elements of the Iranian opposition have since claimed that Rafsanjani himself was involved in supporting the hijacking. It was more logical, however, that the affair was designed to embarrass him and the pragmatists who could not afford, for domestic reasons, to condemn outright an operation by fellow Shia revolutionaries and yet who could recognise that, internationally, Iran's image was likely to suffer further damage from association with yet another terrorist outrage.

The abiding memory of polling day for the third Majlis was not one of Islamic democracy at work but of the Iraqi pilot of the Kuwaiti jet, the captive of Islamic extremists, desperately circling Beirut airport as his fuel ran low and pleading in vain for permission to land.

# 13

# The war at sea: America joins in

One of the great ironies of a war notable for its contradictions and anomalies came in May 1987. The American destroyer *Stark*, one of seven US navy ships then in the Gulf, was sailing alone in the northern part of the waterway when its radar operators detected an Iraqi Mirage plane approaching. There was nothing unusual about that, the navy commander noted later: in the previous nine months the Iraqis had flown 330 missions, launched 90 missiles and hit 40 targets. The Americans were well used to seeing Iraqi planes, and from the briefings of navy headquarters and the state department, looked on Iraq as the friendly power in the Gulf. Even when the Mirage pilot locked his attack radar on to the *Stark*, no more was done than to issue a second warning not to come too close, and only at the last moment was the order given to activate the Phalanx gun, a weapon which spews out hundreds of rounds in a pattern intended to intercept and explode any missile just before it strikes. It was all too late. Two Exocets got through the ship's defences and hit amidships; thirty-seven crewmen were killed and dozens of others injured.

What the Americans did not appear to know was that the *Stark* was being shadowed some miles away by an Iranian gunboat which was sailing on a parallel course. It may have been that the Iraqi pilot had detected the Iranian ship, or that he mistook the *Stark* for a tanker: whatever the reason, he made his attack and helped to change the course of history. But not as might have been expected – there were no calls for vengeance against Iraq from the Americans, no demands even for compensation. Instead, by convoluted logic, Iran was singled out as the author of all America's misfortunes and it was Iran, which played no part in the incident, which became the target of American wrath. Certainly President Hussein wrote to President Reagan assuring him that the attack had been a mistake, apologising for what had happened and sending his condolences, and there was full cooperation with the US Board of Inquiry sent to the Gulf to investigate. Yet the feeling persisted that in other circumstances, other places, the American response would not have been quite what it was. Somehow, the Americans succeeded in transforming the Iraqi mistake into a reason for stepping up pressure against Iran, for justifying their presence in the Gulf and providing a reason for increasing it. 'We've never considered the Iraqis hostile at all,' said Reagan. 'Iran is the villain of the piece.' Very soon, the number of American ships involved in the Gulf increased from seven to nearly eighty.

The attack on the *Stark* marked a turning point in the war, though if it had not occurred, the Americans would by this stage certainly have found another pretext for intervening – or would have done so with no excuse at all. A decision had already been taken, and the attack on the *Stark* was merely a useful trigger. The previous month, Iran had launched what seemed to be its most determined effort to break through the Iraqi defences to Basra, and the series of Kerbala offensives, as they were named, were nibbling away at the Iraqi defences. At huge cost to themselves, the Iranians were gradually pushing the defenders back, using shallow boats to cross the water obstacles, pouring in men to exploit every little opening, keeping up the pressure day after day. All Iraq could do was to hold grimly on as the war moved closer to the country's second city. In Basra, the sounds of war were becoming more audible, the shelling more frequent, the unease more palpable, while in Tehran the mullahs spoke of establishing a new free zone in southern Iraq, a second Islamic Republic which would eventually rule the whole country. So at the beginning of 1987 both sides believed that victory was in the balance: one more heave, one more great offensive, and Iran could break through the Iraqi lines, seize or by-pass Basra and cause such chaos that Saddam Hussein would be swept away to be replaced by others who would be ready to treat with Tehran. For Iraq, there were two imperatives: to hold on, cling to every scrap of land, and make any sacrifice to prevent the Iranian advance, but also to intensify the war at sea, hit any tankers lifting

Iranian oil, and destroy the terminals and the floating storage tanks. If the oil exports could only be stopped, revenues would dry up, supplies could not be obtained, and the whole Iranian war machine would come to a halt.

The balance was fine, and in world capitals no one was sure which way it would tip; what they did know was which way they wanted it to go. Seven years of bloody-minded virulence from Tehran, of regular broadcasts to the Muslim minorities in the USSR who will, by the next century, be the majority, had finally convinced the Russians that they could not allow the Iranians to win. Moscow and Washington were now pursuing parallel policies; both had decided that their strength had to be used to prevent an Iranian victory, and both realised that their pressure would be that much more effective if they acted in concert, not merely in parallel. The professionals on both sides saw a prospect of political gain, too, an opportunity to achieve some of their long-term objectives while dealing with an immediate problem.

One of the signs of common interest came when Richard Murphy, the assistant secretary of state in charge of the Middle East in the state department, paid a visit to Iraq at almost the same time as another important visitor, Soviet deputy foreign minister Vladimir Petrovsky. The superpowers were sending signals, but only the Iraqis seemed to understand; it was with a new confidence that they stepped up their attacks in the Gulf and reinforced the defenders around Basra. They were not going to be abandoned, but instead to be given every help a worried American administration could muster – an administration confident that such actions would not lead to any confrontation with a Russia just as anxious as the United States to hold the line along the Shatt al Arab. In the quiet consultations which went on Afghanistan and Israel, Syria and Egypt, Pakistan and Lebanon all figured. America wanted an accelerated Soviet withdrawal from Kabul, Moscow pressed for a Middle East peace conference, there was the question of support for President Zia ul Huq, arms to the Afghanistan Mujahedin, new weapons systems for Syria, the hostages in Lebanon . . . Officials of the state department and the Soviet Ministry of Foreign Affairs brought up problem after problem, settling a few, making progress here and there, agreeing to differ on many, but reaching consensus on a central theme: Iran had to be stopped. The way in which that was to be achieved emerged too. The United Nations was the easiest instrument for diplomatic action, and the American navy, assured of Soviet neutrality if not actual support, could take action in the Gulf, while both would move to tighten the international embargo on arms to Iran which was supposed to be in force. It was in those few early weeks in 1987 that Iran lost all hope of victory.

The attack on the *Stark* was the perfect excuse. Ignoring all the evidence of US mismanagement, poor seamanship and lack of vigilance, President Reagan went on the offensive, ordering a new 'state of alert' among US forces in the Gulf – a public relations phrase if ever there was one – and, more significantly, declaring that American ships would in future fire on any aircraft flying 'in a pattern that indicates hostile intent', a definition leaving much to individual judgment. Through all the statements and orders and explanations coming out of Washington, the one thing that was clear was that Iran remained the target, in effect the undeclared enemy that America was determined to contain. Rafsanjani, at least, understood the situation. 'We are really at war with the United States now,' he said, and very soon it began to look as if he was right, for once the reflagged Kuwaiti tankers started sailing in convoy incidents proliferated – though the first was more slapstick than tragedy. As it headed north up the Gulf escorted by US destroyers, the supertanker *Bridgeton* hit a mine; it blew a hole in the ship's side, but did not stop the vessel nor set the ship on fire. What it did do was terrify the US naval commanders that they might lose one of their ships, for, unlike the compartmentalised *Bridgeton*, warships could go up in flames or sink; so the world was treated to the spectacle of the US navy huddling in the wake of the supertanker they were supposed to be escorting, to protect themselves from mines. Laughter in the Gulf was about nine on the Richter scale, while in Washington there was a determined effort to avoid the subject.

Quite soon the situation did become more serious. In September 1987 the American navy said that it had detected the small *Iran Ajr* in the act of laying mines; four of the crew were killed, three wounded and the remaining twenty-six captured in the assault. After pictures of the mines aboard the *Iran Ajr* had been shown as well as footage of the prisoners lying face down on the deck of a US ship, their hands bound behind their backs, the Americans sank the Iranian ship and repatriated the prisoners via Oman.

Firm proof had finally been obtained that Iran was laying mines in international waters, while at almost the same time the Americans were giving details of the new Chinese Silkworm missiles which had been test-fired from sites near Bandar Abbas, and were also installed on the Fao peninsula within range of Kuwait.

In October the helicopters were in action once again, this time sinking three of the Boghammar speedboats based at Farsiyeh Island in the northern Gulf. Next Iran scored a remarkable, and certainly accidental, success when it fired a missile from Fao which hit one of the American-flagged Kuwaiti tankers. To guard against such damage, barges with special reflectors had been put in position, and it was apparently one of these which guided the missile in; but the barge which should have been hit was on the far side of the tanker, so that at the last moment the missile struck that instead. In reprisal, the Americans attacked two Iranian oil platforms. And so it went on, until the culmination came in the major naval engagement of the war in April 1988, when the US destroyed much of the Iranian navy in a series of brief battles which began with American attempts to retaliate after the frigate *Samuel B. Roberts* hit a newly laid mine, causing the death of ten US sailors.

The received wisdom in the outside world was still that a negotiated settlement of the war could never be achieved while Khomeini was alive, for the Ayatollah's pledges that Iran would fight to the last house and the last man were taken at face value. By mid-1987, however, it was apparent that Iran's leaders were actively pursuing the possibilities of a negotiated peace. Iran's original war aims – the punishment of Iraq for its aggression, payment of reparations and the downfall of Saddam Hussein – had been whittled down to single demand for international recognition that Iraq had begun the war.

The Kerbala offensives, which were designed to cut off Basra, had failed to achieve the breakthrough that would have brought outright victory. Iran had rallied all its forces for that one 'final' onslaught, so now that it had failed the leaders had to decide how to pursue the war, and in July Rafsanjani revealed that sharp differences existed between those who favoured a war of attrition and those who wanted just one more 'final' offensive – he spoke of this policy split on the eve of the US reflagging operation and it was clearly intended as a signal to Washington that US interference in the Gulf would play into the hands of the hardliners who favoured total war, a mistaken estimate if ever there was one. In another vain attempt to scare off outside powers, the Iranians also went through the motions of preparing for another offensive. President Khamenei and other senior mullahs swapped their clerical robes for military uniforms and spoke at mass rallies throughout the country, calling for volunteers for the next big push, the promised final offensive that never came.

In fact, the war preparations were an exercise in diplomatic shadow-boxing designed to persuade the members of the UN Security Council to improve on the settlement terms offered in Resolution 598, or else to face the prospect that Iran would continue the war indefinitely. Yet the Iranians did not reject 598 out of hand, but instead initiated a twin-track policy aimed at securing the best possible deal, so while the leaders kept up their threats and maintained a strong 'no compromise' line, behind the scenes Iranian diplomats were exploring the prospects for a negotiated settlement that would acknowledge what Tehran regarded as Iran's new-found supremacy in the Gulf. The more pragmatic in the Tehran leadership, notably Rafsanjani, were moving towards the realisation that the conflict could not be won, but even they did not then know the full extent of the corruption and inefficiency that was destroying the Iranian war machine from within.

After the failure of the Kerbala offensives, it became more difficult to enlist volunteers for the fronts. Seven years of conflict and economic hardship, coupled with the people's daily experience of the petty-mindedness of minor officials, had brought about a pervasive war-weariness. While it had been relatively easy to rally tens of thousands of volunteers with the promise that they were setting off to liberate Kerbala and Najjaf, or even Jerusalem, it was harder to sustain enthusiasm for a stalemated war of attrition along the frontier. The regime was forced to respond to the manpower crisis by increasing military service from twenty-four to twenty-eight months, but even then, by the end of 1987, Iraq had, for the first time, more men in the field than Iran. The war of the cities had also inflicted a severe blow to civilian morale: the long-range Iraqi missile bombardments spread terror in Tehran and the other cities which came under fire. But worst of all was the increasing use of chemical weapons on the battlefield, raising the dreadful prospect that Iraq might eventually arm the missiles with mustard and nerve gas; in the capital, civilians began to store gas masks at their homes, and seal the windows of their houses.

Iraqi air raids against Iranian industrial targets were also putting heavy pressure on Iran's capacity to sustain the war – in the final year, Iraqi bombers inflicted as much damage as in the previous seven years, and in June 1988, in the last weeks of the war, they destroyed the new Kangan oil refinery even before it came on stream, and put out of action Iran's largest power station at Mazanderan. On top of all this, money was running out; Iran had financed its war effort from its export earnings with practically no resort to foreign borrowing, and even at the end of the war long-term debt stood at an insignificant $500 million, while short-term debt, most of it acquired in the previous two years, was only about $4 billion. But by 1988 the decline in world oil prices, fiscal inefficiency and even large-scale corruption had deprived Iran of the ability to pay its way, though it was only after the ceasefire that the true extent of mismanagement of the Iranian war effort became apparent.

At a debate in mid-September, Majlis deputies, freed from the constraints imposed on them by the war, recited a catalogue of complaints about the failings of officials at all levels, so that a picture emerged of corruption and amateurism, of officials being appointed because of their ideological purity rather than their organisational abilities, even of troops and Revolutionary Guards dying at the front because of the failings of those whose job it was to supply them. It was discovered that money set aside to develop domestic industrial and military production had been squandered and many of the projects never begun, while conditions at front-line field hospitals were so inadequate that many died of wounds and disease for lack of proper medical attention. Supplies of dressings and surgical thread were allowed to run out entirely before action was taken to replace them. A wounded battalion commander, abandoned without treatment in a provincial hospital, said in a final letter to his parents before he died: 'They have killed us.'

In one incident, an unlabelled drum of mustard gas which had been stored at a warehouse in the centre of Tehran was mistaken for acid and used to clean a blocked sink, killing one person and injuring others. Infected carcasses of sheep were sold or sent to the troops at the front. Ammunition assigned to the Revolutionary Guard Corps was so badly stored that in some cases as many as one in three rounds was damaged, and the effects of shortages were compounded by waste: on the Kurdish front military trucks and road-building equipment lay idle for lack of new tyres while the warehouses of the Revolutionary Guard Corps were stacked high with them.

The inadequacies of the war effort extended to the home front too. It was the policy of the regime to soften the economic impact of the war on ordinary people and to avoid the growth of popular discontent by subsidising staple foods, and in the 1988 budget $2.2 billion was earmarked for the import of basic supplies. But on a local level, distribution was often chaotic and made worse by the corruption of those in charge, leading to the kind of unrest the regime sought to avert. There were bread riots in the north-western town of Orumiyeh, for despite the subsidies there were persistent shortages of basic essentials; one month it might be matches, the next meat or rice, yet goods always seemed to be available on the thriving black market for those with money to pay for them.

The government kept the value of the rial artificially high, but its true value declined to one-fifteenth of its nominal value. By the end of the war, the monthly salary of a minor functionary was about 40,000 rials; this was enough to pay for rationed goods at controlled prices but the rations were never adequate and had to be supplemented from the black market at exorbitant prices – while a kilogram of subsidised chicken cost 400 rials, on the black market it was ten times that amount. Draconian measures ordered by Khomeini against black-marketeers and threats of summary punishment against shopkeepers who overcharged failed to prevent exploitation.

One group did manage to maintain a comfortable lifestyle. The traders and businessmen, a sector which the mullahs could not afford to alienate, had access to hard currency, and so could live well; even in the last months of the war, there were car showrooms in Tehran offering luxury BMWs. Illegal trading in the US dollar, the currency of the Great Satan, became a popular obsession.

By the start of the Iranian new year in March 1988 the economy was in a parlous state. Out of an estimated revenue, mainly from oil, of $10 billion for the year, more than one-third was allocated to military expenditure, so that the cash available for vital power and industrial production was barely enough to keep production going. Having financed the war for more than seven years almost exclusively by cash payments to suppliers and with practically no resort to foreign loans, Iran was increasingly obliged to seek credit for its vital purchases. Inflation was forecast at 32 per cent for the year and was heading higher as prices on the official and black markets spiralled upwards. The inevitable damage to the economy caused by the war had been exacerbated by the uncertainties of economic planning, so that those with money to invest went for a quick profit rather than productive projects because of the fear of expropriation if the regime finally decided to opt for more extensive state control.

After more than seven years of war, Iran had become for most of its inhabitants a dour and joyless place. Many who could afford to leave had gone to make a new life in the United States or Western Europe, joining the tens of thousands who had already fled as political refugees. Among those who remained and who had become disenchanted with the Islamic regime, there was a general recognition that the prospects of political change were hopeless. The mullahs were in control, but seemed to have nothing to offer but endless war.

With all the attention now on the naval conflict in the Gulf, the battle on land reverted to a tiresome stalemate in which Iran appeared only marginally to hold the initiative. The leadership had abandoned the tactic of an annual mass offensive in part because of the huge casualties involved in human-wave attacks. The previous year Rafsanjani outlined a new strategy of attrition involving limited strikes in which casualties would be kept to a minimum, so there were only small gains to report – in one small-scale spring offensive, Iran took the Iraqi Kurdish town of Halabja, now remembered not as an Iranian victory but as a symbol of Iraq's indiscriminate use of gas. And then, in April, disaster struck: the Iraqis recaptured the Fao peninsula in a well-organised attack by units which included Saddam Hussein's élite Presidential Guard.

The capture of the Fao peninsula at the beginning of 1986 was one of Iran's greatest achievements in the land war, but it came about almost by accident. After a year of minimal activity on the ground and conciliatory diplomacy in the Gulf, the Iranians had to demonstrate their continued military ability, their commitment to the battlefield, and to produce for their increasingly restive population some evidence of their army's superiority, a small victory at least to maintain civilian morale. The capture of Fao did all those things, and was a brilliant example of the inventiveness of the Iranian forces and the speed with which they were able to exploit a situation.

In February 1986, Iran had more than 100,000 men massed on the southern front, according to satellite reconnaissance pictures passed on to Iraq by the Americans. It looked as if the long-projected major offensive against Basra, or to split the country, was about to take place. Iraq had its vast static defences fully manned, but assumed that Iran would follow the previous course of launching frontal assaults against its positions, human-wave attacks which could be halted by the superior Iraqi fire power. Instead, the Iranians attempted to move in from the south, sending troops in rubber boats up the Khor Abdullah waterway towards the Iraqi naval base at Umm Qasr, where the small Iraqi navy had been bottled up since the beginning of the war. The eventual aim was to open a new front by threatening Basra from the south, forcing the Iraqis to move some of the city's defenders and making it easier for the frontal attack to take place. The Iranians were prevented from achieving their main objective, but in a brilliant display of the improvisation which had enabled their commanders to do so well back in 1982, the Iranians abandoned their set plan and moved on to the Fao peninsula from both east and west, putting in their main attack under cover of darkness.

Still fearing that this was a feint designed to draw off forces around Basra, the Iraqis were slow to respond, and by the time they launched their first counter-attack, the Iranians had dug in and thrown a pontoon bridge across the Shatt to enable them to reinforce and re-supply. Once convinced that the Iranians intended to hold on to the peninsula, the Iraqis poured men and material into the battle, suffering terrible losses in the process. But so public and so humiliating was the loss of Fao that the Iraqi generals and the Iraqi politicians – Saddam Hussein and his inner circle – felt bound to make a huge effort to retake the place, though its practical value was small: it had been impossible to use the refinery at Fao City for years, the population had been evacuated at the beginning of the war, and Umm Qasr had been out of action because of Iranian naval superiority. Failure to recapture Fao after all the threats from the generals and spokesmen back in Baghdad was a second blow, which forced the Iraqis into a third mistake: the Iraqi army was thrown into a costly offensive on the central front to take the town of Mehran, and did indeed succeed in that objective. Iraqi spokesmen were quick to point out that the Iranian territory they had captured around Mehran was about the same as that the Iranians occupied in Fao, demonstrating that the Mehran attack was very much a civilian strategy designed for propaganda purposes. It proved another example of the trouble caused when the civilians dictated military strategy: within two months the Iranians regained Mehran, throwing the Iraqis out and causing them heavy casualties, while in the south Iran remained in firm control in Fao.

In military terms, the Iranian toe-hold was an irritant, no more. But in political terms, both in Iraq and in the lower Gulf, it was of major importance. For a start, the unexpected success of the 9 February assault brought the Iranian forces to within ten miles of Kuwaiti territory, and put them right opposite Bubiyan Island, a place always claimed by Iraq which the Baghdad government had regularly sought to use during the war. President Khamenei explicitly warned the Kuwaitis against giving in now to Iraqi pressure: 'If you cannot resist the Iraqis and stop their aggression in Bubiyan, we cannot tolerate the enemy behind us, and we will have to defend ourselves with strength.' Kuwait responded by noting the growing danger caused by the Iranian success which, it said, made the danger of superpower intervention all the greater – a coded warning that it might in fact ask for American protection if there was any further movement. Neither Iraq nor Iran did attempt to take Bubiyan, but Iranian 'control' of Kuwait was certainly strengthened by its success in Fao, where it soon installed some of the Silkworm missiles it acquired from China, and SCUD B rockets supplied by Libya. Iran also took the opportunity to set up on Iraqi territory the headquarters of SAIRI, the Supreme Assembly of the Islamic Revolution of Iraq, a symbol of what was intended to be the new government of Iraq. SAIRI was seen by the mullahs in Tehran as the provisional government of Iraq, the group they would have liked to take over in Baghdad if Saddam Hussein were deposed and a Shia revolution swept an Islamic regime into power. It was headed by Hojatoleslam Mohammed

Baqr al-Hakim and was based entirely on the exiled Hakim family; though Iranians sometimes spoke of the SAIRI military arm, this was no more than a group of bodyguards headed by a thug named Abu Ali Mowla.

Once Fao was relatively secure, the SAIRI headquarters was set up there, with much flag-raising and praying, but it was a hollow gesture. Two years later, when Fao was finally re-taken with such ease, the vaunted headquarters of the potential new government of Iraq was seen to be a small house crammed with propaganda material which could not be distributed for lack of clients. The only ones who appeared to have taken advantage of the educational facilities on offer were some of the Iranian soldiers and Revolutionary Guards stationed in Fao, who wanted to continue their studies while doing their military service.

The recapture of Fao in 1988 was one of the early indications of the change in Iran. For the first weeks of the occupation of Fao, the Iranians had held firm against the most powerful counter-attacks the Iraqis could muster, counter-attacks which employed hundreds of guns and tanks plus helicopter gunships and air-force bombing. Now the Iraqis were able to re-take Fao with a much less spectacular effort. One concentrated artillery barrage, steady bombing of the approach roads on the Iranian side of the waterway to prevent reinforcements being thrown in, and a careful spread of activity so that the Iranians would not realise that Fao was the real objective, succeeded within thirty-six hours. The Iranian front line, a remarkably weak affair (reminiscent of the First World War) of trenches, dug-outs and a few concrete block houses, was breached in the first assault so that the Iraqi troops, led by the Republican Guards, were able to move swiftly in on two axes and to spread out and destroy the small number of defenders.

The main reason for the Iraqi success in 1988 was that the lack of troops available to the Iranian commanders had forced them to withdraw considerable numbers from Fao to reinforce their forces opposite Basra, and those who remained were no longer in the mood for suicidal defence. The tour of the battleground we made the day after the Iranians were forced out of Fao showed that the defenders had rarely stood and fought, but had broken from the moment of the first assault, with Iraqi tanks taking out the small pockets of resistance which sought to hold up the main advance as the Iranian troops fled across the pontoon bridge they had established over the Shatt. Interestingly, the Iraqi planes did not take out the bridge as soon as the attack was launched in the hope of bottling up and destroying the Iranian defenders. Instead, the bridge was only bombed after the Iranians had withdrawn, a more intelligent move allowing many Iranians to escape, but also preventing any 'backs to the sea' last stand.

It was a move too, which showed an understanding of the new situation in Iran. No longer were the youngsters queuing up to volunteer when the call went out for a new force to be raised. At the beginning of the year, when it was announced in Tehran that a 100,000-strong Mohammed Corps was to be formed, there was a noticeable lack of enthusiasm, and a good deal of cynicism, and even when the television began showing pictures of boys lining up to sign on, and then setting off for the front, no one took it very seriously. Estimates, satellite pictures and interrogations of prisoners showed that the general assessment was right; instead of 100,000, the mullahs had difficulty in persuading 30,000 to go. The days of willing martyrdom, when every volunteer felt happy to carry Ayatollah Khomeini's key to the hereafter, were long gone. Now the main preoccupation of the middle classes in Tehran and the other cities was to send their sons abroad before they reached the age of sixteen, and even in the provinces the peasants were no longer accepting uncritically the calls to service. The whole country was war-weary and disillusioned, not with the revolution or with Ayatollah Khomeini himself, but with the men who had promised so much and delivered so little, who kept on fighting when it was clear that nothing was going to be achieved, and who so obviously devoted as much effort to their own interests and their own positions as to the jobs they were supposed to do.

The fall of Fao was a setback on a par with Iraq's loss of Khorram-shahr in 1982, but in Iran it was masked by the increased belliger-ence of the Americans in the Gulf – on the night of the Iraqi attack the Iranian navy was preoccupied by nearby American activity. Now Basra, for so long the prime Iranian objective, was once again secure, and within the next two months Iran lost nearly all the Iraqi territory which it had captured in the previous four and a half years. In late May, the Iraqis recovered the Shalamcheh sector which Iran had captured in the winter of 1986 for the loss of 40,000 Iranian lives. Then the Iranians were routed from the Majnoon islands in the marshlands north of Basra and from Kurdish areas, including Halabja, which they had captured only weeks before. It seemed that Iraq's use of poison gas had a decisive effect on Iranian morale, and because of the various Western embargoes on the export of war material to Iran, the country was unable to equip itself with adequate supplies of chemical warfare clothing. Use of the protective suits was, in any event, impractical in the extreme heat of the southern front, so that when faced with a chemical attack, the Iranian forces had little option but to cut and run. It was as if the fervent Revolutionary Guards, who had for so long proclaimed their readiness to die for Islam, had lost the will to fight, and slowly the Iranian war machine ground to a halt, destroyed from within by inefficiency and corruption and squeezed into submission by outside powers, for the US naval escalation in the Gulf was well-timed to put the maximum pressure on Iran.

Even before the Iranian defeat in Fao the Americans knew that Iran was in a perilous position. The US commander in the region, Marine Corps General George B. Crist, told the Senate Armed Services Committee in March that Iran lacked the military wherewithal for another major offensive. He said that Iran had overstretched itself in its last assault on Basra and had not been able to recoup; in addition, he reported that Iran was having problems finding enough new recruits and had been seriously weakened economically by the intensified Iraqi air attacks on more than thirty cities.

All the old antagonisms between the army and the Revolutionary Guard also resurfaced after Fao, with each side accusing the other of responsibility, and there was an immediate search for scapegoats, with a number of army and Guard Corps commanders dismissed, including the chief of staff, Brigadier-General Ismail Sohrabi. Then on 2 June Khomeini appointed Rafsanjani as acting commander-in-chief, but apparently quite out of touch with reality, Khomeini ordered Rafsanjani to end the war militarily within six months. If Rafsanjani did not know before that there was no chance of an Iranian victory, within days of his appointment he learnt that it was impossible, and that his real task, in his few short weeks as a wartime commander, would be to persuade Khomeini to accept peace. Rafsanjani quickly learnt of massive corruption in the Guard Corps, with millions of dollars diverted from essential military projects to private bank accounts abroad; it emerged that money set aside the

previous year to finance major self-sufficiency in arms manufacture
had been either squandered or purloined, and that even the most
elementary projects had not got off the ground.

Within two weeks of his appointment, Rafsanjani did order a
ground offensive to recover the Shalamcheh enclave, and the
Iranian forces made some advances; but Iraq quickly recouped
the situation, turning 'the wicked Iranians, who dreamed of
achieving a victory, into Hell's firewood', in the words of an Iraqi
army spokesman. Then on the morning of Sunday, 3 July 1988
the disaster struck which was to make Rafsanjani's self-imposed
task easier. The cruiser *Vincennes*, crammed with some of the
most sophisticated electronic hardware available to the US navy
and manned by a crew which had for the most part never experienced battle, was involved in a skirmish with Iranian fast motor
boats just inside the Strait of Hormuz. It was the eve of the
Independence Day holiday and American ships in the Gulf were
on high alert in case the Iranians chose to mark 4 July by striking
a US target, but the incident involving the *Vincennes* was routine,
the usual hit-and-run exercise by the Iranians which still raised
the adrenalin levels of the inexperienced operators manning the
cruiser's ultra-modern Aegis radar system – as a US naval officer
was later to remark, nothing in the Aegis training course had
prepared its operators for the excitement and tension of battle.
So in the stress of the moment the radar operators thought that
they detected from the welter of electronic information in front
of them the approach of a hostile F-14 fighter, an air-to-air combat
aircraft not designed for attacking ground or sea targets. Yet
the electronic evidence available to Captain Will C. Rogers III
appeared to offer him no alternative but to assume that his vessel
was under attack, so with only seconds to spare he ordered the
launching of two guided missiles to bring down the plane.

His information was wrong – there was no F-14. The plane
which the missiles hit, exploding its fuselage and sending the
wreckage spiralling 12,000 feet down to the waters of the Gulf,
was an Iranian civilian Airbus with 290 people on board. IranAir
flight 655 had taken off seven minutes earlier from Bandar Abbas
on the Iranian coast for a scheduled forty-five-minute flight to
Dubai in the United Arab Emirates. Most of those on board were
Iranians, but there were also six Yugoslavs and an Italian; a young
Indian doctor living in Tehran was to bury six of his relatives.

The US administration proceeded to compound the appalling consequences of its warship's action with distortion and obfuscation. The tenor of official statements that day and thereafter was that the Iranians themselves were somehow to blame, that the plane had been acting in a hostile manner, or was off course; even the remarkable claim that though it was not an F-14, no one could blame the navy for thinking that the Iranians might use a civilian plane for a suicide mission against the US fleet – an odd reprise of the excuse made years earlier when Israel shot down a Libyan airliner. It was only a month after the disaster that the Pentagon quietly acknowledged that the Airbus had been on the correct flight path and that human error by ship's operators unused to battle had been the real cause. Washington offered compensation – but no apology, and the future president, George Bush, defending the American action at the United Nations, said of the Iranians: 'They allowed a civilian aircraft loaded with passengers to proceed on a path over a warship engaged in battle. That was an irresponsible and a tragic error.'

The Airbus disaster had a traumatic effect on the Iranian leaders. They believed that the plane had been shot down deliberately so they concluded that the United States was now prepared to stop at nothing to support the Iraqi war effort and, if possible, to destroy the revolution. Rafsanjani was later to claim that the shooting down of the airliner was a significant factor in the decision to end the war. Iran, he said, had come to realise that 'world blasphemy and arrogance', which can be read as shorthand for both the superpowers, had decided to deny the Iranians victory. 'An example of this is the strange obduracy displayed by the Americans in the Persian Gulf, with the downing of a passenger plane carrying over 200 passengers; the allegation that a mistake was made is not acceptable in any way. In our opinion, this was to be considered a warning rather than anything else.'

There had been a constant fear of a large-scale US attack on Iran ever since US ships entered the Gulf, and it was this which accounted for the relatively restrained response to the US naval presence. But the Airbus incident was special; Rafsanjani said it convinced Iran that 'insistence by us at this point could lead to extraordinary losses for our people and for the Iraqi people'.

Immediately after the crash, Rafsanjani nevertheless recognised that the incident presented Iran with a new opportunity to present itself in the United Nations as a victim of aggression and to win support from the world community, and Washington's European allies in particular. Iranian diplomats were already making headway in winning over international opinion as a result of the outcry over Iraq's use of poison gas at Halabja, and now the Airbus incident offered a second chance for Iran to claim the moral high ground. So the regime went through the routine diatribes against American aggression: President Khamenei denounced 'the US government and the President of America, Reagan, in person, as criminals and murderers', and pledged a military response on all fronts. But the anticipated threats of direct retaliation never came; the radicals, including Mohtashemi, were for once silent, and it was left to Rafsanjani to tell the Iranians: 'The US may have more crimes in store. Wise men know why we do not take revenge.'

The setbacks of the previous three months, culminating in the shooting down of the Airbus, had brought about a rapprochement between Rafsanjani and the more conservative Khamenei, so as Majlis deputies assembled at the gates of the parliament building to hear a funeral oration for those who died in the IranAir crash, the two men sat cross-legged together on the steps, chatting amiably. And in the immediate aftermath of the crash their public statements contained direct references to the UN in what appeared to be a coordinated attempt to gain maximum diplomatic advantage from the disaster. Hinting heavily that an internationally sponsored peace settlement was now an option, Khamenei spoke of the possibility that 'more proposals might be forthcoming at the UN'.

The next day, Rafsanjani mounted the podium at the Tehran University prayer ground to the cries of '*Jang, jang ba pirouzi*' – 'War, war until victory' – from the 3,000 or so Revolutionary Guards, *basij*, Iraqi prisoners and war-wounded assembled on what had once been the campus football ground, to support the new moderate line. He spoke for an hour, without notes, in the traditional flowery rhetoric of the Shia clergy. His topics were American war crimes, the perfidy of Reagan and Margaret Thatcher and the need to reinforce the front lines. For all that, it was a conciliatory speech directed more at the outside world than at his Iranian audience. 'We must wait to see what the Security Council does,' said Rafsanjani of a forthcoming Security Council debate on the Airbus incident. 'We must see if the Security

Council is prepared to condemn the warmonger. Is the Security Council prepared to tell the US to leave the Persian Gulf?' The only conclusion to be drawn from this unprecedented display of concern for international opinion was that Iran had at last resolved to sue for peace, yet few saw the signs.

Rafsanjani and Khomeini's son Ahmad had always been close, and immediately after the Airbus disaster they decided to act, prompted more by the state of the Ayatollah's health than anything else. A CIA report leaked to the US press in the spring, carried by foreign radio stations and given wide circulation in Iran, suggested that Khomeini was suffering from terminal cancer and had perhaps six months to live. In reality, the main concern among the Imam's entourage was with his recurring migraines, which suggested a brain tumour. The old man was being given plugs of opium to chew, a traditional remedy, in order to relieve the pain.

Rafsanjani and Ahmad told the leader of the revolution that the war had become unwinnable; the shooting down of the airliner, they said, was a signal that the imperialist vultures were gathering. In addition, Iranian military intelligence had received information from agents in Iraq that the enemy was planning a major offensive into Khuzestan with the aim of setting up a puppet government there under Masoud Rajavi of the People's Mujahedin. Lest he be accused at a later date of forcing through the decision to end the war, Rafsanjani took the precaution of presenting Khomeini with signed assessments from Prime Minister Mousavi, the Guards Commander Mohsen Rezai, and other officials detailing the parlous state of the country's finances and military preparedness. With brutal honesty Rafsanjani and Khomeini's son told the old man that the war had to be settled before he died, otherwise the struggle for succession would remain unresolved. The choice was between ending the war now, or continuing it and facing the eventual destruction of the Islamic Republic.

Rarely can so much have rested on the response of one man, but the argument that the continuation of the revolution was at stake won the day, for this was not just Khomeini's life work, but the will of Allah. The triumph of Islam had to be preserved, so Khomeini agreed. Rafsanjani was given the authority to end the war.

That account of the crucial meeting between Khomeini and Rafsanjani is based on information from clerical sources in Iran, but the only detailed account of what followed is that which the opposition Mujahedin claims to have received from its own sources. Stripped of its propagandist content, it does contain a likely scenario. According to this account, on 17 July there was a secret meeting to decide how to put Khomeini's order into effect. The leadership, including Rafsanjani, Khamenei, cabinet ministers, members of the Islamic judiciary and the Council of Guardians, representatives of the armed forces and the Revolutionary Guard Corps, met for eight hours to discuss the implications of the decision to end the war, with Ahmad Khomeini setting the agenda by reading a message from his father which said that the country's military experts were all agreed that Iran could not expect any victories in the near future. It noted that only Rezai, the Guard Corps commander, was prepared to continue the war, though even he acknowledged that the war supplies at his disposal were inadequate.

Khomeini's message recalled that the Guard Corps commander had told him: 'We won't have any victories in the next five years. After 1993, if we have 250 brigades, 2,500 tanks, 3,000 armoured personnel carriers, 300 aircraft and 300 helicopters, we believe, God willing, we will be able to launch offensives.' The Ayatollah's letter added: 'This commander believes our ability to secure sufficient and timely funds and resources to be the most important factor in gaining success and . . . he says we must keep on fighting. But this is a hollow slogan.' He said the Prime Minister had told him that the treasury coffers were empty and that the cost of weapons lost in recent offensives was equal to the entire budget allocated to the army and the Guard Corps. 'The political officials say that the people have no desire to go to the fronts, as they have realised that no victory is in sight.'

According to the Mujahedin account, there was some debate at the meeting, with hardliners arguing that the decision to end the war had been imposed on Khomeini. But none dared challenge the fact that the decision had been made, so in a message dated 18 July 1988 President Khamenei made it public. He wrote to Javier Perez de Cuellar telling him that Iran accepted unconditionally UN Security Council Resolution 598 on the Iran–Iraq war 'in the interests of security and on the basis of justice'. Despite the alarms, the battles and the losses of the next month, the war was effectively over.

# 14

## New battles
## to settle old scores

The sudden announcement by Tehran that it was accepting the ceasefire was greeted with incredulity in the outside world and a resigned bewilderment within Iran. Many could not believe that the decision had been taken in Khomeini's lifetime and therefore assumed that the Imam was already dead. Just ten days earlier the General Command of the Armed Forces, newly established under Rafsanjani's leadership, had issued a general mobilisation order under the slogan: 'Everyone to the front to oppose the rebellion of America.' Now the Iranian people were being asked to accept that, for reasons which the leadership said it was not yet able to reveal, the war which had dominated their lives for eight years was nearing its end. There were no celebrations to match those in Baghdad, where people took to the streets to dance and sing in praise of Saddam Hussein's victory.

Although neither side had achieved its war aims and the opposing armies were now virtually back to where they had been in 1980, Iran's belated acceptance of Resolution 598 could only be seen as an acknowledegment of defeat. Realising that the end of the war was at hand, President Hussein had issued a triumphal statement on 17 July, the anniversary of the 1968 Ba'athist revolution and the day on which the Iranian leaders were summoned to hear of Khomeini's decision to end the war. President Hussein spoke of Iraq as the vanguard of the Arab world, which had stood alone against an international plot to undermine the Iraqi revolution. 'World Zionism and the circles under its influence which have designs against the nation and harbour hatred against it and do not wish the Arab nation to rise and to perform its positive constructive role in the life of humankind have found in this regime in Iran the tool they have been searching for,' the Iraqi leader proclaimed. He said that these external forces had co-opted Islam, 'the Arabs' religion', as a cover for their conspiracies. 'We stand on the ground of victory . . . on the other side, you and the world are watching the fate of the false, suspect experiment produced by the clique of charlatans, jugglers and murderers – the Zionist agents.' It was a persuasive message to a nation which was already scenting victory. Iraq, not Iran, had been the victim of an imposed war and had emerged triumphant as the defender of the Arab cause. 'That,' said Saddam Hussein, 'is the fruit of your sacrifices, efforts and struggle throughout eight years of steadfastness and heroic and honourable fighting against the enemies of God and man.'

In Tehran, the regime's leaders faced a much more difficult task than that of President Hussein in persuading the nation that its sacrifices had not been in vain. Rafsanjani, Khamenei and others in the peace faction had taken a calculated but unavoidable risk in persuading Khomeini to accept the ceasefire, and it made them vulnerable to attack from the radicals. There were murmurings of unrest within the Revolutionary Guard Corps, which was unhappy not only about the decision to end the war but also about being blamed for the defeats at the front – only a few days before the acceptance of Resolution 598, a hit squad believed to be made up of dissident Revolutionary Guards had tried to assassinate Rafsanjani near the Majlis building. There was almost open opposition, too, from Mohtashemi, who a month earlier stepped quite outside his brief as interior minister and stated categorically that Iran rejected 598, declaring: 'The war that began by military action and invasion of our cities cannot have a political conclusion.'

He was slapped down by President Khamenei, who assured him that all foreign policy decisions had Khomeini's prior approval, for the so-called pragmatists knew that they had Khomeini's authority to make peace. But to put that policy over, they needed a public statement from him to quell the anxieties created by the sudden volte-face and to silence their opponents. It came on 20 July in a message to mark the first anniversary, by the Muslim calendar, of the Mecca riots of the previous year. The message, which was broadcast on Khomeini's behalf by a radio announcer, has since been subjected to close textual analysis by a number of

Iranian experts who have sought to prove that it was written by others, but its mix of populism, politics and theology bears the hallmark of Khomeini.

He sought to portray the war as a step on the path to the fulfilment of the ideals of the revolution in which the resurgence of Islam was more important than territorial gain. 'Therefore . . . never talk about the loss of a position with sadness or talk about the capture of another with pride and happiness, since these are as insignificant compared with your goal as the entire world compared with the next world.' Iran had been victorious, he said, in defeating the plots of the United States, the Soviet Union and Israel and the struggle had strengthened the cause of Islam. Nothing had been taken away from the achievements of those who had died in battle, and what had happened was the will of God. 'This is what God wants today. He wanted something different yesterday, and tomorrow, God willing, will be the day of victory for the forces of justice.' Iran's war had been an ideological struggle which did not recognise frontiers and this ideological struggle would continue. 'God willing, the great Iranian nation, through its material and moral support for the revolution, will be compensated for the hardships of the war with the sweetness of the defeat of the enemies of God in the world.'

'The enemies of God' – exactly the phrase used only three days earlier by Saddam Hussein. Both sides had to use religion to justify their shabby shifts and to conceal from their own people the hollow victory on one side, the hollow defeat on the other. President Khamenei said of Khomeini's message: 'It is truly a sign that our Imam, that true son of God's regent and God's Prophet, receives divine inspirations.'

More real help for the cause of the pragmatists came when Iraq decided to continue the war for another month in order to support an abortive invasion by the Iranian National Liberation Army, the NLA, the military wing of the Baghdad-based People's Mujahedin, for the NLA offensive temporarily revived popular enthusiasm in Iran for the fight. Despite the effectiveness of the counter-terror operations of 1981–2, the mullahs always remained wary of the influence of Mujahedin ideology, and the fear that the Iraqis would re-invade Khuzestan and establish a Mujahedin puppet government there had been one of many factors influencing the decision to call a halt to the war. So a number of leaders, including Khomeini, now spoke of the danger of people falling under the influence of the Mujahedin at this critical juncture between war and peace, and on 22 July President Khamenei warned 'that a group of hypocrites, two-faced and evil persons may appear in the country supported by foreign propaganda, who may try to break our national pride'.

The Mujahedin were widely regarded as traitors for having thrown in their lot with Saddam Hussein, so when the Mujahedin invasion came, many civilians rushed to join up, although the numbers fell far short of the mass mobilisation which the regime claimed. But bus drivers in Tehran suspended operations and volunteered to take fighters to the front line, and the offensive did provide the opportunity to close the Majlis in order to allow deputies to join the battle, effectively depriving the pro-war radicals of a forum in which to rally opposition to those who had backed the decision to sue for peace. It was also a chance finally to portray the Mujahedin as aggressors, and in a very Iranian way, to smoke out those still willing to oppose the regime by violent means.

The People's Mujahedin was always better at publicity than at fighting – if half the successes it claimed had proved true, the Tehran regime would have been in serious trouble – but from the time they were defeated in the struggle for power after the revolution, the Mujahedin were never more than nuisances to Iran, assassinating a few officials in provincial cities, occasionally tossing grenades about, or launching small hit-and-run operations in border areas. With their headquarters and most of their people in Paris, the Mujahedin were an insignificant factor. They were entirely dependent on the Iraqis for what operations they were allowed to do, and were used more as scouts, decoys and spies than as a fighting force.

Up to 1986, when Masoud Rajavi and his men were expelled from France as part of the deal by which that country finally settled its dispute with Iran, the main Mujahedin base was only fifty miles from Baghdad, the guerrillas there a scruffy and inefficient lot, and what operations were done inside Iran were usually the work of individuals with no formal links with the movement. There was, too, widespread discontent inside the Mujahedin at one of the most cynical charades when their leader, Rajavi, fell out with his wife and father-in-law, Bani-Sadr, promoted the wife of one of his lieutenants to be co-leader and then married her, carried out what he called an ideological revolution – a purge of all those who saw the whole distasteful affair for what it was – and instituted an even more pronounced personality cult. Many of the better members left the movement at this stage, and it might well have withered away, for all its public relations apparatus and expertise, if the French had not decided to expel Rajavi and his followers. That event, in June 1986, briefly transformed the Mujahedin into something which could have been an influential factor, but in the end the chance was thrown away.

The main trouble, in the eyes of all Iranians, including those dissidents inside the country to whom Rajavi might have appealed, was that the Mujahedin had thrown in their lot so completely with Iraq. It was as if General de Gaulle had set up his headquarters in Nazi Germany to issue his rallying call to the Free French, one disgruntled Iranian said. It was a fatal mistake from which the Mujahedin could never recover; their rationale was that they needed the sort of help, arms and support which only Iraq could give if they were to have a real chance of 'liberating' their country, but even Iranians opposed to the Islamic revolution could not support a man and a movement which sided with their country's enemies at a time of mortal national danger.

Yet for a time it did look as if the French decision to expel Rajavi might have done him and his movement a world of good. Away from the fleshpots of Paris and exposed to the cold survey of Iraqis who had been fighting for years, Rajavi was forced to reassess his situation and that of his men; the result was the formation of the Iranian National Liberation Army, announced in June 1987. By agreement with the Iraqis, this was a force made up of the men who had left Europe with Rajavi, of exiles who had been living in Iraq, and of Iranian defectors and turncoat prisoners of war who could not bring themselves to fight with the Iraqis, but were ready to take up arms against the Khomeini regime with comrades of their own nationality, and under what was always presented as an independent command. It was not, of course; the NLA was allowed to operate only where the Iraqis said they could, when told to do so, and with weapons provided by Iraq. For all that, it did present a credible opposition force in the brief year of its effective existence, it turned out well trained and efficient soldiers. both men and women, and had some sensible commanders who might have played a real part in events if they had been allowed to do so. As it was, the Mujahedin were broken on the wheel when they allowed the Iraqis to use them in this last stage of the war, and the bungled operation into which they were drawn led to the deaths of many of their supporters inside Iran, and to the wave of executions which further sullied Iran's already terrible record.

Seven days after the 18 July acceptance by Iran of Resolution 598, the NLA launched Operation 'Eternal Light', its biggest and effectively its only large-scale offensive into its own country. It was fully supported by Iraq, for the idea was that Rajavi's men should seize a large area of territory on the border around Qasr-e-Shirin, Sar-e-Pol-e-Zahab, Kerend, Islamabad and Kermanshah, set up a provisional Iranian government in this 'liberated' zone, and rally all the dissidents inside Iran. That, it was hoped, would create such chaos in the country that the Khomeini regime would be thrown into disarray, at least, making it much easier for Iraq to gain all it wanted from the peace negotiations which were then supposed to begin – control of the border regions it coveted, and the establishment of a pliant government in Tehran.

It was not to be. The Iranians who should have been demora-lised and dispirited after the shock of their leaders' acceptance of the ceasefire showed themselves very ready to fight against the 'hypocrites' and 'Quislings' as the government portrayed the invaders, 'the tools of the Iraqis' and 'American-Zionist puppets'. Faced with an invasion by people who had spent the eight years of the war under the protection of their enemies, the Iranians fought as they had in the first days of the invasion of their country by Iraq, quickly halting the advance of the NLA-Iraqi forces. Even then, the scheme might have succeeded if Iraq had thrown all its weight into the battle, but instead of doing so the Iraqis pulled out, leaving the NLA to fight alone. The Iraqis quickly decided that their open involvement would be self-defeating, and that if the NLA needed sustained support, the scheme would not work anyway. The Iraqi commanders and the politicians in Baghdad had no hesitation in cutting their losses and leaving their Iranian surrogates to fend for themselves as best they could.

Even when the Iraqis pulled out the Iranians did not stop their warnings of 'a major attack'; in fact, the tone became more shrill even as the Mujahedin found themselves alone, facing larger and

better forces, and so began their precipitate retreat. According to
the Iranian announcements at the time, the threat remained, and
to be specific, the Iranian communiqués mentioned towns deep
inside Iran as having been threatened by the invaders; they even
spoke of revolts in places far from the battle lines. But it was all
a swiftly worked-out plot. What the Iranians were doing was
smoking out Mujahedin sympathisers well away from the border
areas where the actual fighting was going on. And it worked.
Hundreds of men – and women – who were either active supporters of the Mujahedin or who had become disillusioned with
the revolution and were looking for an alternative began speaking
openly of opposing the regime. In some cases, people tried to go
to the towns mentioned in official communiqués to join the
invaders; others sought to rally support for the Mujahedin far
from the area of fighting.

All were rounded up, for this was just what the regime had
planned. Savama, the intelligence organisation which took over
from Savak – in many cases staffed by the same people at the
lower levels – had quickly put into place its plan to identify
anti-regime forces when the Mujahedin invasion began. It worked
brilliantly, with the result that many people were arbitrarily executed, and others were taken before the revolutionary courts to
start the spate of executions which swept across the country in the
autumn of 1988, decimating the opposition and spreading a new
wave of terror, with men who had served minor sentences for
anti-regime activities being hauled before new courts and condemned to death if they did not publicly recant, condemn the
Mujahedin and swear allegiance to the Ayatollah. This final
bloody campaign against internal opposition was more than anything else an admission of the failure of the revolution which had
started with such high hopes. It caused fresh bickering among the
leaders, with Montazeri speaking out more plainly than ever, and
underlined Khomeini's failure to unite his country, to achieve his
purposes, or to make credible his bloody brand of Islam.

The world was largely silent about this wave of mass executions
when it began to be reported from Iran by a number of predominantly left-wing opposition groups, including the Mujahedin,
which alleged that the authorities in Iran had embarked on a
systematic attempt to annihilate their opponents by carrying out
a wholesale slaughter of the political prison population. Accurate

numbers of the victims were hard to come by. The Mujahedin claimed that 12,000 died in the space of four months, although there was reason to believe Tehran's explanation that these included Mujahedin fighters killed on the battlefield in the July offensive. The Iranian leadership veered between denials and justifications. President Khamenei said that the judicial authorities were carrying out God's order, while more urbane officials said privately that, if the Second World War allies had the right to execute war criminals, spies and traitors, why then should Iran not do the same?

The killings were a further sign of the regime's continued instability, for the fear among the clergy was that the underground left would attempt to exploit popular discontent about the outcome of the war to undermine clerical rule. Prisoners who had been held for years were summarily tried and executed; past offenders who had served out their sentences and been released were rearrested and sent to the firing squad. Assadollah Lajavardi, the so-called 'Butcher of Tehran', who was dismissed from his post as head of Evin prison because of his excesses, was reinstated. It was he who was said to have convinced Khomeini that released offenders had tried to join the Mujahedin invasion force and should therefore be rounded up and wiped out. Relatives were barred from making prison visits and would wait for weeks for news of their loved ones, only to be told in the end that they had been killed. In some prisons, the death toll was so high that the authorities resorted to burying the victims of the firing squads in mass graves; it was the biggest purge of the left since the terror and counter-terror of 1981–2. Amnesty International said it believed that at least 1,000 were killed, although the true figure may have been nearer 5,000, among them a number of mullahs, some executed for political crimes, others for corruption, in a gesture by the regime to show its even-handedness.

The plan was to remove the problem of the left by the tenth anniversary of the revolution in February 1989, when an amnesty was declared for a minority of prisoners – including the former Tudeh secretary-general, Kianuri – who were believed to have truly repented. Western governments, eager to push forward the peace process, and equally eager to benefit from the post-war reconstruction boom they expected in Iran, were largely silent. When the Iranian foreign minister, Ali Akbar Velayati, visited

London in February 1989, British officials said the matter of the
mass executions had not been raised with him: they said such a
gesture would have been 'counter-productive'.

Perez de Cuellar, the UN Secretary-General, moved to arrange
a ceasefire as soon as he received Iran's acceptance of Resolution
598, but it was Iraq's turn to procrastinate and to seek to prolong
the conflict now that it had regained the military initiative.
Although the resolution called for a ceasefire as a first step towards
a negotiated settlement, Iraq demanded direct talks with the
Iranians in advance. Baghdad's foreign minister, Tariq Aziz, said
that Iraq considered that the war was still on as long as Tehran
did not clarify its intentions with regard to other aspects of the
resolution. In effect, the Iranians were being asked to set out their
terms for a permanent peace settlement before peace had even
been declared. Khomeini responded by calling on the military to
show no mercy to the tyrannical enemy, and for a while it looked
as if the first real hope of peace in eight years might founder, this
time because of Iraqi intransigence.

Behind the scenes, however, there was indirect contact between
the two sides for the first time since the war had begun. As fighting
continued on the central front, President Hussein telephoned
Colonel Gaddafi in Libya and told him that he wanted Iran's
commitment to direct negotiations on a comprehensive peace
settlement before the fighting would end. Gaddafi then telephoned
President Khamenei and put the Iraqi position to him; Khamenei
rejected it and said that there must be a ceasefire first, making it
clear that no further concessions would be forthcoming from Iran.
The Iranians, who for a year had held up implementation of
Resolution 598 by seeking a re-ordering of its clauses and by
demanding prior condemnation of Iraq as the aggressor, now cast
themselves in the role of peacemakers and defenders of the
authority of the United Nations. The foreign minister, Velayati,
complained of Iraq's violations of Resolution 598 and called on
the Security Council to take action lest Baghdad should 'torpedo
the resolution to which Iran adheres so closely'. Rafsanjani, in an
attempt to make some domestic political capital out of the Iraqi
delaying tactics, claimed that Iran's new image in the world was
one of the victories of the Gulf war. The decision to accept peace,
coupled with Iraq's continued aggression, was proof to the world
that Iran had been victimised, he said.

The first UN officials arrived in Tehran within a week of Iran's acceptance of 598 to investigate the position of prisoners of war, a very tentative first step in the implementation process because neither Perez de Cuellar nor the members of the Security Council were prepared to take any precipitate action, such as trying to impose a ceasefire date, which might upset the whole process, an attitude which contributed to the massacre of the Kurds as, on 19 July, the Baghdad government launched its campaign of poison gas, bombings and forced exodus. Iraq had plans ready to end once and for all the problem of its dissident Kurdish minority, and put them into effect at a time when outside powers could not intervene in case the Gulf war itself was rekindled. The United Nations had, by this time, ample evidence of Iraq's use of chemical and nerve gases in the war against Iran, while there was no proof that Iran had ever used such weapons. But the Security Council decided to ignore Iran's protests at their continued use, even after 18 July, for fear of offending Baghdad. An ambassador of one of the five permanent members, Sir Crispin Tickell of Britain, explained that the Council 'didn't want to upset the applecart' by criticising Iraq before peace talks. The United Nations also held up publication of a report detailing the evidence against Iraq until indirect talks between the belligerents were finally under way, ignoring fears expressed privately by some member states that failure to condemn Iraq would set a precedent for the use of chemical weapons. It certainly contributed to the belief in Baghdad that Iraq could proceed with its chemical attacks on the Kurds with little fear of reproach from the international community.

It was not until 6 August, when the campaign against the Kurds was well under way, that Saddam Hussein finally dropped his demands for prior talks with the Iranians and agreed to the naming of a date for a ceasefire. To mark what they seemed to regard as the opening of peace negotiations, the Iraqi general command two days later issued the 'communiqué of all communiqués', its last official bulletin of the war. D-day for the end of fighting was set for 20 August, one month after Iran's acceptance of Resolution 598, and on 10 August an advance party of the UN Iran–Iraq Military Observer Group (UNIIMOG) arrived in Tehran to prepare for the deployment of the UN observer force along the frontier. The previous day, Rafsanjani had issued an order to the armed forces not to initiate any military action. Now, formally as well as practically, the war was over.

The outside powers which had done nothing to avert the conflict and little, until the final year, to bring it to an end, were quick to try to seize the opportunities presented. Even before Iran had declared its acceptance of Resolution 598, France and Britain moved to improve their relations with Tehran. West Germany was already on good terms with the Iranian regime and had acted as a go-between for Tehran and the Western powers, and after Khamenei's message to Perez de Cuellar, even the hated Americans sent what amounted to a congratulatory message to Tehran, pledging Washington's cooperation in implementing the ceasefire resolution, while in Washington members of the Reagan administration said publicly that America was prepared to have contacts with Tehran as long as it knew it was talking to responsible people there. This sudden display of US goodwill was motivated in part by the proximity of the US presidential elections: if the administration could show that, having helped bring the Gulf war to an end, it could now make progress towards a rapprochement with Iran and perhaps secure the release of the hostages in Lebanon this might help to vindicate its actions during Irangate. Rafsanjani responded by noting that the United States had always taken a hostile attitude towards the Islamic revolution and as long as this persisted there was no point in contemplating discussions with Washington. He repeated a demand that the administration should unblock Iranian assets frozen in the United States since the fall of the Shah.

The Iraqi campaign against the Kurds had obviously been planned well in advance. Whole divisions were quickly sent to reinforce the troops in the north of the country, the air force moved its planes away from the Iranian front to be in a position to strafe the hills and valleys of Kurdistan which the *peshmerga* had made their own for so long, and above all, specialist forces were sent north. Chief among these were the chemical warfare battalions which had already caused such havoc among the Iranians. The muted response by the UN and the international community to Iran's regular – and justified – complaints of the use by Iraq of gas seemed to have emboldened Saddam Hussein and his lieutenants to use chemical weapons against its own population, a ghastly precedent which may yet be repeated.

Iraq had begun preparing its chemical warfare capacity in the 1970s, and again Saddam Hussein as vice-president took personal charge of the enterprise, just as he had direct control of the country's nuclear plant. The first poison-gas factory was built at Samarra, ostensibly as a pesticide plant, but as in Libya a decade later there was never any doubt about what the installation was for. A senior American intelligence official told us:

From very early on, this plant was surrounded by air defences and given maximum security on the ground. It was far bigger than Iraq's demand for pesticides warranted, and anyway, no one ever saw any pesticides produced there – because there weren't any. Right from the start it was designed to produce mustard gas and two nerve gases, sarin and tabun, and the only reason for calling it a pesticide factory was to ease the consciences of those concerned in building it. But no one was fooled; they all knew what they were doing.

An Arab company arranged for the construction to go ahead, and West German firms supplied the components and the expertise, just as they did in Libya ten years later. The odd thing was that on this early occasion there was no outcry, no efforts by America or anyone else to halt the building of the plant, and no publicity at all. Yet America, West Germany, Italy and a number of other countries knew all about it, either from direct involvement or from the evidence of satellite photographs passed on by Washington. No one did anything, no one said anything, no one wanted to know. The Israelis, who took out the Iraqi nuclear plant with their deep penetration raid, made no attempt to destroy the country's chemical warfare capacity; after all, the poison gases produced would only be employed against Iran, or possibly at some future date against Syria. The countries which were later to become so agitated about Libya remained totally calm at the prospect of Iraq using poison gas.

And use it they did. According to Iran, mustard gas was first used on the battlefield as early as 1982, and later proof showed that this was true. What the Iraqis had done was to conduct a field trial, a small-scale use of gas to teach their troops how to handle it, to assess its worth and to see how best to employ it in the future. It was no more than unfortunate in the Iraqi view that the tests had to be conducted on Iranian troops who were not a real threat. After all, they were still the enemy. The first internationally confirmed use of chemical weapons was in the Majnoon marshes in 1984. A Western military attaché in Baghdad at the time who knew of its use said cheerfully that he would probably have done the same if he had been in command. 'Faced with vastly superior numbers and with the enemy forced into certain areas by the terrain, it was a classic situation in which to employ gas,' he said. 'Any commander with gas at his disposal would have used it in those circumstances rather than lose many of his men, or lose the battle.' For all that, Iraq did lose that battle, and with it a valuable source of oil in the Majnoon area.

From that time on, Iran regularly sent soldiers suffering from the effects of gas to Western countries as a way of publicising what was going on, but little attention was paid; it was generally accepted that gas was being used, there were a few ritual denunciations, but there was no international effort to put pressure on Iraq to stop using it. Only the horror of Halabja in March 1988 – when 5,000 Kurdish civilians were killed in a gas attack – seemed to bring any real reaction, and that was merely because the town changed hands just before the gas attack had taken place, so that Iran was able to take TV crews there within hours to record the dreadful scenes of parents dead in mid-stride as they sought to flee with children in their arms, a father trying to shield a baby daughter, mothers killed beside their children. According to some experts, both Iran and Iraq used chemical weapons in Halabja, but this seems unlikely, and appeared to be based solely on the fact that two different types of gas were used on the town. Certainly Iran had the capacity to produce chemical weapons, and did actually build up a stockpile, but, on the direct orders of Khomeini, gas was never used; in a rare display of Islamic principle, the Ayatollah resisted pressure from more worldly Iranian leaders to retaliate against the Iraqis as a way of stopping the dreadful carnage caused by the Iraqi gas attacks. Iran was engaged in a holy struggle, he decreed, and must set an example to other Muslim nations.

So it was after Iranian acceptance of Resolution 598 that the world was forced to recognise that Iraq was using chemical weapons against the Kurdish population which had been giving it trouble for so long. Despite the deportations, the free-fire zones and the regular sweeps by Iraqi troops and attacks by the Iraqi air force, the *peshmerga* kept up the battle throughout the eight years of war, tying down at least 30,000 Iraqi troops. Then in six weeks from 19 July 1988, Iraqi troops killed more than 1,000 *peshmerga* and 3,000 Kurdish civilians in a sustained onslaught in which poison gas was widely and indiscriminately used; more than 100,000 Kurds flew over the border into Turkey and about 20,000 into Iran.

Iraq's attempt to end its Kurdish problem once and for all coincided with the opening of the Iran–Iraq peace talks in Geneva, difficult negotiations in which Perez de Cuellar needed all his skill if collapse was to be avoided. Nothing should be allowed to jeopardise those talks, the outside powers and the UN decided, for, given Iraq's new-found confidence, they believed that there was a real danger of Iraq resuming the war if it were provoked; so, once again, the world turned a blind eye. Only the newspapers of the West paid any attention, and diplomats who at times were very willing to accept evidence gleaned by journalists if it suited their book this time spoke of the need for medical evidence, for scientific proof. But they did nothing to get it. The Americans alone sent members of their Ankara embassy to the border with Iran to interview and photograph the refugees, and there was also CIA information from inside Iraq; but it was only after the most careful weighing of the situation that George Shultz finally went on record as saying that America did have evidence that Iraq had used gas against its Kurdish population. The reason he said this had little to do with what was happening in the mountains of Kurdistan; rather, the decision was taken that America had swung too far towards Iraq, and a pretext needed to be found to redress the balance, in the interests of continued influence and ability to play a role in the Gulf. The criticism of the use of chemical weapons against the Kurds was no more than that, a tilt back towards the centre after America's huge swing towards support of Iraq; the intervention was made for political reasons, not out of humanity.

Iraq was therefore spared more than minimal condemnation of its use of chemical weapons against the Kurds, and a brave attempt within the US Congress to denounce and sanction Iraq ran into strong opposition from the Reagan administration. In mid-September, two staff members of the Senate Foreign Relations Committee, Peter Galbraith and Chris Van Hollen, travelled to

Turkey to see for themselves the plight of the Kurds who had fled from northern Iraq. They compiled a graphic report on Iraq's 'final offensive' against its own Kurdish population and found what they considered to be overwhelming evidence of extensive use of chemical weapons against civilians. The Galbraith–Van Hollen report said that international acquiescence in previous Iraqi use of chemical weapons had undoubtedly been a major factor in Iraq's belief that it could use gas against the Kurds with impunity.

Back in Washington, the Committee's chairman, Senator Claiborne Pell, introduced the Prevention of Genocide Act 1988, which was passed unanimously. Pell told the Senate:

> While a people are gassed, the world is largely silent. There are reasons for this: Iraq's great oil wealth, its military strength, a desire not to upset the delicate negotiations seeking an end to the Iran–Iraq war. Silence, however, is complicity. A half century ago, the world was silent as Hitler began a campaign that culminated in the near extermination of Europe's Jews. We cannot be silent to genocide again.

Pell's stirring words failed to move the White House, which said it found such legislation 'premature' and 'counter-productive' and likely to undercut diplomatic efforts aimed at preventing future use of chemical weapons by Iraq. Although a sanctions bill also gained wide approval in the House of Representatives, there were some dissenting voices who agreed with the administration, among them Congressman Bill Frenzel who said that sanctions were unwise because they would hurt 'American employers and American employees'. In the end, a compromise was worked out by senior US tax negotiators whereby limited sanctions could be imposed on Iraq with US farm products and farming machinery exempted. But legislation was dropped in the dash to wind up Congress before the presidential election and the United States' improved relationship with Baghdad was preserved.

Yet in the case of America, political interest at least coincided with human concern. The Arab countries did not even have that to cloak their cynicism, for far from condemning Iraq for its use of gas, the Arab states criticised America and the West for 'interference in the internal affairs of a country, and calumnies against the Baghdad government'. The Arab states did this not only because they wanted to continue their unquestioning support of Iraq, but also because they had the future in mind: chemical weapons are cheap and relatively easy to produce, 'the poor man's atom bomb', and at least three Arab countries, Syria, Libya and Egypt, had obtained or were in the process of obtaining the capability to produce such weapons. Their rationale and excuse was that they had to be able to negotiate with Israel from a position of strength, and Israel, it was well known, was in possession of nuclear weapons. Hence the need for the Arab move towards chemicals.

The onslaught against the Kurds brought out the worst in many countries. Even Turkey, which after a hesitant start did open its borders and give sanctuary to the tens of thousands of refugees who poured across the frontier, refused to furnish to international bodies the evidence of the use of gas which its own doctors had found, and actively discouraged outsiders from entering the country to seek evidence. Nor did the government in Ankara do more than the minimum for the refugees who arrived, housing them in the most makeshift of accommodation in barren, exposed sites in the middle of winter, with the obvious hope that they would go back to Iraq. Some actually did so, following the announcement of an amnesty by the Baghdad government. Reports from inside northern Iraq said that the few lorry-loads of Kurdish refugees who went back were separated into male and female groups which were taken to different places; the men have not been seen since.

Perhaps more appalling, and totally unremarked, was another phase of Iraqi 'tidying-up' at the end of the war. Republican Guard units, the most dependable forces in the army, were sent to the area of the marshes north of Basra which had become the territory of some 30,000 deserters who preyed on the surrounding countryside. Appeals were made for the deserters to give themselves up, broadcast from helicopters which also gave news of the end of the war. A number did emerge from their hiding places in the marshes and, according to reports, have been imprisoned, though a few officers among them were shot. But many refused to heed the calls for surrender and, given the terrain, the Republican Guards could not mount the kind of sweep which would force them out. So, just as the Iraqi commanders five years before had found the marshes ideal for the use of gas, once again gas was employed, and only an outcry by village leaders of the marsh Arabs who found some of their own loyal people killed in the first experiment prevented a more widespread use. As it was, the threat of gas worked, and few deserters now remain.

# 15

# Islam divided:
# the conflict remains

The guns fell silent, the UN observers moved in, diplomats hurried about their affairs in New York – and nothing else happened; the sudden peace between Iran and Iraq was even colder than that between Egypt and Israel, a ceasefire and nothing more. Yet it was an effective ceasefire. In the first few days, as the UN men took up their positions, there were minor violations as local commanders seized a hill or moved their men to a defensible ridge, but these were the natural reactions of officers concerned with the position on the ground, not part of any plan by either side to gain last-minute advantage, though Iraq, not surprisingly, was the more blatant in its transgressions and the more militant – after all, the Iraqis now saw themselves as the victors, so here and there they overdid things, seizing villages and even besieging a town, and in the process capturing 752 Iranian soldiers. Within days, however, the UN peace-makers were able to sort things out, and very quickly the front was stabilised, and incidents diminished. The war-weariness of both the Iranian and Iraqi peoples had taken over, and without some very strong pretext neither side would have been able to muster the will for new adventures.

Both Iran and Iraq were back roughly where they had started eight years before, but for all the apparent lack of movement on the ground, there had been profound changes in both countries, altering their own make-up, their relations with each other and with the outside world, and the regional balance of power. Iraq, in particular, emerged from the war a united country. In 1980 the Sunni leaders had embarked on their bid to break the Islamic revolution with deep misgivings about the loyalty of the Shia, particularly as Khomeini made his personal appeals to them to put religious solidarity above nationalism. Very few of them did so. Instead, the Shia and the Sunnis of Iraq fought and died together, in the process forging a new unity which made Iraq much more powerful than the sum of its parts, stronger than its physical strength or resources showed. Rather like Israel, the Iraqi leaders knew now that they could call on their armed forces for that extra effort, that special something which in times of crisis distinguishes one country from another.

Yet there was a corollary to that. The leaders in Baghdad had also had to learn the limits of what their people were prepared to do, and of their abilities. Attempts by Israel to present Iraq as a new threat to the Jewish people were patently absurd – certainly the Iraqi army had more battle experience than that of any other Arab country, and it remained hostile to Israel. But the Iraqi experience was purely defensive; in the first two years of the war, with only slightly extended supply lines, but fighting on foreign soil, the Iraqi troops were mediocre at best. Only in defence of their homeland did the Iraqi soldiers fight tenaciously and the Iraqi officers show skill and determination; what Iraqi military genius there was could be seen in the conduct of static warfare, not in any swift deployment of troops at long range, or daring strikes into enemy territory. The Iraqis reflected to the full the teaching of their Soviet mentors. Israeli commanders, for all the ritual words of their political leaders, could still sleep soundly in their beds.

More soundly, probably, than their counterparts in Damascus, for if any one country was weakened by the Gulf war, it was Syria. For eight years, despite a few wobbles in his policy, President Assad had stoutly supported Iran against his fellow-Arabs. He did so for economic and political reasons, for the cheap oil he was given and for the increased authority he believed Iran could give to Syria in its perennial quarrel with Israel, its campaign to recover its captured territory and its efforts to form a credible regional bloc made up of radical states to counter what it saw as the capitulationist policies of the conservative group of Arab countries. In the end, Syria finished up more isolated than ever before, its economy in tatters, its efforts to exert its control in Lebanon thwarted by its Iranian allies, and its voice unheeded in a world increasingly concerned to settle regional problems. Assad,

becoming more isolated from his own people just as his state was
shunned by the outside world, had made the mistake of his life,
and had to pay for it. No sooner was the war over than the
Iraqis began to increase their activity in Lebanon, arming Syria's
Maronite Christian opponents in an effort to undermine that
country's control of its western neighbour.

In the Gulf, the end of the war was naturally greeted with relief,
but there was less than universal joy at the sudden collapse of the
Iranian machine and the strength and solidarity shown by Iraq;
the number of times Kuwaiti ministers and officials protested that
they had no fears of Iraqi expansionism was a fair indicator of
their real feelings. Kuwait, like all the Gulf states, wanted Iraq
to win the war – but not too convincingly; what the Gulf countries
wanted was very similar to the wish of the Israelis – that the two
regional superpowers should exhaust each other, emerging from
the conflict in balance, and in no condition to launch any new
adventures for decades to come. The reality was that Iraq had
come out of it too strong and too united for their liking, seeing
itself as the victor even if it was not, while Iran in the end felt
itself cheated, firmly believing that if it had had to fight Iraq alone,
it would easily have won. It was only the intervention of outside
powers, and the Great Satan in particular, which had allowed the
Iraqis to get away with it.

The end of the fighting left the leaders in both countries curi-
ously untouched; the drama of Iranian acceptance of the ceasefire
resolution was muted for the ordinary people by the endorsement
given to it by the Ayatollah. His word remained law, and his bitter
speech acknowledging the failure of his country's efforts left no
room for debate. Below him too, there was a remarkable una-
nimity of views: left and right, pragmatists and zealots all realised
that they had been given no choice, and so had to make the best
of the situation. They did so by going on much as before, jockeying
for position, arguing over doctrine, yet at the same time carrying
on the business of government with reasonable efficiency, at
least. The Iranian hierarchy was also much more open than its
counterpart in Iraq, publicly acknowledging the mistakes which
had been made – it was a mark of the changed conditions that
some of the criticisms were bound to reflect on the Ayatollah
himself, as the man who had insisted on the 'fight to the finish'
policy. Just as the misguided aim of total surrender by the

Germans in the Second World War led to the devastation of
Western Europe and prolonged the war for years, so the same
policy pursued by Iran meant six unnecessary years of conflict
and victory snatched from it by the efforts of outside powers.
Rafsanjani came as close as anyone to criticising the Imam: 'Some
things have happened that have given rise to questions,' he said.
'The slogan "war, war, to victory" for instance was not a slogan
of the revolution – but we did not start the war. Military victory
was never one of the objectives of the revolution. And cutting
relations with countries, for example, has never been our policy.'

President Khamenei acknowledged the shortcomings of the
state bureaucracy:

> If I wanted to start right now one of the things I would
> certainly do would be to create an organisation that would
> train managers or would search for good managers. Another
> would be to strengthen the universities. Most important of
> all, if we were to start from scratch, would be to give greater
> centralisation to the executive administration.

Chief Justice Ardebili was even more open: 'It is difficult to
make a judgement about everything, but about the war I am
among those who believe that the war should have been stopped
after the liberation of Khorramshahr in 1982.' Rafsanjani went
even further back in time: for the success of the Islamic revolution,
he said, efforts should have been made to prevent the war breaking
out at all – a novel idea, that Iran might have been able to prevent
Iraq invading, and without recourse to arms. But when it was
suggested to him that America was the real victor in the war,
Rafsanjani would have none of it:

> I totally disagree. The real loser has been the US. America
> lost Iran after the revolution, then its ignorant policies led to
> the point where our people were willing to establish relations
> with any country in the world, but not America. In the war,
> we introduced new issues which were in addition to the
> demands of the revolution – military victory, the defeat of
> Iraq, and the total expulsion of America from the region. We
> took too big a bite, yet it was a defeat for the US that it had
> to dispatch seventy or eighty warships to the region. But yes,
> we wanted some things we were not able to get, and that

would have been military victory. But if we had moved with
a bit more planning maybe military victory would not have
been very far away.

All these comments were part of a stock-taking by the leaders
to mark the tenth anniversary of the revolution and the triumphant
return of Khomeini, and perhaps to answer some at least of the
questions being asked by the ordinary people forced to make the
sudden transition from war to peace, a transition which seemed
to leave them no better off than they were during the war. The
change brought about a new, more open and more questioning
mood in the country, with people far less willing to take on trust
the statements of their leaders. This was graphically shown during
a live radio programme in which President Khamenei answered
questions. The first asked why Iran had accepted Resolution 598,
the next why Iran was taking no action in the face of Iraqi
provocations, and another why there was such a delay in exchanging POWs. There was not a single soft question to allow the
President to launch into one of the rambling socio-religious disser-
tations on which the leaders usually depended, but instead, hard
questions about everyday conditions as well as Iran's volte-face.
This was hardly surprising, for the economic situation had certainly played as big a part as any other in the decision to accept
Resolution 598.

Three quite separate problems seemed to have peaked at the
same time to force the hands of the mullahs: falling oil revenues
and lower demand once again limited the country's revenues; the
lack of a coherent agricultural policy meant that millions of acres
of land were lying idle while disputes over ownership meandered
on and the shelves in the shops remained bare; and the rising
birth rate, which gave Iran a population of more than 50 million
in 1989 compared with 42 million eight years earlier, forced the
government to spend more and more on food imports. These
factors allied to the Iraqi successes on land, the activity of the
US navy in the Gulf, and the increasingly effective worldwide
embargo preventing Iran from obtaining the arms it wanted,
forced the government in Tehran to compromise, while the differences in the leadership prevented formulation of any coherent
policy. Ayatollah Montazeri, for so long at odds with Khomeini
though still the old man's designated successor, issued statement

after statement condemning the arbitrary methods of the regime as the zealots instituted a wave of executions, getting rid not only of the Mujahedin sympathisers revealed by the last-minute invasion of Iran by the National Liberation Army, but also of anti-government activists who had served their sentences and been freed. Ardebili boasted that 'the administration of justice' had become so efficient that it now took ten days from commission of the crime to execution – but he did not add that 'the crime' was often no more than failure to toe the line.

The main difficulty facing the Islamic Republic was the same one that had caused so much trouble over the years: who was in charge? Khomeini, old, frail, out of touch and depending on his son Ahmad and other trusted advisers for information and for his words to be passed on, was still the ultimate authority, but could be invoked only rarely. Khamenei and Rafsanjani aided by the technocrats of the foreign ministry – Velayati and Larijani – tried to get some order and discipline into affairs, but were frustrated by Mousavi, Mohtashemi and others manipulating the unsatisfactory constitution. Inflation was worse than ever, the hundreds of thousands of young men returning from the war fronts had to be occupied if trouble was to be avoided, and to make it all worse, Iraq became arrogant with the victory it believed it had gained, and strung out the negotiations designed to bring a definitive peace. It was six months after the ceasefire before the exchange of the estimated 100,000 prisoners of war began, and Baghdad put constant difficulties in the way of negotiations as it sought further advantage, for all the pressure by America and the Soviet Union.

The Iraqi calculation was that by maintaining its occupation of the border areas it wanted, and by its delaying tactics, it could gain maximum advantage when real negotiations did begin, for all the exasperation this caused in the rest of the world. Iraq's long-term objective was still the border; the Baghdad government was determined to try to get control of the Shatt al Arab once and for all, to extend Iraqi authority again right up to the entrances to Iranian ports. In the short term, it wanted to fashion such a commanding position in the UN-sponsored peace talks that it could circumvent that provision of Resolution 598 calling for an independent commission to determine who started the war. The Iraqis were still afraid that they would be labelled the aggressors, with the international difficulties that that would bring and the advantage it would give to Iran if ever the secondary negotiations over reparations began. There was too a genuine fear in Iraq that Iran had merely accepted Resolution 598 as a temporary measure, seeing in it the opportunity to recover from the ravages of eight years of war, to regroup and re-equip, and to prepare for another round of fighting in which it would seek revenge for its humiliation now. Few others shared this idea, but it did colour Iraqi thinking, and made it even more difficult for the UN Secretary-General to get things moving. Equally, Iraqi suggestions that substantive matters should be put aside while work began on clearing the Shatt al Arab of its seventy-five ships and all the detritus of war so that navigation could begin again was totally unacceptable to Iran, which saw in the idea a back-door Iraqi attempt to exercise control over the waterway before it had been legally decided.

In Iraq, Saddam Hussein emerged as he had always hoped, with heightened prestige and totally in control. There was no let-up in the personality cult which had been such a feature of his rule since the early 1980s, and the firm grip of the Ba'ath party remained as tight as ever, but the opportunity was taken to bring in younger and abler men in various ministries and state enterprises, though it was noticeable that personal ties to the President remained as important as ever. The Tikrit clique was now enlarged by those linked to Saddam Hussein through marriage and by young men who had served in the presidential office being promoted to ministerial rank, while the trusted inner cabinet of those who had been with Saddam Hussein since he first seized power – Tariq Aziz, Taha Yassin Ramadan, Adnan Khairallah – all remained as firmly in control as ever. At last, there was no dissent in Iraq. The militant opposition, Dawa and the other Shia groups, and the communists, had all been eliminated; the Kurds had been massacred, brutally forced into exile, deported and harried; the bandits in the marshes were killed, captured or contained. The Ba'ath party, the state in the person of Saddam Hussein, was in total control.

For all that, even the ordinary non-political citizens felt better off: Saddam Hussein had delivered as he said he would – or at least, he was able to present things in that light, to tell the people that together the leader and the state had finally achieved the victory promised back in 1980, and that now they could reap the rewards. And benefits there were. First and foremost, there was swift demobilisation of conscript units, particularly of those recruited in the southern part of the country, so that there could be a large-scale return to the land and an increase in food production. There was too an appreciable programme of economic liberalis- ation, with the private sector allowed to emerge again in business life, individuals less controlled, a freer press and more open discussion of ideas. To maintain the fiction of victory, some of the fruits had to be enjoyed as well.

In the region and in the Arab world in general, the Iraqi position was less clear. The northern Gulf states were returning to their old attitudes of suspicion of Iraq's expansionist tendencies; Saudi Arabia, badly hit by lower oil revenues, wanted to see some repayment by Iraq of its huge war debt, but instead was faced with continued demands for subventions to rebuild Iraq's peacetime economy; and in the lower Gulf, Oman and the Emirates saw a quick opportunity to expand their trade with Iran through im- proved relations now that their lukewarm support of Iraq was no longer in issue. In the wider context, Iraq was in a much better position. Its relations with Jordan had never faltered during the war, and its ties with Egypt had steadily improved, so to capitalise on those gains Saddam Hussein took the initiative in setting up the Arab Co-operation Council, an economic grouping of North Yemen, Iraq, Jordan and Egypt which also had considerable political weight. Except for the addition of North Yemen, which had only recently become an oil producer, the ACC, as it became known, was a formalisation of the close wartime alliance between Iraq, Jordan and Egypt which had kept Iraq supplied with arms and munitions for the previous eight years and, again with the exception of North Yemen, it made sound economic sense.

Its intention went much further than that, however. For Egypt, it was another step on the road to reintegration into the Arab world after being expelled because of its treaty with Israel – an expulsion arranged and announced at a summit conference in Baghdad. For Jordan, it was useful help at a time of economic crisis and a promise of support against its difficult neighbour Syria. For North Yemen it was again a guarantee of help if help should be needed, either against powerful Saudi Arabia or Marxist South Yemen, as well as a source of expertise as the country developed its oilfields, and support in international markets. And for Iraq the ACC was a promise of the labour and technical help it might need, access to the markets of the northern group of countries and a foothold in the southern part of the Arabian peninsula, but above all, an acknowledgement of its new weight in the Arab world. Saddam Hussein was no longer the party strongman, the rabid anti-Zionist and expansionist in the Gulf, but one of the senior statesmen of the Arab world, a man leading a united and prosperous country, the head of the only Arab army hardened and victorious in battle, a statesman to be taken into account on the international stage. It was a remarkable transformation from the party activist and would-be assassin.

If all seemed well with Iraq internally, and its status was high in the Arab world, it still had its troubles; these were mainly economic, for eight years of war had left it with a massive burden of debt. The Gulf states which had been so generous during the war as Iraq fought their battles for them were eager to cut off the flow of cash once the conflict ended; oil revenues were still low and OPEC seemed incapable of adjusting supply and demand as individual members ignored quotas to maximise production. The Gulf countries needed the money, largely to buy off their own restive populations: war in the region had inhibited the activities of the various revolutionary groups, but now subversive activity could recommence, and in Saudi Arabia and the rich sheikhdoms of the Gulf stability depended on maintaining a high standard of living. In Kuwait, the difficult Shia minority was as disaffected as ever, and there was no indication that Iran had given up its dream of spreading militant Islam, for all its defeat at home. The end of the war brought a period of change and uncertainty in the region, a wariness of Iraq's new status and forebodings of an Iran resurgent.

As the stock-taking went on round the world, the realisation slowly emerged that the outcome of it all was profoundly unsatisfactory for most. Iran was still a revolutionary state, apparently with the extremists in control and thus still hoping to export their dangerous ideas. Iraq had emerged stronger than anyone would have liked, a difficult neighbour to the other Gulf states, though a useful addition to the conservative bloc in the Arab world, possibly ready to tip the balance towards moderation in the accelerating negotiations with Israel. The length of the war had forced both countries to diversify their means of exporting their oil, so that increased supplies could be expected on the world market if O P E C continued to show itself to be such an ineffectual cartel. And the superpowers were left with a nagging situation, an area of the world where neither was in control though both were vulnerable. The Soviet Union still wanted a stable neighbour on its southern borders and a friendly government in Tehran which would not seek to subvert the growing Muslim population of the central Asian republics, and had not got it. America wanted a powerful regional ally capable of maintaining the peace of the area as Britain had in its imperial days, and this too was missing. Saudi Arabia still felt threatened, though it would probably throw in its lot with Iraq, relying on its own strength to prevent domination by that country, and preferring the Arab neighbour it believed it understood to the Persian regional rival it feared. Iran itself seemed to be looking more to the east: the settlement in Afghanistan presented it with opportunities, and held out the prospect of a potentially useful and powerful political and economic grouping with that country and with Pakistan.

In many ways, 1988 was rightly called an *annus mirabilis*, the year in which the new-found consensus between the superpowers fostered progress towards ending a variety of regional conflicts – Angola, Cambodia and Afghanistan, as well as the Gulf. Yet Iran and Iraq remained in a situation, not of peace, but of non-war long after the guns had fallen silent. Behind the hope of UN Secretary-General Javier Perez de Cuellar that the international cooperation which led to the ceasefire might serve as the model for the solution of other conflicts, there was the nagging fear that the war could all too easily flare up again, that both sides were retiring to lick their wounds and would at some future date resume the battle. The ceasefire represented only one half of one clause of the ten-point Resolution 598 and there was little progress in the wary contacts between Iraq and Iran towards the comprehensive settlement which the Security Council wanted. There was, however, optimism in the outside world that the two belligerents, exhausted by eight years of total war, with Iraq saddled with foreign debts of $60 billion and Iran with its economic infrastructure in ruins, might quietly settle down to a period of consolidation and reconstruction. The war had cost the two sides a total of $350 billion and now oil revenues for each were down to below $12 billion a year. But the harsh economic realities did not dampen the tone of triumph in Iraq, nor cool the radicalism and factionalism of the Iranian revolution, with Baghdad again pressuring Kuwait to give it greater territorial access to the Gulf, reaffirming its claim of sovereignty over the whole of the Shatt al Arab and, despite the empty coffers, announcing a grandiose scheme to divert the waters of the estuary westwards into Iraqi territory.

The Iranians had been severely shaken by the decision to accept peace but, in the West, there was a widespread belief that they would now put war and revolution behind them and begin the monumental task of reconstruction. Instead, it soon became clear that eight years of war, rather than consolidating the revolution, had only prolonged the revolutionary process and that few of the contradictions within Iranian society which had led to the movement to overthrow the Shah had been resolved. The disagreements among the rival factions over economic policy and relations with the outside world remained unresolved, and the methods and aims of post-war reconstruction became the key subject of internal dissent. Rafsanjani and his political allies were perhaps too visibly eager to renew ties with the West, alarming the diehards of the regime who, as time went by, showed mounting success in the competition for the ear of Khomeini. 'I am keeping a watchful eye on the internal and external policies of the country and as long as I am alive I will not let the course of our real policy change,' Khomeini said ten weeks after the end of the war. He warned against the visible and invisible hands of West and East which were devising new plots against the revolution.

Both Iran and Iraq had to face the challenge of rising expectations among populations which had suffered eight years of economic and political constraints. Iraqis had been more sheltered from the economic effects of the war than had their Iranian enemies, but political controls had been tighter and, although Saddam Hussein announced a projected liberalisation of Iraqi political life, there were persistent reports that purges in the armed forces were continuing long after the war was over. It still seemed doubtful that Iraq could ever evolve towards a more open society while Saddam Hussein remained in power. In Iran there seemed little prospect of an improvement in living standards unless the regime could resolve its differences on economic policy, specifically the desirability of resorting to foreign borrowing for reconstruction after fighting the war for eight years without outside help. The pragmatists argued that Iran had no alternative but to open up to the West, while the radicals demanded why Iran should reward those who had conspired against it during the war. Iran was also faced by a demographic problem of alarming proportions with one of the highest birthrates in the world. In revolutionary terms, the exploding population offered the prospect of new young minds ready to be moulded to the ideals of the Islamic Republic, but it also meant new young mouths waiting to be fed.

Like all social upheavals, the Iranian revolution sought to create the New Man: 'The biggest achievement of the Islamic revolution is that it has transformed the mentality of the people,' President Khamenei boasted, but the main change was that Iran had become a nation of drug-takers; drug abuse was a major social problem during the war years, despite draconian penalties, and by the end one in fifty Iranians was an addict. In that remarkably frank series of interviews which the leaders gave to mark the tenth anniversary of the revolution, there were admissions of such faults, but there was also the now characteristic tendency to blame Iran's ills on the outside world – low oil prices were part of a US-inspired plot to destabilise the economy, and Western complaints about human rights abuses were an attempt to sow discord within the regime.

The truth was that the decision to end the war had a profound effect on the Iranian leadership because it represented an open challenge to the infallibility of the *ulema*. The certainties of the wartime slogans were replaced by the perils of the internal debate about Iran's future role in the region and the world. The claim that the Islamic Republic had proved its independence by fighting an eight-year conventional war without outside help was a valid one, but it was an argument which obscured the fact that both superpowers had been committed, first separately and later jointly, to the geopolitical concept that neither Iran nor Iraq should be allowed to go under. As relations improved between Washington and Moscow, the paranoid fear in Iran and elsewhere in the Middle East, which in many ways reflected the outside world's fear of fundamentalist Islam, was that the superpowers were heading towards a new Yalta in which the Third World would be carved up into mutually agreed spheres of influence. This was a scenario which particularly touched Iran, wedged between the Soviet Union and the pro-Western regimes of the southern Gulf and an increasingly Western-oriented Iraq, so that future relations with the superpowers became the pivotal element of the post-war debate. Rafsanjani and the pragmatists were committed to better and more equitable links with the West, Western Europe in particular; the United States was excluded from this process but an eventual renewal of ties with Washington was considered to be only a matter of time. The radicals and advocates of centralised control, including Prime Minister Mousavi and Mohtashemi, the interior minister, took every opportunity to oppose this trend and to question the need for any approach to the West.

As the bickering and recriminations went on in Iran, with Ayatollah Montazeri an increasingly vocal critic of the regime and Rafsanjani and the other moderates overborne by the harder men who wanted no truck with compromise, any accommodation with the outside powers seemed unlikely despite the ignominious end to the war. Just as the expected reconstruction in Iraq was inhibited by lack of resources, so in Iran few foreign companies went in because of the continuing uncertainty of the political situation. This came to a head in the bizarre affair of *The Satanic Verses*, Salman Rushdie's opaque novel taken in Muslim countries as an attack on Islam and on the Prophet himself. In December 1988 there was a damning review of the book in Tehran's leading cultural weekly, but no one took much notice. It was in Pakistan and India, and even in Britain, that dislike of the book erupted into violence: copies were burned in Bradford, five people died in a riot in Pakistan, and two more in an Indian protest. There was evidence that Saudi Arabia, keen to assert its moral authority in the Islamic world, was encouraging the wave of protest against the book.

It was after these protests, two months after the book had been noticed in Iran, that Ayatollah Khomeini stepped into the affair, delivering a brief *fatwa* condemning Rushdie to death for his impiety. For all the world outrage caused, Britain reacted moderately, merely freezing the projected up-grading of diplomatic relations between the two countries, and for a time this quiet response seemed to be paying off, as several figures in the Iranian hierarchy, notably President Khamenei, suggested that an apology from Rushdie would end the affair. Just when things seemed to be going well, Khomeini spoke again. The sentence of death would stand, he said, even if Rushdie became the most pious Muslim in the world; and anyone carrying out that death penalty and suffering for it would be a martyr sure of a place in paradise. Not surprisingly, this caused uproar, with Western ambassadors recalled from Tehran and Iranian diplomats taken out of Europe, an end to high-level contacts with ministers, and general condemnation of Iran as a barbaric throwback to the Middle Ages. President Khamenei became more vitriolic than Khomeini in his damnation of Rushdie, and Iran emerged once more as the pariah of the Western world – though Arab and Muslim countries were notably silent on the issue.

Post-war Iran's attitudes towards the Soviet Union were, if anything, even more ambivalent than its attitudes towards the West. The level of wartime Iranian rhetoric against the Soviet Union, which placed the 'atheist' Russians almost on a par with the Great Satan, never truly reflected the actual relationship between the two countries, which remained relatively normal compared with Iran's relations with much of the West. A consistent element of Iranian foreign policy since the days when Britain and Russia competed for influence was never to confront both powers at the same time or indeed confront one without at least the tacit support of the other. When the war ended, the Soviet Union was more eager than ever to ensure a sound relationship with Tehran in view of the withdrawal from Afghanistan and the threat of ethnic unrest within its own borders; for, although the war between Arab Iraq and Persian Iran had helped to contain the spread of Khomeinism in the Arab world, it appeared to have done nothing to dull the attraction of Islamic fundamentalism to Muslims in central Asia and the sub-continent. During the ethnic unrest in Soviet Armenia and Azerbaijan in 1988, Shia Azerbaijani demonstrators held aloft portraits of Khomeini to the familiar chant of '*Allahu akhbar*'. The Russian desire not to offend the Tehran regime resulted in a stunning piece of sophistry on the part of the Soviet ambassador, Alexei Gudov, when he was questioned about the events in Azerbaijan:

Even if we assume that the demonstrators were carrying pictures of the leader of a friendly country, there is nothing wrong in it. If, for argument's sake, there were demonstrations outside the Soviet embassy in Tehran and one of the demonstrators was carrying a picture of Mr Gorbachev, we would do nothing about it. If all the demonstrators were to carry pictures of leaders of friendly countries it would help to improve relations.

An indication that Iran's military failure in the war had done nothing to curb Ayatollah Khomeini's enthusiasm for exporting the revolution came in January 1989 when, in a remarkable epistle to Mikhail Gorbachev, he urged the Soviet leader to study Islam. It was a letter reminiscent of the messages sent by the Prophet Mohammed to the emperors of Persia and Byzantium and contained many high-handed phrases which caused the otherwise impassive Gorbachev to colour slightly as it was read to him by a member of an Iranian delegation. Khomeini wrote that, in view of international developments, particularly within the Soviet Union, which might revolutionise the present world order, 'I have found it necessary to remind you of certain issues.' He went on to assert that communism was dead but warned Gorbachev against turning towards the West's capitalist system, for 'your principal problem is a long and futile combat with God, the origin of existence and creation'. After a lengthy philosophical discourse on the nature of matter and hidden reality during which he offered Gorbachev an Islamic reading list and invited him to send experts to study at Qom in order to understand the stages of mysticism, Khomeini concluded: 'I openly announce that the Islamic Republic of Iran, as the greatest and most powerful base of the Islamic world, can easily fill the ideological vacuum of your system. . . . Peace be upon those who follow the truth.'

Despite the novel nature of Khomeini's message, it was not one which the Soviet Union could afford to dismiss out of hand in view of the sensitivities of its large and growing Muslim population and of Iran's increasingly high profile in Afghan affairs, so the following month Eduard Shevardnadze, the foreign minister, was dispatched to Tehran to deliver Gorbachev's reply during an unprecedented audience with Khomeini in which both sides expressed a desire for good relations. Shevardnadze said diplomatically that there were many points of agreement in the Ayatollah's letter as well as others on which differences remained.

The epistle to Gorbachev and the furore caused by Khomeini's intervention in the Salman Rushdie affair, with the challenge it posed to the leaders of conservative Muslim regimes, were indications that the Islamic Republic could continue to play a destabilising role in an intrinsically shaky region. The immediate post-war optimism that the Iranian revolution would somehow settle down and cease to be a threat to Western or indeed Soviet interests proved to be premature, while the continued factional strife in Iran cast doubt on the future course of reconstruction, despite Khomeini's attempts to lay down guidelines which would appease all sides in the debate; the essence of his intervention was that Iran should avoid relying on 'the criminal Soviets or world-devouring America'. But Iranian leaders of all factions faced some stark choices: either they accepted credits or grants from the outside world to rebuild the badly shattered infrastructure – some estimates put the destruction at as much as $300 billion – or they retained their economic independence within the confines of a virtual siege economy.

Despite the political shift in early 1989 towards Moscow, the best Iran could hope for from the Eastern bloc and its Third World partners were barter deals, with the value of imported goods and services set against oil exports, or participation agreements in productive sectors such as mining. In the longer term, Iran also had to determine its role in the region after a war in which it had alienated the entire Arab world, despite the tactical support it received from Syria and, less consistently, Libya. Khomeini's Islamic Republic had proved to be no more to the liking of the Arabs than was the Shah's Iran, a phenomenon which the Iranians appeared to accept despite their adherence to the long-term goal of extending the frontiers of the true Islam in the Middle East. Tehran's rapprochement with the Soviet Union, its desire to win a role for itself in Afghanistan and its concern about the tribulations of Islam in the sub-continent, were signs that Iran once more saw itself as a central Asian rather than a Middle Eastern power.

Iran's sudden emergence as a power-broker in Afghanistan was an example of this heightened involvement in Asian as opposed to Middle Eastern affairs. Despite the war, Tehran had managed to play a major role in Lebanese affairs, but the Mujahedin in Afghanistan, even the Shia, had received only minimal assistance. At the time of the Soviet withdrawal, however, Tehran increased its backing for the eight Iranian-based Shia resistance groups and demanded a central role for them in a future Afghan regime. This Iranian interference deepened the rift between the rival groups and indirectly, although perhaps in a deliberate gesture towards Moscow, played into the hands of the Kabul government and the Soviet Union. There was also heightened interest in relations with Pakistan, despite the distress which it must have caused the mullahs when a woman, Benazir Bhutto, was elected to the premiership of a neighbouring Islamic country. The post-war period also saw a revival of Iranian interest in the Tehran-based Economic Co-operation Organisation, linking Iran, Pakistan and Turkey, with Afghanistan as a possible future member. There was discussion of joint defence projects with Pakistan, and the new Revolutionary Guards minister, Ali Shamkhani, said after a visit to Pakistan that 'Iran, in collaboration with Pakistan, will form an important part of the Islamic defence line in the region'. Whatever the outcome of the internal political debate in Iran, it appeared likely that the trend would continue away from the Middle East and towards a central Asian alliance, grouping Iran, Pakistan and Afghanistan – countries with intimate religious and cultural links.

For eight years the Gulf war had confronted outside strategists, particularly in the West, with one of their worse geopolitical nightmares – a sustained conflict between two major oil producers in a region of intense superpower rivalry. In the event, the rest of the world was only dragged into the conflict at a military level to a very minimal degree. Oil continued to reach Western markets and, after the initial shock, world oil prices actually fell. The attacks on tankers were costly and in human terms distressing, but the economic effects of the war on the rest of the world were, in the unemotional terminology of the international financial system, discounted by the markets.

Despite some of the more blood-chilling rhetoric of the Iranian clergy and their periodic threats to close the Strait of Hormuz and starve the West of oil, in practice Iran behaved with cool-headed pragmatism, realising that it had at least as much to lose as anyone else if it turned off the oil tap. The fact that there was a glut of oil on the market for most of the 1980s, despite the war raging in the Gulf, may have lulled many people in the Western consuming nations into a false sense of security and into the mistaken belief that Gulf oil was no longer as important to their economies as it had been. In fact, although production by the thirteen OPEC countries, Iran and Iraq included, declined as a proportion of the

West's energy needs, the remaining oil reserves in the world were increasingly concentrated in the Gulf as wells elsewhere ran dry. The oil glut of the 1980s resulted in part from economic recession in the West and also from successful efforts to find alternative energy sources, but other sources of energy are expensive and, in the case of nuclear energy, potentially dangerous, as Chernobyl showed all too well. For the time being, until such time as scientists make the breakthrough to the production of fusion energy, Gulf oil will remain the largest and most cheaply produced energy supply in the world.

The conventional wisdom in the West used to be that the main threat to Western access to the oil of the Gulf came from the Soviet Union. This doctrine was at the heart of US strategic planning which saw regional conflicts primarily in an East–West context. But the Gorbachev era and the rapprochement between the Soviet Union and the United States have given rise to optimism about a new era of East–West cooperation which would remove the threat both of direct superpower rivalry or of indirect surrogate conflicts in the Third World. The danger now is seen as coming more from the inherent internal contradictions of the Gulf states, coupled with the potentially destabilising influence of Islamic fundamentalism. The power vacuum created in the Gulf by the fall of the Shah which the Gulf war might have resolved, had it led to outright victory by either side, is still there. While there is an anti-Western regime in Tehran, the Americans cannot re-establish a permanent and effective military presence in the Gulf capable of guaranteeing the security of oil supplies without risking the new-found relationship with the Soviet Union, which says it is eager to see all foreign fleets withdraw.

The temptation therefore is to foster pro-Western alliances, particularly among the conservative Arab states of the Middle East and the southern Gulf, in order to halt the spread of revolution and confront any direct military threat; hence the West's massive arms sales to Saudi Arabia and other Gulf states. But the fate of the Shah serves to illustrate the drawbacks and limitations of relying on surrogate military power. The rational alternative – a neutral, non-aligned Gulf where regional relationships are based on co-operation rather than conflict – may not be attainable in the short term. The ancient Arab–Persian antagonism, now heightened by eight years of bloody war, will not die away quickly. And the doctrinal, theological conflict between Khomeinism and the Saudis and the threat which it poses to Western interests in the Gulf, is something which is beyond the scope of the outside world to resolve.

# Chronology

**1979**

17 January: Shah leaves Iran.
1 February: Ayatollah Khomeini returns from exile in France.
30–31 March: Iranians vote for Islamic Republic to replace monarchy.
16 July: Saddam Hussein becomes President of Iraq.
30 October: Iraq demands revision of the 1975 Algiers agreement defining the border and giving Iran control of the Shatt al Arab.
4 November: Militant students seize the US embassy in Tehran, taking the diplomats there hostage.
2 December: Referendum in Iran approves new Islamic Constitution.
26 December: Soviet troops enter Afghanistan.

**1980**

3 April: Assassination attempt on Tariq Aziz, Iraqi deputy premier.
7 April: Execution in Iraq of Ayatollah Mohammed Bakr al-Sadr.
25 April: US aircraft collide on Iranian desert airstrip after hostage rescue mission aborted.
30 April: Dissident Iranian Arabs seize Iran's embassy in London.
20 July: Rafsanjani elected speaker of the Iranian parliament.
27 July: Shah dies in exile in Egypt.
July and August: cross-border incidents intensify.
4 September: Iranian shelling of Khaneqin and Mandali; the day on which Iraq claims the war began.
17 September: Iraq abrogates the Algiers agreement.
22 September: Iraqi troops invade Iran.
24 October: Iraq captures Khorramshahr.
11 November: Olof Palme appointed UN special representative to mediate in the Gulf war.

**1981**

20 January: Iranians free fifty-two hostages held since the seizure of the US embassy in Tehran.

7 June: Israeli jets bomb Iraq's Osirak nuclear reactor.

10 June: Bani-Sadr removed as commander-in-chief of Iranian forces.

21 June: Bani-Sadr removed as President.

28 June: Bomb kills seventy-four in Tehran in attack on leaders of Islamic Republican Party.

29 September: Iraqi forces pushed back across Karun river and forced to break off siege of Abadan.

**1982**

10 April: Syria stops transit of Iraqi oil through Mediterranean pipeline.

3 May: Algerian foreign minister, Mohamed Benyahiya, killed near the frontier when his plane shot down by unidentified fire.

24 May: Iran recaptures Khorramshahr.

6 June: Israel invades Lebanon.

30 June: Iraq announces its unilateral withdrawal from Iranian territory.

12 August: Iraq declares a maritime exclusion zone around Iran's Kharg Island oil terminal.

1 November: Iran captures Iraqi territory in the Musian area.

17 November: Supreme Assembly of the Islamic Revolution in Iraq formed in Tehran.

**1983**

2 March: Iraqi planes bomb Iran's Nowruz oilfield.

30 April: Tudeh leader Kianuri admits spying for Moscow.

23 July: Iran drives Iraqi troops out of Kurdish area around Haj Omran and out of Mehran.

23 October: Suicide bomber causes death of 241 US Marines in Beirut.

**1984**

1 March: Iraqi troops driven out of the Majnoon marshes and oilfield.

1 March: Missile strike on British vessel *Charming* begins series of Iraqi attacks on Gulf shipping – the start of the tanker war.

1 March: First confirmed use of poison gas by Iraq.

5 June: Saudi air force shoots down intruding Iranian F4.

**1985**

4 March: Beginning of first 'war of the cities', with Iraq bombing Ahwaz and Iran firing missiles at Baghdad.

14 June: Iraq announces fifteen-day truce in the war of the cities and, when Iran halts attacks, does not resume after that period.

June: Robert McFarlane suggests in secret internal memo that US should approach Iran with view to exchanging arms for hostages.

14 July: Iran warns that ships sailing into the Gulf may be stopped and searched.

23 November: Ayatollah Hossein Ali Montazeri designated as Khomeini's successor.

## 1986

10 February: Iranian troops capture the Fao peninsula.

March: UN report confirms that Iraq has used chemical weapons.

25 May: McFarlane, Oliver North and others visit Tehran.

3 November: *Al Shiraa* weekly in Beirut breaks story of US arms-for-hostages deal.

25 November: First Iraqi attack on Larak oil terminal.

## 1987

10 January: War of the cities resumes.

17 May: Iraqi plane attacks USS *Stark*, killing thirty-seven American servicemen.

17 July: France breaks diplomatic relations with Iran.

20 July: UN Security Council approves Resolution 598, calling for ceasefire, withdrawal of troops to the internationally recognised border and the establishment of a commission to decide responsibility for the war.

22 July: US navy begins escorting reflagged Kuwaiti tankers.

31 July: Clashes between Iranian pilgrims and Saudi security forces at Mecca leave more than 400 dead.

21 September: US attacks *Iran Ajr* while it allegedly lays mines in the Gulf.

3 October: Iran and Iraq formally break diplomatic relations.

11 November: Special Arab League summit in Amman to discuss Gulf war.

## 1988

28 March: Some 5,000 killed in Iraqi chemical attack on Halabja.

18 April: Iranian forces driven out of Fao peninsula.

25 May: Iraq recaptures territory opposite Basra.

2 June: Rafsanjani appointed acting commander-in-chief.

25 June: Iraq drives Iranian forces out of the Majnoon islands.

3 July: All 290 civilians on Iranian Airbus killed when it is shot down by USS *Vincennes*.

17 July: Iranian hierarchy meets to implement Khomeini's order to
  end war.
18 July: Perez de Cuellar receives Iran's formal acceptance of
  Resolution 598.

# Glossary

*asr*: the mid-afternoon prayer (of the five daily prayers prescribed in the *Koran*).

**Assad, Hafez**: president of Syria and Iran's only consistent ally in the Arab world.

**Ayatollah**: sign of Allah; the most senior title in the Shia religious–legal hierarchy of which the holder is a source of guidance and emulation.

**Aziz, Tariq**: Iraqi foreign minister who escaped assassination in April 1979.

**Ba'ath party**: pan-Arab socialist movement of which two rival wings now govern Iraq and Syria.

**Bani-Sadr, Abolhassan**: Iran's first President; elected January 1980, deposed June 1981.

*basij*: an Iranian all-volunteer force set up to boost the wartime manpower of the Revolutionary Guards.

**Basra**: Iraq's second city and largest port; main target of Iranian offensives after 1982.

**Dawa**: underground clergy-led Shia group opposed to Saddam Hussein.

**Fao**: Iraqi peninsula and oil port, south of Basra, captured by Iran in 1986.

**Fadlallah, Sheikh Mohammed Hussein**: spiritual leader of Iranian-backed Hizbollah organisation in Lebanon.

*fatwa*: a religious edict.

**Gulf Cooperation Council (GCC)**: formed after outbreak of war by Saudi Arabia, Bahrain, Kuwait, Oman, Qatar and UAE to enhance joint security.

*haj*: the annual pilgrimage to Mecca.

**Halabja**: Iraqi Kurdish town where 5,000 were killed in Iraqi chemical weapons raid in March 1988.

**Hizbollah**: the Party of God, an unstructured grouping of Shia extremists who, in Iran, acted as street fighters for the clergy factions; in Lebanon, an Iranian-backed militia held responsible for the kidnapping of Westerners.

**Hojatoleslam**: proof of Islam; a Shia clerical title below Ayatollah.

**Hussein al-Tikriti, Saddam**: President of Iraq from July 1979.

**Huyser, Robert**: US general dispatched to Iran in the last months of the revolution to rally the Imperial armed forces.

**Imam**: Muslim religious leader; Mosque prayer leader.

*intifada*: uprising, in particular, the Palestinian revolt against the Israeli occupation.

**Irangate**: the shorthand term for secret operations, directed from the White House, to supply Iran with arms in return for Western hostages and to divert the profits to right-wing Contra rebels in Nicaragua.

**Islamic Jihad**: a group claiming responsibility for kidnappings of Westerners in Lebanon.

**Islamic Republic**: on 30–31 March 1979, more than 98 per cent voted in a referendum to replace the Iranian monarchy with an Islamic Republic.

**Islamic Republican party (IRP)**: founded February 1979; the main political grouping of the Shia clergy.

**Islamic Revolution Guard Corps (IRGC) or Sepah-ye-Pasdaran**: set up to protect the revolution from internal and external enemies; grew into major fighting force during war.

*jihad*: holy war.

*keffiyeh*: Arab headdress, usually of black-and-white or red-and-white chequered cloth.

**Kerbala**: holy city and centre of pilgrimage for the Shia, in Iraq.

**Khamenei, Ayatollah Ali**: president of Iran 1981–9.

**Khomeini, Ayatollah al-Ozma Sayyed Ruhollah Mousavi**: founder of the Islamic Republic and supreme leader by virtue of a theocratic constitution.

**Khorramshahr**: Iranian port and naval base on the Karun river.

**Khuzestan**: known by the Arabs as Arabistan, Iran's most southwesterly province and home to its ethnic Arab minority.

**Kianuri, Nureddin**: secretary-general of Iran's Tudeh (communist) party; jailed but later pardoned after confessing to spying for Moscow.

*komiteh*: self-appointed group of local activists running an area of a city or town in Iran after the Islamic revolution.

**Kurds**: Indo-European race inhabiting border areas of Iran, Iraq, Turkey, Syria and the Soviet Union.

**Madani, Ahmad**: Iranian navy commander and governor-general of Khuzestan.

**Majlis**: a council of elders or advisers; in Iran, the parliament.

**Mohtashemi, Hojatoleslam Ali Akbar**: Iranian ambassador to Damascus and later interior minister; a leading hardliner.

**Montazeri, Ayatollah Hossein Ali**: a clerical leader of the revolution; Khomeini's successor until 1989.

**Mousavi, Mir Hossein**: Iranian Prime Minister from 1981; a hardliner.

**mullah**: Muslim cleric or preacher.

**Najjaf**: holy city and centre of pilgrimage for the Shia, in Iraq.

**National Liberation Army**: the Iraqi-based military wing of the People's Mujahedin.

**OPEC**: Organisation of Petroleum Exporting Countries; Iran and Iraq are among its thirteen members.

**Pasdaran**: Revolutionary Guards, the special force raised in Iran after the revolution to act as a counterbalance to the regular army and to protect the Islamic revolution.

**People's Mujahedin**: left-wing Muslim guerrilla movement which helped overthrow the Shah but went underground in 1981 with the aim of ousting Khomeini.

**Persians**: Indo-European race which predominates in Iran and historically exerted widespread cultural influence on Middle East and sub-continent.

*peshmerga*: 'those who face death' – the armed guerrillas of the Kurdish autonomy movement.

**Qaddissiya**: a battle in 633 AD in which the armies of Islam defeated the forces of Zoroastrian Persia.

**Rafsanjani, Hojatoleslam Ali Akbar Hashemi**: speaker of the Iranian parliament and, from June 1988, acting commander-in-chief.

**Rajavi, Masoud**: leader of the People's Mujahedin.

**Ramadan, Taha Yassin**: Iraqi deputy prime minister.

**Republican Guard Corps**: élite Iraqi corps entrusted with protecting the President; played central role in successful Iraqi offensives in final months of war.

**Resolution 598**: unanimously adopted by the UN Security Council on 20 June 1987; the resolution called for an immediate ceasefire.

**Revolutionary Command Council (RCC)**: the ruling body of the Iraqi regime, under the presidency of Saddam Hussein.

**Shatt al Arab**: disputed estuary between Iran and Iraq, formed by the confluence of the Tigris and the Euphrates.

**Shia**: numbering about 10 per cent of all Muslims, and more than 90 per cent of Iranians and about 60 per cent of Iraqis, the Shia are partisans of the descendants of the Prophet Mohamed who, it is believed, were usurped; the Shia await the return of the missing twelfth Imam; unlike mainstream Sunnism, Shi'ism has a hierarchical clergy and a tradition of dissent and theological debate.

**Strait of Hormuz**: twenty-five-mile strait between Iran and Oman; the narrowest point for vessels entering or leaving the Gulf.

**Sunnism**: the predominant doctrine of Islam in which the Koran and the traditions of the Prophet are less subject to interpretation than among the Shia.

**Supreme Assembly of the Islamic Revolution of Iraq (SAIRI)**: Iranian-sponsored organisation intended to form the basis of an Islamic government in Iraq.

**Tikrit**: home town of Saddam Hussein and many of his closest collaborators.

**Tudeh party**: pro-Moscow party and successor to the communist party of Iran, the oldest communist party in the Middle East.

*Ulema*: collective term for Muslim religious and legal scholars.

**UNIIMOG**: UN Iran–Iraq Military Observer Group.

**US embassy hostage crisis**: 444-day crisis which followed capture of embassy on 4 November 1979 by Iranian students loyal to Khomeini, demanding the extradition of the Shah.

**Velayat-e-faqih**: doctrine of the guardianship the Islamic jurisprudent formulated by Khomeini during his exile in Iraq; the basis of Iran's theocratic constitution and of Khomeini's supreme role.

**Velayati, Ali Akbar**: US-trained physician; Iranian foreign minister from 1981.

**Vorontsov, Yuli**: Soviet deputy foreign minister and subsequently ambassador to Kabul who undertook Moscow's shuttle diplomacy in the Gulf.

**Wahhabis**: an extreme, puritanical sect of Sunnism which backed the ascendancy of the ruling Saud dynasty in the Arabian peninsula and which is antipathetic to the Shia.

# Select bibliography

Aburish, Said K., *Pay-Off* (André Deutsch, 1985)

Arthur Andersen and Co. and Cambridge Energy Research Associates, *World Oil Trends* (1987–8)

Bakhash, Shaul, *The Reign of the Ayatollahs* (I. B.Tauris, 1985)

Barnaby, Frank, *The Invisible Bomb* (I. B.Tauris, 1989)

Belgrave, Ebinger and Okino, *Energy Security to 2000* (Gower, 1987)

de Bock, Walter and Jean-Charles Deniau, *Des Armes Pour l'Iran* (Gallimard, 1988)

Brzezinski, Zbigniew, *Power and Principle: Memoirs of the National Security Adviser 1977–1981* (Weidenfeld and Nicolson, 1983)

CARDRI (ed.), *Saddam's Iraq* (Zed Books, 1986)

Chubin, Shahram, *Iran and its Neighbours* (Centre for Security and Conflict Studies, 1987)

Chubin, Litwak and Plascov, *Security in the Gulf* (IISS, 1982)

Chubin and Tripp, *Iran and Iraq at War* (I. B.Tauris, 1988)

Cordesman, A.H., *The Gulf and the Search for Strategic Stability* (Westview, 1984)

Cordesman, A.H., *The Iran–Iraq War and Western Security* (RUSI, 1987)

Cunningham, Michael, *Hostages to Fortune: the Future of Western Interests in the Arabian Gulf* (Brassey's Defence Publishers, 1988)

Diba, Farhad, *Mossadegh* (Croom Helm, 1986)

Farouk-Sluglett, Marion and Peter Sluglett, *Iraq Since 1958* (KPI, 1987)

Heikal, Mohamed, *The Return of the Ayatollah* (André Deutsch, 1981)

Hiro, Dilip, *Iran under the Ayatollahs* (Routledge and Kegan Paul, 1985)

Hiro, Dilip, *Islamic Fundamentalism* (Paladin, 1988)

Hussain, Asaf, *Islamic Iran* (Frances Pinter, 1985)

Huyser, General Robert E., *Mission to Tehran* (André Deutsch, 1986)

Iraq, Foreign Ministry of, *The Iraqi-Iranian Dispute* (1981)

Islamic Republic of Iran, War Information HQ, *The Imposed War* (volumes published annually)

Ismael, Tareq Y. and Jacqueline S., *Government and Politics in Islam* (Frances Pinter, 1985)

Joffe, George and Keith McLachan, *Iran and Iraq* (EIU, 1987)

Kapuscinski, Ryszard, *Shah of Shahs* (Quartet, 1985)

King, Ralph, *The Iran–Iraq War* (IISS, 1987)

Laing, Margaret, *The Shah* (Sidgwick and Jackson, 1977)

Laurent, Annie and Antoine Basmous, *Guerres Secrètes au Liban* (Gallimard, 1988)

Limbert, John W., *Iran: at War with History* (Croom Helm, 1987)

McLachan, Keith and George Joffe, *The Gulf War* (EIU, 1984)

Mostyn, Trevor (ed.), *The Middle East* (Cambridge University Press, 1988)

Mottahedeh, Roy, *The Mantle of the Prophet: Religion and Politics in Iran* (Chatto and Windus 1986)

Muslim Students Following the Line of the Imam, *Documents from the US Espionage Den* (The Centre for the Publication of the US Espionage Den's Documents, Tehran, 1987)

Nogee, Joseph I. and Robert H.Donaldson, *Soviet Foreign Policy Since World War II* (Pergamon Press, 1988)

O'Ballance, Edgar, *The Kurdish Revolt* (Faber, 1973)

Seale, Patrick, *Asad* (I. B.Tauris, 1988)

Segev, Samuel, *The Iranian Triangle* (The Free Press, 1988)

Seton-Watson, Hugh, *The Russian Empire 1801–1917* (Oxford, 1967)

Sick, Gary, *All Fall Down: America's Fateful Encounter with Iran* (Random House/I. B.Tauris, 1985)

Tower, John, *The Tower Commission Report* (Bantam, 1987)

Whitehall Papers, *The War in the Gulf* (RUSI, 1987 and 1988)

Wright, Denis, *The English Among the Persians* (Heinemann, 1977)

Yorke, Valerie, *The Gulf in the 1980s* (RUSI, 1980)

Yorke, Valerie and Turner, Louis, *European Interests and Gulf Oil* (RUSI, 1986)

Zabih, Sepehr, *The Iranian Military in Revolution and War* (Routledge, 1988)

Zemzemi, Abdel-Majid Trab, *The Iran–Iraq War: Islam and Nationalisms* (United States Publishing Co., 1986)

# Index

Abadan (oil refinery town), 36, 50; Iraqi assault on, 19, 40, 41, 53, 101; lifting of siege, 110–11
Abu Ghraib prison, 71, 74
Abu Musa island, 24, 37, 195
Abu Nidal group, attempt on Argov's life by, 81–3, 86–7
Abu Nuwas, 186
Abu Widad, executioner, 71
Afghan peace accord (1988), 212
Afghanistan, 141, 212, 213, 233; British influence (1900s), 201; Iranian role in, 207–11, 276, 281, 282–3; Mujahedin guerrillas, 10, 199, 207, 209, 210, 211, 228, 233, 282; Soviet occupation of (1980), xvii, 4, 6–7, 137, 141, 165, 199, 200, 207–11, 213; and Soviet withdrawal from (1989), xvii, 208, 210–11, 213, 280
Ahwaz (Iran), 19, 41, 45, 51–2, 53, 101–2, 111
Alattiyah, Sadiq, 74
Alawi, Youssef, 44
Algeria, 37, 133, 114–15, 117, 221
Algiers: Bazargan–Brzezinski meeting (1979), 133–4; OPEC Conference (1975), 37
Algiers agreement (1975), 34, 35, 36, 37, 38, 79, 114, 118, 198
Ali (Prophet's cousin), 107, 108
Amal militia, 90, 91, 92, 93, 94
American–Israeli Public Affairs Committee, 184
Ames, Robert, 92–3
Amir-Baqeri, General Bahman, 139
Amnesty International, 70, 72, 73, 74, 257
Anglo-Iranian Oil Company, nationalisation of (1951), 126
Anglo-Persian Agreement (1919), 202, 203

Anglo-Russian Agreement (1907), 201
Aoun, General Michel, 92
Aqaba, 32
Arab Co-operation Council, 274–5
Arab–Israeli conflict, 119–20, 198; Israeli invasion of Lebanon (1982), 81, 83–9; 1967 War, 44; October (1973) War, 5; see also Israel; PLO
Arab League, 117, 119, 120
Arafat, Yasser, 52, 82, 85, 89, 90, 119–20
Ardebili, Chief Justice, 106, 270, 272
Argentina, 192
Argov, Shlomo, attempted murder in London of, 81–3, 86–7
Armenia, Soviet, unrest in, 280
Armenians in Iran, 35
Armilla Patrol, British, 174
Assad, Hafez, President of Syria, 31, 92, 94, 96–7, 119, 156, 268–9
Assembly of Discernment, Iranian, 216
Assembly of Experts, Iranian, 60
Association of Friday Prayer Leaders, 105
Atapour, General, 203
Atomic Energy Authority, International, 180–1, 183
Atropin (anti-nerve gas drug), 172
El Azhary, M. S., 69
Azerbaijan, Azerbaijanis, 23, 35, 125, 205; Autonomous Republic, 205; Soviet, 280–1
Aziz, Tariq, 40, 258, 273; attempted assassination of (1979), 22, 29

Baalbek (Lebanon), 89, 94, 96, 97
Ba'ath party/regime, Iraq, xx, 18, 25, 26–30, 31, 38, 39, 45, 70, 71, 74, 146, 148, 194, 273; conflict between Shi'ites and, 26–9; Iraqi Popular Army forced from members of, 46; Ninth Party

Mohtazemi, Reza, 45
Mokri, Mohammad, 47
Mombasa, 141
Montazeri, Ayatollah Hossein Ali, 90, 96,
  98, 219, 227, 256, 271–2, 279
Morocco, 14
Mossadeq, Mohammad, 126, 205
Mostansirya University, Baghdad, 22, 23
Mottahedeh, Roy, 11
Musa Sadr, Imam, 18, 89–91
Mousavi, Mir Hossein, Prime Minister of
  Iran, 98, 99, 106, 111, 215, 219, 248,
  272, 279
Mubarak, Hosni, Egyptian President, 55,
  190
Mughniyeh, Imad, 95
Mujahedin guerrillas in Afghanistan, 10,
  199, 207, 209, 210, 211, 228, 233, 282;
  see also Iraqi Mujahedin Movement;
  People's Mujahedin
Mukhabarat (Iraqi intelligence), 82, 144
Multinational Peace Force in Lebanon,
  88, 93, 222
Murphy, Richard, 178, 233
Muskie, Edmund, 4, 142
Muslim Brotherhood, 14

Naft-e-Shah (Iran), 24
Najafabbadi, Hadi, 98
Najjaf (Shia holy city), 15, 75–6, 77, 109,
  203, 236; Ayatollah Khomeini's exile in,
  12–13, 77–80, 95; and expulsion of
  Khomeini from (1978), 28, 80; Shia
  Islam Association, 27
al-Naqib, General Hassan, 74
Naraghi, Ehsan, 67–8
Nasser, Egyptian President Gamal
  Abdul, 31, 158, 204, 206
Nasserism, 14, 90
Nassreddin Shah, 200, 201
National Democratic Front (NDF), Iran,
  61
National Front, Iranian, 51
National Iranian Oil Company, 188
National Liberation Army (NLA),
  abortive invasion of Iran by (1988),
  252–6, 257, 272
National Security Council, US, 95, 138
NATO, 15
Nehru, Jawaharlal, 203
nerve gas see poison and nerve gas
Nicaragua and Irangate affair, xvii, 95–6
Nir, Amiram, 99
Nixon, US President Richard M., 9, 178;
  Tehran visits, and close relations with
  Shah, 125, 126, 127–9
Non-Aligned Movement, 117, 119, 158

Non-Aligned Summit Conference (1982),
  54, 76, 158, 159
Noor-Ali, Samir, 22
North, Colonel Oliver, 96, 226
North Korea, xviii, 192
North Yemen, 141, 274
nuclear energy, 284
Nuclear Non-Proliferation Treaty, 180
nuclear weapons: Iraqi programme,
  180–4, 181; Israeli possession of, 180,
  181

Ocalan, Abdullah, 116
oil industry/oilfields, xv, xvl, xvii, 4–6, 24,
  36, 73, 125, 127, 141–2, 152, 225, 275–6;
  Abadan attacked by Iraq, 19, 40, 41,
  53, 101; Arab oil embargo (1973), 5;
  effect of Gulf War on, 41–2, 53, 55,
  152, 153, 159–60, 169, 170, 172,
  173–4, 185–6, 233, 283; effect of
  Iranian Revolution on, 5, 42; falling
  prices (1980s), 160, 237, 271, 283;
  importance of Gulf oil, 4–5, 10,
  283–4; Kangan refinery destroyed by
  Iraq, 237; Kharg Island terminal
  attacked by Iraq, xviii, 151, 152, 153,
  172, 173; nationalisation of AIOC
  (1951), 126; pipeline from Kirkuk
  closed down by Syria, 152, 159; price
  explosion (1970s), 5–6, 37;
  Soviet-Iranian agreement (1987), 211;
  and tanker war, xviii, 161, 172–8, 233,
  235
Olympic Games (Moscow, 1980), 6
Oman, 43–4, 152, 165, 178, 274
Omani Navy, 174
OPEC (Organisation of Petroleum
  Exporting Countries), 5, 37, 41–2,
  160, 275, 276, 283
Operation Ajax (1953), 126
Operation 'Eternal Light' (1988), 255
Operation Peace for Galilee (1982), 84
Operation Red Alert, 140–1
Operation Staunch, 188
Organisation of African Unity, 38
Orumiyeh, bread riots in, 238
Osirak nuclear reactor, Israel bombing
  attacks on, 182–3
Ottoman Empire, 14, 22, 35–6, 90, 200,
  203
Oveissi, General Gholam Ali, 48–9
Ozal, Turgut, 120

Pahlavi, Mohammed Reza, Shah of Iran
  (1941–79), 5, 10, 14, 15, 32, 33, 36, 37,
  50, 78, 79, 90, 124, 125, 126–7, 193,

Republican Guard Corps, Iraqi, 18–19, 46, 47, 149, 265
Reuter, Baron Julius de, 201
Revolutionary Command Council (RCC), Iraq, xvi, 46, 74, 76, 77, 84, 146, 153, 155
Revolutionary Council, Iranian, 59–60
Revolutionary Court, Iran, 70
Revolutionary Guard Corps, Iran (IRGC: Pasdaran), xv, xvi, 24, 34, 41, 42, 50, 52, 63, 64, 66, 67, 68, 72, 85, 93, 94, 102, 103, 104, 106, 110–11, 112, 135, 169, 194–5, 199, 208, 210, 218, 225, 228, 238, 249, 251; antagonism between regular army and, 102, 244; Boghammar patrol boats manned by, 195, 235; clashes between Mujahedin and, 66, 67; in Lebanon, 89, 91, 94, 222; massive corruption within, 244–5
Revolutionary Justice Organisation, 223
Reza Khan/Reza Shah Pahlavi, 49–50, 108, 124, 201, 202–3, 205
Reza Pahlavi, Mohammed see Pahlavi
Rezai, Mohsen, 111, 248, 249
Rochot, Philippe, 223
Rogers, Captain Will C., III, 245
Roosevelt, President Franklin D., 124
Rosan, Nawaf, 82
Rushdie, Salman, *The Satanic Verses*, 279–80, 281
Ruthbah poison gas plant, 194

Sabra refugee camp massacre, 89
Sadat, Anwar, President of Egypt, 14; assassination of, 14
al-Sadr, Ayatollah Mohammed Baqr, 27, 28, 29; execution of (1980), 23, 25, 27, 29, 71
Safronchuk, Vasily, 198
Said, Hussein, 82, 83
Said, Nuri, 25
SAIRI (Supreme Assembly of the Islamic Revolution of Iraq), 71, 241–2
SALT I and II treaties, 6
Samarra poison-gas factory, 194, 261
*Sambow Banner* (cargo ship), 151
*Samuel B. Roberts* (US frigate), hits mine, 235
SAPO (Swedish secret police), 117
Sarabgarm refugee camp, Iran, 21, 22
Sar-e-Pol-e-Zahab, 24, 255
SAS, British, 23
Saud, King of Saudi Arabia, 166
Saudi Arabia, 9, 94, 119, 141, 142, 162–3, 163–5, 175, 275, 276; arms build-up of, 164; causeway linking Bahrain with,

166; GCC established by, 164; and Hashemi assassination plot, 226; Iranian campaign against, 163; Iranian F4 shot down by, 172–3; Iraq supported by, 32, 41, 43, 159, 160, 163, 165, 172, 184, 185, 274; and Mecca riots (1987), 226, 227–9; oil industry, 5, 13, 15, 41, 42, 160, 274; Pakistani troops in, 15, 165; Shia in, 13, 162–3, 175; and tanker war, 172, 174, 175; US relations with, 164, 172; Wahhabism, 229
Savak (Iranian secret police), 50, 78, 79
Savama (Iranian secret police), 256
Shevardnadze, Eduard, 213, 281
Schmidt, Alfred, 222
Seale, Patrick, 96, 97
Senegal, 119
Shah of Iran see Pahlavi
al Shahristani, Dr Husain, 74
Shalamcheh sector (Iraq), 112, 243, 245
Shamkhani, Ali, 283
Shariawtmadari, Grand Ayatollah Kazem, 114
Sharon, Ariel, 83, 84, 85, 86–7
Shatt al Arab, 32, 50, 101, 112, 151, 157, 168, 208, 233, 272, 273, 277; foreign ships trapped in, 53, 115–16; territorial dispute over, 14, 35–7, 38
Sheikholeslamzadeh, Hossein, 95, 135
al Shenshan, General Abdul-Jabbar, 46
Shia Islam association, Najjaf, 27
Shia Muslims, Shi'ism: in Afghanistan, 208, 209, 282; in Bahrein, 13, 43, 165–6; fundamentalists, 13–15, 18, 21; hijacking of Kuwaiti 747 aircraft by, 230; in Khuzestan, 50; kidnapping of Western hostages by Islamic Jihad, 222; in Kuwait, 13, 94, 162, 167, 275; in Lebanon, 89–91, 92, 94–5, 222, 230; in Saudi Arab, 13, 162–3, 175; in Soviet Azerbaijan, 280
Shia Muslims in Iran, 104–8, 109, 200, 203, 208, 273; in Army, 149; conflict between Wahhabism and, 229; as dominant religion, 107; Friday prayer meetings, 105–7, 220; martyrdom complex, 104–5, 107, 110; and Mecca riots (1987), 226, 227–9; mosque as political centre of life, 106–7
Shia Muslims in Iraq, 14–15, 19, 20–2, 23, 25, 26, 27–9, 31, 45, 46, 71, 74, 75, 76, 77–8, 146, 148, 154, 158, 173, 185, 267–8; Ba'ath regime's conflict with, 27–9, 30, 71–2; in Army, 45, 46, 149–50; expulsion of Baghdad bazaaris, 20–2; government posts held by, 46; see also Dawa Al Shiraa (Beirut weekly), 96, 97, 99